Debt Management in India

The key objective in macroeconomics is to achieve steady growth. Monetary and fiscal policy are the two instruments through which macro stability can be achieved. The focus of monetary policy is inflation and financial stability while fiscal policy concentrates on employment and growth. Since Independence in India, both fiscal and monetary policy have undergone significant changes.

In any emerging country where rapid development is pursued, financial resources are generally scarce. In a country like India, which is not resource-rich in oil or commodities, and a significant part of the population is illiterate as well as below the poverty line, tax collection is low and dependence on tax revenue is limited. In such cases, the process of development is associated with financing projects and infrastructure through large borrowings. In the planning era, initially, external borrowings played a significant role but domestic borrowings assumed significance since the 1970s. Over the years, increased borrowings have led to higher interest payments which account for nearly one-third of the tax revenue. Borrowings reflect the nexus between monetary and fiscal policy.

Any borrowing, external or internal, has inter-generational implications and therefore many countries consider imposing limits on debt. In this context, Ricardian Equivalence implies that taxes and borrowings are, inter-temporally, similar, assuming that economic agents behave rationally. However, though theoretically a sound argument, empirically, in most cases, rational expectations may not hold.

This book is a comprehensive analysis of the implications of rising public debt in India. It studies data on debt in India from 1951 to 2017, and covers a wide canvas of issues related to debt management and important developments in the government securities market. It specifically investigates the implications of domestic debt on consumption, effect of monetised debt on prices, the long-term relationship between domestic debt and growth, and separation of debt and monetary management. By examining the hypothesis of Ricardian Equivalence in India, it argues and concludes that debt management should be separated from monetary management, and delineates the implications of domestic debt.

Charan Singh teaches economics to graduate students and executives at the Indian Institute of Management Bangalore, India. He has been the Reserve Bank of India Chair Professor at IIM Bangalore, and Senior Economist at the Independent Evaluation Office of the International Monetary Fund, Washington DC. Earlier, he was the Research Director in Internal Debt Management Department of the Reserve Bank of India. Along with his official assignments and in-house policy research, he has published extensively in reputed national and international journals, and regularly in national dailies.

Debt Management in India

Charan Singh

CAMBRIDGE
UNIVERSITY PRESS

CAMBRIDGE
UNIVERSITY PRESS

University Printing House, Cambridge CB2 8BS, United Kingdom

One Liberty Plaza, 20th Floor, New York, NY 10006, USA

477 Williamstown Road, Port Melbourne, vic 3207, Australia

314 to 321, 3rd Floor, Plot No.3, Splendor Forum, Jasola District Centre, New Delhi 110025, India

79 Anson Road, #06–04/06, Singapore 079906

Cambridge University Press is part of the University of Cambridge.

It furthers the University's mission by disseminating knowledge in the pursuit of education, learning and research at the highest international levels of excellence.

www.cambridge.org
Information on this title: www.cambridge.org/9781107191273

© Charan Singh 2018

This publication is in copyright. Subject to statutory exception and to the provisions of relevant collective licensing agreements, no reproduction of any part may take place without the written permission of Cambridge University Press.

First published 2018
Printed in India by Rajkamal Electric Press, Kundli, Haryana.

A catalogue record for this publication is available from the British Library

Library of Congress Cataloging-in-Publication Data
Names: Singh, Charan (Economist), author.
Title: Debt management in India / Charan Singh.
Description: New York : Cambridge University Press, 2018. | Includes bibliographical references and index.
Identifiers: LCCN 2017059468 | ISBN 9781107191273 (hardback)
Subjects: LCSH: Debts, Public--India. | Economic development--India. | Rational expectations (Economic theory) | Ricardo, David, 1772-1823.
Classification: LCC HJ8782 .S55 2018 | DDC 339.5/230954--dc23 LC record available at https://lccn.loc.gov/2017059468

ISBN 978-1-107-19127-3 Hardback

Cambridge University Press has no responsibility for the persistence or accuracy of URLs for external or third-party internet websites referred to in this publication, and does not guarantee that any content on such websites is, or will remain, accurate or appropriate.

Contents

List of Tables and Figures   *vii*

Preface   *xi*

1. Introduction   1
2. Public Debt in India   8
3. Ricardian Equivalence: Introduction   62
4. Ricardian Equivalence: Empirical Studies Utilising Consumption Function   76
5. Ricardian Equivalence and Consumption in India   130
6. Monetisation of Debt in India   145
7. Domestic Debt and Economic Growth in India   184
8. Separation of Debt from Monetary Management   211
9. Conclusions and Policy Implications   259

Bibliography   265

Index   289

List of Tables and Figures

Tables

Table 2.1:	Public debt of the government (1952–2016)	9
Table 2.2:	Decadal rate of growth in select debt indicators (1952–2016)	10
Table 2.3:	Share of borrowings in the financing pattern of the Five Year Plans of the government	12
Table 2.4:	Net interest payments	15
Table 2.5:	Ratio of net interest payment to select macro indicators	16
Table 2.6:	Five-year averages of inflation-adjusted growth rates of revenue and capital accounts of central government (1951–2016)	17
Table 2.7:	Annual average growth in the components of domestic debt of the government (1952–2016)	19
Table 2.8:	Components of internal debt of the government as per cent of total (1952–2016)	20
Table 2.9:	Maturity pattern of market loans and bonds (1958–2016)	27
Table 2.10:	Ownership pattern of market loans and bonds (1958–2016)	29
Table 2.11:	Structure of interest rates – long term (1960–2016)	30
Table 2.12:	Devolvement of government securities on primary dealers and RBI (1988–2015)	34
Table 2.13:	Structure of interest rates – short term (1961–2016)	37
Table 2.14:	Ownership pattern of 91-day Treasury bills (1952–2016)	38
Table 2.15:	Recommendations by various committees	44
Table 2.16:	Minimum balance and limit of WMA for state governments	46
Table 2.17:	Components of small savings (1952–2016)	49
Table 2.18:	Small savings schemes	51
Table 2.19:	Components of provident funds and other accounts	54
Table 2.20:	Reserve funds and deposits of the government	56
Table 2.21:	Fiscal responsibility legislation in India	59
Table 4.1:	Summary of some important studies on Ricardian Equivalence Hypothesis and consumption function	92
Table 4.2:	Kochin's original results and attempted replications	102
Table 4.3:	Buiter and Tobin's original results and attempted replications	104
Table 4.4 :	Feldstein's original results and attempted replications	106

Table 4.5:	Kormendi's original results and attempted replications	109
Table 4.6:	Aschauer's original results and attempted replications	111
Table 4.7:	Modigliani and Sterling's original results and attempted replications	112
Table 4.8:	Examining the issue of par and market value of debt	116
Table 4.9:	Testing for unit roots – Augmented Dickey-Fuller test	120
Table 4.10:	Estimating the wealth function	122
Table 4.11:	Estimating the government debt function	123
Table 4.12:	Testing for stationarity in the anticipated and the unanticipated components of wealth and government debt – Augmented Dickey-Fuller test	124
Table 4.13:	Test for Ricardian equivalence and consumption – The model developed in this study	125
Table 4.14:	Test for Ricardian equivalence and consumption – The modified model	126
Table 5.1:	Empirical studies on Ricardian Equivalence Hypothesis and consumption in India	132
Table 5.2:	Testing for unit roots – Augmented Dickey-Fuller test (1971–95)	137
Table 5.3:	Estimating the wealth and the domestic debt functions (1971–95)	138
Table 5.4:	Testing for stationarity in the anticipated and the unanticipated components of domestic debt and the unanticipated component of wealth-augmented Dickey-Fuller Test (1971–95)	139
Table 5.5:	Empirical results of the estimation of Ricardian equivalence and consumption – The model developed in this study (1971–95)	140
Table 5.6:	Testing the robustness of results of Ricardian equivalence in India (1971–95)	141
Table 6.1:	Sources of reserve money	152
Table 6.2:	Monetary ratios	156
Table 6.3:	Important empirical studies on causality between the monetary aggregates and the price level in India	161
Table 6.4:	Testing for stationarity of the series – The unit roots-augmented Dickey-Fuller test	164
Table 6.5:	FPE of autoregressive process for the variables	166
Table 6.6:	Autoregressive equations of variables for 1951–95, annual	167
Table 6.7:	Autoregressive equations of variables for 1971–95, quarterly	168
Table 6.8:	Minimum FPE and the optimal lag structures of the variables	169

Table 6.9:	Granger causality test: Monetised debt (MD) and reserve money (RM)	170
Table 6.10:	Granger causality test: Monetised debt (MD) and narrow money (M1)	172
Table 6.11:	Granger causality test: Monetised debt (MD) and broad money (M3)	173
Table 6.12:	Granger causality test: Monetised debt (MD) and prices (P)	174
Table 6.13:	Granger causality test: Reserve money (RM) and narrow money (M1)	175
Table 6.14:	Granger causality test: Reserve money (RM) and broad money (M3)	176
Table 6.15:	Granger causality test: Reserve money (RM) and prices (P)	178
Table 6.16:	Granger causality test: Narrow money (M1) and prices (P)	179
Table 6.17:	Granger causality test: Broad money (M3) and prices (P)	180
Table 6.18:	Summary of conclusions: Test for Granger causality	182
Table 7.1:	Role of public sector in national accounts aggregates (as per cent of GDP)	197
Table 7.2:	Testing for stationarity of domestic debt and GDP – The unit roots-augmented Dickey-Fuller test	199
Table 7.3:	FPE of autoregressive process for domestic debt and GDP	200
Table 7.4:	Autoregressive equations of domestic debt and GDP	201
Table 7.5:	Minimum FPE and the optimal lag structures of domestic debt and GDP	202
Table 7.6:	Engle-Granger cointegration test for domestic debt and growth	203
Table 7.7:	Granger causality test – Domestic debt and growth	204
Table 7.8:	Summary of conclusions emerging from the Granger causality test for domestic debt and growth	205
Table 7.9:	Testing for stationarity of unanticipated domestic debt and GDP – The unit roots-augmented Dickey-Fuller test	206
Table 7.10:	FPE of autoregressive process for unanticipated domestic debt and GDP	206
Table 7.11:	Autoregressive equations of unanticipated domestic debt and GDP	207
Table 7.12:	Minimum FPE and the optimal lag structures of unanticipated domestic debt and GDP	208
Table 7.13:	Granger causality test – unanticipated domestic debt and GDP	208
Table 7.14:	Summary of conclusions emerging from the Granger causality test – unanticipated domestic debt and GDP	209
Table 8.1:	Location of debt management office in select countries	215
Table 8.2:	General government gross debt of select countries	218
Table 8.3:	Select country practices relating to distribution of profit	223

Table 8.4:	Profits of RBI transferred to central government (per cent of GDP)	228
Table 8.5:	Management of public debt in India	229
Table 8.6:	Interest earnings from domestic securities	231
Table 8.7:	Timeline: Separation of debt management	233

Figures

Figure 2.1:	Domestic debt, external debt and GDP – annual growth (1952–2016)	10
Figure 2.2:	Net annual domestic liabilities, total expenditure and tax revenue as per cent of GDP (1960–61 to 2015–16)	13
Figure 2.3a:	Direct taxes of centre and states as a percentage of GDP (1950–2016)	13
Figure 2.3b:	Indirect taxes of centre and states as a percentage of GDP (1950–2016)	13
Figure 2.4:	Tax revenues, revenue and capital expenditure of centre and states (1982–2016)	14
Figure 2.5:	Total tax revenues, gross fiscal deficit and revenue deficit of centre and states (1982–2016)	14
Figure 2.6:	Ratio of revenue and capital receipts and expenditure of central government (1951–2016)	16
Figure 2.7:	Components of domestic debt as per cent to total internal liabilities of combined central and state governments (1952–2016)	18
Figure 2.8:	Net market borrowings of the government through loans and bonds as per cent of GDP (current at market prices) (1952–2016)	26
Figure 2.9:	Cut off yields of central government securities (1988–2015)	33
Figure 2.10:	Contingent liabilities of the government as percentage of GDP	57
Figure 6.1:	Monetised debt and reserve money: Annual growth (1952–95)	153
Figure 6.2:	Monetised debt and money supply: Annual growth (1952–95)	154
Figure 6.3:	Reserve money and money supply: Annual growth (1952–95)	154
Figure 6.4:	Monetised debt, reserve money and prices: Annual growth (1952–95)	156
Figure 6.5:	Money supply and prices: Annual growth (1952–95)	157
Figure 7.1:	Annual accruals in domestic debt held by public (ADBP) and total tax revenue (TTR) of the government as percentage of total expenditure (TE) and non-developmental expenditure (NDE), (1961–95)	194
Figure 7.2	Domestic debt held by the public (DDP) and GDP – Annual growth (1960–95)	195
Figure 7.3	Gross domestic product – public and the private sector – annual growth (1962–95)	197
Figure 8.1	Combined market borrowings of centre and state (as a per cent of GDP)	238

Preface

In India, fiscal policy has undergone significant changes since start of the planning era in 1951. Initially, external debt played an important role but by 1970s, India became aware of the risks associated with borrowings from external sector. The development process, requiring significant amount of financial resources was financed by domestic sources. The rising domestic debt led to high interest payments pre-empting resources for investment purposes, given the constraint of limited taxable capacity of the economy. Soon, the discussion on having a fiscal rule resulted in legislations at the centre and states.

The debt management is done by the Reserve Bank of India (RBI), the monetary authority of India. To ensure independence of monetary policy and transparency in debt management, the key issue of separating debt from monetary management was extensively discussed. The initial steps of separating the two functions were taken hesitantly and even those were stalled when the great recession of 2008 occurred. RBI argued against the separation, given the fragile economic situation, domestically and globally.

I have been part of the fascinating story of debt management in India from 1987 onwards when I was introduced to the subject by Professor I. S. Gulati. This book is a result of my academic research for about a decade, and then working in the Debt Management Department of RBI for more than five years, first in the initial stages and then as Director of Research. The experience and interaction with the best minds in the country, nay the world, is unparalleled. Hence, I owe my sincerest gratitude to my professors and colleagues.

I also would like to thank Cambridge University Press for persistently pursuing me and ensuring that I publish this work on Debt Management in India.

1

Introduction

Public debt as an important instrument of public finance policy is of a relatively recent origin, but has already assumed great significance. Though its origin can be traced back to war finance, it has only recently become an integral part of the fiscal and monetary policies of the developed as well as the developing countries. In the case of the developed economies, the implications of rising public debt have been analysed and critically evaluated. However, the economic literature on developing countries is lacking on this critical issue. The need for financial resources has led many developing countries to increasingly resort to public debt, in the context of public investment.

This study examines the economic impact of public debt in India. Public borrowing in India is a recognised source of public finance. The central and state governments derive the power to borrow from Articles 292 and 293 of the Indian Constitution, respectively. Article 292 of the Constitution empowers the union (federal) government to borrow on the security of the Consolidated Fund of India within such limits, if any, as may be fixed by the Parliament. Article 293 confers similar powers on the state governments within the limits fixed by the State Legislative Assemblies. States can only borrow domestically, whether from the centre or from other sources. However, if a state has any loans outstanding from the centre, or for which the centre is a guarantor, it must obtain the centre's consent before borrowing from any other source. As a consequence, in effect, almost all states today need union governments consent before they can borrow funds.

Under the Constitution of India, union government's debt is a 'union subject', while state government' debt is a 'state subject', i.e., the centre cannot legislate how state governments should manage state borrowings. Article 246(1) of the Constitution read that Entries 35 and 37 of List I provides that Parliament has exclusive power to make laws regarding public debt of India and foreign loans. Article 246(3) of the Constitution read that Entry 43 of List II provides that state legislatures have exclusive power to make laws regarding the public debt of states. However, the Constitution limits sources from which state governments can borrow, and gives the centre power under certain circumstances to influence whether a state can borrow from sources other than the centre. Therefore, the Constitution implicitly empowers the centre to place limits on the amount and sources of state government borrowing.

No separate law has been enacted under Article 292 to regulate central government borrowing. However, the Fiscal Responsibility and Budget Management (FRBM) Act, 2003 and FRBM Rules, 2004 lay down a framework for fiscal management. The FRBM Act aims to ensure inter-generational equity in fiscal management and long-term macroeconomic stability. This requires sufficient revenue surpluses, reducing fiscal deficit, removing fiscal impediments in the effective conduct of monetary policy and prudential debt management consistent with fiscal sustainability through limits on central government borrowings, debt and deficits, and greater transparency in fiscal operations. The FRBM Act, 2003 prohibited participation of the Reserve Bank of India (RBI) in the primary government securities market with effect from 1 April 2006, except under special circumstances. The FRBM Rules, 2004 specified annual targets for reduction of fiscal and revenue deficits, annual targets for accumulating contingent liabilities in the form of guarantees, and accruing of additional liabilities as a percentage of gross domestic product (GDP).

Central and state government borrowing is constitutionally secured against the Consolidated Fund of India and of state governments, respectively. Article 112(3)(c) provides that expenditure in respect of 'debt charges for which the Government of India is liable, including interest, sinking fund charges and redemption charges and other expenditure relating to the raising of loans and the service and redemption of debt' shall be charged on the Consolidated Fund of India. Article 202(3)(c) makes the parallel provision for states, and provides that a state's cost of borrowing is charged on the Consolidated Fund of the state.

The RBI is legally obliged to manage central government debt but it agrees to manage state government's debts also through a formal agreement. Under Section 20 of the RBI Act 1934, the RBI is obliged to manage central government's public debt. Section 21 of the RBI Act 1934, provides that the central government shall entrust debt management to the RBI. Section 21A of the RBI Act 1934 provides that a state government may agree to let the RBI manage its debt. Under Section 17(11) of the RBI Act, the RBI is empowered to act as an agent of, *inter alia*, the central government and state governments, in managing public debt, and issuing and managing bonds and debentures.

Historically, the public debt was being managed by the erstwhile Imperial Bank of India before the establishment of RBI. Since the establishment of RBI on 1 April 1935, it was entrusted with the management of public debt and issue of new loans of the central and state governments.

Public debt has been an important source of mobilising financial resources for economic development in India. The increasing need of financial resources for development purposes could not be met through other fiscal instruments like tax revenues due to weak income base and, therefore, the reliance placed on public debt increased. The planned economic development of India was initiated in the form of five year plans in 1951 and government mobilised domestic borrowings for investment purposes, arguably. The share of domestic borrowings was generally around one-half or less of the total plan outlay in the initial Five Year Plans. But since the early 1970s, due to economic reasons and political prudence, reliance on external borrowings declined and domestic borrowing was encouraged. The increasing use of domestic borrowing as a fiscal instrument has resulted in a rapidly rising domestic debt, especially since 1980s. The gross fiscal deficit of the government increased to 9.5 per cent of GDP in 1986–87 from 6.0 per cent in 1981–82. Consequently, domestic debt situation became critical in the late 80s and debt to GDP ratio increased to 72.9 per cent as on end March 1992 from 48.9 per cent in 1982.

The increasing reliance on domestic debt has varied macroeconomic implications. The rising domestic debt would have an effect on the consumption pattern of the consumer through interest rates, price level and the path of growth in the economy. In a developing country like India, these issues gain paramount importance.

There have been a few studies since 1965 investigating the rising domestic debt in India. In many of these studies, the emphasis lies on the descriptive review of the debt situation in India. Few other studies attempt an empirical analysis of some of the issues. The empirical literature in India is lacking in a comprehensive study of the implications of the domestic debt situation in India.

In view of the above discussion, a comprehensive analysis of the implications of rising public debt in India is attempted in this study which tries to probe into the subject of domestic debt of India more closely. This research, specifically, investigates the following issues:

- implications of domestic debt on consumption;
- effect of monetised debt on prices;

- long term relationship between domestic debt and growth; and
- separation of debt and monetary management.

It is important to mention that the scope of this study is mainly restricted to domestic debt of the government, both central (federal) and state (provincial) governments. Domestic debt of the government comprises loans raised in open markets, Treasury bills, special securities issued to the RBI, ways and means advances, special floating loans and compensation, and other bonds. Besides these, the government has other liabilities on account of funds raised through small savings schemes, provident funds, and reserve funds and deposits.

The book has analysed data from 1951 to 2017, and covers a wide canvas on issues related to debt management and important developments in government securities market. However, technical work contained in Chapters 4, 5, 6 and 7 are restricted to the extensive doctoral work completed in July 1997 at University of New South Wales, Sydney. The period of this study is largely guided by the availability of data on a consistent basis. The ownership pattern of domestic debt was available from 1959, while the data on components of consumption expenditure was available from 1971. Therefore, the period of the study will be 1971 to 1995 for the analysis of effect of domestic debt on the consumption pattern. In the case of the chapter investigating the impact of monetisation of debt and the price level, data was available since 1951 and, therefore, the span of analysis was the longest, 1951–95 (annual). The quarterly data on monetary aggregates, on consistent basis was available from 1970 onwards. Therefore, the results based on the quarterly series are presented for the period 1970–95. In case of analysing the relationship between debt and growth, where data was consistently available from 1959, the period under study will be 1959–95.

The study mainly draws data from the publications of the RBI and the Government of India. In case of data gaps, other sources like the Central Government Budget (Explanatory Memorandum to the Budget), and the Economic and Functional Classification of the Central Government Budget, both publications of the Ministry of Finance, Government of India, were also extensively used.

In the study, trend in domestic debt is discussed and a descriptive review of the major components is presented. This is followed by a theoretical discussion on the Ricardian Equivalence Hypothesis which is the most important concept, historically and in contemporary literature, on public debt. Then, the implications of domestic debt delineated in the objectives are empirically analysed. There is a vast literature, both theoretical and empirical, which studies the relationship between domestic debt and consumption. In contrast, there is a relatively small amount of literature on analysing the effect of monetised debt on prices, and on the relationship between domestic debt and growth. Accordingly, the next two chapters concentrate on domestic debt and consumption followed by a chapter each on monetised debt and prices, and domestic debt and growth. Finally, the issue of reparation of debt and monetary management, widely debated in India since 1992, is discussed. The discussion on the chapter scheme is briefly presented in the following paragraphs.

The debt situation in India is discussed in Chapter 2. Domestic debt is defined and its trend analysed *vis-a-vis* the national aggregates and other instruments of public finance. A discussion on causes of rising expenditure leading to a rise in domestic debt follows. In this chapter, the composition of domestic debt is analysed and the trend for each major component is separately probed in detail.

A theoretical perspective for study on public debt in the historical concept of Ricardian Equivalence is set in Chapter 3. An insight into the various theoretical issues pertaining to the Ricardian Equivalence Hypothesis is provided. The concept is explained in detail along with its assumptions. The important assumptions like the finite lives and intergenerational transfers, imperfect capital markets, and uncertainty and taxes are discussed in detail. An important conclusion that emerges from the discussion is that even if the assumptions do not hold perfectly, the concept remains valid for theoretical and empirical purposes.

In Chapter 4, the need to conduct empirical tests for the Ricardian Equivalence Hypothesis in an appropriate consumption function is emphasised. This is followed by a discussion on the existing consumption functions in the literature. The relationship between the permanent income hypothesis incorporating rational expectations and the Ricardian Equivalence Hypothesis, which assumes rational behaviour on the part of the consumer, is demonstrated. Having established the relationship, a new model is then derived, following the neoclassical approach, to empirically test the Ricardian Equivalence Hypothesis in the consumption function. The literature on domestic debt and consumption is critically reviewed and some of the major studies are replicated to examine for the robustness of the results. A very important issue in empirical work pertains to the use of par or market value of government debt. In the context of the US, most of the studies make use of the market value of government debt rather than the par value, but in case of India the market value series has not yet been computed. Therefore, in this chapter an attempt has been made to examine the sensitivity of the results to the use of market and par value of debt. As most of the empirical literature on Ricardian Equivalence and consumption is based on the data from the developed countries and specially the USA, the application of the theoretically-derived model is empirically tested for the US economy before applying it to India.

The application of the Ricardian Equivalence Hypothesis to the consumption pattern in India is explored in Chapter 5. A critical review of the existing empirical literature in India is presented. The limitations of the available data in the Indian context are discussed. This is followed by the empirical estimation of our model developed in the previous chapter.

The relationship between domestic debt and inflation is investigated in Chapter 6. The rising trend in monetisation of debt in India and its implications for the monetary aggregates and the price level is discussed. A large part of government debt is purchased by the RBI. This is mainly due to the lack of demand in the open market due to the low coupon rates on government bonds. The result of such purchases by the RBI is an increase in reserve money and the money supply. Though the RBI attempts to partially sterilise these purchases through the use of the instruments like cash and statutory reserve ratios, success is limited. In India, many studies have established the relationship between the money supply and prices, but in this chapter the investigation is extended to monetised debt and inflation. The open economy model is discussed and a testable hypothesis is formulated. In the empirical section, tests of Granger causality are used to examine the effect of rising monetised debt on money supply and prices, and their inter-relationships.

The analysis is further extended to study the relationship between rising domestic debt and growth in Chapter 7. The traditional view considers that in the long run, domestic debt has a negative impact on economic growth while the Ricardian Equivalence Hypothesis implies the neutrality of domestic debt to growth. The issue is empirically examined using the Granger causality test and the Cointegration test.

The need for separation of debt and monetary management is discussed in Chapter 8. In the aftermath of recent global crisis, the issue of separation of monetary policy, fiscal policy and debt management has re-emerged especially for the advanced economies. In many countries, during the period of crisis, scope of fiscal policy was expanded and debt to GDP ratios increased significantly. Consequently, debt management, in general, became difficult and coordination between monetary and debt management assumed significance. Historically, a number of countries with liberalised financial markets and high levels of government debt sought to adopt professional debt management techniques to save cost and to provide policy signals to the market. In India, traditionally, management of debt is diffused in different layers of different governments. Hence, it is argued that in India, debt management should be separated from monetary management. The setting up of separate debt management office will help to establish transparency, and assign specific responsibility and accountability on the debt manager. This could lead to an integrated and more professional management of all government liabilities, with a focused mandate to operate on sound economic and commercial principles. The strategy could ensure that resources are available to the government at competitive market rates of interest prompting expenditure prioritisation and fiscal discipline in budget making.

Finally, a summary and conclusions drawn from the study are presented in Chapter 9.

2

Public Debt in India

In India, domestic debt has been rising at a higher rate than the national income since 1952. The rise in domestic debt has been a result of large domestic borrowings resorted to by the government to achieve a higher rate of economic development. Therefore, the pattern, trend and the components of domestic debt need to be analysed. In this chapter, a discussion on the domestic debt of the government in India is presented.

In India, domestic debt of the central and the state governments are separately published and analysed. But in order to analyse the impact of domestic debt on macro aggregates in the economy, it is important to have a consolidated debt position of the government. Therefore, in this chapter, a consolidated position of the debt situation of the government, both the central and the states, is computed and presented.

2.1. Trends in the domestic debt of India

India's public debt, as a percentage of GDP, steadily increased between 1952 and 1990 and then after some respite started rising again from 1999–2000 to reach a peak by 2003–04 (Table 2.1).[1]

The pattern in the rise of public debt reveals that external debt rose rapidly until 1971, with a quantum increase in 1966–67 and since then has been taken over by domestic debt. The trend in annual growth rates of domestic and external debt, and GDP are presented in Figure 2.1. External debt increased by an annual average rate of 23.7 per cent from 1952 to 1980 while domestic debt increased by 10.1 per cent. In the period 1980–81 to 1990–91, both external and internal increased by nearly 19.2 per cent. Since 1991–92, the rate of annual increase of domestic debt is higher than external debt.

---

1 The financial year in India refers to the period, 1 April to 31 March. The figures for debt refer to end-March of the year.

Table 2.1: Public debt of the government (1952–2016)

Year (end-March)	Total public debt (₹ in billion)	Percentage to public debt			Percentage of GDP		
		Domestic liabilities	External liabilities	Total public debt	Domestic liabilities	External liabilities	Total public debt
1	2	3	4	5	6	7	8
1951–52	32.4	95.8	4.2	100.0	28.1	1.2	29.3
1960–61	76.3	89.7	10.3	100.0	38.2	4.4	42.5
1970–71	222.5	70.9	29.1	100.0	33.1	13.6	46.7
1980–81	717.3	81.2	18.8	100.0	38.9	9.0	47.9
1990–91	4036.1	83.6	16.4	100.0	57.5	11.3	68.9
2000–01	16041.0	88.2	11.8	100.0	64.9	8.7	73.7
2010–11	51076.4	94.5	5.5	100.0	62.0	3.6	65.6
2011–12	58845.6	94.5	5.5	100.0	63.7	3.7	67.4
2012–13	66235.6	95.0	5.0	100.0	63.2	3.3	66.6
2013–14	75331.6	95.0	5.0	100.0	63.5	3.3	66.8
2014–15	84204.7	95.7	4.3	100.0	64.5	2.9	67.4
2015–16	93073.2	95.8	4.2	100.0	65.6	2.9	68.6

Note: From 2011–12 onwards, GDP Current at Market Price taken with base year as 2011–12.
Source: RBI and Government of India.

The rise in public debt is mainly due to the domestic debt. India's domestic debt has been steadily increasing since 1952.[2] The domestic debt rose from ₹ 31.0 billion in 1952 to ₹ 89.1 trillion by end March 2016, an annual average growth of 13.27 per cent during the period. The domestic debt as a per cent of GDP rose from 32.7 per cent in 1952 to 76.8 per cent in 31 March 2004 and since then has declined to reach 65.6 per cent in March 2016 (Table 2.1). The annual growth in domestic debt as a per cent of GDP rose from 0.6 per cent in 1952–53 to nearly 10.0 per cent in 1966–67, 1980–81, 1985–86 to 1989–90, 1991–92, 1999–2000 and 2001–02 (Figure 2.1).

---

2   Domestic debt of government is computed from the debt of the central (federal) government and the state (provincial) governments. The debt position of the state governments is available only from 1952 onwards. The intragovernment debt like the loans and advances from the central government to the state governments has been excluded in our computations.

Figure 2.1: Domestic debt, external debt and GDP – annual growth (1952–2016)

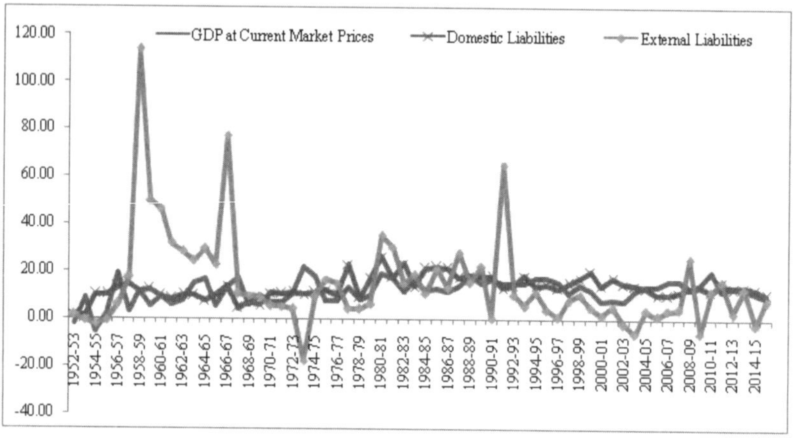

Note: From 2011–12 onwards, GDP at current market prices taken with base year as 2011–12.
Source: RBI.

The decadal rate of growth in select debt indicators reveals that annual average growth rate in domestic debt has been significantly higher than external debt since 1971 (Table 2.2). The increase in public debt has been higher than GDP in all decades except 2001–11, mainly because growth suffered due to great recession. The persistently higher rate of growth of domestic debt as compared to GDP implies a higher burden of debt.[3]

Table 2.2: Decadal rate of growth in select debt indicators (1952–2016)

Year	GDP current at market prices	Domestic liabilities	External liabilities	Total public debt
1	2	3	4	5
1952–61	5.8	9.3	25.7	10.1
1961–71	10.3	8.7	24.9	11.4
1971–81	12.2	14.1	8.3	12.6
1981–91	14.7	19.2	17.6	18.9
1991–01	14.1	15.4	12.3	14.8
2001–11	13.6	13.1	4.2	12.3
2011–16	11.9	13.0	7.5	12.8

Source: RBI.

---

3   As Domar (1944, 822–823) observes 'It is hoped … the problem of debt burden is essentially a problem of achieving a growing national income. A rising income is of course desired on general grounds, but in addition to its many other advantages it also solves the most important aspects of the problem of the debt. The faster income grows, the lighter will be the burden of the debt.'

The increase in domestic debt is mainly due to heavy reliance on domestic borrowings since 1951, mainly because of developmental activities. The Planning Commission,[4] since the First Five Year Plan had strongly favoured the expansion of the debt base, anticipating an important role for borrowing in economic development.[5] This was necessitated due to the weak economic base of the economy. The share of domestic borrowing in the total plan outlay has consistently been high since 1951 (Table 2.3). The share further rose in the Sixth and the Seventh Plans. The Planning Commission realised the implications of the rising dependence on borrowing by mid 1980s while recognising the existing resource crunch, and therefore considered restructuring the pattern of development financing so as to maintain sound financial planning. The share of borrowings increased until the Seventh Five Year Plan, reduced in Eighth and touched a peak in Ninth Plan, reflecting a shrinking share of contribution from public enterprises. Since then, given the financial sector reforms, the share of domestic borrowings has declined in the plan outlay.

The major cause of rising domestic debt is the limited scope for further expansion of the tax revenue to meet growing expenditure, and inadequate returns from large investments made in public enterprises. The tax to GDP ratio has already increased from 7.5 per cent in 1961 to nearly 14.2 per cent in the 1990s to nearly 17.3 per cent in 2016. The major cause, over the years, of rise in expenditure is the increased outlay on defence, interest payments, general administration and food subsidies.[6] Interest payments increased from 2.4 per cent of GDP in 1980–81 to 7.0 per cent in 2003–04 and still were around 5.40 per cent in 2015–16. Defence expenditure increased from 2.4 per cent of GDP in 1980–81 to 3.3 per cent by 1987–88 but since then has been declining and was 2.2 per cent in 2009–10 and 1.7 per cent in 2015–16. The expenditure on administrative services had increased to 1.9 per cent of GDP in 1990–91 from 1.6 per cent in 1980–81, while that on food subsidy increased from 0.4 per cent in 1980–81 to 1.10 per cent in 2009–10

---

4   Planning Commission, Government of India, was responsible for long term planning in the country until it was abolished in 2014.

5   Rao (1953).

6   These represent broadly the non-developmental expenditure of the government. The other items of non-developmental expenditure are tax collection charges, police, subsidy on controlled cloth, grants and loans to foreign countries, and famine relief (Ministry of Finance, Government of India).

and continues to be in that range. In addition to these causes, the restrictions on external borrowing due to the high servicing cost has led to increasing reliance on domestic borrowing, especially since 1970.[7]

Table 2.3: Share of borrowings in the financing pattern of the Five Year Plans of the government

(per cent)

Five Year Plans	Period of the plans	Total plan outlay	Total borrowing (5+6)	Domestic borrowing	External borrowing
1	2	3	4	5	6
First	1951–56	100.00	61.63	51.99	9.64
Second	1956–61	100.00	73.67	51.22	22.45
Third	1961–66	100.00	66.10	37.85	28.25
Annual	1966–69	100.00	75.99	40.08	35.91
Fourth	1969–74	100.00	66.12	53.21	12.91
Fifth	1974–79	100.00	47.99	33.14	14.84
Annual	1979–80	100.00	52.16	43.54	8.62
Sixth	1980–85	100.00	63.30	55.60	7.70
Seventh	1985–90	100.00	81.09	71.96	9.14
Annual	1990–92	100.00	95.93	83.44	12.49
Eighth	1992–97	100.00	74.98	70.06	4.92
Ninth	1997–02	100.00	97.57	95.10	2.47
Tenth	2002–07	100.00	74.91	73.93	0.98
Eleventh	2007–12	100.00	68.90	66.77	2.13
Twelfth*	2012–17	100.00	45.96	45.96	-

Note: '*' Estimates; '-' Not available.
Source: RBI, Planning Commission and Government of India.

The trend in annual domestic borrowing, total expenditure and tax revenue, as a per cent of GDP, is presented in Figure 2.2.

---

[7] The major reasons for foreign exchange crunch were the two oil shocks and the consequent high import bill.

Figure 2.2: Net annual domestic liabilities, total expenditure and tax revenue as per cent of GDP (1960–61 to 2015–16)

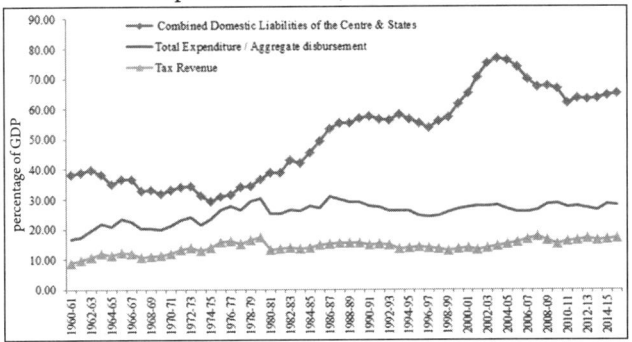

Source: RBI.

Of the tax revenue, the amount collect by central government is significantly larger than that of states (Figure 2.3a and 2.3b).

Figure 2.3a: Direct taxes of centre and states as a percentage of GDP (1950–2016)

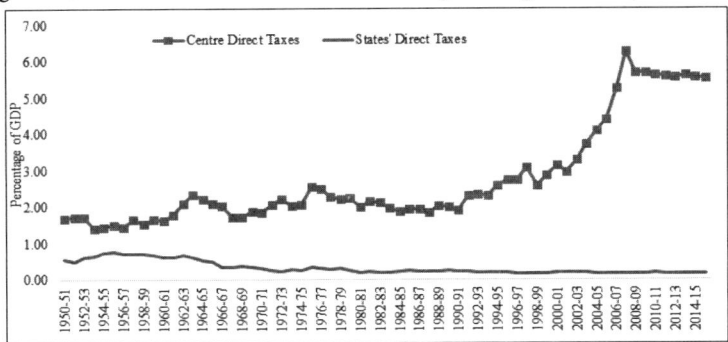

Source: GOI.

Figure 2.3b: Indirect taxes of centre and states as a percentage of GDP (1950–2016)

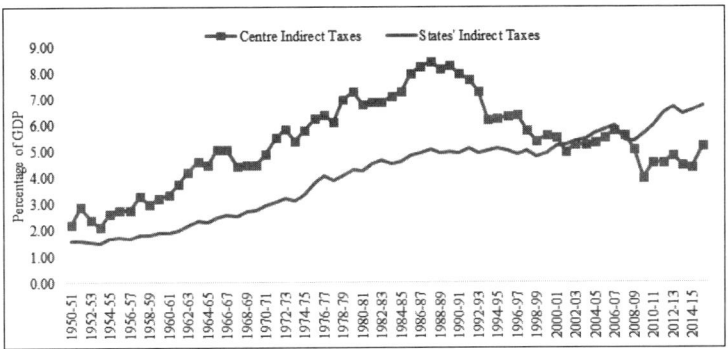

Source: GOI.

In the years since 1981–82, revenue expenditure has increased significantly compared to capital expenditure but tax revenue has not increased accordingly (Figure 2.4).

Figure 2.4: Tax revenues, revenue and capital expenditure of centre and states (1982–2016)

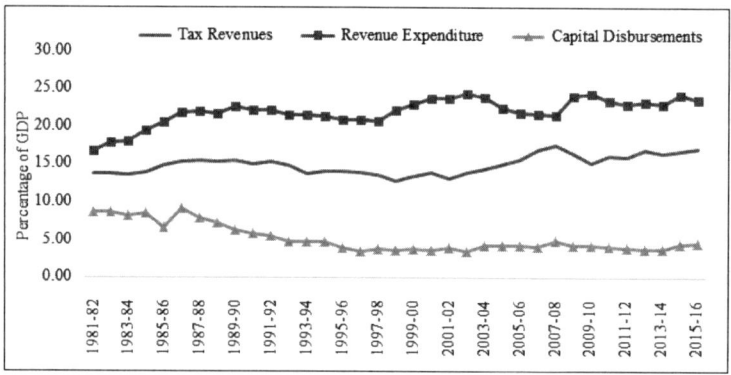

Source: RBI.

Comparatively, when tax revenues are low, deficits increase significantly (Figure 2.5).

Figure 2.5: Total tax revenues, gross fiscal deficit and revenue deficit of centre and states (1982–2016)

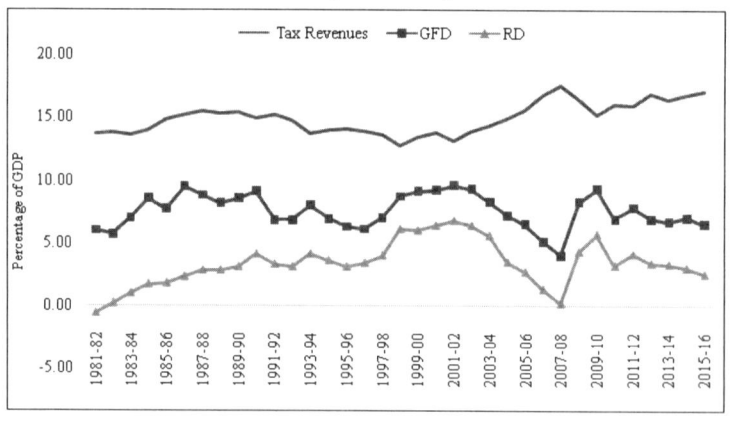

Note: GFD: gross fiscal deficit; RD: revenue deficit.
Source: RBI.

Net interest payments of the central government (difference between the interest payments and interest receipts) in India have been increasing since 1970–71 (Table 2.4) and the amounts are sizeable in recent years.

Table 2.4: Net interest payments

(Rupees billion)

Year	Net interest payments#	Revenue receipts	Revenue expenditure
1	2	3	4
1970–71*	0	33	31
1980–81	8	124	144
1990–91	128	550	735
2000–01	665	1926	2778
2010–11	2143	7885	10407
2011–12	2529	7514	11458
2012–13	2924	8792	12435
2013–14	3524	10147	13718
2014–15	3892	11263	14888
2015–16	4325	11416	15360

* Net interest payments in 1970–71 were ₹ 170 million approximately; # Interest payments - Interest receipts.

Source: RBI.

Table 2.5 presents net interest payments as percentage of the tax revenues, revenue receipts, total receipts, revenue expenditure, total expenditure and the GDP. The change in the ratios is very stark. In 1970–71, all the net interest payments ratios were less than a per cent, and in 1980–81 the ratios were in single digits. During 1970–71 and 2000–01, all these ratios indicate a considerably rising trend. In comparison with the 2000–01 levels, the ratios are lower in 2010–11, after which, other than Net IP to GDP, the other ratios have generally increased. A large chunk of tax revenues, nearly 50 per cent, gets absorbed by interest payments (Kanagasabapathy, Singh and Shimpi, 2016).

In India, the ratio of revenue to capital expenditure has been rising since 1956–57 but the volatility has been the largest in the last decade (Figure 2.6). Similarly, the ratio of revenue to capital receipt has generally been stable except in the last two decades reflecting the trend in government borrowings.

16   Debt Management in India

Table 2.5: Ratio of net interest payment to select macro indicators

(Per cent)

Year	Net IP/ revenue receipts	Net IP/ tax revenue	Net IP/ total receipts	Net IP/ revenue expenditure	Net IP/ total expenditure	Net IP/ GDP at market prices (current prices)
1	2	3	4	5	6	7
1970–71	0.5	0.7	0.3	0.5	0.3	0.0
1980–81	6.5	8.6	4.0	5.6	3.6	0.5
1990–91	23.2	29.7	13.6	17.4	12.1	2.2
2000–01	34.5	48.7	20.4	23.9	20.4	3.1
2010–11	27.2	37.6	18.0	20.6	17.9	2.8
2011–12	33.7	40.2	19.2	22.1	19.4	2.9
2012–13	33.3	39.4	20.0	23.5	20.7	2.9
2013–14	34.7	43.2	22.3	25.7	22.6	3.1
2014–15	34.6	42.8	22.9	26.1	23.1	3.1
2015-16*	37.9	47.0	24.5	28.2	24.3	3.1

IP: Interest payments; *GDP computed.

Source: RBI.

Figure 2.6: Ratio of revenue and capital receipts and expenditure of central government (1951–2016)

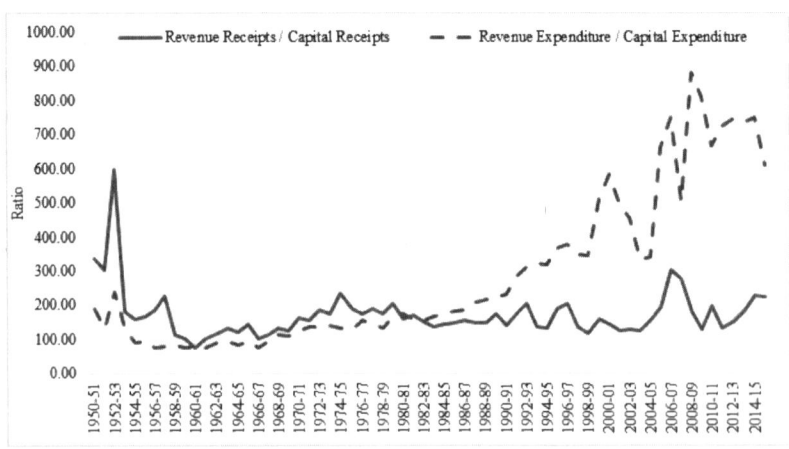

Source: RBI and Government of India.

The increase in capital receipts and revenue expenditure is significantly larger than revenue receipts and capital expenditure (Table 2.6).

Table 2.6: Five-year averages of inflation-adjusted growth rates of revenue and capital accounts of central government (1951–2016)

Year	Revenue expenditure	Capital expenditure	Revenue receipts	Capital receipts
1	2	3	4	5
1951–56	6.8	33.3	6.4	47.3
1956–61	8.7	12.1	7.9	31.4
1961–66	13.5	9.5	15.5	1.6
1966–71	3.6	-0.6	1.3	1.4
1971–76	8.3	7.7	9.8	7.4
1976–81	7.5	1.9	1.4	7.5
1981–86	10.2	9.0	9.2	11.1
1986–91	8.0	2.5	5.8	6.7
1991–96	3.4	-6.1	4.9	0.7
1996–01	9.0	0.1	6.2	14.8
2001–06	5.5	7.6	8.5	2.6
2006–11	11.9	16.0	11.5	14.6
2011–16	3.2	3.8	4.1	5.0

Source: RBI and Government of India.

2.2. Composition of domestic debt

The study of composition of domestic debt becomes essential in an analysis of the implications of rising obligations. The significance of domestic debt is an important feature of fiscal policy in India. In this section, a discussion on the composition of the domestic debt of the government is presented.

The composition of domestic debt can be broadly presented in the following form (Chart 2.1).

Chart 2.1: Domestic debt of the government

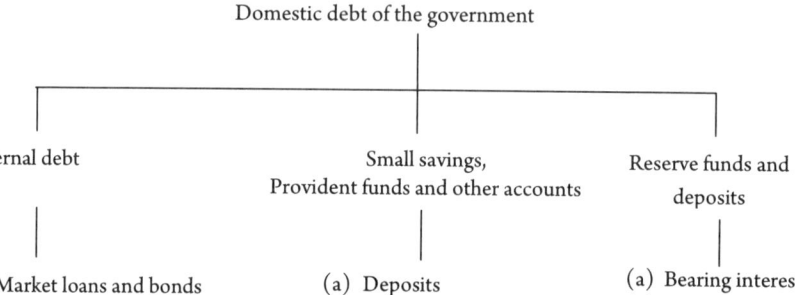

The composition of domestic debt has been changing over the period. The share of internal debt in domestic debt had declined from 67.8 per cent in 1952 to 51.4 per cent in 1995 but then rose to 77.8 per cent in 2016 (Figure 2.7). The kink in 1999, explained later, is due to the formation of National Small Savings Fund (NSSF).

Figure 2.7: Components of domestic debt as per cent to total internal liabilities of combined central and state governments (1952–2016)

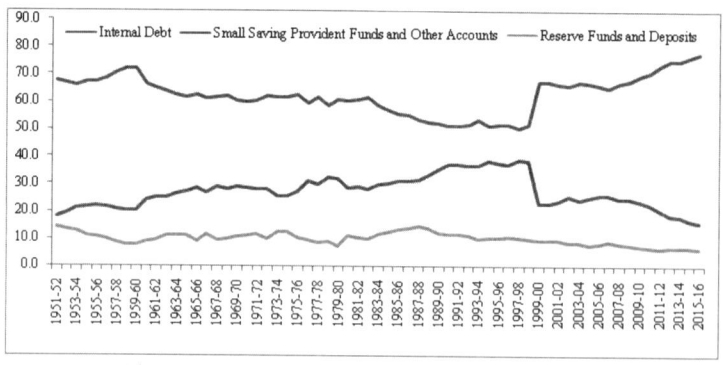

Source: RBI and Government of India.

The highest increase during the period was recorded by internal debt (Table 2.7). The annual average growth rate in all the components of domestic debt was the highest during 1981–91 but since then the rate has generally declined except in case of internal debt.

Table 2.7: Annual average growth in the components of domestic debt of the government (1952–2016)

(per cent)

Year (end of march)	Internal debt	Small saving provident funds and other accounts	Reserve funds and deposits	Domestic liabilities
1	2	3	4	5
1952–2016	13.9	13.5	12.9	13.4
1952–61	9.2	13.0	4.5	9.3
1961–71	7.6	10.6	12.3	8.7
1971–81	14.3	14.1	16.3	14.1
1981–91	17.3	22.4	20.3	19.2
1991–01	19.5	11.5	13.6	15.4
2001–11	14.7	14.0	10.8	13.1
2011–16	14.1	4.6	9.9	13.0

Source: RBI and Government of India.

2.2.1. Internal debt

The important components of internal debt are market loans and bonds, and Treasury bills. Amongst the components, the share of Treasury bills, and special floating and other loans has declined over the period (Table 2.8).[8]

The share of Treasury bills has to be considered along with special securities issued to RBI, as these mainly represent the funding of Treasury bills in the form of special securities issued to the RBI since 1981–82. Considered thus, the share of these two combined components has been increasing over the period. The components of internal debt are discussed in detail as follows.

---

8 Treasury bills, special securities issued to RBI, and special floating and other loans belong exclusively to the central government. Loans from banks and other institutions belong exclusively to state governments. Ways and mean advances and market loans and bonds belong to both, the central and the state governments.

Table 2.8: Components of internal debt of the government
as per cent of total (1952–2016)

(per cent)

Year (end March)	Market loans and bonds	Treasury bills	Special securities issued to RBI	Special floating and other loans	Ways and means advances	Loans from banks and other from RBI institutions	Total internal debt (2 to 7)
1	2	3	4	5	6	7	8
1952	73.93	14.92	0.00	10.41	0.75	0.00	100.00
1961	67.79	24.20	0.00	6.00	0.92	1.09	100.00
1971	59.68	26.45	0.00	7.41	3.94	2.51	100.00
1981	53.62	36.40	1.66	4.36	1.37	2.60	100.00
1991	51.30	4.65	38.84	3.80	0.39	1.02	100.00
2001	74.30	2.62	14.67	3.26	0.95	4.21	100.00
2011	91.58	4.59	0.00	1.00	0.05	2.78	100.00
2012	89.58	7.32	0.00	0.81	0.02	2.28	100.00
2013	90.25	7.00	0.00	0.75	0.01	1.99	100.00
2014	90.64	6.83	0.00	0.71	0.03	1.79	100.00
2015	91.16	6.17	0.00	0.82	0.02	1.84	100.00
2016	90.09	6.46	0.00	1.53	0.02	1.89	100.00

Source: RBI and Government of India.

2.2.1.1. Market loans and bonds

The market loans, also called rupee loans, consist of three kinds of obligation: (a) loans floated by the government; (b) loans issued by the government in exchange for the *ad hoc* Treasury bills outstanding with the RBI;[9] and (c) compensation and other bonds.[10] In this subsection we look into the trends, maturity and ownership pattern of the rupee loans.

Market loans: Market loans, also called as Rupee loans, generally comprise of three kinds of obligations: (a) marketable debt; (b) dated loans issued by

---

9   This refers to the funding operations, which began in 1958–59, amounting to ₹ 19.3 billion until 1980–1981. These loans, offered in conversion, could be subscribed to by the Public.

10 Refers to miscellaneous debts, such as the Hyderabad State Loans, and bonds including five-year Interest Free Prize Bonds; Premium Prize Bonds, 1963 and 1964; National Defence Bonds, 1972; Gold Bonds, 1977; National Defence Gold Bonds (A and B Series), 1980; Bonds (Voluntary Disclosures), 1985; Banks (Acquisition and Transfer) Compensation Bonds, 1979, 1990, and 1999; Jayanti Shipping Company (Acquisition of Shares) Compensation Bonds, 1981; Special Bearer Bonds, 1991; Gold Bonds, 1998; Land Ceiling Compensation Bonds of the state governments, etc.

the government to the RBI in exchange for *ad hoc* Treasury bills outstanding; (c) miscellaneous debts such as, the Hyderabad State Loans, National Defence Bonds, Gold Bonds, etc.

Historically, during earlier years of the First Five Year Plan (FYP), repayments exceeded borrowings mainly due to deflationary conditions in the economy and bearish trends on the money and capital markets. It was only after 1953, that the government was able to float more loans (with stability and revival of confidence in the market). Substantial outlay envisaged in the Second FYP required increased borrowing operations of the government. This is when the technique of market borrowing was reoriented by way of floating multiple loans with varying maturity patterns and rates of interest, in order to cater to a wider range of investment preferences. The loans were raised by the government, both central and state, from the market on fixed coupons and prices till 1992. As a part of financial sector reforms, borrowings for the central government have been undertaken through auctions of government securities of different maturities since 3 June 1992. Since then new instruments have been regularly introduced for example, zero coupon bonds, floating rate bonds and capital indexed bonds. In the case of state governments, the auction system has been initiated from January 1999 and now all states are resorting to borrowing through the auction system.

The amount of market borrowings was decided in consultation with the Planning Commission (until 2014), Ministry of Finance (MoF), state governments, the central government and the RBI. While the RBI prepared a monetary budget taking into account growth in deposits, the Planning Commission, earlier, and the Ministry of Finance now takes into account the overall plan finance over the next few years. The state governments complete a budget exercise, finalise an estimate of market borrowings for the year, and send this estimate to the central government. The central government takes into account all the inputs and finally decides on the allocations, in consultation with the state governments. Thereafter, the overall market borrowings to be undertaken during the year are advised to the RBI. RBI is a debt manager of the central as well as the state governments, except for Jammu and Kashmir, and Sikkim. So, market borrowings for the states are on arbitrary basis, though negotiated, and not on the basis on any formula. Formula based allocation of market borrowings, as is the case for Ways and Means Advances, explained later, would not be appropriate for state borrowings. Primarily because each state would have its specific requirements, at different time periods, and that the requirements (both, the reason as well the time of the requirement) of all states would not necessarily be alike.

To coordinate the activities of debt management with fiscal authorities, various committees function in the RBI and the government. The Cash and Debt Management Committee, consisting of officials from the MoF and the RBI meets regularly to discuss operational details of market borrowings for the central government. The issues pertaining to state governments are discussed in a semi-annual meeting with the officials from MoF, Department of Finance (state) and the RBI.

RBI also advises the central and the state governments on the quantum, timing and terms of issue of new loans. While formulating the borrowing programme for the year the government and the RBI takes into account a number of considerations such as the central and state loans maturing for redemption during the year, the estimate of available resources (based on the growth in deposits with banks, premium income of insurance companies and accretion to provident funds) and absorptive capacity of the market. The normal practice was to float loans inviting subscriptions from the public either in cash or conversion of maturing stock. But on some occasions earlier, such as when individual issues were small or market conditions were not conducive to the success of the issue, the RBI initially took up the entire issue in its portfolio for sale at a later date when demand developed. In carrying out the loan operations, the RBI endeavoured on one hand to minimise the effects on money markets caused by the operations and obtain the best possible terms for the government concerned. Since the introduction of auction system, the RBI mainly looks at the timing of borrowing. In recent years, since 2003, a calendar for borrowings has been introduced which is released to the public on half-yearly basis.

The RBI coordinates the borrowing program of the central and state governments. Normally the central and state governments float loans separately. Consolidated loans were issued in 1954--55 and 1963–64. The states were permitted to issue their own loans mainly because, apart from the difficulty of allocating shares to the various states, centralised borrowing did not offer much scope to the state governments to use their local influences and tap their local resources. In earlier years, generally, all states entered market on identical terms and at same time, with the interest of having an orderly market for public borrowings. To secure the floatation of government loans at reasonable rates of interest, the RBI coordinated the terms on which the direct loans were raised and guaranteed by the state governments.

Since the start of planning in India in 1951, the amount of market loans mobilised annually has been rising rapidly. Market loans of central and state governments increased from 2.1 per cent of GDP in 1980-81 to 7.5 per cent of GDP in 2011-12. The share of state governments, in total market borrowings, varies and ranged from 7.3 per cent in 1980-81 to 42.5 per cent in 2004-05. Market borrowings by the central government were larger in comparison with the state governments. Also, the coupon rates on market bonds floated by the central government were lower than those floated by state governments. In earlier years, because of interest rate advantage, large borrowings were done by the centre and distributed to states and developmental institutions. In view of the rising gross fiscal deficit, and market related rates of interest since 1992 with the introduction of auction system of borrowing, the proportion of market borrowings by the states has generally increased. This is mainly because of two reasons. Firstly, the central government's borrowing costs were rising and to on-lend to states it would generally add a premium, which would make borrowings by the states more expensive. Secondly, many state governments were eager to test the markets themselves and avail of lower interest rates, given their reputation of high growth and regularity in servicing of debt. There was another reason too – the large borrowings by the central government (though on-lent to the states and financial institutions) implied higher gross fiscal deficit for the centre, which was being closely watched by rating and multi-lateral agencies.

There have been innovations in market borrowing policy of the government. Both, the central and state governments have regularly resorted to market loans, which was enhanced during difficult periods. Factors such as rising interest burden, process of financial liberalisation, resulted in lower market borrowing by the central government during 1990-93. The central government brought out a debt swap scheme, which has benefited state governments and, in some way, also the central government. The states have been able to swap their high cost debt to the centre with low cost market borrowings. These additional recoveries have enabled the centre to repay some of its own high cost debt to the NSSF, among others.

In India, a variant of Inflation Indexed Bonds, that is the Capital Indexed Bonds, were first issued in 1997, in which the principal repayment at the time of redemption was indexed to inflation (RBI, 2013b).[11] The Union Budget

---

11   No further issuance of indexed bond was made after the 1997 issuance for nearly a decade and a half, primarily because this instrument received a dull response in primary and secondary markets. Complexities in pricing and, the factor that only the principal was protected from inflation, were brought up as some of the reasons for such lacklustre response (RBI, 2004a). Ghose (2013) observed that, since the bonds issued in June 2013

of 2013–14 made an announcement regarding launch of instruments so as to protect the savings of the poor and middle classes, from inflation, and referred to financial instruments such as the Inflation Indexed Bonds and, the Inflation Indexed National Security Certificates (GoI, 2013b). Consequently, in June 2013, IIBs linked to the Wholesale Price Index were issued by the Government of India, through the RBI. After this issuance, these bonds were issued on a monthly basis, till December 2013 (RBI, 2015a). Unlike Capital Indexed Bonds, the IIBs provide protection to both, the principal and interest payments (Kanagasabapathy, Singh and Shimpi, 2016).

While the IIBs launched in June 2013 were for institutional investors, later in December 2013, Inflation Indexed National Saving Securities-Cumulative (IINSS-C), were launched for retail investors. In IINSS-C, inflation compensation is linked to combined CPI. The interest rate had two components, a fixed rate of 1.5 per cent per annum, and an inflation rate based on CPI, with a lag of three months (RBI, 2014b).

The 'When Issued' market was introduced in India on 3 May 2006 to facilitate the price discovery process and to insulate the PDs from asset fluctuations. Initially, only PDs were allowed to take short positions in WI markets and these transactions were allowed only on re-issue of securities. Now, this market is accessible by all members of the Negotiated Dealing System-Order Matching.[12] On 25 September 2015, the RBI's Bi-Monthly Monetary Policy Statement had given scheduled commercial banks the right to take a short position in the WI market for both new and re-issued securities.[13] The WI Market smoothens the issue process by granting time to participants to consume a large issue of G-secs. Currently, the WI Market is open to most financial institutions including mutual funds, insurance companies, pension funds and NBFCs to take long positions.

The market loans have not been much popular outside the captive market, mainly general public, due to the low rates of interest on these instruments.

---

were linked to the WPI, and not the CPI, these could provide only partial hedge against inflation. Further, Ghose observed that these IIBs received a lacklustre response from medium and small investors, suggesting the view of these investors about the inability of such bonds to offer complete hedge against inflation. RBI (2014a) mentions that the bonds issued in December 2013 also garnered a subdued response as a result of some of the design features, as also because the timing coincided with the issue of various tax free bonds by PSUs, and due to the retail investors' lack of awareness about the product.

12 NDS-OM was introduced by the RBI in August 2005.
13 RBI Circular (2015).

The market for government securities is narrow, being confined to institutional investors comprising mainly the RBI, commercial banks, LIC, PF schemes and other trust funds.

2.2.1.1.1. Trends in the growth of market loans and bonds

Since the start of planning in India in 1951, the amount of market loans mobilised annually has been rising rapidly.[14] The share of market loans was declining until 1993 but since then has consistently been increasing as a share of total internal debt.

The central and state governments have regularly resorted to market loans. The rising trend in the annual average growth rate is perceptible from 1971–72 onwards and then again from 1978–79.[15] The rising interest burden, the process of financial liberalisation beginning from 1991, and the move towards market related rates of interest resulted in lower market borrowing by the central government during 1990–93. The central government compared to state governments has been borrowing large amounts through the market loans due to its stronger resource base and its past record of regularly servicing the loans. In addition, coupon rates on market bonds floated by the central government were lower than those floated by the state governments.[16] Thus the central government was borrowing funds at a lower cost than the state governments.

The trend in the net market borrowing of the central and state governments as per cent of GDP is presented in Figure 2.8. In the figure, the break in the trend for the central government in 1954 and 1993, and for the state governments in 1958 and 1964 is explained as follows. In 1954, the central government repaid its existing debt and no net borrowings were incurred, while in 1993 an increasing reliance was placed on borrowing through the Treasury bills. In 1958, the net borrowing by the state governments was low due to stringent conditions prevailing in the market and only two states floated market bonds. In 1964, the state governments

---

14   In the earlier years, repayments exceeded the borrowing mainly due to the deflationary conditions in the economy and the bearish trends on the money and capital markets. It was only after 1953, with the establishment of stability and revival of confidence in the market that the government was able to float substantial amount of loans (Dalaya, 1966, 23).

15   This corresponds to the increased financial requirements by the government due to the war with Pakistan in December 1971, followed by the two oil shocks. The external borrowings declined after the war.

16   Normally, the central and the state governments float market loans separately. Consolidated loans were, however, issued in 1963–64 (RBI, 1970, 26).

did not borrow from the market directly, but received a portion from the combined borrowing by the central government.

Figure 2.8: Net market borrowings of the government through loans and bonds as per cent of GDP (current at market prices) (1952–2016)

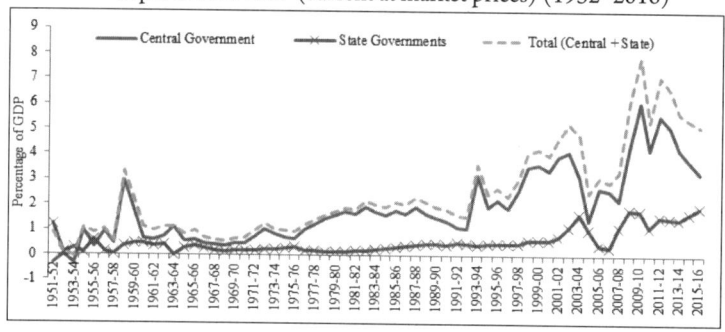

Note: From 2011–12 onwards, the base year was revised as 2011–12.
Source: RBI.

2.2.1.1.2. Maturity pattern of market loans and bonds

The maturity pattern of rupee loans is an important indicator in assessing the impact of the domestic debt. The maturity pattern of market loans and bonds has also been changing. In the 1950s, market loans with a maturity period of less than ten years were popular. But to secure funds for investment in long term projects for capital formation, bonds with a longer maturity period were floated from 1959 onwards.[17] The maximum maturity period of bonds was raised to twenty years from 1959–60 and to thirty years from 1969–70. From 1986–87, on the basis of the recommendations of the Monetary Committee Report,[18] the maximum maturity period was reduced to 20 years. On introduction of auction system, the central government loans, with a maximum maturity period of ten years, were floated where the coupon rates were determined by the market. The maturity period was once again raised to 20 years in 1998–99, 25 years in 2001–02, 30 years in 2002–03 and 40 years in 2017.

The maturity pattern of government securities, on the basis of the data collected from the survey, is presented in Table 2.9.[19] The data reveals that the

---

17 The large developmental outlay envisaged in the Second Five Year Plan necessitated increased borrowing operations of the government. The technique of market borrowing was reoriented then to cater for a wider range of investment preferences. Instead of a single medium dated loan as was usually the case in the earlier periods, multiple loans with varying maturity patterns and coupon rates were floated.

18 Report of the Committee to Review the Working of the Monetary System, RBI (1985).

19 The data was collected from the survey on ownership pattern of government securities

share of short-term loans (less than five years) and long term loans (more than ten years) is declining, while that of five to ten years is on the increase.

Table 2.9: Maturity pattern of market loans and bonds (1958–2016)

(per cent)

Year (end March)	0–5 years	5–10 years	10 years and above	Non-terminals	Total
1	2	3	4	6	7
1958*	35.90	32.60	20.00	11.50	100.00
1968	44.00	17.00	33.00	6.00	100.00
1978	17.53	27.98	52.25	2.21	100.00
1982	18.41	17.87	62.53	1.17	100.00
1990	10.56	9.92	78.92	0.07	100.00
2001	29.36	40.99	29.65	0.00	100.00
2010	31.24	35.83	32.93	0.00	100.00
2016	28.03	39.62	32.35	0.00	100.00

* End-December.

Note: Government Securities for over 10 years for 1978 and 1982 include non-terminables for state governments. The total for 1990 includes the investments of provident funds of scheduled and non-scheduled commercial banks in case of which maturity pattern is not available. Therefore the maturity-wise break-up will not add up to the total.

Source: RBI.

2.2.1.1.3. Ownership pattern of market loans and bonds

The major investors in rupee loans are RBI,[20] banks, insurance companies and provident funds (Table 2.10). A large number of these institutions are nationalised

which was initiated by RBI in 1957. These surveys were conducted on an annual basis until 1971 but since then, have been placed on an *ad hoc* basis. The last such survey was conducted for the period 1990. The survey provides detailed data, not available elsewhere. The surveys for the period 1957 and 1958 provide data as at the end of December, while the surveys since 1959 provide data as at the end of March. The data at the end of March is consistent with other data in India, as India follows a fiscal year, April to March. The data for 2001 and 2016 were compiled from the publications of the RBI.

20 The RBI holds securities on its own account, as also for the purpose of conducting open market operations. RBI traditionally avoids subscribing to the market loans floated by the state governments. Though in the 1950s it did hold state government loans, it has not held these since then. It also holds a negligible amount of government securities on behalf of others.

and help transfer private saving to the government and these generally constitute the captive market.[21] The existence of the captive market helps in the successful operation of fiscal and monetary policy as it constitutes a stable source of demand for government securities.[22] The captivity operates through the Statutory Liquidity Ratio (SLR). SLR was originally introduced as a means of imposing financial discipline on the banks and providing some measure of protection to the depositors. Subsequently, the definition of SLR was modified to strengthen the effectiveness of the cash reserve ratio as a tool of monetary policy. Since 1970, it came to be used as a tool to pre-empt a given proportion of resources mobilised by banks. Since the yields on government bonds were lagging behind, it was impossible to market government bonds without the compulsion of SLR.[23] SLR rose from 20.0 per cent in 1949–50 to 25.0 per cent in 1964–65, 35.0 per cent in 1981–82 and to 38.5 per cent in 1990–91. It was reduced to 29.5 per cent in 1994–95 to make the banking operations more flexible, and as part of the liberalisation process of the financial markets initiated since 1991. The rate was lowered to 24 per cent in December 2010, 23 per cent in August 2012, 21 per cent in July 2016, 20.5 per cent in January 2017 and 20.0 per cent in June 2017.

The share of banks had doubled by 1990 while the share of government and the Provident Funds had declined over the period. In recent years, the share of banks has declined but the share of issuances companies, foreign portfolio investors, corporate, mutual funds and DDs (covered under others) has been increasing. The sharp decline in the share of provident funds in 1990 was due to a change in statutory requirements since 1986.

The share of the RBI varies widely as it is entrusted with the task of managing public debt on behalf of the government and therefore had to provide an initial market for the loans until 2006. The conditions prevailing in the Indian money market, in the initial years, when markets were developing justified the large scale

---

21 Captive market refers to the concept under which the specified financial institutions have to statutorily subscribe to government bonds and have to maintain a minimum balance of these in their portfolios. This market consists of commercial banks, provident funds, insurance companies, industrial finance corporation, state finance corporations and the RBI.

22 Tobin (1963, 211) observes, '..costs could be lowered, without sacrifice of monetary effect, by enlarging the captive market for government debt through a secondary reserve requirement on Banks, and through reserve requirements on other financial intermediaries. These requirements would also improve the efficiency of monetary control.'

23 Rao (1980).

Table 2.10: Ownership pattern of market loans and bonds (1958–2016)

(per cent)

Year (end of March)	Government	RBI (Own account)	Banks	Insurance	Provident funds	Others	Total
1	2	3	4	5	6	7	8
1958*	10.14	13.68	28.58	13.48	5.96	28.15	100.00
1968	7.80	30.14	23.49	14.00	16.86	7.71	100.00
1978	1.81	18.54	41.70	16.13	19.53	2.30	100.00
1982	0.98	23.34	44.11	13.80	16.34	1.43	100.00
1990	0.37	18.67	57.88	14.35	2.70	6.02	100.00
2000	0.00**	6.98	60.86	18.06	2.04	12.05	100.00
2010	0.00**	10.13	59.12	20.76	4.89	5.10	100.00
2016	1.35	9.91	41.89	24.91	8.64	13.29	100.00

* End-December; ** Not separately available.

Note: Others include investments by financial institutions, electricity boards, transport corporations, joint stock companies, trusts, and individuals.

Source: RBI.

buying of government securities by the RBI at the time of floating the loan in the market and then selling them to the public later. This resulted in large holdings of government securities by the RBI of India at certain times.[24] The monetary policy required to sterilise this had to be very flexible, but such flexibility did not exist in India, and therefore it had adverse monetary implications. The RBI's participation in the primary auctions of dated securities was discontinued from 14 April 2006 except under exceptional circumstances as per the Fiscal Responsibility and Budget Management Act, 2003.

Thus, the market for government securities was narrow for a long time as they were developing. It has been generally observed in less developed countries, unlike the developed countries, that non-bank investors tend to hold only a small part of their assets in liquid form. The government finances itself mainly by recourse

---

24 As discussed in the RBI (1960, 4), 'In India where the money market is characterised by a sharply defined seasonal pattern, it is not convenient for the Government to enter the market with new loans time and again or to keep loans on tap indefinitely. It becomes necessary, therefore for the Reserve Bank to acquire a reasonable stock of Government securities of varying maturities for meeting the requirements of the investors all the year round. The RBI may be compared to a wholesale merchant who acquires a large stock at the time of harvest.'

to the banking system.[25] This has also been the experience of many developing countries, including India.[26]

The major reason for the ownership pattern showing a restrictive trend initially was due to the low yield on market loans. The coupon rates on government securities were out of alignment with other rates prevailing in the economy from the early 1970s to the mid-1980s (Table 2.11). Though, since 1978–79, coupon rates on government securities were raised in phases, yet these continued to be low as compared with the other rates in the economy until mid-1980s. In recent years, especially after the reforms of 1991, the coupon rates are more aligned with the market which reflected in the wider ownership pattern with loans being subscribed by mutual funds, and corporate, explained earlier.

Table 2.11: Structure of interest rates – long term (1960–2016)

(per cent)

Year	Commercial bank rates		Coupon rates on market loans and bonds		
	3-5 years	Over 5 years	0-5 years	5-10 years	Over 10 years
1	2	3	4	5	6
1960–61	4.0	4.5	-	4.0	4.0
1970–71	7.0	7.25	-	4.5	5.75
1980–81	10.0	10.0	-	6.5	7.5
1990–91	11.0	11.0	10.5	10.75	11.5
2000–01	9.50–10.00	8.50–10.00	9.47–10.95	9.88–11.69	10.47–11.70
2010–11	8.25–8.75	8.50–8.75	5.98–8.67	7.17–8.19	7.64–8.63
2011–12	9.00–9.25	8.50–9.25	8.21–8.49	7.80–10.01	8.25–9.28
2012–13	8.75–9.00	8.50–9.00	8.82–8.21	7.86–8.72	7.91–8.06
2013–14	8.75–9.10	8.50–9.10	7.22–9.00	7.16–9.40	7.36–9.40
2014–15	8.50–8.75	8.25–8.50	*	7.66–9.28	7.65–9.42
2015–16	7.00–7.50	7.00–7.30	*	7.54–8.10	7.59–8.27

'-' Interest rates unavailable; '*' Not Floated.
Source: RBI.

---

25 Sreekantaradhya (1972), 124.
26 Seshadri (1976), 633.

The reforms in debt management were initiated in 1986 with the objective of spreading the ownership of market loans.[27] The maximum maturity period of the government loans was reduced from the prevalent 30 years to 20 years and the coupon rates were raised in phases to more market related rates. The primary and satellite dealers were introduced and auction system of raising resources at market-related rates of interest was used.

Primary and satellite dealers: The primary objective of a Primary Dealer system is to create an institutional mechanism and provide the infrastructure for smooth functioning and development of the primary and secondary market for government securities. In India, this was intended at marketisation of government borrowings. The guidelines and procedures of the primary dealer system were issued by the RBI on 25 March 1995. Primary dealers were appointed in November 1995 and have been operating since 1 February 1996. The licenses were granted first to Securities Trading Corporation of India Ltd. (STCI), Discount and Finance House of India Ltd. (DFHI), ICICI Securities and Finance Company Ltd. (I-SEC) which were stand-alone PDs and three commercial banks, State Bank of India, Punjab National Bank and Canara Bank which set up subsidiaries for the same purpose. They were the six PDs that operated in 1996, which then rose to a total of 13 during 1998–99. In March 2006 when there was an overhaul of the PD system, there were 17 PDs.[28] There are 21 registered, as on 31 May 2017, with the Primary Dealers Association of India (PDAI), a self-regulatory body for PDs that was incorporated in December 1997.

Given the high levels of uncertainty in PD funding and the vagaries of the interest rate movement, the RBI saw the need to nurture primary dealers to allow them to be competitive in the market. By virtue of the Fiscal Responsibility and Budget Management Act, 2003 the RBI was mandated to stop continuing as underwriter of last resort and withdrew its services from primary issues of government securities. An Internal technical group on central government securities market was constituted in December 2004 by the RBI with the purpose of 'examining the implications of the RBI's withdrawal under the FRBM Act from participation in primary issues for the conduct of the RBI's debt management function'.[29] The group's report published in July 2005 recommended a fresh approach towards developing the government securities market by allowing PDs to

---

27 Following the Monetary Committee Report, RBI (1985).
28 Gomez (2008), 145.
29 Report on internal Technical Group on Central Government Securities Market (2005).

exercise greater freedom in operation. Thus, PDs have become sole underwriters of government debt since 2006.

Primary dealers play an active role in both primary and secondary markets of government securities. The primary obligations of a PD include: supporting auctions of government bonds by giving annual bidding commitments to the RBI after negotiations, underwriting the primary issuance and to offer two-way quotes in select government securities through the Negotiated Dealing System-Order Matching (NDS-OM), over-the-counter market and recognised stock exchanges. Serious bidding is ensured through a stipulated success ratio, and PDs also take principal positions in the secondary market.[30]

The RBI currently extends facilities to PDs to enable them to effectively fulfil their obligations, such as: access to Current Account facility with RBI; access to Subsidiary General Ledger (SGL) account facility; permission to borrow and lend in the money market including call money market and to trade in all money market instruments; and, access to the Liquidity Adjustment Facility (LAF) whereby the RBI operates in the market through repos and reverse repos.

To assist PDs, satellite dealer system was introduced by the RBI with the fundamental intention of broadening the scope of the government securities market by focusing on trading, distribution and dealing of government securities in the secondary market. The secondary market was projected to distribute securities at the retail level and thereby widen the investor profile. The system was launched on 31 December 1996 following successful functioning of PDs but was discontinued on 31 May 2002 due to failure of achieving anticipated results. Before the system was scrapped, there were 14 dealers that had been granted approval to participate in the secondary market.[31]

Auction method of government securities: The RBI experimented with both the multiple price (European) and uniform price (Dutch) auction method, although preference was given to multiple price auction method. The government felt that it could maximise revenues because of the advantage posed by this method, which ensured that bidders paid the price that they quoted. Although economists preferred the uniform price method, the only major constraint with multiple price auctions was that the winning bidder would incur losses in a low priced auctions, termed as 'winners' curse'.

---

30 GOI, 2012.
31 Ghose and Rajaram (2015), 9.

Akin to the multiple and uniform price experiments, yield-based auctions were tested along with price-based auctions, finally resorting to the latter due to the odd fractional yields and odd coupon rates that confused market participants. Communication of results of auctions also became a matter of concern given the fact that some market participants with in-house treasury departments had an unfair advantage over others. However, in 1996, the weighted average yield, a key piece of information, was also disclosed along cut-off yield, balanced unsubscribed and amount accepted in the auction.

Another development that led to the auction method being adopted for state government securities was the discovery of yields for state government securities being higher than central government securities. And since many state governments' securities were floated together at fixed coupon rates, states with better fiscal responsibility would have to settle for mediocre treatment of their securities. Thus, to safeguard the interests of states and to rewards their fiscal restraint, the auction method was adopted.[32]

Consequent to the auction system, yield on government securities were market determined and have narrowed with development of the market (Figure 2.9).

Figure 2.9: Cut off yields of central government securities (1988–2015)

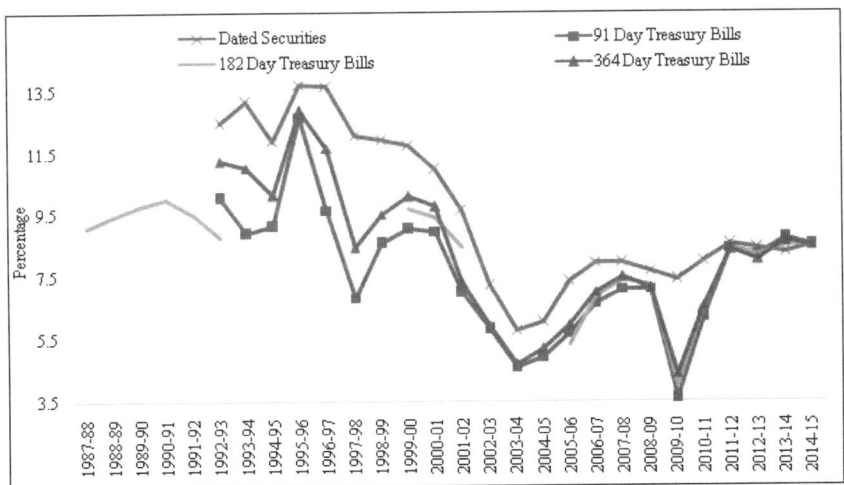

Source: RBI and Government of India.

---

32 In 1992, the RBI Governor suggested another key reform in the form of auctioning of government securities with a reserve price and with RBI intervention. The rationale behind this suggestion lay in the contradiction posed by interest rate caps and open market operations. The reserve price mechanism would allow the RBI to more actively intervene in markets and more importantly, moderate any jump in interest rates.

The development of the market also reflects in the lower devolvement on PDs and the RBI (Table 2.12).

Table 2.12: Devolvement of government securities on primary dealers and RBI (1988–2015)

(₹ crore)

Year	Dated securities		91 day Treasury bills		182 day Treasury bills		364 day Treasury bills	
	on PDs	on RBI	on PDs	on RBI	on PDs	on RBI	on PDs	on RBI
1	2	3	4	5	6	7	8	9
1987–88	-	-	-	-	0	0	-	-
1988–89	-	-	-	-	0	0	-	-
1989–90	-	-	-	-	0	0	-	-
1990–91	-	-	-	-	0	0	-	-
1991–92	-	-	-	-	0	0	-	-
1992–93	0	2215	0	1149	0	0	0	0
1993–94	0	435	0	3235	-	-	0	0
1994–95	0	157	0	2406	-	-	0	0
1995–96	0	12729	0	7791	-	-	0	0
1996–97	357	3697	523	3370	-	-	0	0
1997–98	1903	13027	869	1089	-	-	0	0
1998–99	3125	38205	1160	3015	-	-	514	1572
1999–00	2792	27000	57	1525	0	556	0	2267
2000–01	7381	31151	0	856	0	250	0	1827
2001–02	735	28892	0	0	0	0	0	0
2002–03	2722	36175	0	0	-	-	0	0
2003–04	0	21500	0	0	-	-	0	0
2004–05	985	1197	0	0	-	-	0	0
2005–06	0	10000	0	0	0	0	0	0
2006–07	5605	0	0	0	0	0	0	0
2007–08	957	0	0	0	0	0	0	0
2008–09	10775	0	0	0	0	0	0	0
2009–10	7219	0	0	0	0	0	0	0

Table continued

Table 2.12: Devolvement of government securities on primary dealers and RBI (1988–2015)

(₹ crore)

Year	Dated securities		91 day Treasury bills		182 day Treasury bills		364 day Treasury bills	
	on PDs	on RBI	on PDs	on RBI	on PDs	on RBI	on PDs	on RBI
1	2	3	4	5	6	7	8	9
2010–11	5772	0	0	0	0	0	0	0
2011–12	12112	0	0	0	0	0	0	0
2012–13	1828	0	0	0	0	0	0	0
2013–14	17450	0	0	0	0	0	0	0
2014–15	5272	0	0	0	0	0	0	0

Source: RBI and Government of India.

Market stabilisation scheme: Large-scale capital inflows from 2003–04 onwards, on account of growing foreign direct investment and foreign portfolio inflows, led to a progressive decline in the quantum of government securities owned by the RBI.[33] It was found that the RBI's efforts to manage the forex movement and liquidity through various methods such as liquidity adjustment facility and open market operations resulted in a significant depletion in the quantity of government securities present with the RBI. The major problem that the RBI faced was that with this impending shortage, the OMO's ability to sterilise large forex inflows would be rendered useless. The RBI and government even resorted to non-market measures such as pre-payment of high costing external debt to the US, ADB and World Bank, liberalisation of capital outflows, encouraging domestic companies to retain foreign earnings abroad, discouraging non-resident deposits and external commercial borrowings and restricting debt inflows.[34]

Finally, Market Stabilisation Scheme was introduced on 23 February 2004, and launched on 23 April 2004. The Working Group thus saw the need for effectively managing monetary policy 'by "sterilising" the expansionary impact of forex inflows'.[35]

In an effort to strengthen the RBI's ability to freely conduct monetary policy and stabilise the effects of foreign exchange markets, the Government of India

---

33　Subbarao, D. (2011).
34　RBI (2003a).
35　RBI (2003a).

entered into a Memorandum of Understanding (MoU) with the RBI to authorise the issuance of existing debt instruments and securities such as Treasury bills and dated securities. The bonds, bills and dated securities that are issued by way of auction through the RBI have a specified ceiling limit that is agreed upon by the government and RBI from time to time. However, tenure, timing, amount and other conditions are left to RBI's discretion. The amount under MSS is part of internal debt.

The initial amount of outstanding obligations held by the government in 2004 was not allowed to exceed ₹ 60,000 crore and was ₹ 30,000 crore for 2016–17.[36] However, in the follow-up to central government's demonetisation directive, banking system's liquidity increased due to a surge in deposits. As a result, the ceiling of MSS was raised to ₹ 6,00,000 crore.[37] To mitigate any impact of this scheme on revenue and fiscal deficits, equivalent cash balance would be maintained by the government for all bills and bonds issued and recorded separately in the budget for transparency.

2.2.1.2. Treasury bills

Treasury bills are the most short-term issues of the central government, generally for a period of three months.[38] In India, 91-day Treasury bills have been in the market since 1917,[39] while the 182-day Treasury bills were introduced in November 1986 and the 364-day Treasury bills in April 1992.

The share of Treasury bills in internal debt increased from 14.9 per cent in 1952 to 36.4 per cent during 1981. However, the share of Treasury bills has since declined and is now in the range of 6.5 per cent (Table 2.8). The various types of Treasury bills prevalent in India are briefly discussed in this sub-section.

2.2.1.2.1. 91-day Treasury Bills

In India, 91-day Treasury bills are of two kinds – (a) *ad hoc* Treasury bills; and (b) Normal Treasury bills. The *ad hoc* Treasury bills are issued by the central government in favour of the RBI for the purpose of replenishing the cash balances maintained by it with the RBI.[40] The normal Treasury bills are sold in auctions or

---

36 RBI Press Release (2016a).

37 RBI Press Release (2016b).

38 Treasury bills on behalf of the state governments were sold infrequently in the past. Since 1950, no Treasury bills have been issued by the state governments (RBI, 1970, 26).

39 Barman (1978), 81 and Velayudham (1986), 39.

40 The origin of *ad hoc* Treasury bills dates back to 1940–41 when the sterling debt had to be repatriated. As the sterling used for repatriation of the Government of India debt

on tap, and are intended to be primarily an investment outlet for short-term funds. These were offered through weekly auctions until 1965. However, 'intermediate' sale of Treasury bills were also made by the RBI at a discount fixed by it. The auction system was discontinued from July 1965 and the Treasury bills were made available on tap from the RB at a fixed discount rate.

In July 1965, when the auction system was discontinued, the discount rate was fixed at 3.5 per cent per annum. This was raised in phases to 4.6 per cent per annum in April 1974 where it continued until 1997. In recent years, with introduction of auctions, discount rate on Treasury bills is market related (Table 2.13).

Table 2.13: Structure of interest rates – short term (1961–2016)

(per cent)

Year	Bank rate	Treasury bills - 91-day (Tap)	Call money rate – Bombay
1	2	3	4
1960–61	4.0	2.65	4.24
1970–71	6.0	3.08	6.38
1980–81	9.0	4.6	7.12
1990–91	10.0	4.6	15.85
2000–01	7.0	6.2	9.15
2010–11	6.0	8.4	5.89
2011–12	9.5	8.2	8.22
2012–13	8.5	8.9	8.09
2013–14	9.0	8.5	8.28
2014–15	8.5	7.4	7.97
2015–16	7.75	7.3	6.98

Source: RBI.

belonged to the RBI, arrangements had to be made to provide the Bank with alternative eligible rupee assets. The rupee finance was provided in part by the issue of *ad hoc* Treasury bills. The *ad hocs* were retired when the government's dated securities loan programme was undertaken.

The present use of *ad hocs*, resulting in automatic creation when the central government's cash balance falls below the minimum stipulated amount, has been in vogue since 1954–55 (RBI, 1994c, 4–5). The amount of these bills was restricted under an agreement between the central government and the RBI (RBI, 1995, VIII-3). These *ad hoc* Treasury Bills were discontinued from 1 April 1997.

In initial years, before 1997, the discount rate on Treasury bills was lower than the interest rates prevalent in the market for short term notes. As a result of the low discount rate this instrument was traditionally supported by RBI (Table 2.14).

Table 2.14: Ownership pattern of 91-day Treasury bills (1952–2016)

(per cent)

Year (end of March)	RBI	Banks	State governments*	Others #	Foreign banks	Total
1	2	3	4	5	6	7
1952	85.35	-	14.65	0.0	-	100.00
1961	80.11	-	17.27	2.62	-	100.00
1971	88.09	1.59	8.38	1.95	-	100.00
1981	92.16	4.05	3.38	0.40	-	100.00
1991	71.59	0.14	27.04	1.22	-	100.00
2001	4.07	50.58	-	8.72	36.63	100.00
2011	-	33.85	16.65	49.50	-	100.00
2012	-	39.18	17.32	40.16	3.34	100.00
2013	-	43.09	35.16	21.75	-	100.00
2014	-	29.54	39.44	31.02	-	100.00
2015	-	41.38	34.10	24.53	-	100.00
2016	-	34.85	36.20	28.96	-	100.00

* Refers to state governments and other approved bodies until 1969\70; # Other is the residual item until 1969/70; - Not Available.

Note: The outstanding amount shown against different holders from 1981 are net of bills rediscounted with the RBI.

Source: RBI.

The low discount rate on 91-day Treasury bills on tap and the resultant concentration of holdings with the RBI restricted the operation of monetary policy, raised the reserve money and inhibited the development of the secondary market in these bills. Therefore, the auction system was revived in January 1993.

Ad hoc Treasury bills: The RBI is authorised to grant advances to central and state governments that are repayable in three months. While these WMAs were aimed at enabling the government to maintain the minimum prescribed balance with the RBI, it was found that the WMAs were not availed from 1944 to 1954.

However, from 1954-55 onwards, the government was allowed to purchase *ad hoc* Treasury bills from the RBI. Both the RBI and Government officials agreed to create *ad hocs* to automatically replenish the balances of the government to match the stipulated amount. The RBI also used this mechanism by purchasing *ad hocs* from the government to facilitate currency expansion in times of need.

However, the excessive issuance of *ad hocs* resulted in uncontrolled and automatic monetisation of government deficits, immobilising the RBI's efforts to rein in inflation. It must be noted that this matter was a subject of discussion between the RBI and MoF as early as 1957. The then Governor, H.V.R. Iyengar had pointed out that there was no means of stopping the government from increasing the currency if it wished increase to expenditure. This 'merely mechanical' process, he pointed out, would prevent the RBI from achieving its statutory responsibility of 'securing monetary stability'. The then Finance Minister, T. T. Krishnamachari, replied that the setting up of any rigid procedures on creation of *ad hoc* Treasury bills was unnecessary.

In 1984, the RBI urged for an increase in the Treasury bill rates which had stagnated since 1974 whereas rates on other dated securities' had risen during this period. In 1985, as the RBI realised that the volume of outstanding Treasury bills had reached a record high back at the time, a suggestion was made to the government to either finance these bills or increase the interest rates on them. Similarly in 1989, as suggested in earlier years, the RBI renewed its pitch to request the government to go in for large-scale funding of outstanding 91-day Treasury bills as there was 'no purpose served' in renewing this bills regularly. The RBI pointed out that a short-term instrument such as the Treasury bills were being used for meeting long-term requirements of government along with open-ended monetisation of government deficits. This was undermining the role and effectiveness of monetary policy.

In 1993, the then RBI Governor, Dr C. Rangarajan charted a plan for phasing out of *ad hoc* Treasury bills. In the Union Budget speech of 1994–95, Finance Minister announced that *ad hoc* Treasury bills were to be phased as per an agreement signed by the RBI and government on 9 September 1994. It was also decided that government's budget deficit would be delinked from automatic and unlimited monetisation owing to *ad hoc* Treasury bills by 1997–98. It was then agreed between the RBI and government that the year 1996–97 was the final year for the adjustment programme that would phase out *ad hoc* Treasury bills and from 1 April 1997, and the mechanism would be replaced by WMAs limited to the bank rate and repayable at the end of the financial year. On 31 March 1997, all outstanding *ad hoc* Treasury bills were converted into special securities without any specific maturity. Finally, from 1 April 1997, WMAs were extended to the government at a mutually agreed interest rate. In the event of an overdraft, the RBI would calculate daily overdrawn balances and charge interest on the same. The amount advanced would have to be repaid within three months' time, failing which the government would have to issue securities to raise the money to cover the WMA outstanding balance.

2.2.1.2.2.182-day/364-day Treasury bills

The 182-day Treasury bills were introduced in 1986 to develop the bill market. The 182-day Treasury bills were offered to the public,[41] in auctions, from November 1986 to April 1992. This instrument was devised to provide an alternative avenue for short term investments and facilitate the development of a secondary market. The discount rate on these bills moved in the range of 6.8–9.6 per cent during 1986–92. This instrument was popular in the market and accounted for 31.1 per cent of outstanding Treasury bills in 1992.

The success of the 182-day Treasury bills led to its replacement by the 364-day Treasury bills in April 1992 with a view to providing financial instruments with varying short-term maturities to cater for the needs of different investors. 182-day bills were restarted in June 1999 and again discontinued in May 2001. Once again, 182-day bills were re-introduced in 2005. In March 2016, of the two, 364-day Treasury bills accounted for 66.4 per cent of total outstanding. The discount rate on 182-day bills, over 1987–2016 ranged between 4 per cent and 10 per cent, while 364-day bills ranged between 4.4 and 12.9 per cent during 1992 to 2016.

2.2.1.3. Special securities issued to RBI

Special securities issued to RBI mainly represent the funding of *ad hoc* Treasury bills (91-day) and have no specific maturity period.[42] The share of these securities in internal debt increased from 1.7 per cent in 1981 to 38.8 per cent in 1991 and since then has been declining. The amount of special securities was liquidated by

---

41 Other than the government and RBI.
42 Refers to conversion of 91-day Treasury Bills into long-term government securities. These are different from those referred earlier. The difference lies in the fact, that those could be subscribed by the public while in the present case, these were issued specifically to the RBI.

end-March 2003 (Table 2.8).[43] These securities earned interest at the rate of 4.6 per cent per annum, until liquidation similar to the discount rate on the *ad hoc* Treasury bills that were converted/ funded. Thus, this conversion enabled the government to borrow at low cost for a longer period of time.

2.2.1.4. Special floating and other loans

Special Floating and other loans refer to non-negotiable, non-interest bearing rupee securities issued to International Financial Institutions to meet certain obligations.[44] Its share in internal debt consistently declined from 10.4 per cent in 1952 to 0.7 per cent in 2014, before rising to 1.5 per cent in 2016 (Table 2.8).[45]

2.2.1.5. Ways and means advances

The RBI provides Ways and Means Advances (WMA) to the government to tide over temporary financial imbalances. The central government had not resorted to this instrument between 1943–44 and 1997.[46] The state governments have used this facility regularly to tide over a temporary mismatch in the cash flow of receipts and expenditure.[47] The WMA to the state governments are of two types *viz.*, Special and Normal. The special WMA is provided against the pledge of Government of India securities while the normal WMA is provided without

---

43   Also includes a marginal amount of securities issued to the RBI against compulsory deposits held in RBI.

44   They are issued in making subscriptions to the international financial institutions like International Monetary Fund (IMF), International Bank for Reconstruction and Development (IBRD) and International Development Association (IDA). Special rupee securities are also issued in making contributions towards the share capital of the Asian Development Bank (ADB). They are also issued whenever the subscription quotas or the share capital in these are revised.

45   This increase in special floating loans was necessitated under the 'maintenance of value' provision of the Funds Article of Agreement, under which the value of the currencies of members held in the General Resources Account is to be maintained in terms of Special Drawing Rights.

46   RBI (1970), 28.

47   Each state government (except Jammu and Kashmir, and Sikkim) has entered into a separate agreement with the RBI to keep a minimum cash balance with the bank in order to facilitate its financial transactions (Gopalakrishnan 1989, 92–94). The state governments may sometimes resort to overdrafts, i.e., withdrawls beyond the normal and special WMA. Such overdrafts are considered unauthorised and have to be cleared within a specific number of days, presently, in ten working days.

such cover. The share of WMA in domestic debt is marginal during the period under review.[48]

Central government WMA: The central government obtained ways and means advances (WMA) from the Imperial Bank of India till 1935 and from the RBI thereafter. Since 1943–44 for about a decade, the central government did not have recourse to the RBI for WMA in view of large cash balances accumulated during the war years. But from 1954–55, the government has resorted to the RBI for accommodation on an increasing scale to meet the growing development expenditure under the Five Year Plans. However, this had taken the form of sales of *ad hoc* Treasury bills to the RBI rather than WMA.

A system of providing WMA to the Government of India under section 17(5) of the RBI Act, 1934, was considered as a possible means of accommodating temporary mismatches in government receipts and payments from 1 April 1997 onwards after the practice of issuing *ad hoc* Treasury bills was discontinued. The scheme would contribute to strengthening fiscal and monetary policy co-ordination in several directions: (a) It would prevent unplanned creation of money through uncontrolled expansion of *ad hoc* Treasury bills and improve the degree of monetary control in the economy; (b) It would reflect the true level of the government's credit requirement from the market and strengthen the interest rate mechanism; and (c) It would improve the credibility of macro-economic policies and dampen the adverse inflationary expectations that arose from the uncertainty inherent in the automatic monetisation of the fiscal deficit.

The rate of interest on WMA to the central government during 1997–98 (for any quarter) was set as a transitional measure, at 3 per cent points below the average of the implicit yield at the cut-off price of 91-day Treasury bill auctions held during the previous quarter. Since April 1998, however, the interest rate on WMA has been linked to the Bank Rate as in the case of state governments.

As per the provisions of the agreement dated 26 March 1997 between the central government and the RBI, overdrafts beyond ten consecutive working days was not allowed from 1 April 1999. The minimum balance required to be maintained by the central government with the RBI has also been revised from not less than ₹ 50 crore to ₹ 100 crore on Fridays and from not less than ₹ 4 crore to ₹ 10 crore on other days.

---

48 Includes cash credit from the State Bank of India and other commercial banks until 1967–68, which have since been combined with loans from banks and other institutions. The amount of such cash credit was negligible.

State governments WMA: In terms of Section 17(5) of the Reserve Bank of India Act, 1934, the RBI is authorised to make, to the central and state governments, ways and means advances which are repayable not later than three months from the date of making the advance. There are two types of ways and means advances: (i) Normal WMA or clean advance, which was introduced in 1937; and (ii) Special WMA instituted in 1953, which is secured advance provided against the collateral of GoI securities. From 1 April 1938, the provincial governments assumed full responsibility for their own ways and means requirements and also agreed to keep a specified minimum balance with the RBI (Tables 2.15 and 2.16).

The ways and means advances to the state governments are subject to limits, which are related to the minimum balances to be maintained by them with the RBI. Initially, during the period April 1938 to March 1953, the limits were equal to the minimum balances of the respective provinces and such advances were granted as clean advances, that is, without any collateral security. The aggregate limits for normal and special ways and means advances have been periodically revised, beginning the early 1950s, in the light of the perceived requirements of the state governments, keeping in view the evolving fiscal, financial and institutional developments as well as the objectives of monetary and fiscal management. The revision of the limits for ways and means advances in general was based on, the increase in the aggregate receipts and expenditure on both revenue and capital accounts of the states over the year.

Besides the clean and secured ways and means advances, the RBI, at its discretion, also allows additional special ways and means advances in very exceptional cases against the pledge of central government securities to meet any unforeseen difficulties of a state government such as drought, flood or any other natural calamity, provided the resources for clearing the advance would be available within a short period. If state government is indebted to the RBI for a period of 45 days even within the prescribed limit of normal ways and means advances, the central government will initiate discussions with it to rectify the imbalance.

Table 2.15: Recommendations by various committees

Item	Prior to Vithal Committee	Vithal Committee (1998)	Group of State Finance Secretaries (2000)	Ramachandran Committee (2003)	Bezbaruah Committee (2005)	Sumit Bose Committee (2015)
1	2	3	4	5	6	7
Normal WMA (NWMA)						
Methodology for Computation of WMA Limit	Limit was fixed at twice the minimum balances of states in 1953, increased to 12 times in 1967 and further revised to 168 times in 1996.	Limit fixed at a ratio of 2.25% for non-special category and 2.75% for special category states multiplied by last three years' average of revenue receipts and capital expenditure.	Average of revenue receipts and capital expenditure of the latest three years multiplied by a ratio of 2.4% for non-special category and 2.9% for special category states.	Ratio of 3.19% for non-special category and 3.84% for special category states multiplied by latest three year averages of revenue receipts and capital expenditure.	Average of revenue expenditure and capital expenditure of the latest three years adjusted for *ad hoc* expenditure and multiplied by a ratio of 3.1% for non-special category and 4.1% for special category states.	Average of total expenditure excluding lottery expenditure of the previous three years multiplied by a ratio of 2.78% for Himalayan states and north eastern states and 2.03% for other states.
Aggregate WMA Limits	₹ 2,234 crore	₹ 3,941 crore	₹ 5,283 crore	₹ 7,170 crore	₹ 9,875 crore	₹ 32,225 crore
(i) Non-Special Category States	₹ 2,033 crore	₹ 3,589 crore	₹ 4,794 crore	₹ 6,445 crore	₹ 8,820 crore	₹ 28,035 crore#
(ii) Special Category States	₹ 202 crore	₹ 352 crore	₹ 489 crore	₹ 725 crore	₹ 1,055 crore	₹ 4,060 crore#

Table continued

Table 2.15: Recommendations by various committees

Item	Prior to Vithal Committee	Vithal Committee (1998)	Group of State Finance Secretaries (2000)	Ramachandran Committee (2003)	Bezbaruah Committee (2005)	Sumit Bose Committee (2015)
1	2	3	4	5	6	7
Special Drawing Facility (SDF)						
Computation of limits (Margin)	Limits were placed at 64 times the minimum balances.	Investment in G-Secs 15 %* 10 %**	Investment in G-Secs 15 %* 10 %**	Investment in G-Secs 5% uniformly.	Investments in GoI securities plus incremental investment of CSF and GRF subject to a maximum of NWMA limit.	Investments in GOI dated securities, ATBs and incremental investment of CSF and GRF.
Use of SDF	Availed of after NWMA	Availed of after NWMA	Availed of after NWMA	To be availed of before utilising NWMA limit.	To be availed of before utilising NWMA limit.	To be availed of before utilising NWMA limit.
Overdraft scheme						
No. of consecutive working days	10	10	12	14	14	14
No. of days in a quarter	-	-	-	36	36	36
No. of consecutive working days in excess of NWMA limit	-	3	5	5	5	5

CSF – Consolidated Sinking Fund; GRF – Guarantee Redemption Fund.

* For securities with residual maturity of more than 10 years; ** For securities with residual maturity of less than ten years; # To be in conformity with the NITI Aayog's classification of states in October 2015, the Advisory Committee on ways and means advances to state governments (Chairman: Sumit Bose) revised the nomenclature from special category states to Himalayan and north eastern states.

Source: RBI.

Table 2.16: Minimum balance and limit of WMA for state governments

(₹ Crore)

Sl. No.	Date of revision	Minimum balance (Total for all States)	WMA limits (In multiples of minimum balance)	
			normal WMA	SDF (special WMA)
1	2	3	4	5
1	1 April 1937 (effective 1 April 1938) (Provincial Government/ Part A states)	1.95	1 (1.95)	*
2	1 April 1953 (Part A and Part B states)	a) 3.94 on Friday b) 3.38 on day other than Friday c) 4.50 before repayment of WMA	2 (7.88)	2.00 for each State
3	1 March 1967	6.25	3 (18.75)	6 (37.50)
4	1 May 1972	6.50+	12 (78.0)	6 (42.66)
5	1 May 1976	13.00	10 (130.0)	10 (130.0)
6	1 October 1978	13.00	20 (260.0)	10 (130.0)
7	1 July 1982	13.00	40 (520.0)	20 (260.0)
8	1 October 1986			
	(a) April–September	13.00	52 (676.0)	20 (260.0)
	(b) October–March	13.00	48 (624.0)	20 (260.0)
9	1 March 1988	13.30##	56 (744.80)	20 (266.0)
10	1 November 1993	13.30	84 (1,117.20)	32 (425.60)
11	1 August 1996	13.30	168 (2,234.40)	64 (852.20)
12	1 March 1999	41.04**	3,941.00 #	++
13	1 February 2001	41.04	5,283.00	++
14	1 April 2002	41.04	6,035.00	++
15	1 April 2003	41.04	7,170.00	++
16	1 April 2005	41.04	8,935.00	++
17	1 April 2006	41.04	9,875.00	++
18	17 December 2007	41.19***	9,925.00	++
19	1 April 2011	42.33****	10,240.00	++
20	11 November 2013	42.33	15,360.00	++
21	29 January 2016	42.33	32,225.00	++

* Secured ways and means advances were occasionally granted on an *ad hoc* basis.

+ The increase of ₹ 0.25 crore over the figure for 1967 was due to the fixation of minimum balance for four States *viz.* Himachal Pradesh, Manipur, Meghalaya and Tripura. There was no revision for other states.

** The minimum balance revised upwards linking it to the same base as for WMA.

++ The limits for special WMA liberalised, no upper limit on Special WMA, which is being provided against the actual holdings of central government sSecurities subject to margin.

The aggregate amount applicable in March 1999 was ₹ 685 crore on the basis of the recommendation of IAC. On bifurcation of Bihar, Madhya Pradesh and Uttar Pradesh, interim limits were granted to the six recognized States effective November 2000.

##Joining of Goa raised the minimum balance by ₹ 0.30 crore.

Joining of UT of Puducherry raised the minimum balance by ₹ 0.15 crore.

Joining of Jammu & Kashmir raised the minimum balance by ₹ 1.14 crore.

Note: Figures in brackets in columns 4 and 5 are the total monetary limits for all the states.

Source: RBI.

2.2.1.6. Loans from banks and other institutions

Loans from banks and other institutions refer to the borrowings made only by the state governments. The state governments are authorised to take advances from banks to meet financial requirements for purchases of food grains and fertilisers.[49] From the other term lending institutions, the state governments take loans to meet such capital expenditures as construction of bridges, housing quarters, laying of pipe-lines, etc. It constituted a marginal component of domestic debt with its share in the total being less than 2.0 per cent generally in the period but during 2003–05, the share rose to nearly 6 per cent.

2.2.2. Small savings

Small savings as a source of government borrowing is of special significance as it taps the savings of the public directly without any financial intermediation. Hence, the Government of India, has been pursuing a policy of promoting small savings since the beginning of the planning period. This subsection briefly looks at the small savings movement historically, before analysing the trends.

The small saving scheme was started in India in 1833 in the Presidency Banks. In 1870, to popularise the scheme, the savings bank was opened in selected district treasuries. It was from 1882 that the government extended it to the post offices, and by 1896 the post office system emerged as the sole savings

---

49   The data on loans from banks and other institutions is available from 1957. Refer to loans from the State Bank of India and other banks as also from the National Rural Credit (Long-term operations), Fund of the National Bank for Agriculture and Rural Development (NABARD), National Co-operative Development Corporation, Life Insurance Corporation of India and Khadi and Village Industries commission, etc. Loans from banks were included in this component from 1968–69. Until then these constituted a part of ways and means advances.

bank agency mobilising small savings.[50] Initially, small savings collections were appropriated by the state governments. However, since World War II, a process of centralisation was initiated which was completed by 1948. To encourage the state governments to co-operate with the central government, a scheme of sharing the collections in the form of long term loans was formulated in October 1952. In the initial stages the loans against small savings were linked with the market borrowing of the state governments, but in 1958 this link was discontinued. In later arrangement, collections were made by the central government and a certain portion was distributed to the state governments in the proportion which was mutually determined from time to time.[51]

Small savings as a percentage of GDP rose from 3.9 per cent in 1952 to 4.4 per cent in 2016. The high rates of interest offered along with numerous fiscal concessions have contributed to the popularity of the small savings in the initial years. But in recent years the stock markets, with the liberalisation of the economy, have attracted funds away from the small saving schemes. The interest rates on small savings were rationalised from 2002 on the recommendations made by the Committee on Administered Rates on Small Savings (Chairman: Dr Y. V. Reddy) in 2001. The committee had recommended that market determined yields on government securities should be used as a benchmark. This recommendation has been subsequently endorsed by various committees and even the Thirteenth Finance Commission.

The small savings instruments comprise savings deposits and certificates (Table 2.17).[52] The government has regularly been effecting diversification in the instruments, considering the need for funds and market requirements.[53] In the 1970's, financial institutions invested in small savings instruments, but more

---

50   Gopalakrishnan (1989), 64–65.
51   Two thirds of the net small savings collections in each state are passed on to them in the form of 25 year loans. Besides, as an incentive for mobilising collections, for every 5 per cent in excess of the national average of net to gross collections, the states are entitled to receive 2.5 per cent over and above their normal share of two-third of net collections. Similarly, two-third of the increase in the net small savings collections in union territories over the net collection in the previous year goes towards augmenting their plans. From 1973–74, the state governments have been entitled to additional loan assistance equal to 25 per cent of the amount of individual savings collected in excess of the target fixed for that state.
52   Certificates, distinct from deposits, are characterised by fixed lock-in period of funds.
53   Presently, the important ones amongst these are One to five years Time Deposits and Recurring Time Deposits, Post Office Monthly Income Scheme, National Savings Certificates, Kisan Vikas Patras and Sukanya Samriddhi accounts.

recently mainly households are buying them.[54] Amongst the deposits, time deposits and savings bank deposits are popular while amongst the certificates, the most popular ones are the Kisan Vikas Patras followed by National Savings Certificates. The amount of small savings increased from ₹ 3.7 billion in 1952 to ₹ 5,938.4 billion as at end March 2016.

Table 2.17: Components of small savings (1952–2016)

(per cent)

Year	Total deposits	Total certificates	Total
1	2	3	4
1951–52	53.95	46.05	100
1960–61	44.71	55.29	100
1970–71	53.32	46.68	100
1980–81	82.45	17.55	100
1990–91	33.86	66.14	100
2000–01	36.88	63.12	100
2010–11	63.59	36.41	100
2011–12	63.22	36.78	100
2012–13	65.26	34.74	100
2013–14	67.25	32.75	100
2014–15	68.36	31.64	100
2015–16	68.82	31.18	100

Source: RBI.

A number of instruments of small savings with varying features continue to attract financial resources across the country (Table 2.18).

National small savings fund: There has been a significant change in the scheme of small savings since 1999. The National Small Savings Fund was established on 1 April 1999 following the recommendations of a committee set-up by the government.[55] The aim of creating this fund was to clearly depict government's fiscal deficit, providing transparency in assessing viability of various small saving

---

54 Chelliah (1991), 17.

55 Committee on Small Savings (Chairman: R. V. Gupta), set-up in January 1999, submitted its report in February.

schemes and to accept deposits made to numerous schemes so as to reduce cost of management. The outstanding balances under small savings amounting to ₹1802.7 billion were converted into central government special securities which formed part of internal debt. In fact, all investments by NSSF in central government special securities are part of internal debt since 1999–2000. The amount outstanding as of end-March 2016 was ₹313.9 billion.

The accumulated balance in this fund is invested in special securities issued by state governments and balance in special central government securities through a specific sharing formula, after accounting for withdrawals and interest payments.[56] The liabilities of the central government, which includes borrowings from NSSF, is shown through Public Account Liabilities in the Union Budget. However, Fourteenth Finance Commission (FFC) recommended that since states incur higher cost through borrowing from NSSF in comparison to market borrowings, they should be excluded from operations of schemes and NSSF. The FFC also noted that states complained of the involuntary nature of NSSF borrowings, fall in collections over the years, insignificant contribution to total borrowings and secular decline in deficit being financed by NSSF. Consequently, in a decision taken by the Union Cabinet in January 2017,[57] state governments (except Arunachal Pradesh, Madhya Pradesh, Delhi and Kerala) have been excluded from receiving loans through NSSF with effect from 1 April, 2016. The government intends to use NSSF to invest in expenditures that are ultimately borne by the government in the Union Budget. This implies that the market borrowing of the 26 excluded states will rise, whereas the government will see an increase in investible funds through NSSF.

2.2.3 Provident funds and other accounts

Provident Funds and other accounts increased from ₹1.9 billion to ₹4,676.4 billion during 1952–2016. Provident Funds and other accounts, as a per cent of GDP, also rose from 2.0 per cent in March 1952 to 3.4 per cent in March 2016. Amongst the components, the share of State Provident Funds has declined sharply in favour of other accounts (Table 2.19).

State provident funds are the Provident Funds of the government.[58] The

---

56   Sub-Committee of National Development Council (Chairman: P. Chidambaram), set-up on 16 September 2005 and recommendations endorsed by NDC on 9 December 2006.

57   GOI, (2017).

58   State provident funds consist of civil, defence, railways and other provident funds. The Civil Provident Funds consist of General P.F.; contributory P.F's; ICS P.F's and All India

Public Debt in India 51

Table 2.18: Small savings schemes

Name of the scheme	Date of launch of scheme	Date of closure of scheme	Limits of investment	Maturity period (years)		Rate of interest (per cent per annum)				Outstanding balance in April 2016 (₹ billion)
				April 1991	April 2017	April 1991	April 2001	Dec 2011	April 2017	
1	2	3	4	5	6	7	8	9	10	11
12	Launched on 1 April 1882	-	Minimum ₹ 20 for opening	#	#	5.5	3.5 ##	4	4.0	550.82
Post Office Time Deposit Account	Launched on 1 April 1982	-	Minimum ₹ 200 and no Maximum Limit	1,2,3 and 5	1,2,3 and 5	-	-	-	-	706.32
(i) 1 Year	-	-	-	-	-	9.5	7.5	7.7	7.1	-
(ii) 2 Year	-	-	-	-	-	10.0	8.0	7.8	7.2	-
(iii) 3 Year	-	-	-	-	-	11.0	9.0	8	7.4	-
(iv) 5 Year	-	-	-	-	-	11.5	9.0	8.3	7.9	-
Post Office Recurring Deposit Account	Launched on 17 December 1981	-	Minimum ₹10 per month or any amount in multiples of ₹5 and no Maximum Limit	5	5	11.5	9.0	8	7.4	761.82

Table continued

Table 2.18: Small savings schemes

Name of the scheme	Date of launch of scheme	Date of closure of scheme	Limits of investment	Maturity period (years)		Rate of interest (per cent per annum)				Outstanding balance in April 2016 (₹ billion)
				April 1991	April 2017	April 1991	April 2001	Dec 2011	April 2017	
1	2	3	4	5	6	7	8	9	10	11
National Savings Scheme 1992	a) Launched on 1 April 1987 b) Launched on 1 October 1992	a) Discontinued from 1 April 1992 b) Discontinued on 1 November 2002	Discontinued	4	4	11.0	9.0	-	-	9.50
Post Office Monthly Income Scheme	Launched on 15 August 1987	-	Minimum ₹1500 and maximum ₹4.5 Lakh in single account and ₹9 Lakh in joint account	6	6+	12.0	9.5	8.2	7.8	1938.06
Indira Vikas Patra	Launched on 19 November 1986	Discontinued on 17 July 1999	Discontinued	5	6	14.9 @	-	-	-	8.87
Kisan Vikas Patra	a) Launched on 1 April 1988 b) Relaunched on 18 November 2014	a) Discontinued on 1 December 2011	Minimum ₹1000, no upper limit	5 1/2	6@@	13.4 @	10.0 @	-	7.8	848.41

Table continued

Table 2.18: Small savings schemes

Name of the scheme	Date of launch of scheme	Date of closure of scheme	Limits of investment	Maturity period (years)		Rate of interest (per cent per annum)				Outstanding balance in April 2016 (₹ billion)
				April 1991	April 2017	April 1991	April 2001	Dec 2011	April 2017	
1	2	3	4	5	6	7	8	9	10	11
Senior Citizens Saving Scheme	Launched on 1 November 2004	-	Minimum ₹1000 and maximum ₹15 Lakh	-	5	-	-	-	8.6	228.76
NSC VIII issue (For 5 years)	Launched on 8 May 1989	-	Minimum ₹100 and No maximum Limit	6	6	12.0	9.5	8.4	8.1	352.64
Sukanya Samriddhi Accounts	Launched on 22 January 2015	-	Minimum ₹1,000 and maximum ₹1.5 Lakh	-	-	-	-	-	8.6	642.60
NSC IX issue (For 10 years)	Launched on 1 December 2011	Discontinued on 20 December 2015	Discontinued		10	-	-	8.7	-	-

Open ended scheme; ## 4.5 per cent for individual/joint and group account, 4 per cent for public account and security deposit accounts – for purchase of motor vehicles or tractors, 3 per cent for official capacity accounts and other accounts; + Maturity period is 5 years from 1 December 2011; @ Compounded Interest Rate; @@ Maturity period was raised to 6 1/2 years with effect from January 15, 2000, 7 years 3 months from March 1, 2001, 7 years 8 months from 1 March 2002 and 8 years 7 months from 1 March 2003.

Source: RBI.

Table 2.19: Components of provident funds and other accounts

Year (end of march)	State provident funds	Other accounts	Public provident funds	Total
1	2	3	4	5
1951–52	85.74	0.00	14.26	100
1960–61	58.77	0.00	41.23	100
1970–71	57.37	0.17	42.46	100
1980–81	54.99	2.24	42.77	100
1990–91	31.03	3.85	65.12	100
2010–11	45.09	50.24	4.67	100
2011–12	49.05	45.74	5.22	100
2012–13	52.20	42.02	5.78	100
2013–14	49.65	44.61	5.75	100
2014–15	51.29	42.56	6.15	100
2015–16	52.95	40.64	6.41	100

Source: RBI.

outstanding amount increased from ₹ 1.6 billion in 1952 to ₹ 3,780.6 billion in March 2016. The Public Provident Fund, has gradually increased to ₹ 576 billion, in March 2016.[59] The Other accounts refer to funds in the trust and endowment accounts, insurance and pension funds, and special deposits and accounts.[60]

Services PF. The Defence Provident Funds include Defence Savings PF; Defence Service Officers and Personnel PF and Indian Ordinance Factories Workmen PF. The other provident funds refer to workmen's contributory PF; Contributory Provident Pension Fund and other Miscellaneous PF's.

59 The Public Provident Fund Scheme is framed with the objective of attracting voluntary savings, mainly, from self employed public.

60 The Trust and Endowment Funds includes Hyderabad Endowment Fund. The Insurance and Pension Funds includes Postal and Life Annuity Fund; Family Pension Fund; Other Insurance and Pension Funds; Central Government Employees Group Insurance Scheme; Union Territories Employees Group Insurance Schemes; etc. Special Deposits and other Accounts comprise of Special Securities issued to Rural Electrification Corporation; Special deposits by Provident Superannuation and Gratuity Funds; Income-Tax Annuity Deposits; Compulsory Deposits; deposits by Unit Trust of India, Life Insurance Corporation, General Insurance Corporation and its subsidiaries; Deposits by Industrial Development Bank of India, National Bank for Agriculture and Rural Development, Special securities to Nationalised Banks and National Deposit Scheme.

The debt under this group has increased at the highest rate with the amount outstanding rising from ₹ 0.3 billion to ₹ 319.8 billion over the period 1952–2016. The major increase is due to special securities in lieu of subsidies to oil marketing companies, fertiliser companies and Food Corporation of India.

2.2.4. Reserve funds and deposits

The reserve funds and deposits rose from ₹ 4.4 billion in 1952 to ₹ 6,028.6 billion in March 2016. Their share in domestic debt, however, declined from 14.1 per cent in 1952 to 6.4 per cent in 2016 after reaching a peak of 14.7 per cent in 1987–88. Reserve funds and deposits, comprising mainly of depreciation and reserve funds of government departments and deposits of local funds, departmental and judicial deposits, and civil deposits.[61] For the central government, the share of interest-bearing[62] and non-interest bearing[63] components has generally remained the same, with the interest-bearing component accounting for more than half of total outstanding.

Reserve funds and deposits are controversial in their inclusion as a component of domestic debt.[64] The perusal of the components of reserve funds reveal that these are generally depreciation, developmental, contingency or similar funds of

---

61   Reserve Funds and deposits came to be included as a part of total internal debt of the Government of India in 1965–66. The figures for the purpose of this study have been computed from Finance Accounts, Government of India, for the period 1952 to 1965.

62   The Reserve Funds bearing interest are Depreciation Funds of Railways; Commercial and Non-commercial departmental undertakings; Revenue Reserve Fund; Development Funds of Railways and Post and Telegraphs; General and other Reserve Funds like Railway Pension Fund; Staff Benefit Funds; Railways Accident Compensation Fund; Safety and Passenger Amenities Fund; Contingency Reserve Fund (electricity) and General Insurance Fund. The Deposits bearing interest are the Security deposits; Railway deposits; National Defence Fund; deposits of shipping development funds; deposits of government companies and corporations; own your telephone exchange deposits; telephone application deposits; etc.

63   The Non-Interest bearing Reserve Funds include Famine Relief Fund; Central Road Fund; Development Funds for Education, Medical and Public Health, Agriculture and Industry purposes; Mining Areas Development Funds; Special Development Funds; Railway Reserve Funds; Railway Safety Works Funds; Foodgrains Reserve Funds; etc. The non-interest bearing deposits are Revenue Deposits, Securities Deposits, Court Deposits, deposits of Police Funds; Forest Deposits; deposits under Central and State Acts, Liquidation Accounts Companies, Provident Societies, deposits of Educational institutions, Unclaimed Deposits of General Provident Funds, Provident Funds, Savings Banks, etc.

64   Seshan (1987) excludes Reserve Funds, Rangarajan, Basu and Jadhav (1989), Gopalakrishnan (1989 and 1991) and Bhattacharya and Guha (1990) exclude Reserve Funds and Deposits.

the central and state governments. These are created from revenue and are held by the government for various specific purposes. They, in some cases, seem to represent intra-governmental liabilities. Deposits refer to money received by the government in the course of its business. It consists of diverse items like court deposits, telephone deposits, shipping deposits, and deposits of government companies/corporations/departments, etc. In the strict sense, these are more in the nature of financial obligations rather than liabilities.

In view of (*a*) the nature of the components; and (*b*) the difficulty in fixing the ownership pattern of these funds and deposits accurately,[65] though broadly they seem to belong to government, these have been excluded from domestic debt while analysing its implications on macro-economic aggregates in the study in Chapters 4, 5, 6 and 7.

Table 2.20: Reserve funds and deposits of the government

Year	Centre		State (%)	Total centre and state (₹ in billion)
	Bearing interest (%)	Not bearing interest (%)		
1	2	3	4	5
1951–52	56.2	43.8	-	4.4
1960–61	22.8	77.2	-	6.2
1970–71	15.2	84.8	-	17.6
1980–81	28.4	27.9	43.7	64.6
1990–91	26.2	28.0	45.8	404.2
2000–01	19.9	21.5	58.6	1414.5
2010–11	18.1	15.0	66.9	3889.6
2015–16	20.6	12.3	67.1	6028.6

Note: Data for state government was only available from 1981 onwards.
Source: RBI and Government of India.

Contingent liabilities of the government: In India, contingent liabilities are not considered as part of domestic debt. However, these have been declining over the years (Figure 2.10).

---

65 Bhattacharya and Guha, 1990.

Figure 2.10: Contingent liabilities of the government as percentage of GDP

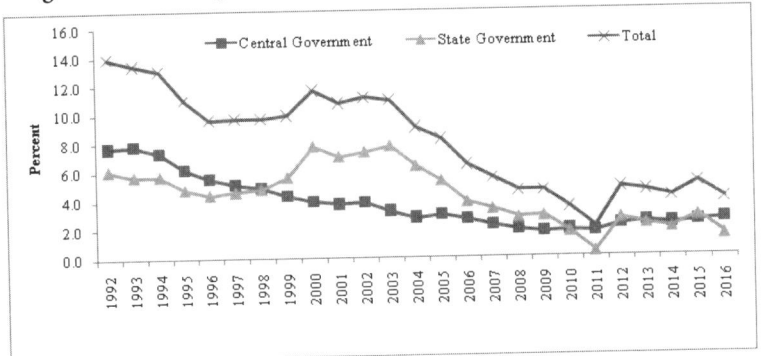

Source: RBI and Government of India.

A rise in contingent liabilities of state governments essentially reflects the practice to set up corporations to borrow from the market to undertake departmental projects. In view of low user charges and inefficient operations of state public sector undertakings, these contingent liabilities are a cause of concern. The rising trend and its implications were examined by the state governments and remedial measures were taken – 25 states have legislated ceilings on guarantees[66] and 11 states have set up a guarantee redemption fund.[67] The RBI, which regulates and supervises the government securities market as well as the commercial banking activity, has specifically directed the banks and financial institutions to extend loans only on the basis of commercial viability and not on the basis of the government guarantees. The banks and financial institutions have been advised by the RBI to make adequate provisions for the guaranteed bonds. This stipulation has helped partially in containing the rise in state government guarantees.

Fiscal responsibility and Budget Management Act: Fiscal Responsibility and Budget Management Act (FRBMA) was introduced in Parliament as the FRBM Bill in December 2000 with the intention of fostering fiscal discipline; efficient management of expenditure, revenue and debt; and achieving a balanced budget.

While the Act was passed on 26 August 2003, FRBMA was brought into effect from July 5, 2004. The objectives of FRBMA were elimination of revenue deficit by 2008–09 and reduction of fiscal deficit to no more than 3 per cent of GDP at

---

66 All states except Jammu and Kashmir, Jharkhand and Uttar Pradesh.

67 Andhra Pradesh, Assam, Goa, Gujarat, Haryana, Madhya Pradesh, Manipur, Mizoram, Nagaland, Orissa and Uttarakhand.

the end of 2008–09. However, global financial crisis led the government to infuse resources in economy as fiscal stimulus in 2008 and therefore fiscal targets had to be postponed temporarily in view of the global crisis. Later, the Budget for 2012–13 introduced amendments to FRBM Act.[68] The central government introduced a medium-term fiscal adjustment road map on 16 March 2012 to improve fiscal situation at federal level. The concept of effective revenue deficit was introduced, which excluded grants to states for creation of capital assets from conventional revenue deficit.[69] The second important feature was the introduction of provision for 'Medium Term Expenditure Framework Statement' in the FRBMA.[70]

The implementation of FRBM Act has been stalled four times since its enactment in 2003. With more than a decade of experience, including regular pauses, there was a critical need to evaluate the implementation of provisions of FRBMA. Since FRBMA enactment in 2003, its role has been discussed continuously in controlling fiscal and revenue deficit. Recently, a special FRBM Committee submitted a report on its findings to the Finance Minister.[71] Finally, the report was made public in April 2017.

The Preamble to the FRBM Act 2003 sheds light on some of its key features. The Act seeks to achieve long-term macroeconomic stability, while generating budget surpluses, prudential debt management, limiting borrowings to cut down deficits and debt, greater transparency, removal of fiscal impediments and providing a medium-term framework for budgetary implementation (Singh, Prasad, Sharma and Reddy, 2017).

The state governments have also fiscal responsibility legislations since 2003 (Table 2.21).

---

68 Singh, 2013, 23.

69 This was an important development for the reason that while the revenue deficit of the consolidated general government fully reflected total capital expenditure incurred, in the accounts of centre; these transfers were shown as revenue expenditure. Therefore, the mandate of eliminating the conventional revenue deficit of centre became problematic. With this amendment, the endeavour of the government under the FRBM Act was to eliminate the effective revenue deficit (GoI, 2013).

70 Singh, 2013, 23.

71 The Committee (Chairman: N. K. Singh), set up in May 2016, submitted Report in January 2017.

Table 2.21: Fiscal responsibility legislation in India

Year	State	Original documents			Ceiling on guarantee imposed
		RD by 31 March	GFD as per cent of GSDP/GDP as on 31 March 31	Debt as per cent of GSDP/GDP as on 31 March	
1	2	3	4	5	6
2002	Karnataka	Nil; 2006	3; 2006	25; 2015.	Yes
2003	India	Nil; 2008	3; 2008	Reduction Rule	Yes
	Kerala	Nil; 2009	3; 2008	-	Yes
	Tamil Nadu	Nil; 2009	3; 2008	-	Yes
	Punjab	Nil; 2009	3; 2008		Yes
2004	Uttar Pradesh	Nil; 2009	3; 2009	25; 2018.	No
2005	Andhra Pradesh	Nil; 2009	3	35; 2010	Yes
	Assam	Nil; 2010	3; 2010	45; 2010	Yes
	Chhattisgarh	Nil; 2009	3; 2009	-	Yes
	Gujarat	Nil; 2008	3; 2009	30; 2008	Yes
	Haryana	Nil; 2009	3; 2010	28; 2010	Yes
	Himachal Pradesh	Nil; 2009		-	Yes
	Madhya Pradesh	Nil; 2009	4; 2010	40	Yes
	Maharashtra	Nil; 2009	3; 2009		Yes
	Manipur	Nil; 2010	3	-	Yes
	Tripura	-	3; 2010	40; 2010.	Yes
	Uttarakhand	Nil; 2009	3; 2009	25; 2015.	Yes
	Odisha	Nil; 2009	3; 2009	Debt stock limited to 300 per cent of total revenue receipt ; 2008	Yes
	Rajasthan	Nil; 2009	3	Debt should not exceed twice consolidated fund receipt.	Yes

Table continued

Table 2.21: Fiscal responsibility legislation in India

Year	State	Original documents			Ceiling on guarantee imposed
		RD by 31 March	GFD as per cent of GSDP/GDP as on 31 March 31	Debt as per cent of GSDP/GDP as on 31 March	
1	2	3	4	5	6
2006	Arunachal Pradesh	Nil; 2009	3; 2010	-	Yes
	Bihar	Nil; 2008	3; 2008	-	Yes
	Goa	Nil; 2009	3; 2009	30; 2009	Yes
	Jammu & Kashmir			55; 2010	No
	Meghalaya	Nil	3	28	Yes
	Mizoram	Nil; 2009	3; 2009	Debt should not exceed twice consolidated fund receipts.	Yes
	Nagaland	Nil	3; 2009	40; 2010	Yes
2007	Jharkhand	Nil; 2009	3; 2009	Debt stock limited to 300 per cent of total revenue receipt.	No
2010	Sikkim	-	3; 2014		Yes
	West Bengal	Nil; 2015	3; 2015	34.3; 2015	Yes

Note: Reduction rule: The government shall not assume additional liabilities (including external debt at current exchange rate) in excess of 9 per cent of GDP for financial year 2004–05 and in each subsequent financial year, the limit of 9 per cent of GDP shall be progressively reduced by at least one percentage point of GDP.

RD: Revenue Deficit; GFD: Gross Fiscal Deficit; GSDP: Gross State Domestic Product; GDP: Gross Domestic Product.

Source: Various FRBM Acts of States.

2.4. Conclusions

The domestic debt of India, as a per cent of GDP, has been rising over the years. The increasing reliance on domestic debt was encouraged as it was argued by the government and economic planners that borrowed funds would be utilised for capital formation in development planning initiated since 1951. The trend in the financing pattern of such five year development plans reveal that nearly 70 to 80 per cent of the plans were financed by incurring domestic debt. The emergent fiscal situation suggests that domestic debt is being used to finance current government expenditure in view of the inelastic tax revenue and inadequate surplus generated in public enterprises. Thus, the borrowed funds are not being utilised for capital formation as envisaged initially when development planning was initiated. The annual rise in domestic debt is higher than the annual growth rate in gross domestic product.

The rise in the domestic debt has been contributed to by all the components though the shares of the major components have undergone changes. The share of internal debt in domestic debt has increased over the years, mainly because of market loans. The share of debt held within the government has declined in favour of the public, including the banks. The domestic debt held by the public may bear a negative relation with the inflationary pressure as they mop up the extra purchasing power available with the people or may encourage further consumption through the wealth effect. The debt held by the RBI has pronounced implications leading to a rise in reserve money and money supply, and influencing the price level.

3

Ricardian Equivalence: Introduction

In this chapter, the concept of Ricardian equivalence is introduced and discussed in a theoretical framework. In Section 3.1, the concept of Ricardian equivalence is introduced followed by a brief discussion in Section 3.2. The Ricardian equivalence holds under special assumptions which are delineated in Section 3.3. In Section 3.4, the assumption of finite lives and intergenerational transfer is discussed in detail. This is followed by a discussion on imperfect capital markets in Section 3.5 and on uncertainty and taxes in Section 3.6. In Section 3.7, other assumptions for Ricardian equivalence are discussed.

3.1. The concept of Ricardian equivalence

The Ricardian Equivalence Theorem is the proposition that a public loan and a lump-sum tax exert equivalent effects upon the economy.[1] More precisely, the choice between levying lump-sum taxes and issuing government bonds to finance government spending does not affect the consumption pattern of any household nor does it affect capital formation. The fundamental logic underlying this argument was presented by Ricardo (1951, 244–45) as follows:

> "When, for the expenses of a year's war, twenty millions are raised by means of a loan, it is the twenty millions which are withdrawn from the productive capital of the nation. ... Government might at once have required the twenty millions in the shape of taxes; in which case it would not have been necessary to raise annual taxes to the amount of a million. This, however, would not have changed the nature of the transaction. An individual instead of being called upon to pay 100 per annum, might have been obliged to pay 2000 once and for all."

Ricardo assumes that the creation of public debt implies a stream of future interest payments and possible repayments of principal. These future payments

---

[1] The term Ricardian Equivalence Theorem was introduced by Buchanan (1976). However, O'Driscoll (1977) has documented Ricardo's reservations about this result.

have to be financed by future taxes. It is argued, that a rational individual living during the time when the expenditure decision is made will fully capitalise all future tax payments arising due to debt and will consequently write down the value of the income-earning assets which he owns by the amount of the present value of these future payments. The present values of assets will be reduced by the present value of the tax obligations created by the future service charges. Present values will be identical in the two cases.

3.2. Ricardian Equivalence Theorem – simple explanation

The argument of Ricardian equivalence is simple. If government expenditure is not financed by current taxes then it can be financed by incurring debt. In case of debt, rational individuals must know that taxes will be levied in future to pay the interest as well as the principal. To provide for future taxes, the households will save more, precisely enough to purchase new government bonds. As a result, aggregate wealth and consumption remain the same. The increase in private saving just offsets the decrease in public saving and national saving remains the same. Thus, given the present value of tax, the timing of the taxes makes no difference.

The underlying logic of Ricardian equivalence can be illustrated by a simple example. Consider a reduction in current (lump-sum) taxes of $100 per capita. This reduction in tax revenue is financed by the sale of government bonds of one-year maturity with a coupon rate of 5 per cent, suppose of the amount of $100 per capita. Further supposing that the population is constant, then in the year following tax cut, the taxes have to be raised by $105 per capita to pay for the tax as well as the principal. Now considering the response of the household to this intertemporal arrangement of tax liabilities. The households increase current savings in the first year and hold government bonds while in the second year they use the same bonds to pay the higher taxes.. Thus, the consumption pattern of the consumer is invariant to the switch between tax finance and debt finance for a given government expenditure.

Mathematically, the concept of Ricardian equivalence can also be explained in simple terms. Suppose the present value of a future income stream is PV* which can be denoted as:

$$PV^* = y^1 + y^2 + y^3 + \ldots \qquad \text{Equation 3.1}$$

where y denotes discounted values of future income streams Y. The superscripts to y or Y, show the number of years beginning from the current year. The discount rate is r and it is assumed that government as well private consumers can borrow and lend at the same rate, r. Now, suppose that the government needs to fund an extraordinary project of the amount, g. It has the option to raise the amount in the current year either through tax (lump-sum) or through the sale of bonds. In case of bond finance, the government would have to collect tax, t, from the public from year two to pay the annual interest, rg. The present value of the income stream under the two options can be shown as:

Case 3.1: Tax finance in current year

$PV = y^1 - g + y^2 + y^3 + ...$ Equation 3.2

or $PV = (y^1 + y^2 + y^3 + ...) - g$ Equation 3.3

or $PV = PV^* - g$ Equation 3.4

Case 3.2: Bond finance in current year

$PV = Y^1 + (Y^2 - t)/(1+r) + (Y^3 - t)/(1+r)^2 + ...$ Equation 3.5

or $PV = Y^1 + (Y^2 - rg)/(1+r) + (Y^3 - rg)/(1+r)^2 + ...$ Equation 3.6

or $PV = [Y^1 + Y^2/(1+r) + Y^3/(1+r)^2 + ..] - [rg/(1+r) + rg/(1+r)^2 + ..]$ Equation 3.7

or $PV = PV^* - g$ Equation 3.8

Thus, the result is similar in both the options as the present value in the two cases is the same.

3.3. Assumptions of the Ricardian equivalence proposition

The Ricardian equivalence proposition equating tax finance and bond finance would hold under the following assumptions:

a. There is no possibility of escaping part of the perpetual tax liability, either by dying or by leaving the jurisdiction of the government.

b. Everyone can borrow and lend funds at the same interest rate as the government.

c. There is uncertainty about future tax shares, which might be due to uncertainty about individual income or other characteristics that determine tax shares.

d. Future tax liabilities implied by public debt are accurately perceived.

e. The volume of government expenditures is independent of the method of finance.

f. No other channels exist for effects of the choice of finance method on the prices, rates of return, etc., faced by individuals.

These conditions are important and any deviation from these could result in the invalidation of the Ricardian equivalence proposition. Tobin (1980) provides a clear overview of why the Ricardian equivalence conditions may not provide an accurate description of the actual effects of debt finance *vs.* tax finance. These restrictive assumptions have been keenly debated in the macroeconomic literature in the last two decades. As a result, new interpretation of some of these assumptions has emerged which seem to be a good approximation of reality and therefore strengthens the proposition of Ricardian equivalence. The two most important conditions which have generated much literature are the first two – assumptions regarding finite lives and imperfect capital markets, respectively. The assumption regarding the lack of certainty about future tax shares has also resulted in some empirical work. These three assumptions have been discussed in detail in the next three sections followed by a section where brief discussion on other assumptions is presented.

3.4. Ricardian Equivalence and finite lives and Barro's intergenerational model

In Ricardian equivalence, a key assumption is that the individual cannot escape the tax liability by virtue of having a finite life unlike in the life-cycle models where individuals capitalise only those taxes that they expect to face during their lifetimes. Supposing that interest payments and associated tax liabilities, due to the issue of government debt, extend beyond the expected lifetime of the representative current taxpayer (presuming that the debt principal is never paid off), then the net wealth of the current taxpayer rises and households react by increasing consumption demand. This would invalidate Ricardian equivalence. But, if the added liabilities on descendants were fully counted in wealth calculations by current taxpayers, then the present distinction between debt and tax options would disappear. The individual may react to the debt with a compensating increase in voluntary transfers to their descendants. The households may capitalise the entire array of expected future taxes, and thereby plan with an infinite horizon. Thus, the Ricardian result could remain valid even in a model with finite lifetimes.

Barro (1974) examines the effect of finite lives using a version of the Samuelson (1958)-Diamond (1965) overlapping-generations model with physical capital to analyse whether an increase in government debt constitutes an increase in perceived household wealth. The model developed by Barro is explained in detail in the following paragraphs.

3.4.1. Assumptions of Barro's intergenerational model

a. Each individual lives two periods – young (superscripts y) and old (superscripts o).

b. Generations are numbered consecutively beginning with the generation which is currently old (subscript 1) followed by its descendants which are currently young (subscript 2), followed by its descendants and so on.

c. Each generation has the same number of people, N, and all individuals are identical in terms of tastes and productivity. The members of each generation work a fixed amount of time only while young and receive a wage income of w, at the start of the young period. Expectations on w for future periods are to be static at the current value.

d. Asset holdings (A) take the form of equity capital (K). The rate of return on assets is r and is paid out once every period. Expectations on r are static at the current value.

e. The asset holding while old constitutes the bequest provision which is assumed to go to the immediate descendant, a member of generation $i+1$. A member of the ith generation holds the amount of assets A^y_i while young and the amount A^o_i while old.

f. Government neither demands commodities nor provides public services.

g. Consumption (c) and receipt of interest income occur at the start of the period.

h. Utility of a member of generation i depends solely on own two-period consumption, c^y_i and c^o_i and on the attainable utility of his immediate descendant, U^*_{i+1}, where * denotes the maximum value of utility, conditional on given values of endowment and prices.

i. No technological change occurs over time.

j. The production function follows constant returns to scale and depends on the amounts of capital and labour input, and equates the marginal products of capital and labour to r and w, respectively.

3.4.2. Basic model without government debt

The budget equation for a member of generation 1, which is currently old, is:

$$A^y_1 + A^o_0 = c^o_1 + (1-r)A^o_1 \qquad \text{Equation 3.9}$$

where the total resources available are the assets held while young, A^y_1, and the bequest from the previous generation, A_0^o. The total expenditure is consumption while old, c_1^o and the bequest provision, A_1^o, which goes to a member of generation 2, less interest earnings at rate r on this asset holding.

The budget equation for members of generation 2 when young is:

$$w = c_2^y + (1-r) A_2^y \qquad \text{Equation 3.10}$$

where the wage payments and the interest income have been assumed to occur at the start of the young period. The total expenditure is consumption while young, c_2^y, and the savings in the form of asset holdings, A_2^y.

The budget equation of generation 2, when old, which is similar to 3.9, is:

$$A_2^y + A_1^o = c_2^o + (1-r) A_2^o \qquad \text{Equation 3.11}$$

where A_1^o represents the bequest provision received from generation 1, while A_2^o represents the bequest provision for the descendant generation 3.

The bequest provision of a member of generation i is motivated by a concern for a member of generation $i+1$. This concern can be modelled by introducing either the anticipated consumption levels or the attainable utility of a member of generation $i+1$ into the utility function for a member of the ith generation. Assuming, for the sake of convenience, that the utility of a member of generation i depends solely on own two-period consumption – young and old, and on the attainable utility of his immediate descendant, U^*_{i+1}. Then the utility function of the member of the ith generation has the form:

$$U_i = U_i(c_i^y, c_i^o, U^*_{i+1}) \qquad \text{Equation 3.12}$$

Each member of generation 1 determines his allocation of resources to maximise U_1, subject to Equations 3.9–3.12 and to the inequality conditions, (c_i^y, c_i^o, A_i^y) $>= 0$ for all i. The key restriction imposed here is that the bequest to the member of the next generation cannot be negative. The choice of bequest, takes into account the effect of A_1^o on generation 2's resources, the impact of U^*_2 on U_1, and the chain dependence of U_2 on U^*_3 and so on. The solution to this problem for members of generation 1, which is old, takes the general form:

$$c_1^o = c_1^o(A_1^y + A_0^o, w, r)$$
$$A_1^o = (1/1-r)(A_1^y + A_0^o - c_1^o) = A_1^o(A_1^y + A_0^o, w, r) \qquad \text{Equation 3.13}$$

Similarly for members of generation 2 (and for members of any generation $i>2$), the solution would be:

$$c_2^y = c_2^y(A_1^o, w, r)$$
$$A_2^y = (1/1-r)(w - c_2^y) = A_2^y(A_1^o, w, r)$$

$$c_2^o = c_2^o(A_2^y + A_1^o, w, r)$$

Equation 3.14

$$A_2^o = (1/1 - r)(A_2^y + A_1^o - c_2^o) = A_2^o(A_2^y + A_1^o, w, r)$$

The consumption and asset holding of members of generation 2, when young, depends on wage rate, interest rate and bequest received from the earlier generation. And the consumption and bequest provision by members of generation 2, when old, depends on wage rate, interest rate, bequest received from the earlier generation and asset holdings while young.

The model can be closed by assuming a, constant returns to scale, production function that depends on capital and labour input and equating the marginal products of capital and labour to r and w, respectively. The value of r for the current period, would then be determined in order to equate the supply of assets to demand:

$$K(r, w) = A_1^o + A_2^y$$

Equation 3.15

where, $K(r, w)$ is such as to equate the marginal product of capital to r. The current demand for assets, $A_1^o + A_2^y$, depends on r, w, and the previous period's value of $K(A_1^y + A_0^o)$. Since the number of people in each generation, N, is constant and technical change is not considered, the current and previous periods' values of K would be equal in a steady state. With the marginal product of labour equated to w and with constant returns to scale, output, y, is given by:

$$y = rK + w$$

Equation 3.16

The commodity market clearing condition is implied by the Equation system 3.10, 3.11, 3.15 and 3.16:

$$c_1^o + c_2^y + \Delta K = y$$

Equation 3.17

where ΔK denotes a change in capital stock from the previous to the current period.

3.4.3. Basic model with government debt

To incorporate government debt in the model, it is assumed that the government issues an amount of debt, B, in the form of one-period, real valued bonds. These bonds pay the specified amount of real interest, rB, in the current period and the specified real principal, B, in the next period. It is assumed that asset holders regard equity and government bonds as perfect substitutes and that the government bond issue takes the form of a helicopter drop to currently old (generation 1) households. The assumption here is that the current period's interest payments are financed by a lump-sum tax levy on generation 2 households (while young)

Ricardian Equivalence: Introduction

and the principal is paid off at the beginning of the next period by an additional lump-sum tax levy on generation 2 households (while old).

The budget constraint Equations 3.9–3.11, of the two generations need to be modified with the inclusion of the bond issue. The generation 1 budget constraint now is:

$$A_1^y + A_0^o + B = c_1^o + (1-r)A_1^o \qquad \text{Equation 3.18}$$

where B represents the lump-sum transfer payment through the bond issue. The budget constraint in Equation 3.18 is similar to that in Equation 3.9 except for the inclusion of the amount of bond issue.

The current budget constraint for generation 2 is:

$$w = c_2^y + (1-r)A_2^y + rB \qquad \text{Equation 3.19}$$

where rB represents the tax levy for the interest payments assumed to be imposed on generation 2 (while young). This equation is similar to Equation 3.10 except for the inclusion of tax levy.

The next period's budget constraint for generation 2 is:

$$A_2^y + A_1^o = c_2^o + (1-r)A_2^o + B \qquad \text{Equation 3.20}$$

where B represents the tax levy for repayment of principal. Similarly, the above equation is similar to Equation 3.11 except for the inclusion of the amount of transfer payment. The two constraints on generation 2 can be combined into a single two-period budget equation:

$$w + (1-r)A_1^o - B = c_2^y + (1-r)c_2^y + (1-r)c_2^o + (1-r)^2 A_2^o \qquad \text{Equation 3.21}$$

The form of Equation 3.21 implies that the utility attainable by a member of generation 2 can be written as follows:

$$U_2^* = f_2^* \left[(1-r)A_1^o - B, w, r \right] \qquad \text{Equation 3.22}$$

where $[(1-r)A_1^o - B]$ is the net bequest and determines the endowment for members of generation 2. From Equation 3.18 it emerges that c_1^o varies inversely with $[(1-r)A_1^o - B]$, for a given value of $A_1^Y + A_0^o$. Hence, given the predetermined value of c_1^y and using Equations 3.12, 3.18 and 3.22 U_1 can be written as follows:

$$U_1 = U_1 (c_1^y, c_1^o, U_2^*) = f_1 [(1-r)A_1^o - B; c_1^y, A_1^y + A_0^o; w, r] \qquad \text{Equation 3.23}$$

The choice problem for members of generation 1 amounts to the optimal selection of the net bequest, $[(1-r)A_1^o - B]$, subject to the constraint that the gross bequest, A_1^o, be non-negative, for the given values of $c_1^y, A_1^y + A_0^o, w$, and r. Any change in B would be met by a change in A_1^o that maintains the value of the net bequest, $(1-r)A_1^o - B$. This response in A_1^o will keep unchanged the values of c_1^o, c_2^y, c_2^o and A_2^o. Hence, the utility levels attained by members of any generation will be unaffected by the shift in B.

To determine the value of r, the current asset market clearing condition is now modified from Equation 3.15 to:

$$K(r, w) + B = A_1^o + A_2^y \qquad \text{Equation 3.24}$$

The increase in B implies a similar increase in asset supply on the left hand side of Equation 3.24. On the demand side, A_1^o rises by $1/1-r$ times change in B in order to maintain the size of the net bequest, $(1-r)A_1^o - B$. Further, with c_2^y fixed, the increase in rB (tax) in Equation 3.19 implies that A_2^y falls by $r/1-r$ times the change in B. On balance, total asset demand on the right hand side also rises one-to-one with B, so that no change in r is required to clear the asset market. The commodity market clearing condition as given in Equation 3.17 continues to hold at the initial value of r, as the bond issue has no impact on aggregate demand.

Thus, the model stresses the bequest motive but the crucial issue is the intergenerational transfer which may occur because of any motive – altruistic or otherwise. This transfer could be in any form like expenditure on education, gifts, etc. (Barro, 1989b). The model can be successfully extended to incorporate social security payments and other imposed intergenerational transfers as well as the incidence of inheritance taxes. The other issue is of persons without children, as such people are not connected to the future generations, as has been argued by Tobin (1980), and Tobin and Buiter (1980a). But in any model the averages are considered and so if there are a few childless persons in the economy, so would there be persons with more than the average number of children which would compensate on the whole. Empirical evidence from Darby (1979) and Kotlikoff and Summers (1981) shows that the accumulation of households' assets in the US for the purpose of intergenerational transfers is more important than that associated with the life cycle approach. A taxpayer can also escape some part of the future taxes associated with debt by leaving the jurisdiction of the government. However, this would arise only where the government-owned real capital was not sufficient to generate income offsetting the debt-finance costs and where out-migration costs are low.

3.5. Ricardian Equivalence and imperfect private capital markets

The Ricardian Equivalence Theorem also requires that everyone should be able to borrow or lend at the same rate as the government. In the simple mathematical example in Section 3.2, it was shown that debt finance and tax finance would yield same results, but the crucial assumption there was that the government as well as the individual could borrow or lend at the same rate. In case of violation of that assumption, it can be shown that the present value of a future stream of income would no longer be $PV^* - g$, as shown therein, but $PV^* - (r/e)g$, where e is the discount factor of the individual different from that of the government's rate of interest, r.[2] Mundell (1971) argues that because of high discount rates for some individuals, the taxes which finance the government debt will not be fully capitalised and hence government debt will involve a net wealth effect invalidating Ricardian equivalence.

In the real world, discount rates could differ for the high risk and the low risk individuals. To analyse this effect, following Barro (1974), suppose that there are two types of individuals – those with a low discount rate, r_l and those with a high discount rate, r_h. Individuals with a high discount rate have relatively bad collateral and this is reflected in high borrowing rates. It is also supposed that the two discount rates are: related by

$r_h = (1 + \lambda)r_l$ Equation 3.25

where $\lambda > 0$ represents the proportional transaction costs involved in the loan process. Suppose that the government debt now takes the form of a perpetuity that carries a real interest payment of i per year. This bond would be subscribed to by a low-discount-rate individuals and would be evaluated as $B = i/r_l$. Suppose that the government uses the lump-sum proceeds from this sale, B, to effect a lump-sum transfer to individuals, with a fraction 'a' of this transfer going to r_l individuals and a fraction $1 - a$ going to r_h individuals. Further, the taxes for financing the government interest payments are $(1 + \gamma)i$, where 'γ' represents the proportional transaction costs associated with the government bond sale and tax collection. Suppose that these taxes are distributed amongst discount rate individuals in the same manner as the lump-sum proceeds.

Now consider the wealth effects for the r_l and r_h groups. The bond sale itself does not involve any wealth effect for the r_l group. The lump-sum transfer to r_l individuals is $aB = ai/r_l$, while the present value of the r_l share of tax liabilities, discounted at rate r_l is $(1+\gamma) ai/r_l$. If $\gamma > 0$, the net wealth effect for r_l individuals is

---

2   $PV = Y^1 + (Y^2 - t)/(1+r) + (Y^3 - t)/(1+r)^2 + ...$ F3.1
or $PV = Y^1 + (Y^2 - eg)/(1+r) + (Y^3 - eg)/(1+r)^2 + ...$ F3.2
or $PV = [Y^1 + Y^2 /(1+r) + Y^3 /(1+r)^2 + ...] - [eg)/(1+r) + eg/(1+r)^2 + ...]$ F3.3
or $PV = PV^* - (r/e)g$ F3.4
where PV^* is the discounted value of the future income streams (Equation 3.1).

negative. For the r_h group, the lump-sum proceeds are $(1-a)B = (1-a)i/r_l$, while the present value of the tax liability, discounted at rate r_h, is $(1+\gamma)(1-a)i/r_h$. Using $r_h = (1+\lambda)r_l$, the net wealth effect would be:

$$\frac{(1-a)i}{r_l}\left(1 - \frac{1+\gamma}{1+\lambda}\right) = \frac{(1-a)i}{r_l(1+\lambda)}(\lambda - \gamma) \qquad \text{Equation 3.26}$$

which is positive if $\lambda > \gamma$. To the extent that the transfer payment and tax liability involve the r_h group, the government bond issue amounts to effecting a loan from the r_l individuals to r_h individuals. The government induced transfer implied by its bond issue can raise net wealth only if the government is more efficient than the private capital market in carrying out this sort of lending and borrowing operations. In such a case, the results are non-neutral and therefore non-Ricardian.

Barro (1974) however argues that the government may be more efficient than the private market only over a certain range of B. There may be a sufficiently large value of B such that, at the margin, the net wealth effect of government debt is zero. If the public choice process leads to this value of B, then the net wealth effect of government debt would be zero despite the existence of imperfect private capital markets and Ricardian equivalence would still hold. Barro (1989d) argues that the implication of the inclusion of imperfect capital market is that the government's issue of public debt can amount to a useful form of financial intermediation. The government encourages people with good access to credit markets to hold more than their due share of the extra public debt.[3]

A different approach followed by Yotsuzuka (1987) allows for adverse selection among borrowers with different risk characteristics. Individuals know their probabilities of default, but the lenders' can only learn about these probabilities by observing the chosen levels of borrowing at going interest rates. In this setting, the government's borrowing amounts to a loan to a group that pools the various risk classes. Such borrowing is important, particularly if the private sector equilibrium does not involve similar pooling. Yotsuzuka argues that the private equilibrium typically involves a pooled loan of limited quantity at a relatively low interest rate. Then the high risk types may borrow additional amounts at a high interest rate. The assumption is that the additional borrowing is not observable by other lenders. In this case, the government's borrowing replaces the private pooled lending and leads to no real effects. Thus, as Barro (1989d) concludes that Ricardian equivalence holds despite the imperfect private capital market where high risk individuals face high marginal borrowing rates.

---

3   page 213.

3.6. Ricardian equivalence and uncertainty about future taxes and incomes

It is often argued that the uncertainty about individuals' future taxes implies a high rate of discount in capitalising these future liabilities (Bailey, 1971; Buchanan and Wagner, 1977). The substitution of a budget deficit for current taxes raises net wealth as the present value of the higher expected future taxes falls short of the current tax cut. Hence, it follows that budget deficits raise aggregate consumer demand and violate Ricardian equivalence.

A proper treatment of uncertainty, however, leads to different conclusions. Chan (1983) first considers the case of lump-sum taxes that have a known distribution across households. However, future taxes and the real value of future payments on public debt are subject to uncertainty. In this case a deficit-financed tax cut has no real effects. Individuals hold their share of the extra debt as it is a perfect hedge against uncertainty of the future taxes. He then considers another case where taxes are still lump sum but have an uncertain incidence across individuals. Then a budget deficit tends to increase the uncertainty about each individual's future disposable income. This leads to people reacting by reducing current consumption and thereby raising current private saving by more than the tax cut.

Barsky, Mankiw and Zeldes (1986) consider income tax and uncertainty – individual as well as intergenerational. They emphasise that variation in individual fortunes is large relative to aggregate uncertainty and a general feature of an optimal consumption plan is a precautionary demand for saving of any individual. In this case, a tax cut would lead to increased consumption, on the condition that claims on human capital cannot be traded. The reason for this stimulatory effect is that a tax cut provides certain wealth while the future tax increase is contingent upon future income. Considered together, these effects would reduce income uncertainty without changing the present value of expected tax payments. Their development follows that of Chan (1983) and using a two-period utility maximising consumption model they conclude that the marginal propensity to consume (MPC) out of a tax cut, with associated future income taxes, is likely to be large. In their model, the positive and large MPC is due to the reduction in precautionary saving when the government, by reducing the variance of future income, provides insurance to individuals that is not available in the private market.

The conclusion depends on the net effect of higher average future tax collections on the uncertainty associated with individuals future disposable incomes. If this uncertainty increases, then the budget deficit tends to raise desired national saving, and vice versa.

3.7. Ricardian equivalence and other assumptions

The other assumptions of the Ricardian Equivalence Hypothesis regarding the misperception of future taxes, volume of government expenditure and the timing of taxation are discussed in this section.

3.7.1. Misperception of future taxes

It is also argued that the future taxes implied by public debt are difficult to estimate due to the complexities involved (Feldstein, 1976; Buchanan and Wagner, 1977). It is generally considered that such misperceptions would call particularly for underestimation of future taxes. It can be argued that government deficits, which are well publicised, make people nervous and induce them to feel poorer. This could be because people could temporarily misperceive unusual movements in government deficits or in government expenditure changes, etc.

3.7.2. The volume of government expenditure

It is also generally argued that the existence of the debt-finance option effectively 'cheapens' government expenditure programs, because deficits are politically more popular than taxes (Buchanan and Wagner, 1977). Therefore, the volume of government expenditure generally does not remain independent of the method of finance. The argument implies that a shift, at the margin, from taxes to debt would substantially raise perceived private sector wealth, since a move toward deficit finance would only be politically popular in this circumstance.

3.7.3. The timing of taxation

Ricardian equivalence may not hold if taxes are not lump-sum. The tax structure may change with the budget deficit and thereby may affect people's incentive to work and save in different periods. This implies that changes in deficits are non-neutral. Tobin (1980) argues that taxation of wealth or income from wealth makes a 'gaping hole' in the Ricardian case. This is obvious if current lump-sum transfer payments are financed by debt issues to be serviced by future wealth taxes. This results in increased consumption.

Barro (1989b) argues that it is possible in a world of distorting taxes to determine the optimal path of budget deficit corresponding to the optimal time pattern of taxes. One of the ways could be to use deficits to smooth tax rates over time, despite fluctuations in government spending and the tax base (Barro, 1979 and 1986; Pigou, 1928). This would require budget deficits when government spending is unusually high, and surpluses when spending is unusually low. In the case of perfect foresight, tax smoothing implies constant tax rates over time though, realistically, some revisions may be necessary as more information becomes available. And in the presence of uncertainty, tax smoothing would imply tax rates behaving roughly like random walks

3.8. Conclusions

In this chapter, the theoretical aspect of the concept of Ricardian equivalence is discussed in detail. Ricardian equivalence considers that the consumers are rational and are able to perceive the rise in domestic debt as equivalent to the present discounted value of future government taxes. Therefore, the consumer does not consider domestic debt as a component of wealth. Hence, with the rise in domestic debt, the household consumption pattern in the economy does not change, but only the private savings rise to match the decline in government saving. Thus, the rise in domestic debt would not have any impact on the national macro aggregates. The concept has restrictive assumptions which have been discussed in detail. These assumptions are important to the Ricardian equivalence and have been critically evaluated in the literature.

4

Ricardian Equivalence: Empirical Studies Utilising Consumption Function

The Ricardian Equivalence Hypothesis asserts that consumers respond in exactly the same way to a change in taxes as to a change in the government deficit. Therefore, a tax cut that leads to an equivalent increase in the government debt, would finally have no effect on the consumption pattern.

In this chapter, the implications of the Ricardian Equivalence Hypothesis on consumption behaviour is examined. In Section 4.1, the need for an appropriate consumption function to test for Ricardian Equivalence Hypothesis is emphasised. In Section 4.2, a brief discussion on consumption functions and the related empirical work is presented. The extension of the permanent income hypothesis to incorporate the rational expectations model is discussed in Section 4.3. In this section, the relationship between the Ricardian Equivalence Hypothesis and the Permanent Income Hypothesis under rational expectations emerges. Once this relationship is established, a consumption equation is then derived incorporating the fiscal variables to empirically test for the Ricardian Equivalence Hypothesis. In Section 4.4, a critical review of the existing literature on Ricardian Equivalence is presented. In Section 4.5, six major studies have been replicated to test for the robustness of the specification of the respective models given a common data set. A major issue in empirical work pertains to the market and par value of government debt. This is also empirically examined in this section. The model that has been developed in Section 4.3 of this chapter is empirically estimated in Section 4.6. Finally, conclusions from the chapter are presented in Section 4.7.

4.1. Ricardian Equivalence Hypothesis and consumption

In this section, the importance of an appropriate underlying consumption function which can be used for testing the Ricardian Equivalence Hypothesis is briefly discussed.

The major empirical work on Ricardian equivalence has generally been based on an *ad hoc* specification of the consumption function. It is not usually established whether the underlying consumption function itself is supported by the data. It is crucial for tests of Ricardian equivalence to assure that the consumption function in itself is robust and has an appropriate theoretical basis. Otherwise, the result with respect to Ricardian equivalence may be caused by misspecification of the consumption function itself. One of the important assumptions about Ricardian equivalence is that people can rationally forecast the future implications of decisions taken today and accordingly adjust their consumption. Therefore, the consumption function used for testing the Ricardian Equivalence Hypothesis should itself also be consistent with the rational expectation hypothesis.

4.2. Ricardian equivalence and form of consumption function

In this section, various consumption theories which have been proposed and empirically verified in the economic literature are briefly examined.

In macro-economic models, traditionally, consumption was modelled on the basis of the Keynesian consumption function. The important feature of this theory is that aggregate consumption is related to aggregate income. The Keynesian consumption function, thus establishes a direct relationship between consumption and income,

$C = \beta YD$ Equation 4.1

or

$C = a + \beta YD$ Equation 4.2

where, C is consumption, YD is disposable income and β is the marginal propensity to consume. In the simplest models, an increase in income leads to a somewhat smaller increase in consumption, implying that the marginal propensity to consume is less than unity ($0<\beta<1$).

Another consumption function specifies consumption not only as a function of income but also of non-human real wealth (W). The consumption function then takes the form,

$C = a + \beta YD + \gamma W$ Equation 4.3

where, γ is the marginal propensity to consume out of wealth.

Still another consumption theory, which is most widely accepted and has been empirically tested, is the permanent income hypothesis, enunciated by Friedman (1957). Permanent income is defined as the steady rate of consumption a person could maintain for the rest of his life, given the present level of wealth and income earned now and in the future. The permanent income hypothesis considers consumption to be an intertemporal decision and that the effect of a change in current income on consumption will depend on whether the change is viewed by an economic agent as being permanent or temporary. If the increase is seen as permanent (i.e., occurring in every future period), only then is there an impact on the individual's lifetime budget constraint, leading to a change in current and future consumption.

In its simplest form, the permanent income hypothesis argues that consumption (C_t) is proportional to permanent income (Y_t^p),

$$C_t = \beta Y_t^p \qquad \text{Equation 4.4}$$

Permanent income can be defined as the constant stream of income which flows from the present discounted value of the agent's life time resources,

$$Y_t^p = \left(\frac{r}{1+r}\right)\left\{A_t + YD_t + \sum_{i=1}^{\infty} \frac{_t YD_{t+i}}{(1+r)^i}\right\} \qquad \text{Equation 4.5}$$

where, A_t is current assets (or wealth), YD_t is current labour income (disposable income), $_t YD_{t+i}$ is the forecast of future labour income (disposable income) based on information at time 't', and r is the real interest rate (assumed to be constant). Consumption, which is a function of permanent income, then can be shown as follows,

$$C_t = \beta \left[\left(\frac{r}{1+r}\right)\left\{A_t + YD_t + \sum_{i=1}^{\infty} \frac{_t YD_{t+i}}{(1+r)^i}\right\}\right] \qquad \text{Equation 4.6}$$

where, $\beta (r/1+r)$ is the marginal propensity to consume out of current income.

Another theory, the life cycle hypothesis can be considered similar to the permanent income hypothesis. The life cycle hypothesis views individuals as planning their consumption and saving behaviour over a long period, with the intention of allocating their consumption in the best possible way over their lifetimes – very similar to the assumption of the permanent income hypothesis. The life cycle hypothesis focuses on the motives for savings, and provides convincing reasons to include wealth as well as income in the consumption function. The permanent income hypothesis, on the other hand, concentrates on the way in which individuals form expectations about future income.

The similarity of the permanent income hypothesis with the Ricardian Equivalence Hypothesis can now be emphasised. The basic emphasis of the Ricardian Equivalence Hypothesis (REH) is to focus on the household's long term budget equation or more specifically the permanent income. The important issue in the Ricardian Equivalence Hypothesis concerns the household's response to a tax cut, given no change in government spending, thereby implying a rise in deficit. It is argued that a tax cut, generally, would not affect the household's ability to spend in the long run – lower taxes now would imply an equal increase in future taxes (on a present value basis). Accordingly, the household's consumption would not change if, fundamentally, the expectation of their permanent income does not change.

In this section, three consumption functions which are prevalent in theoretical and empirical work have been briefly discussed. However, the most important and widely accepted consumption function in the empirical literature is the permanent income hypothesis. The similarity between the permanent income hypothesis and the Ricardian Equivalence Hypothesis emerges in this section.

4.3. Ricardian equivalence and permanent income hypothesis incorporating rational expectations

In the previous section, it was mentioned that the emphasis of the permanent income hypothesis is on the way in which individuals form expectations about future income. In the present section, the permanent income hypothesis is extended to incorporate rational expectations in subsection 4.3.1. Then, given the consumption function incorporating the rational expectations, a model is developed in subsection 4.3.2, which can then be used to test for the Ricardian Equivalence Hypothesis.

4.3.1. Permanent income hypothesis incorporating rational expectations

The consumption function under the permanent income hypothesis can be extended to incorporate the implications of rational expectations.[1] Consider, again, the equation for permanent income,

$$Y_t^p = \left(\frac{r}{1+r}\right)\left\{A_t + YD_t + \sum_{i=1}^{\infty} \frac{_t YD_{t+i}}{(1+r)^i}\right\}$$

Equation 4.7

Taking expectations based on the information set at '$t - 1$', for permanent income,

---

[1] Modern research in this area originated with the work of Hall (1978), wherein, the combined implications of rational expectations and permanent income theory of consumption were derived.

$$_{t-1}Y^p_t = \left(\frac{r}{1+r}\right)\left\{_{t-1}A_t + _{t-1}YD_t + \sum_{i=1}^{\infty}\frac{_{t-1}YD_{t+i}}{(1+r)^i}\right\} \qquad \text{Equation 4.8}$$

The rational expectations hypothesis assumes that all the information at time 't-1' must have been taken into consideration before any expectation of permanent income would have been made at time 't'. Thus, $_{t-1}Y^p_t = Y^p_{t-1}$, as permanent income at 't - 1' would be the same as that at 't'. Therefore,

$$Y^p_{t-1} = \left(\frac{r}{1+r}\right)\left\{_{t-1}A_t + _{t-1}YD_t + \sum_{i=1}^{\infty}\frac{_{t-1}YD_{t+i}}{(1+r)^i}\right\} \qquad \text{Equation 4.9}$$

Considering the change in permanent income between 't - 1' and 't', then

$$Y^p_t - Y^p_{t-1} = \left(\frac{r}{1+r}\right)\left\{A_t - _{t-1}A_t + YD_t - _{t-1}YD_t + \sum_{i=1}^{\infty}\frac{_tYD_{t+i} - _{t-1}YD_{t+i}}{(1+r)^i}\right\} \text{Equation 4.10}$$

where, $(A_t - _{t-1}A_t)$, $(YD_t - _{t-1}YD_t)$, and $(_tYD_{t+i} - _{t-1}YD_{t+i})$ must be an innovation or unanticipated change (denoted by superscript 'u'), under the rational expectations approach, given the information set at 't - 1'. This can be represented as,

$$Y^p_t - Y^p_{t-1} = \left(\frac{r}{1+r}\right)\left\{A^u_t + YD^u_t + \sum_{i=1}^{\infty}\frac{_tYD^u_{t+i}}{(1+r)^i}\right\} \qquad \text{Equation 4.11}$$

where, A^u_t is the unanticipated asset position at time 't' and can be called as an asset surprise. At time 't - 1', $A^u_t = 0$, and so are the other terms like YD^u_t and $_tYD^u_{t+i}$.

The unanticipated change in assets can be derived as follows:

$$\Delta A_t = A_t - A_{t-1}$$
$$\Delta A^a_t = A^a_t - A^a_{t-1} \qquad \text{Equation 4.12}$$
$$A^u_t = A_t - A^a_t$$
$$\Delta A^u_t = \Delta A_t - \Delta A^a_t$$

where, superscript 'a' denotes the anticipated change in assets.

In a situation when there are no innovations or unanticipated changes in the variables, Equation 4.11 can be written as,

$$Y^p_t - Y^p_{t-1} = \left(\frac{r}{1+r}\right)\eta_t = \varepsilon_t \qquad \text{Equation 4.13}$$

where, $_{t-1}\eta_t = 0$. Thus, it implies that under rational expectations, permanent income follows a martingale. At time 't - 1', the best predictor of next period's permanent income, (at time 't'), is the current period's permanent income.

Since, according to permanent income hypothesis, consumption is just a linear function of permanent income, it can be derived that

$$C_t = \beta Y_t^p \qquad \text{Equation 4.14}$$

or

$$Y_t^p = \frac{C_t}{\beta} \qquad \text{Equation 4.15}$$

As in the case of the permanent income, the change in consumption from '$t-1$' to 't' would be a function of unanticipated changes in assets and disposable income,

$$\frac{C_t}{\beta} - \frac{C_{t-1}}{\beta} = \left(\frac{r}{1+r}\right)\left\{A_t^u + YD_t^u + \sum_{i=1}^{\infty} \frac{{}_tYD_{t+i}^u}{(1+r)^i}\right\} \qquad \text{Equation 4.16}$$

or

$$C_t = C_{t-1} + \beta\left[\left(\frac{r}{1+r}\right)\left\{A_t^u + YD_t^u + \sum_{i=1}^{\infty} \frac{{}_tYD_{t+i}^u}{(1+r)^i}\right\}\right] \qquad \text{Equation 4.17}$$

Thus, the change in consumption, between '$t-1$' and 't', is a function of the unanticipated changes in assets, and current and future disposable income.[2] In case there are no unanticipated changes in permanent income, then consumption, as well, follows a random walk:

$$C_t = C_{t-1} + v_t \qquad \text{Equation 4.18}$$

where, $v_t = \beta \varepsilon_t$ and ${}_{t-1}v_t = 0$.

Hall (1978) observed that rational consumption behaviour at time 't' would be based on expectations about future income that already takes into account all the available relevant economic information at that point of time. Therefore, consumption in the next period would differ from that in the current period only by a random component which would be serially uncorrelated. Hence, consumption variables that are lagged for more than one period, should not add to the predictive power of the current period consumption equation. Hall focused on US quarterly data for the period 1947–77, and found support for the above derived implications of the permanent income hypothesis under rational expectations.[3]

---

[2] Lucas (1976) pointed out that under rational expectations, the permanent income hypothesis does not lead to a structural relationship between consumption and income but to a statistical relationship that could change. The Lucas critique, thus, called for estimation methods that treat consumption and income jointly. Hall (1978) sharpened the implications of the permanent income hypothesis by showing that under rational expectations only surprises in permanent income should affect current consumption, once lagged consumption is accounted for. Thus, a new dichotomy was added in the consumption literature, that of anticipated and unanticipated changes in income.

[3] However, other studies attempting to test Hall's hypothesis, yield mixed results (Bilson, 1980; Flavin, 1981; Cuddington, 1982; Muellbauer, 1983; Wilcox, 1989; Zeldes, 1989).

4.3.2. Testing Ricardian equivalence under the permanent income hypothesis incorporating rational expectations

The consumption equation, combining rational expectations and the permanent income hypothesis, derived in the previous subsection, can now be extended to test the Ricardian Equivalence Hypothesis.

In Ricardian Equivalence Hypothesis, it is assumed that households take into consideration the tax payments that will have to be made in future while calculating their life-time wealth or permanent income. Therefore, when the government reduces taxes to run a deficit, financed only through bonds, individuals recognise that their taxes will rise in the future. The resultant higher taxes in future would be used for interest payments as well as for repayments of the debt. The permanent income of the households would thus be unaffected by the government's substitution of taxes from time 't' to '$t+i$', where $i=1..\infty$. Therefore, their consumption does not undergo any change. Since the tax cut increases disposable income, but consumption does not change, savings must rise. Ricardian equivalence implies that an increase in the budget deficit unaccompanied by cuts in government spending should lead to an increase in private savings that precisely matches the deficit (negative government saving).

In the consumption function, net assets or wealth of the private sector, A_t, can be defined as

$$A_t = K_t + R_t + GB_t \qquad \text{Equation 4.19}$$

where, K_t is the value of capital stock measured by the total value of stockholder's equity plus the value of the housing stock, land, and consumer durables. R_t is the value of reserves held at the central bank which are a private sector claim on the government, and GB_t is the value of government bonds which are held by the public. Considering that the private sector wealth or assets can be divided into government bonds (GB_t) and others (Z_t, where $Z_t = K_t + R_t$). Then,

$$A_t = Z_t + GB_t \qquad \text{Equation 4.20}$$

and the unanticipated component in the assets can be shown as follows:

$$A_t^u = Z_t^u + GB_t^u \qquad \text{Equation 4.21}$$

Substituting Equation 4.21 in the consumption Equation 4.17 yields

$$C_t = C_{t-1} + \beta \left[\left(\frac{r}{1+r}\right) \left\{ GB_t^u + Z_t^u + YD_t^u + \sum_{i=1}^{\infty} \frac{YD_{t+i}^u}{(1+r)^i} \right\} \right] \qquad \text{Equation 4.22}$$

In Equation 4.22 the unanticipated change in government bonds (GB_t^u) at time 't' implies that a stream of future taxes will go up by rGB_t^u, where r is the rate of interest on the bonds. Therefore, the unanticipated change in disposable income, due to the unanticipated change in the bond holdings, will be equal to the interest payments on these unanticipated bonds, ie.,

$$YD^u = -rGB^u \qquad \text{Equation 4.23}$$

Therefore, the consumption function would now simply reduce to the following form,

$$C_t = C_{t-1} + \beta \left[\left(\frac{r}{1+r}\right)\{Z_t^u\}\right] \qquad \text{Equation 4.24}$$

where, $GB^u_t = YD^u_t$, and $\sum_{i=1}^{\infty} \frac{YD^u_{t+i}}{(1+r)^i} = 0$, as $YD^u = -rGB^u$.

It can be implied from the above equation, that consumption at time 't' is a function of consumption lagged by one period and any unanticipated changes in other assets.

Thus, in a consumption regression, under the rational expectations and permanent income hypotheses, neither anticipated nor unanticipated government bonds, if included, should have a significant coefficient. Consequently, in the following regression,

$$C_t = a_1 C_{t-1} + a_2 Z_t^u + a_3 GB_t^u + a_4 GB_t^a \qquad \text{Equation 4.25}$$

the coefficients of both unanticipated and the anticipated government bonds are expected to be insignificant ($a_3 = 0$ and $a_4 = 0$). This equation can be used for testing the Ricardian Equivalence Hypothesis.

Thus, in this section, it has been shown that the permanent income consumption function, under rational expectations, follows a random walk. Therefore, the best predictor of consumption in period 't + 1', is consumption itself in period 't'. The consumer has foresight, complete information, and therefore behaves rationally, by incorporating all available information in his consumption function in any period. The Ricardian Equivalence Hypothesis stresses that under the assumption of rational expectations, the consumer is indifferent between bond finance and tax finance. The consumer realises that bond finance in the current period implies future tax liabilities, the present value of the two being the same, and therefore permanent income and consumption do not change. The permanent income hypothesis under rational expectations, is therefore considered appropriate, in deriving a reliable consumption equation for testing the Ricardian Equivalence Hypothesis.

4.4: Review of literature

Initially, the empirical work on the Ricardian Equivalence Hypothesis was scanty but since Barro's seminal paper in 1974, a large number of empirical studies have been conducted to test the hypothesis. The growth in the empirical literature has been accompanied by an increasing sophistication of the techniques employed to test the proposition. In this section, a critical review of the empirical studies investigating the impact of budget deficits on consumption is presented. Most of these studies rely on estimates of coefficients in the consumption function. The overall evidence is in favour of the Ricardian equivalence proposition.

In view of the large number of studies and issues, this section has been divided into two subsections for a better focus. In subsection 4.4.1, a discussion on the general issues emerging from the literature is presented. This is followed by a detailed and specific discussion of the empirical work in subsection 4.4.2.

4.4.1. General issues on Ricardian equivalence and consumption studies

In this subsection, some of the major problems which are shared virtually by all studies attempting to study the effects of deficits on consumption are summarised. These are, broadly, issues pertaining to measurement, methodology and the appropriate choice of the equation to be tested. Though technically, the choice of equation forms part of methodology, it is being considered separately due to its importance in this work.

In most of the studies attempting to test for the Ricardian Equivalence Hypothesis, consumption in the current period is considered as the dependent variable. The explanatory variables generally considered are national income, personal or private disposable income, private wealth, social security wealth, taxes, government expenditure, transfer payments to individuals, government debt and deficit. Thus, the emphasis is to regress consumption on various variables which proxy income, wealth and fiscal policy instruments.

4.4.1.1. Measurement

Most of the studies suffer from this problem. Measurement issues include adjustments from par value to market value of government debt, use of deflators, proper accounting for government assets, investments, contingent liabilities, etc. Many of these issues involve serious conceptual problems and the right measure is not easily obvious (Kotlikoff, 1986). And, econometric estimates appear highly sensitive to the set of corrections that are then made. Two of the important measurement issues are discussed as follows.

4.4.1.1.1. Appropriate measure of government debt

Theoretically, under Ricardian equivalence, bond finance is a substitute for tax finance. Therefore, total government debt in the economy is the appropriate measure to model for Ricardian equivalence rather than federal debt, to study the impact of bonds and taxes on aggregate consumption. In addition, no study seems to have attempted to assess the relationship between the federal, state and the local debt, and their implications. There are, however, only a few studies showing a significant relationship between federal fiscal activity, and state and local fiscal activity (Feldstein and Metcalf, 1987).

4.4.1.1.2. Market and par value of government debt

The issue of using data on debt series in terms of par values or market values is also controversial in the literature. The official statistics on outstanding debt are presented on nominal par values. It is agreed that in the period of rapid changes in interest rates, market value and not the par value of government debt is an appropriate measure. In the earlier studies, in absence of any market value of debt series, par value of debt has been used (Tanner, 1970; Kochin, 1974). A large number of latter studies have used the market value of debt in their consumption functions. The most widely used market value of debt series is that constructed by Seater (1981)[4] for the United States on an annual basis, and updated and extended by Cox and Hirschhorn (1983)[5] and Cox (1985) on a monthly basis. These calculations are exact measures of market value as actual price quotes for each issue are considered. Butkiewicz (1983) provides a simpler method using averages, which yields results similar to that by Seater (1981) and Cox-Hirschhorn (1983).[6] This issue is empirically analysed in Section 4.5.2.

4.4.1.2. Methodology

Several issues pertaining to econometric methodology are important for the proper evaluation of the results. These issues are identification, data specification, differencing, simultaneity and treatment of expectations.

---

4   The correlation between the par value and market value, in levels is 0.974, and between annual changes is 0.871, for 1947-74.

5   The correlation between the levels of market and par value is 0.9918 and between their first differences is 0.6902, for the period January 1975 to December 1980.

6   The correlation between the series generated by Butkiewicz's method and that of Seater's, and Cox-Hirschhorn is 0.99, respectively.

4.4.1.2.1. Problems of identification

Problems of identification are really complex in any economic series, as it is difficult to distinguish between the economic effects of different fiscal policy variables. For example, government deficits and spending move together very closely, especially during unusual years like wars and famines. If government debt is included in the regression but government expenditure omitted, then this exclusion can introduce omitted variable bias in the results. Many of the initial studies suffered precisely from such a bias (Tanner, 1970, 1979a, 1979b; Kochin, 1974; Yawitz and Meyer, 1976).

Again, most of the studies include income, government spending, transfers, taxes, deficits and debt in their regressions. Each of these variables affect economic activity independently. For example, generally, it is assumed that, since taxes decrease disposable income, the tax coefficient should equal the negative of the income coefficient. But this assumption can only be valid when taxes are non-distortionary. To identify such econometric models precisely, it is important to have a data series on marginal tax rates for various incomes. Even marginal tax rates may closely follow movements in revenue, making identification more difficult. All the studies under review have ignored marginal tax rates except that by Seater (1982), and Seater and Mariano (1985), implying an omitted variable bias.

4.4.1.2.2. Data specification

The issues of data specifications like inclusion/exclusion of some variables, period of the study, and data breaks are crucial for the results. They could bias the results and many consumption functions are sensitive to the period of study, mainly the inclusion/exclusion of abnormal years like the war years (Seater, 1982; Feldstein and Elmendorf, 1990; Kormendi and Meguire, 1990; Haug, 1990).

The literature on Ricardian equivalence is ambiguous on the use of the various measures of consumption and national income in the regressions, the two most important variables in any consumption function. Many of the studies specify the dependent variable as consumer expenditure rather than an estimate of consumption, wherein the implicit annual rental from durables is imputed and added to the expenditure on nondurables and services.

heoretically, consumption expenditure would be an appropriate measure in the consumption function but it could result in a bias through subjectivity in fixation of implicit annual rental rates.[7] Kormendi (1983) uses the Bureau of Economic Analysis' measure of stock of consumer durables while Modigliani and Sterling (1986) use the Federal Reserve Bank series and get different results for the United States. Darby (1978) argues that the errors in classifying consumer expenditures as durables or non-durables suggest that the use of consumer expenditure is substantially less subject to specification error than the alternative approach. However, many studies consider only the consumer expenditure on non-durables and services or only consumer expenditure on non-durables in their consumption functions.

In the case of the income variable, Feldstein (1982) argues that the disposable personal income is the correct measure of income and not the national income. He contends that national income includes corporate retained earnings, and is not adjusted for taxes and transfers, and therefore is closer to the Ricardian equivalence proposition that the household's cash receipts are not directly relevant to consumption. However, Kormendi (1983) argues that the consumption function wherein it is assumed that individuals rationally perceive the benefits of government expenditure as well as future tax liabilities implicit in the debt instrument, it is the total income generated in the economy, which is an appropriate measure, rather than disposable income. Kormendi (1983), Barth, Iden and Russek (1986), and Modigliani and Sterling (1986) and many other later studies consider national income as the appropriate measure of income.

In the case of government purchases, permanent and transitory changes are likely to have different effects on consumption (Barro, 1981a; Seater and Mariano, 1985). However, debt is likely to be positively correlated with transitory purchases due to the preferential process of tax smoothing by the government (Barro, 1989b, 1989d). In a regression equation with government purchases and the deficit as regressors, but with no decomposition of government purchases into permanent and transitory components, the deficit may proxy for transitory purchases and may have a significant coefficient when actually it would not. However, this problem does not seem to be serious and the inclusion of the decomposed variable does not yield different results (Seater and Mariano, 1985).

In the case of decomposition of taxes into permanent and transitory, the results may vary sharply and exhibit sensitivity to the period and methodology of the study (Modigliani and Sterling, 1986, 1990; Kormendi and Meguire, 1986, 1990).

---

7   Hayashi (1982) concludes that his test for permanent income hypothesis is rejected when consumer expenditure is used, but is accepted when consumption series which includes service flows from consumer durables is used.

However, the practise of decomposing some variables explicitly into permanent and transitory components but ignoring to consider the same decomposition for other appropriate variables in the same consumption equation can yield spurious results (Modigliani and Sterling, 1990; Kormendi and Meguire, 1990; Seater, 1993).

4.4.1.2.3. Treatment of trend in the model

The issue of treatment of trend in the empirical estimation is also important. In the case of deterministic trend, it would be proper to include time as an independent explanatory variable but with the random trend, first differences of the data becomes necessary. Kormendi (1983), Kormendi and Meguire (1986, 1990) as well as Haug (1990) adopt first-differencing in their studies, after testing for cointegration, as an appropriate tool for eliminating the random trend in the variables and making the data stationary. Modigliani and Sterling (1986, 1990) argue that the data should not be differenced when the variables in the regression are cointegrated. Feldstein and Elmendorf (1990) consider differencing less efficient than performing a regression in levels with an autoregressive transformation. A closely related issue pertains to stationarity of the data series. Nelson and Plosser (1982) argue that most of the data series are $I(1)$, but very few studies have considered and tested for it except Modigliani and Sterling (1986), Kormendi and Meguire (1986 and 1990) and Haug (1990). The results of the other studies, specially conducted in levels could therefore yield spurious inferences.

4.4.1.2.4. Simultaneity in the model

Another methodological issue concerns simultaneity. Generally, most of the consumption specifications include variables like deficits, government spending, income, interest rates, tax revenue and transfer payment. All these variables may be endogenous, so estimation techniques need to be concerned with simultaneity (Flavin, 1987). Only a few studies have made use of instrumental variables and even in these the exogeneity of these variables is not certain (Feldstein, 1982; Seater and Mariano, 1985). No study has used the three-stage least square method, and only one study (Aschauer, 1985) makes use of the full information maximum likelihood method.

4.4.1.2.5. Decomposition of the variables

In the consumption studies, it is important to distinguish between the expected and unexpected movements of explanatory variables. In the stochastic permanent income hypothesis, only unexpected changes matter. In the empirical literature, only a few studies adopt this methodology. Also, there is some problem in estimating expectations. Usually, distributed lags of past variables are used in some way to capture the formation of expectations of the future values (Barro, 1977; Aschauer, 1985; Modigliani and Sterling, 1986, 1990).

Another method to distinguish unexpected changes in the deficit is to use statistical models to define the evolution of deficits, and relate deficit innovations to consumption innovations (VAR models). But this technique would only be useful if the consumers really form expectations as defined in the models. Otherwise these models create a bias in favour of Ricardian Equivalence Hypothesis (Plosser, 1982; Bernheim, 1987).

4.4.1.3. Choice of the equation to be tested

The choice of an appropriate equation is perhaps the most important problem in the estimation of the consumption function to test for the Ricardian Equivalence Hypothesis. In order for the Ricardian equivalence to hold, the economic agents are expected to maximise intertemporal utility and form expectations rationally. These two assumptions are the basis of the permanent income hypothesis under rational expectations using the Euler equation, and therefore it seems to be an appropriate framework to test for the Ricardian equivalence (Flavin, 1987).

The advantage of Euler equation method as used by Hall (1978), following Flavin (1987), is that it is based on the first order condition,

$$E_t\left(\frac{1+r_t}{1+\delta}U'(C_{t+1})\right) = U'(C_t) \qquad \text{Equation 4.26}$$

where C is consumption, E_t is the mathematical expectation operator conditional on information known at t, r is the rate of interest and δ is the agent's subjective discount rate. The Euler equation, assuming that the utility function exhibits constant relative risk aversion and making standard distributional assumptions, would take the following form,

$$\log C_{t+1} - \log C_t = \alpha_0 + \alpha_1^{-1} E_t \log(1+r_t) + (\log C_{t+1} - E_t \log C_t) \qquad \text{Equation 4.27}$$

where α_1^{-1} is the coefficient of relative risk aversion. Thus, the Euler equation decomposes the growth rate of consumption into a forecastable component, depending on the intercept, interest rate and the expectational error term.

On the other hand, the consumption function not incorporating rational expectations, can be represented in first differences, in the following form

$$\Delta C_t = \beta_0 + \beta_1 \Delta Y_t + \beta_2 \Delta DF_t + \eta_t \qquad \text{Equation 4.28}$$

where Y and DF are income and deficit, respectively. In Equation 4.28, the coefficients of both income and deficit should also be insignificant, given the assumptions of rational expectations.

In case the data is generated in the Ricardian sense, then, apart from the specific issues of log transformation and the omission of the interest rate variable in Equation 4.28 compared to Equation 4.27, the error term needs to be carefully analysed.[8] Only the variables which help in revising the forecast of future disposable income, taxes, deficit, interest rates, etc. will help determine the expectational error in consumption. Thus, the expectational error term can be represented as follows,

$$C_t - E_{t-1}C_t = \phi_y \varepsilon_y + \phi_t \varepsilon_t + \phi_0 \varepsilon_0 \qquad \text{Equation 4.29}$$

where the epsilons are the innovations in income (ε_y) or taxes (ε_t) or any other (ε_0) variables which help revise the expectations pertaining to consumption. In the studies which use the consumption functions without incorporating rational expectations, the equations are prone to the simultaneity bias affecting the results even if the instrumental variables are used (Flavin, 1987).[9]

The Euler equation tests are, however, criticised as unfavourable to the stochastic permanent income model of aggregate consumption in the case of uncertain future income (Hayashi, 1985b) or liquidity constraints (Zeldes, 1986). For example, in the face of uncertain future income, a closed form solution is unobtainable for future consumption from the Euler equation. Hence the implied testable restrictions would also be unobtainable.

It has to be recognised that it is difficult to derive restrictions that are both testable and measurable in any economic model. Economic models are expected to provide close approximations in terms of the true theoretical relationships. Therefore, theoretically, the rational expectations model of the permanent income hypothesis, using the Euler equation, can be considered appropriate.

---

8   The log transformation of the consumption data should not make important difference to the results in the two equations (Flavin, 1987). Similarly, the expected interest rate variable in Equation 4.27 may be assumed to not making a significant contribution to the change in consumption, given the basic assumption of rational expectations and Ricardian equivalence.

9   Even if contemporaneous values of exogenous variables are used as instruments, the bias still persists. These instruments may ameliorate the problem of simultaneity between consumption and income, but the exogenous variables may still be correlated with the expectational error under the null hypothesis.

4.4.2. Specific consumption studies on Ricardian Equivalence Hypothesis

The empirical literature on Ricardian equivalence reveals the progress of techniques from simple regressions in studies conducted in the 1970s to sophisticated cointegration methods being adopted now. The emphasis on the choice of testable equation has also changed from the traditional aggregate consumption function to the permanent income consumption function incorporating rational expectations. Accordingly, the discussion here follows a similar pattern.

A summary of important studies testing for the impact of deficits on consumption is presented in Table 4.1. The statement provides information on the data specifications, variables used, technique employed, instruments used and the conclusions derived from these studies.

4.4.2.1. Ricardian equivalence and traditional aggregate consumption function

In the traditional aggregate consumption function approach two distinct patterns emerge. These are, Keynesian consumption functions, and the permanent income-life cycle specifications not incorporating rational expectations. There are nine studies which follow the aggregate consumption function approach and the majority of them yield evidence in favour of the Ricardian Equivalence Hypothesis. However, as the aggregate consumption function specifications do not incorporate the role of rational expectations, these studies cannot be considered to lend much support to a hypothesis which requires rational expectations (See Sections 4.2 and 4.3). The two types of consumption functions are discussed separately.

4.4.2.1.1. Keynesian specification of the consumption function

The initial empirical work uses the Keynesian consumption function (Studies 1, 3, 4 and 5, marked '*' in Table 4.1). In these studies, as mentioned in section 4.2, consumption is expected to be a linear function of income and the existing wealth. The consumption equation generally takes the following form

$$C_t = \alpha_0 + \alpha_1 Y_t + \alpha_2 W_t + \alpha_3 DF_t + \alpha_4 D_t + \alpha_5 Z_t \qquad \text{Equation 4.30}$$

where, C is consumption expenditure, Y is disposable income, W is private sector holding of wealth net of government debt, DF is the deficit, D is government debt, and Z is a vector of any other variable.

Table 4.1: Summary of some important studies on Ricardian Equivalence Hypothesis and consumption function

S.No	Study and year	Data specifications	Dependent variable	Independent variables	Technique employed	Instruments used	Parameter restrictions (Null hypothesis: Ricardian equivalence)	Conclusion
1	2	3	4	5	6	7	8	9
1.	Tanner (1970)*	1951–67, Canada, Quarterly.	S	YD, r, W, D.	OLS, levels.	None	$\alpha W = \alpha D$.	Supports Ricardian equivalence.
2.	Kochin (1974) ***	1952–71, USA, Annual.	C_{ns}	YD, DF, UFD, MB, C_{t-1}.	OLS, levels, differences.	None	$\alpha DF = 0$.	Supports Ricardian equivalence.
3.	Yawitz and Meyer (1976)*	1953–69, USA, Annual.	C	YD, PD, W.	OLS, Levels.	None	$\alpha PD = \alpha W$.	Refutes Ricardian equivalence.
4.	Tanner (1979a)*	1929–40, 1947–74, USA, Annual.	C	$YD, YD_{t-1}, RE, U, DR_{t-1}, W_{t-1}, DF$.	OLS, levels.	None	$\alpha DF = 0$	Supports Ricardian equivalence.
5.	Tanner (1979b)*	1947–74, USA, Annual.	C	$YD, YD_{t-1}, RE, U, DR_{t-1}, W_{t-1}, DF, D_{t-1}$.	OLS, levels.	None	$\alpha DF = 0$; $\alpha D_{t-1} = \alpha W_{t-1}$.	Supports Ricardian equivalence.

Table continued

Table 4.1: Summary of some important studies on Ricardian Equivalence Hypothesis and consumption function

S.No	Study and year	Data specifications	Dependent variable	Independent variables	Technique employed	Instruments used	Parameter restrictions (Null hypothesis: Ricardian equivalence)	Conclusion
1	2	3	4	5	6	7	8	9
6.	Seater (1982)**	1930–40, 1947–74; 1947–74, USA., Annual	C and C_n	YD, RE, U, MTR DR, W, MB, r, MCD, PCD, D, SSW, NDM, CGD.	OLS, levels.	None	$aPCD, aMCD<0; aD=aSSW = aNDM = aCGD = 0.$	Mixed. supports when only C is used.
7.	Buiter and Tobin 1980)***	1949–76, USA, Annual.	C and C_{ns}	YD, DF, G, T, C_{t-1}, C_{nst-1}.	OLS, levels.	None	$aYD = aDF = aT.$	Inconclusive.
8.	Feldstein (1982)**	1930–40, 1947–77, USA, Annual.	C	Y, YD, A, G, SSW, T, TR, D.	OLS, 2SLS, levels.	$T_{t-1}, Y_{t-1}.$	$aSSW = aT = aTR = aA + aD = 0.\#$	Refutes Ricardian equivalence.
9.	Kormendi (1983)***	1930–76, USA, Annual.	C_{nds}	Y, Y_{t-1}, G, W, TR, T, RE, GI, D.	OLS, differences.	None	$aT = aRE = aGI = aD = 0; aG < 0.$	Supports Ricardian equivalence.
10.	Aschaer (1985)***	1948–81, USA, Quarterly.	C, C_{ns}	DF, G, C_{t-1}, C_{nst-1}.	Full information maximum likelihood, differences.	None	$aDF_{t-i} = 0, where\ i = 1..n.$	Supports Ricardian equivalence.

Table continued

Table 4.1: Summary of some important studies on Ricardian Equivalence Hypothesis and consumption function

S.No	Study and year	Data specifications	Dependent variable	Independent variables	Technique employed	Instruments used	Parameter restrictions (Null hypothesis: Ricardian equivalence)	Conclusion
1	2	3	4	5	6	7	8	9
11.	Seater and Mariano (1985)**	1929–75, USA, Annual.	C and C_{ns}	$Y, YP, G, GP, MTR, r_s, r_l, T, TR, D, SSW$.	2SLS, levels.	CAS, DMR, D, GIT.	$\alpha D = \alpha T = \alpha TR = \alpha SSW = 0$.	Supports Ricardian equivalence.
12.	Evans (1985)**	1901–29, USA, Annual.	C	YD, DF, G, GT, Y, D.	Generalised method of moments, levels, differences.	$MTR, G, MS, M2$.	$\alpha D = \alpha DF = 0$.	Supports Ricardian equivalence.
13.	Barth, Iden, and Russek (1986)***	1931–83, USA, Annual.	C_{nds}	$Y, Y_{t-1}, G, W, TR, T, RE, GI, D, DFD, DS$.	OLS, differences.	None	$T = \alpha RE = \alpha GI = \alpha D = 0$; $\alpha G < 0$.	Supports Ricardian equivalence.
14.	Modigliani and Sterling (1986,1990)**	1952–84, USA, Annual.	C_{nds}	A, D, Y, T, DF.	Almon distributed lag function, levels.	None	$\alpha A = -\alpha D, \alpha G < 0, \alpha T = 0$.	Refutes Ricardian equivalence.

Table continued

Table 4.1: Summary of some important studies on Ricardian Equivalence Hypothesis and consumption function

S.No	Study and year	Data specifications	Dependent variable	Independent variables	Technique employed	Instruments used	Parameter restrictions (Null hypothesis: Ricardian equivalence)	Conclusion
1	2	3	4	5	6	7	8	9
15.	Evans (1988)***	1947–85, USA, Quarterly.	C_{ns}	$A_{t-1}, C_{nst-1}, G.$	2SLS, levels.	$C_{nst-2}, A_{t-2}.$	$\alpha A_{t-1}=0.$	Supports Ricardian equivalence.
16.	Poterba (1988)***	1959–87, USA, Monthly.	C_{nf}, C_s and C_{nso}	$C_{t-1}, T, r, s, S.$	OLS, differences.	None	$\alpha T=0.$	Refutes Ricardian equivalence.
17	Feldstein and Elmendorf (1990)***	1931–40,1947–85, USA, Annual.	C_{nds}	$Y, Y_{t-1}, G, W, TR, T, RE, GI, D.$	OLS, 2SLS levels, ratios, differences	$G, T, D.$	$\alpha T=\alpha RE=\alpha GI=\alpha D=0; \alpha G<0.$	Refutes Ricardian equivalence.
18	Haug(1990)***	1929–85, USA, Annual.	$C_{ns}, G, Y.$	$D, T, TR,$	Generalised method of moments. differences.	$D, G, TR.$	$\alpha D=0.$	Mixed. supports if World War II period is included.

* Keynesian consumption function. ** Permanent income - Life cycle consumption function without Rational expectations.
*** Permanent income - Life cycle consumption function incorporating rational expectations. α refers to the coefficient of the variable. # when Y is used. If YD is used then $\alpha SSW=\alpha A+\alpha D=0, \alpha G<0, \alpha TR<0.$

Table continued

Table 4.1: Summary of some important studies on Ricardian Equivalence Hypothesis and consumption function

C	: Total consumption expenditure
C_n	: Consumption expenditure on nondurables
C_s	: Consumption expenditure on services
C_{ns}	: Consumption expenditure on nondurables and services
C_{nso}	: Consumption expenditure on nondurables, services and others like clothing, shoes and nontax payments
C_{nds}	: Consumption expenditure on nondurables, durables and services
S	: Personal net savings

Independent variables

CAS	: wartime casualty rates	MTR	: Marginal tax rate
D	: Debt	MS	: Size of military
DF	: Deficit	r	: Rate of interest
DFD	: Federal deficit	s_s	: Stock market returns
DMR	: Unexpected money growth	S	: Salaries and wages
DR	: Stock of consumer durables	SSW	: Social security wealth
DS	: Deficit of the states	T	: Tax
G	: Government spending	TR	: Transfers
GI	: Interest on govt. debt	TT	: Temporary taxes
GP	: Permanent govt. spending	UFD	: Full employment deficit
GT	: Transitory govt. spending	Y	: National income
M_2	: Money stock M_2	YD	: Disposable income
MB	: Monetary base	YP	: Permanent income
A	: Stock of pvt. sector assets including government bonds		
CGD	: Capital gain on government debt		
GIT	: Graduated income tax function		
MCD	: Monetised current deficit		
NDM	: Non deficit related monetary changes		
PCD	: Non-monetised current deficit		
PD	: Private sector holdings of government debt		
RE	: Retained earnings of corporations		
r_s	: Short-term rate of interest		
r_l	: Long-term rate of interest		
U	: Unemployment rate adjusted with disposable income		
W	: Stock of pvt. sector wealth net of government bonds		

The test for Ricardian equivalence involves simply testing for the coefficient of the deficit or the debt variable which is included in the regression equation. The initial empirical studies were simple regressions but the results they yield are mixed. Tanner (1970, 1979a, 1979b) finds support for Ricardian equivalence, while Yawitz and Meyer (1976) refute it. Though the results show that three of the four studies support Ricardian equivalence, this support cannot be considered strong as the underlying consumption function is not appropriate.

4.4.2.1.2. Permanent income – Life cycle hypothesis not incorporating rational expectations

In this specification, consumption is based on the simple permanent income – life cycle hypothesis not incorporating rational expectations. The equation, which is generally estimated under this approach, is as follows,

$$C_t = a_0 + a_1 Y_t + a_{12} Y_{t-1} + a_2 T_t + a_3 G_t + a_4 D_t + a_5 W_t + a_6 Z_t \qquad \text{Equation 4.31}$$

where, C is consumption expenditure, Y is income, T is taxes, G is government spending, D is government debt, W is the private sector holding of wealth net of government debt, and Z is a vector of any other variable such as deficit, social security wealth, transfer payments, monetary base, taxes (permanent and/or temporary), government spending (permanent and/or temporary) or any other exogenous variables.

Total income is gross income in some studies or disposable income in others. In case gross income is considered in the regression equation, then the tax coefficient is expected to be insignificant ($a_2 = 0$) while if disposable income is considered then it is expected to be positive and significant ($a_2 > 0$) to get the Ricardian equivalence result.

The coefficient of government spending, a_3, is expected to be negative (Barro, 1983; Seater and Mariano, 1985) and small under Ricardian equivalence, as it reflects the first year response of the households whose economic life is considered to be infinite. If $a_3 = -1$, then it implies a strong form of fiscal impotence (Feldstein, 1982).

The coefficient of transfer payments, if included in the regression, would be insignificant as these are considered analogous to a reduction in taxes (Feldstein, 1982; Seater and Mariano, 1985). Kormendi (1983) argues that as transfer payments shift wealth from high income individuals to low income individuals, it can be significantly related to an increase in private sector consumption.[10]

There are five important studies following this specification (Studies 6, 8,

---

10 The magnitude of the coefficient will depend on the propensities to consume and the anticipation of the consumers as to the permanence of such transfers.

11, 12, and 14 marked as '**' in Table 4.1). The results are even, with two clearly supporting, two decisively rejecting the Ricardian Equivalence Hypothesis, and one yielding mixed results. These studies are briefly discussed as follows.

In the study by Seater (1982) the results are mixed and are sensitive to the choice of the dependent variable – total consumption expenditure or consumption expenditure on nondurables. The study by Feldstein (1982) was path-breaking in two ways. Firstly, it logically argued about the generalisations that should follow Ricardian equivalence. Secondly, it recognised the problem of simultaneity and tried to correct it through the use of instrumental variables.[11] Feldstein concludes that the United States data strongly refutes Ricardian equivalence during the period, 1930–77.[12]

Seater and Mariano (1985) use an extended version of Barro (1983) and decompose income, government expenditure, and taxes into permanent and transitory components and also use marginal tax rates in their regressions. Their results are in support of the Ricardian Equivalence Hypothesis.[13] The other studies are by Evans (1985) which supports the Ricardian Hypothesis while Modigliani and Sterling (1986, 1990) refute it.

4.4.2.2. Ricardian equivalence and permanent income hypothesis incorporating rational expectations

The permanent income hypothesis incorporating rational expectations implies that consumption follows a random walk. It is only the unexpected changes in the variables which influence current and future consumption. The studies reviewed

---

11   The instrument used is the once-lagged value of the variable itself.

12   Seater and Mariano (1985) criticise Feldstein's study on two issues – use of once-lagged values as instrumental variables and the interpretation of the significant coefficient of transfers. They conduct the exogeneity tests (Hausman, 1978) and find that current and once-lagged income, taxes and social security wealth are endogenous and therefore conclude that Feldstein's equation may still suffer from the simultaneity bias. The significant coefficient of transfers, Seater and Mariano argue, is due to its acting as a proxy for omitted or mismeasured variables. They suggest that the inclusion of the business cycle indicator, reduces the significance of the transfers. Seater and Mariano repeat Feldstein's regressions with corrected variables and report different results suggesting that the original estimates are affected by misspecification of variables and improper correction of simultaneity bias. Leimer and Lesnoy (1982) argue that Feldstein's measure of social security wealth arbitrarily and incorrectly adjusts for changes in the law.

13   The results indicate that the marginal tax rate is a significant variable. However, their results are qualitatively the same as the results they obtain from replications of Feldstein (1982) and Kormendi (1983), two important studies which omit marginal tax rates, suggesting that the bias arising from omission may not be severe.

in this section either explicitly contain a lagged consumption variable when the consumption equation is specified in levels, or else the consumption function is specified in first differences.

There are nine studies which make use of this approach, with five clearly supporting Ricardian equivalence, two refuting it, one yielding mixed results and the other drawing inconclusive results (Studies 2, 7, 9, 10, 13, 15, 16, 17 and 18 marked as '***' in Table 4.1). These studies are briefly discussed as follows.

Kochin's (1974) study was the first to include a lagged value of consumption in the regression.[14] His results based on United States data for the period 1952–71 support the Ricardian Equivalence Hypothesis. Kochin's study was criticised by Buiter and Tobin (1980) on the issue of misspecification of the data series.[15] Buiter and Tobin (1980) use lagged consumption in their equation for the United States data for the period 1949–76. Their results are inconclusive as the coefficients of the important variables in their equation (deficit, government spending and taxes on which the null hypothesis depends) lack statistical significance. Kormendi (1983) generated a large number of comments, replies and extensions. The result of the OLS regression, in the first differences, on the United States annual data for 1931–76, generally supports the Ricardian Equivalence Hypothesis. Later extensions with revised data definitions, a longer sample period and the use of 2SLS estimation also yield robust results supporting Ricardian equivalence (Kormendi and Meguire, 1986, 1990).

Modigliani and Sterling (1986, 1990) criticise Kormendi (1983) on ignoring the role of temporary taxes, and specifying the variables in first differences, especially when they are cointegrated.[16] Barth, Iden and Russek (1986) explored

---

14 Kochin (1974, 390) argued that, 'It can be shown that if permanent income is formed by taking a weighted average of past incomes in which the weights on past incomes decline at a constant percentage rate, then current consumption is a function of current income and the level of consumption in the previous period.'

15 They were critical of the use of (a) consumption expenditure on only nondurables and services rather than the total consumption expenditure; (b) federal deficit rather than total deficit; (c) personal disposable income rather than private disposable income; and finally, (d) data series in the aggregate form rather than in per capita terms.

16 Kormendi and Meguire (1990) conduct a Monte Carlo exercise and report contrary results. Haug (1990) also concludes similarly that his consumption equation with government spending and bonds is not cointegrated. This result contrasts with other empirical findings that income and consumption are cointegrated (surveyed in Stock and Watson, 1988). Kormendi and Meguire (1990) argue that such findings are generally derived from specifications that use disposable income instead of unrestricted fiscal variables, and for the post-war period only rather than the longer period starting from 1929.

the sensitivity of Kormendi's results to, *(a)* time period specification; *(b)* differentiation between federal, and state and local government debt; and *(c)* measurement of government debt (par and market value). Their results generally support Ricardian equivalence. Feldstein and Elmendorf (1990) criticise Kormendi (1983) on misspecification errors and inappropriate correction for simultaneity bias. Their results refute Ricardian equivalence.

Aschauer (1985) following Hall's (1978) approach, and using the Euler equation method for the quarterly US data for 1948:I – 1981:IV, finds evidence supporting Ricardian equivalence. Evans (1988) derives from Blanchard's (1985) model an Euler equation condition for testing Ricardian equivalence. The results based on the United States quarterly data for 1947:II – 1985:IV support the Ricardian Equivalence Hypothesis.[17] Haug (1990) follows Hall's (1978) Euler equation approach to investigate for Ricardian equivalence through the generalised method of moments. The results for the annual United States data, specified in first differences, are mixed and are in support of Ricardian equivalence only if the World War II period is included. In case the World War II period is excluded, then the Ricardian Equivalence Hypothesis is accepted only if the rate of return is measured by the stock market return, but is rejected if the rate of return is measured by Aaa or Baa bond rates.[18]

Thus, in this subsection, the literature on Ricardian equivalence and consumption has been reviewed. As argued earlier, the most appropriate method to test for Ricardian equivalence is under the settings of the permanent income hypothesis incorporating rational expectations. The empirical evidence under this approach, in majority, is in favour of the Ricardian equivalence.

4.5. Replication of some studies on Ricardian equivalence

In this section, in view of the mixed evidence on Ricardian equivalence and consumption, some major studies have been replicated to test for the robustness of the equations\models, given a certain common data set. The objective of this exercise is to see if any of the differences of results is due to data specifications or specific sample periods, given the common data set. In Subsection 4.5.1 the

---

17 Leiderman and Razin (1988) also draw on and extend the model of Blanchard (1985). Using monthly time series data for Israel for only five years 1980:9 – 1985:12, they conclude in favour of Ricardian equivalence.

18 Haug does not specify the reasons for considering the years 1942–49 as the World War II period and not the years 1941–46, which are generally considered as the War years in the empirical literature.

respective specifications in the studies are replicated. In Subsection 4.5.2, the issue of par and market value of government debt is empirically analysed, replicating the equations specified in Kormendi (1983) – the most widely debated study in the literature.

4.5.1. Replication of some major studies on Ricardian equivalence

In this subsection, six major studies which have been path breaking in the literature on Ricardian equivalence have been replicated. The major problem in replication pertains to the definition of the variables and their respective construction.[19] Throughout this exercise, the definition of the variables is closely followed, as given in the respective original studies. The studies are arranged sequentially in the order of their appearance in the literature and therefore follow a pattern of simple regressions to complex equation systems. The expected sign of the coefficients, in each study, under the null hypothesis of Ricardian equivalence, are provided in the respective tables.

The first study which explicitly tests for Ricardian equivalence (R.E.) was attempted by Kochin (1974). To test for Ricardian equivalence, Kochin (1974) estimates the following equation in levels and first differences

$$C_t = \beta_0 + \beta_1 Y_t + \beta_2 FDF_t + \beta 3 C_{t-1} \qquad \text{Equation 4.32}$$

where, C_t is consumption expenditure on non-durables and services, Y_t is disposable income and FDF_t is the federal deficit. Each of these variables is deflated by the implicit price index for consumption expenditure. Kochin considers that if consumers take into account future taxes then the federal deficit should bear a negative relationship with consumption.

It can be argued that if the equation is specified in levels, then the lagged value of consumption in the regression amounts to estimating the permanent income hypothesis under rational expectations. In such a specification, the coefficient of federal deficit as well as that of disposable income should be insignificant. In contrast, if the equation is specified in first differences, then the changes in lagged consumption reflect habit formation and can be significant, while the coefficients of any other variables in the equation are still expected to be insignificant.[20]

The original results and that of our replication, along with the expected sign of

---

19 The major revision in data series by NIPA in 1985, however, does not cause any change in results.

20 However, this study precedes that of Lucas (1976), Hall (1978) and Flavin (1981) and hence, probably, these theoretical shortcomings.

the coefficients under the null hypothesis of Ricardian equivalence, are presented in Table 4.2.

Table 4.2: Kochin's original results and attempted replications

Period	H_o:RE. expected sign	O.Eq. 1952–71	O.Eq. 1952–71	R.Eq. 1952–71	R.Eq. 1952–71	R.Eq. 1952–93	R.Eq. 1930–71	R.Eq. 1930–93
		Levels	Differ.	Levels	Differ.	Differ.	Differ.	Differ.
1	2	3	4	5	6	7	8	9
Cons.		5.56 (1.8)	2.88 (3.4)	18.79 (2.3)	8.22 (2.0)	15.25 (2.5)	3.99 (1.8)	6.51 (2.1)
Y_t		0.28 (3.8)	0.39 (7.8)	0.42 (5.5)	0.48 (6.8)	0.38 (5.9)	0.43 (9.8)	0.40 (8.7)
FDF_t	<0	-0.22 (2.6)	-0.11 (2.9)	0.18 (2.2)	0.10 (1.7)	0.10 (1.3)	0.15 (5.4)	0.11 (3.0)
C_{t-1}		0.64 (5.1)	0.22 (2.4)	0.46 (4.3)	0.19 (1.6)	0.27 (2.7)	0.30 (4.3)	0.37 (5.3)
R^2-Adj.		0.99	0.89	0.99	0.85	0.66	0.86	0.79
SEE		2.23	1.26	6.88	6.46	14.50	8.32	13.66
h-stat				1.95	-1.32	-1.13	-1.20	-1.49
DW		0.68	1.79	1.16	2.28	2.20	2.33	2.25

The dependent variable is the consumption expenditure on nondurables and services (C_t). Y_t is disposable income, FDF_t is federal deficit. H_o:RE. refers to the null hypothesis under Ricardian equivalence. O.Eq. is the original equation. R.Eq. is the replicated equation. Differ. refers to the equation specified in first differences.

The *t-statistics* are shown in parentheses. DW is presented for the columns 5 to 9 for comparison with the original results in columns 3 and 4.

Source: Kochin (1974) and author's compilation and calculation.

In both the original equations, at levels and differences, the coefficient of the federal deficit is negative and significant (Columns 3 and 4) while our attempted replications for different time periods, yield mixed results (Columns 5 through 9).[21] In particular, we get a different sign on FDF_t in all our replications. In the

---

21 This is the only study which yields contrary results in replication as compared with the original results. To investigate the cause of this discrepancy, a request was made to Proffessor Kochin for the data set used in his original work. The data set was not made available.

Ricardian Equivalence: Empirical Studies Utilising Consumption Function

original equations as well as our replications, the coefficient of lagged consumption is significant in levels and differences. In levels, the coefficient of income is also significant which can imply the excess sensitivity of current consumption, in contradiction to the permanent income hypothesis under rational expectations (Flavin, 1981, 1985).

Buiter and Tobin (1980) use the following specification to test for Ricardian equivalence:

$$C_t = \beta_0 + \beta_1 Y_t + \beta_2 T_t + \beta_3 DF_t + \beta_4 C_{t-1}$$ Equation 4.33

$$C_t = a_0 + a_1 Y_t + a_2 G_t + a_3 C_{t-1}$$ Equation 4.34

$$C_t = \lambda_0 + \lambda_1 (Y_t - G_t) + \lambda_2 C_{t-1}$$ Equation 4.35

where, C_t is consumption expenditure, Y_t is national income, T_t is tax net of transfers, DF_t is deficit and G_t is government purchases of goods and services. Consumption (C_t) is measured as the consumption expenditure on non-durables and services (C_{ns}), and total consumption expenditure (C). All variables are in real per capita terms.

Buiter and Tobin argue that, from the point of view of the private sector, the appropriate per capita real income concept is $Y_t - T_t - DF_t = Y_t - G_t$. They regard a significantly negative coefficient of DF_t as evidence of debt neutrality and test the hypothesis that Y_t, T_t, and DF_t have equivalent coefficients. In the equation system 4.33 - 4.35, they test for (a) $Y_t = T_t = DF_t$ (Equation 4.33 versus 4.35); (b) $T_t = DF_t$ (Equation 4.33 versus 4.34); and (c) $Y_t = G_t$ (Equation 4.34 versus 4.35).

The issues critical to Kochin (1974) are also applicable to this model. Most importantly, these equations could suffer from simultaneity bias as argued by Flavin (1987).[22] The estimation of equation 4.33 by Buiter and Tobin, as well as our attempted replications of the same equation are presented in Table 4.3.[23] On the basis of insignificance of the coefficients of public sector deficit (Columns 3 and 4, Table 4.3), Buiter and Tobin express their inability to conclusively reject the hypothesis that the coefficients are the same.

---

22 Refer sub-section 4.4.1.3 for detail discussion.
23 The other two Equations 4.34 and 4.35, are estimated but the results are not presented in Table 4.3.

Table 4.3: Buiter and Tobin's original results and attempted replications

Period	H_o:RE expected sign	O. Eq. 1949–76 Level	O. Eq. 1949–76 Level	R. Eq 1949–76 Level	R. Eq. 1949–76 Level	R. Eq. 1949–93 Level	R. Eq. 1930–76 Level	R. Eq. 1930–93 Level
D. Var		C	C_{ns}	C	C_{ns}	C	C	C
1	2	3	4	5	6	7	8	9
						$	$	$
Cons.		-218.81 (1.3)	-133.14 (1.6)	-927.49 (5.3)	-482.72 (4.5)	-1112.50 (5.9)	1764.30 (1.9)	-385.41 (2.3)
Y_t	>0	0.42 (4.1)	0.22 (4.4)	0.56 (5.3)	0.30 (4.2)	0.74 (8.5)	0.50 (7.9)	0.53 (7.8)
T_t	<0	-0.68 (1.3)	-0.34 (1.3)	-0.63 (3.8)	-0.26 (2.3)	-0.80 (5.2)	-0.63 (5.3)	-0.73 (5.6)
DF_t	<0	-0.50 (1.0)	-0.25 (1.0)	-0.21 (1.8)	-0.07 (0.8)	-0.14 (1.2)	-0.38 (8.3)	-0.36 (7.2)
$C_{t-1}/(C_{ns})_{t-1}$		0.65 (6.2)	0.80 (13.5)	0.59 (7.2)	0.73 (11.4)	0.42 (5.9)	0.29 (3.6)	0.59 (11.3)
R^2-Adj.		0.99	0.99	0.99	0.99	0.99	0.99	0.99
SEE		40.23	19.34	88.51	59.93	92.03	101.58	115.99
F-stat				11.24*	9.39*	25.88*	26.46*	23.98*
h-Stat				1.25	0.65	1.70	-0.51	0.57
DW		1.44	1.73	1.54	1.70	1.70	1.40	1.80

The dependent variable (D.Var) is C_{ns} when consumption expenditure on nondurables and services is used and C when total consumption expenditure is used. Y_t is national income, T_t is taxes net of transfers, DF_t is the public sector deficit

H_o:RE refers to the null hypothesis under Ricardian equivalence. $ Corrected for autocorrelation using the Cochrane-Orcutt procedure. O.Eq. is the original equation. R.Eq. is the replicated equation. The t-statistics are shown in parentheses. The F-statistics tests for $Y_t = T_t = DF_t$. * Significant at the level of 1 per cent.

Source: Buiter and Tobin (1980) and author's compilation and calculation.

The replications for the same period are presented in Columns 5 and 6. In the case of total consumption expenditure the hypothesis that $Y_t = T_t = DF_t$ is rejected but the other two hypothesis that $T_t = DF_t$ and $Y_t = G_t$ cannot be rejected. In the case of consumption expenditure on non-durables and services, the hypothesis $Y_t = T_t = DF_t$ and $Y_t = G_t$ is rejected. Further, the results are sensitive to the period specification as the coefficients of deficit and taxes become significant (Columns 7 through 9). The results, however, are not affected by the choice of the dependent variable.[24]

Another empirical work replicated here is by Feldstein (1982), who estimates the following equation to test for Ricardian equivalence.

$$C_t = \beta_0 + \beta_1 Y_t + \beta_{12} Y_{t-1} + \beta_2 W_t + \beta_3 SW_t + \beta_4 G_t + \beta_5 T_t + \beta_6 TR_t + \beta_7 D_t$$
Equation 4.36

where, C_t is consumer expenditure, Y_t is income,[25] W_t is privately owned wealth at market value, SW_t is a measure of the value of future social security benefits, G_t is government spending on goods and services, T_t is tax revenue, TR_t is government transfers to individuals, and D_t is the net debt of the federal, state and local governments. Feldstein chooses the lagged value of tax as an instrument to reduce the simultaneity bias in the equation. All variables are measured in real per capita basis.

The model is specified in levels and the non-stationarity in the data could yield spurious results. More importantly, the absence of lagged consumption in the equation is contradictory to the permanent income hypothesis under rational expectations. The presence of lagged income variable in the equation also is considered unnecessary if consumption series evolves under the assumption of rational expectations.

Feldstein estimates the equation for the period 1930–77, with the years 1941–46 being omitted. First, the results with total national income are considered as the income variable (Columns 3 and 4, Table 4.4). The results are mixed, mainly supporting Ricardian equivalence in Column 3 (OLS) and refuting it in Column 4 (2SLS).

---

24 The results of regressions where the dependent variable is total consumption expenditure are only reported here. The results are mixed, and similar in that sense, with those obtained by using only the consumption expenditure on nondurables and services.

25 Feldstein uses both disposable personal income and national income in the estimation of the equation.

Table 4.4 : Feldstein's original results and attempted replications

	H_o:R.E. expected sign	O.Eq.	O.Eq.	O.Eq.	R.Eq.	R.Eq.	R.Eq.	R.Eq.	R.Eq.
Income	NI / DPI	NI	NI	DPI	NI	NI	DPI	DPI	DPI
Method		OLS	INV	INV	OLS	INV	INV	INV	INV
Period		1930–40 /47–77	1930–40 /47–77	1930–40 /47–77	1930–40 /47–76	1930–40 /47–76	1930–40 /47–76	1930–76	1947–76
1	2	3	4	5	6	7	8	9	10
					$	$	$		
cons.		0.613 (13.6)	0.544 (5.8)	-0.413 (0.5)	1315.812 (5.6)	1375.212 (6.6)	404.412 (2.3)	187.781 (0.6)	-399.973 (1.1)
Y_t		0.466 (14.6)	0.479 (12.3)	0.582 (2.9)	0.423 (7.9)	0.390 (7.3)	0.580 (9.5)	0.675 (7.5)	0.689 (8.3)
Y_{t-1}		0.033 (1.7)	0.024 (1.0)	0.053 (0.4)	-0.002 (0.1)	0.047 (1.1)	0.079 (1.7)	0.142 (1.6)	0.094 (1.1)
W_t	>0@ @ >0	0.017 (2.8)	0.025 (2.3)	0.102 (1.0)	0.087 (3.2)	0.076 (3.0)	0.076 (3.8)	0.073 (2.4)	0.067 (3.0)
SW_t	=0 =0	-0.001 (0.2)	0.005 (0.5)	0.064 (0.8)	0.056 (2.0)	0.042 (1.6)	0.034 (1.7)	0.009 (0.3)	-0.011 (0.4)
G_t	<0 <0	-0.102 (1.8)	-0.001 (0.1)	0.927 (0.8)	-0.08 (1.0)	-0.104 (1.3)	0.086 (1.6)	-0.246 (10.9)	0.084 (1.3)
T_t	=0 >0	-0.021 (0.3)	-0.222 (0.9)	-1.734 (0.8)	-0.152 (1.4)	-0.098 (1.1)	-0.154 (2.5)	0.102 (1.0)	-0.151 (1.8)
TR_t	=0 <0	1.206 (15.5)	1.315 (8.6)	1.256 (1.0)	1.265 (11.3)	1.260 (11.2)	0.450 (3.5)	-0.240 (1.5)	0.374 (2.1)
D_t	<0@ @<0	-0.015 (1.4)	-0.002 (0.1)	0.175 (1.0)	-0.001 (0.1)	-0.013 (0.8)	0.046 (4.4)	0.012 (0.7)	0.089 (2.6)
R^2-Adj.		#	#	#	0.99	0.99	0.99	0.99	0.99
SEE		0.02	0.02	0.07	59.1	59.56	50.22	102.43	53.26
F-stat					4.60**	2.92***	21.49*	4.29**	11.02**
DW		1.54	1.53	1.76	1.42	1.49	1.7	1.43	1.87

The dependent variable is the consumer expenditure. Y_t is the income variable with *NI* being the national income and *DPI* being the personal income, W_t is privately owned wealth at market value, SW_t is social security benefits, G_t is government expenditure on goods and services, T_t is tax revenue, TR_t is government transfers to individuals, and D_t is debt of the government. INV = Instrumental variable estimation.

H_0:RE. refers to the null hypothesis under Ricardian equivalence. O.Eq. is the original equation. R.Eq. is the replicated equation. # Not reported. $ Corrected for autocorrelation using the Cochrane-Orcutt procedure. @ Expected under the null hypothesis: D = -W. The *t-statistics* are shown in parentheses. The *F-statistics* tests for D + W = 0. * Significant at the level of 1 per cent. ** Significant at the level of 5 per cent. *** Significant at the level of 10 per cent.

Source: Feldstein (1984) and author's compilation and calculation.

In Column 5, the income variable is now disposable personal income. The results show that the signs of these coefficients are contrary to those expected for Ricardian equivalence but the coefficients are not significant.[26] In addition, the equations suffer from serial correlation. On the basis of the superiority of the instrumental variable estimation, Feldstein concludes that empirical evidence rejects Ricardian equivalence.

This analysis has attempted to replicate Feldstein's study. Though the construction of all the variables is not precisely defined in his study, Feldstein does provide data on fungible wealth and social security wealth at 1972 prices for the period 1930–76.[27] The attempted replication therefore is restricted to the period of the study, 1930–76. The replication here has been extended to include the war years, 1941–46, and also to only the post-war period, 1947–76. The dependent variable is total personal consumption expenditure in all the replicated regressions.

The replication for the period 1930–76, with the period 1941–46 omitted, is presented in Columns 6 through 8 (Table 4.4). The results of our replication are similar to the original results. We then extended the exercise to the period 1930–76, inclusive of the war years (Column 9), and to the post-war period, 1947–76 (Column 10). The results are still mixed but are not similar to those obtained in the original time specification. Thus, the results of our replications are inconclusive but sensitive to the sample period.[28]

---

26 The regression suffers from multi-collinearity. To correct for this collinearity another regression is run omitting debt. This reduces the standard errors but the results remain the same, the insignificant coefficients have contrary signs to those expected for Ricardian equivalence.

27 The deflator that has been used to deflate these series, and whether the series are at the end-of-period or beginning-of-period is not explicit.

28 We also experimented with the set of data before the major revision in 1985, and also with all the data at 1972 prices. The results continued to be mixed. Finally, considering that the wealth series included in the appendix, may be at the end-of-year basis, and therefore, to make it at the beginning of the period, the lag values of it were considered. Still the results were the same.

Another study replicated here is by Kormendi (1983). Kormendi estimates the following two equations, in first differences, for the annual data from the United States, to test for the Ricardian equivalence.

$$C_t = \beta_0 + \beta_1 Y_t + \beta_{12} Y_{t-1} + \beta_2 G_t + \beta_3 W_t + \beta_4 TR_t + \beta_5 T_t + \beta_6 RE_t + \beta_7 GINT_t + \beta_8 D_1 \quad \text{Equation 4.37}$$

$$C_t = \beta_0 + \beta_1 Y_t + \beta_{12} Y_{t-1} + \beta_2 G_t + \beta_3 W_t + \beta_4 TR_t + \beta_5 D_1 \quad \text{Equation 4.38}$$

where C_t is private sector consumption, Y_t is net national product, G_t is government (federal, state and local) spending on goods and services, W_t is private wealth, TR_t is transfer payments, T_t is tax payments, RE_t is corporate retained earnings, $GINT_t$ is net interest payment by government on its outstanding debt and D_t is the stock of government debt.[29] Kormendi hypothesises that the test for Ricardian equivalence implies that $\beta_2 < 0$ and $\beta_5 = \beta_6 = \beta_7 = \beta_8 = 0$ in Equation 4.37.

In this specification, Kormendi uses the first differences and therefore the two equations are appropriately measuring the rational expectations in the permanent income hypothesis. But the inclusion of current and lagged income would be testing for the excess sensitivity of consumption to income in contradiction to the permanent income hypothesis under rational expectations.[30]

The original results for the period 1931–76, inclusive and exclusive of the war years, are presented in Columns 3 through 5 (Table 4.5) for the Equations 4.37 and 4.38. The negatively significant coefficient of government debt, which is an exception to the expected coefficients under the null hypothesis, is explained in terms of uncertainty of the future effects of debt.[31]

In an attempted replication of the two equations for the two period specification, one including and the other excluding the war years, 1941–46,

---

29   Kormendi uses the market value of government debt as given in Seater (1981). This series in Seater is available only till 1976.

30   Flavin (1981) argues this in detail.

31   Kormendi (1983, 1005) explains: 'The real income stream deriving from government debt involves inflation risk and some default risk to holders of the debt. The future tax stream implied by the debt, on the other hand, involves that same inflation and default risk plus considerable additional risk as to both its intertemporal and cross-sectional incidence. Thus, in rationally assessing the future tax consequences of government debt, the current certainty equivalent value of the future taxes may exceed the current certainty equivalent value of the income stream (which is simply the market value of debt). In such a case, the net wealth of the private sector is adversely affected by government debt, implying a negative effect for ΔGB_t (and a positive effect for ΔTx_t) on private consumption.' Barro (1976, 346) also argues on similar lines that individual uncertainty with respect to the future effects of government deficits may make people nervous and this may result in reducing consumption demand.

(Columns 6 through 9, Table 4.5) the results are generally similar to that of Kormendi (1983).³² In the post-war period, 1947–76, the coefficient of government spending is negative but significant in Column 11 but not in Column 10, while the coefficient of government debt is insignificant. Thus, the results are sensitive to the period specification.

Table 4.5: Kormendi's original results and attempted replications

Period	H_o:R.E. expected sign	O.Eq. 1931–76	O.Eq. 1931–76	O.Eq. 1931–40 /47–76	R.Eq. 1931–76	R.Eq. 1931–76	R.Eq.@ 1931–40 /47–76	R.Eq. 1931–40 /47–76	R.Eq. 1947–76	R.Eq. 1947–76
1	2	3	4	5	6	7	8	9	10	11
					$	$	$	$	$	$
Cons.		#	#	#	18.43 (1.3)	20.75 (1.4)	14.52 (0.8)	12.21 (0.7)	53.40 (1.8)	8.55 (1.8)
Y_t		0.29 (7.3)	0.32 (14.8)	0.33 (14.1)	0.32 (7.9)	0.32 (12.2)	0.31 (7.2)	0.31 (12.2)	0.21 (2.7)	0.28 (6.0)
Y_{t-1}		0.07 (3.3)	0.06 (3.0)	0.05 (2.2)	0.06 (2.8)	0.05 (2.5)	0.05 (1.9)	0.04 (1.7)	0.03 (0.8)	0.02 (0.7)
G_t	<0	-0.23 (12.8)	-0.23 (13.2)	-0.21 (3.5)	-0.27 (12.6)	-0.27 (12.5)	-0.16 (2.7)	-0.18 (3.1)	-0.14 (1.6)	-0.18 (2.2)
W_t	>0	0.03 (3.0)	0.03 (3.4)	0.03 (3.5)	0.02 (2.7)	0.02 (3.2)	0.02 (3.0)	0.03 (3.7)	0.02 (1.7)	0.02 (2.1)
TR_t		0.83 (5.6)	0.78 (5.6)	0.74 (3.5)	0.60 (3.7)	0.54 (3.6)	0.56 (3.3)	0.53 (3.6)	0.44 (1.9)	0.37 (1.6)
T_t	=0	0.07 (0.9)			0.02 (0.3)		-0.02 (0.2)		0.09 (0.7)	
RE_t	=0	0.10 (0.9)			0.03 (0.2)		0.06 (0.5)		0.13 (0.8)	
$GINT_t$	=0	1.15 (1.3)			1.47 (1.6)		1.30 (1.3)		1.84 (1.6)	
D_t	=0	-0.06 (2.9)	-0.04 (2.4)	-0.03 (1.6)	-0.06 (2.8)	-0.03 (2.0)	-0.01 (0.8)	-0.01 (0.7)	-0.02 (0.5)	-0.01 (0.4)
R^2-Adj		0.91	0.90	0.91	0.85	0.85	0.87	0.87	0.74	0.74

Table continued

---

32 The data definitions, as suggested by Kormendi and Meguire (1986 and 1990), have been adopted from Barth, Iden, and Russek (1986). The replication could not extend the time period in these equations because of the non-availability of market value of government debt beyond 1976.

Table 4.5: Kormendi's original results and attempted replications

Period	H₀:R.E. expected sign	O.Eq. 1931–76	O.Eq. 1931–76	O.Eq. 1931–40 /47–76	R.Eq. 1931–76	R.Eq. 1931–76	R.Eq.@ 1931–40 /47–76	R.Eq. 1931–40 /47–76	R.Eq. 1947–76	R.Eq. 1947–76
1	2	3	4	5	6	7	8	9	10	11
					$	$	$	$	$	$
SEE		0.02	0.02	0.02	50.07	49.72	49.51	48.63	53.13	53.40
F-stat		1.20			0.91		0.64		1.08	
DW		#	#	1.60	1.90	1.85	1.92	1.81	2.02	1.92

The dependent variable is private consumption expenditure. Y_t is net national product, G_t is government expenditure on goods and services, W_t is private wealth, TR_t is transfer payments, T_t is current taxation, RE_t is corporate retained earnings, $GINT_t$ is net interest payments by government omits outstanding debt, and D_t is stock of government debt.

H_0: R.E. is the null hypothesis under the Ricardian Equivalence Hypothesis. O.Eq. refers to the original equation. R.Eq. refers to the replicated equation. # Calculated but not reported. $ Corrected for autocorrelation using the Cochrane-Orcutt method. @ Similar equation is not estimated in Kormendi (1983). The *t-statistics* are shown in parentheses. The *F-statistics* tests for $T_t = RE_t = GINT_t = 0$.

Source: Kormendi (1983) and author's compilation and calculation.

Another replication is of the study by Aschauer (1985). Aschauer follows Hall's specification of the permanent income hypothesis and estimates the following equation for the United States, using the quarterly data,

$$C_t = \beta_0 + \beta_1 C_{t-1} + \beta_2 DF_{t-1} + \beta_3 DF_{t-2} + \beta_4 DF_{t-3} + \beta_5 DF_{t-4} \qquad \text{Equation 4.39}$$

where, C_t is real per capita consumer expenditure on non-durable goods and services, and DF_t is the per capita net deficit of the total government sector. Aschauer argues that given the consumption specification under permanent income, the lagged deficit variables would make insignificant contribution to the equation ($\beta_2 = \beta_3 = \beta_4 = \beta_5 = 0$).

In Table 4.6, the original results of Aschauer (Column 3) and attempted replications (Columns 4 through 6) are presented. In Column 1, the deficit variable makes a statistically important contribution to the equation, especially the first and second lagged values.[33]

---

[33] Aschauer goes on from here to formulate another equation incorporating the government spending variable and using the method of full-information maximum likelihood (FIML) to find support for Ricardian equivalence.

Ricardian Equivalence: Empirical Studies Utilising Consumption Function

Table 4.6: Aschauer's original results and attempted replications

Period	Ho:R.E. expected sign	Original equation 1948:1 to 1981:IV	Replicated equation 1948:1 to 1981:IV	Replicated equation 1947:1 to 1981:IV	Replicated equation 1947:1 to 1993:III
1	2	3	4	5	6
			$	$	$
Cons.		#	36.172 (1.7)	37.244 (1.8)	61.998 (3.2)
C_{t-1}		0.990 (330.0)	0.999 (338.6)	0.999 (340.8)	0.995 (374.2)
DF_{t-1}	=0	-0.540 (2.2)	-0.067 (1.9)	-0.052 (1.6)	-0.024 (0.9)
DF_{t-2}	=0	0.066 (1.8)	0.043 (0.9)	0.041 (0.9)	0.004 (0.1)
DF_{t-3}	=0	-0.042 (1.2)	0.005 (0.1)	-0.011 (0.3)	-0.001 (0.1)
DF_{t-4}	=0	-0.026 (1.0)	-0.073 (2.1)	-0.051 (1.6)	-0.042 (1.6)
R^2-Adj.		0.99	0.99	0.99	0.99
SEE		2.09	38.04	38.12	38.20
F-stat		4.17	3.31**	2.72**	2.74**
h-stat		0.88	-1.10	-1.02	-1.19

The dependent variable is consumer expenditure on nondurable goods and services (C). DF is the net deficit of the government.

H_0: R.E. is the null hypothesis under Ricardian equivalence. # Not reported. $ Corrected for autocorrelation using the Cochrane-Orcutt method. The *t-statistics* are shown in parentheses. The *F-statistics* tests for $DF_{t-1} = DF_{t-2} = DF_{t-3} = DF_{t-4} = 0$. ** Significant at the level of 5 per cent

Source: Aschauer (1985) and author's compilation and calculation.

This study found similar results to Aschauer's at the 5 per cent level of significance. In addition, these equations were estimated in levels and therefore could yield spurious results due to the problem of non-stationarity in data.

Finally, the study by Modigliani and Sterling (1986) is replicated. Modigliani and Sterling test the following equation:

$$C_t = \beta_0 + \beta_1 W_t + \beta_2 D_t + \sum_{i=1}^{L} \beta_{3i}(Y_{t-i} - T_{t-i}) + \sum_{i=1}^{L} \beta_{4i} DF_{t-i} \qquad \text{Equation 4.40}$$

where, C_t is consumption, W_t is aggregate non-human wealth, D_t is government debt, Y_t is the net national product, T_t is government taxes, net of transfers including government net domestic interest payments[34] and DF_t is government deficit. The β_{3i} and β_{4i}, $i=1,...,L$ distributed lag coefficients in Equation 4.40 reflect both the expectations formation mechanism and the behavioural parameters. The distributed lag coefficients are constrained to lie on a first-degree polynomial with five lags (including the current term). The test is based on annual data from the United States.

Modigliani and Sterling hypothise that, in the case of Ricardian equivalence, the estimated sum of the coefficients of the deficit should be negative and equal to the sum of the income coefficients ($\Sigma\beta_{4I} = -\Sigma\beta_{3i}$), while the coefficient of government debt should be negative and close to the coefficient of wealth, $\beta_2 = -\beta_1$.

The equations are specified in levels and are therefore subject to the problem of non-stationarity in data. In addition, the rational expectations in permanent income hypothesis are ignored in the specification.

The original equation and the attempted replications are presented in Table 4.7. In the Table, only the sum of current and lagged coefficients is presented. The estimated coefficients of deficit as well as that of debt are positive and therefore the results contradict the Ricardian Equivalence Hypothesis (Columns 3 and 4).

Table 4.7: Modigliani and Sterling's original results and attempted replications

Data set	H_0:R.E. expected sign	O.Eq. MS	O.Eq. MS	R.Eq. MS	R.Eq. MS	R.Eq. C	R.Eq. C	R.Eq. C	R.Eq. C
Period		1952–84	1952–76	1953–84	1953–76	1953–84	1953–76	1953–93	1933–93
1	2	3	4	5	6	7	8	9	10
						$	$	$	$
Cons.		-0.38 (6.3)	-0.39 (2.6)	-0.37 (5.8)	-0.38 (2.4)	-2.39 (3.4)	0.15 (0.3)	1.44 (1.4)	-1.35 (2.9)
W	>0	0.02 (4.6)	0.03 #	0.02 (5.1)	0.03 (4.7)	-0.01 (0.7)	-0.02 (2.9)	0.01 (1.3)	0.01 (1.1)
D	<0	0.07 (3.1)	0.07 (1.3)	0.07 (2.6)	0.05 (0.9)	0.19 (3.1)	-0.06 (0.8)	0.10 (3.9)	0.15 (4.4)

Table continued

---

34 Net interest payments to the domestic sector equal the ex-post real payments, calculated by subtracting the product of the actual rate of inflation and the stock of net government debt from net interest payments.

Table 4.7: Modigliani and Sterling's original results and attempted replications

Data set	H_0:R.E. expected sign	O.Eq. MS	O.Eq. MS	R.Eq. MS	R.Eq. MS	R.Eq. C	R.Eq. C	R.Eq. C	R.Eq. C
Period		1952–84	1952–76	1953–84	1953–76	1953–84	1953–76	1953–93	1933–93
1	2	3	4	5	6	7	8	9	10
						$	$	$	$
$\Sigma Y@$	>0	0.92 (46.1)	0.90 (32.0)	0.92 (46.1)	0.89 (26.9)	1.14 (7.9)	1.16 (19.0)	0.69 (7.5)	0.90 (7.8)
$\Sigma T@$		-0.92 (46.1)	-0.90 (32.0)	-0.92 (46.1)	-0.89 (26.9)	-1.14 (7.9)	-1.16 (19.0)	-0.69 (7.5)	-0.90 (7.8)
ΣDF	<0	0.17 (2.1)	0.02 (1.3)	0.20 (2.0)	-0.03 (0.2)	-0.86 (2.1)	-1.72 (8.6)	-0.73 (8.2)	-0.68 (1.9)
R^2-Adj		#	#	0.99	0.99	0.99	0.99	0.99	0.99
SEE		0.02	0.02	0.02	0.02	0.09	0.05	0.09	0.09
F-stat(a)				57.45*	11.56*	1.54	7.07**	2.70***	1.28
F-stat(b)				7.17**	1.92	6.60**	0.43	2.52	8.43*
D.W.		1.43	1.50	1.45	1.49	1.53	2.09	1.04	1.28

The dependent variable is consumption expenditure. W is wealth, D is government debt, Y is net national product, T is taxes net of transfers and real interest payments, and DF is current deficit. Σ refers to the sum of current and lagged coefficients. Data Set: MS – Modigliani and Sterling (1986), Table-3; data in real values: 1972 Dollars per capita terms. C – The data was constructed following the methodology given in the Appendix to the Study; The data was constructed in real values: 1987 Dollars per capita terms.

H_0: R.E. is the null hypothesis under the Ricardian Equivalence Hypothesis. O.Eq. refers to the original equation. R.Eq. refers to the replicated equation. @ The coefficient of taxes are constrained to equal the negative of the income coefficients. # Not Reported. $ Corrected for autocorrelation using the Cochrane-Orcutt method. The t-statistics are shown in parentheses. The F-statistics tests for (a) $\Sigma Y + \Sigma DF=0$ and (b) $W + D = 0$. * Significant at the level of 1 per cent. ** Significant at the level of 5 per cent. *** Significant at the level of 10 per cent.

Source: Modigliani and Sterling (1986) and author's compilation and calculation.

Similar results are obtained from the replication (Columns 5 and 6) except for the period 1953–76, where the coefficient of the deficit is negative but not equal to that of income.[35] The exercise is extended to the specifications on the basis of data

---

35 The data set for the period 1949–84 is provided by Modigliani and Sterling (1986) in the study. However, the data set is confusing regarding the period of the study. The five

constructed in this study, to test for the robustness of the specification (Columns 7 through 10).[36] The perusal of these results reveals that they are sensitive to the sample period and also suffer from serial correlation.

The conclusion that follows from this section, is that the specification of the models are not appropriate to test for Ricardian equivalence. The data revisions do not seem to make any difference to the results. The techniques used are generally OLS regressions, though instrumental variables as well as distributed lag models are also used. The studies replicated here are sensitive to the time period specifications or the inclusion/exclusion of the war years. In most of the studies, the value of the DW is very low, suggesting the presence of misspecification errors.

4.5.2. Issue of par and market value of government debt

In this subsection, an attempt has been made to empirically analyse whether the consumption function testing for Ricardian equivalence is sensitive to the use of par or the market value of government debt. The specification under which this issue is being examined is adopted from Kormendi (1983), the most widely debated study in the literature on Ricardian equivalence.

The issue of par and market value is empirically examined here for two reasons. Firstly, the market value of debt may not be available for many countries,[37] and as computing it involves a huge investment, par values may emerge as useful proxies. The other reason is more fundamental. Government debt in the form of small saving bonds, which are not traded on any market and therefore no price quotations are available for them even for the United States, may be appropriately estimated at the

---

    year lag structure would imply that the study is for the period beginning 1953. In case the replication is attempted for the period beginning 1952 as given in the original tables, instead of 1949, the results are different from the original. Hence, it is replicated on the basis of data beginning from 1949, implying the period of study, given the five year lag, beginning from 1953.

36   The data set given in the study is for the period 1949–84 only. The appendix to the study does not provide an exact definition of the variables and their method of construction. This study has tried to be as close as possible to the data specifications given in the appendix.

37   Market value of debt, computed in a comprehensive and accurate manner, is only available for the United States.

par value.[38] The difficulty is accentuated in countries with underdeveloped money markets. Therefore, it may be safe to assume that consumers would generally value the saving bonds in their portfolios only at the par value and not at any 'notional market value', due to the non-availability of any market price on these. In addition, the assumption of rational expectations should imply that the par value of the saving bond truly reflects the capitalised value of the bond.[39]

Theoretically, the issue of par and market value should not lead to a significant difference in the results as the correlation between the two series is 0.974 at levels and 0.871 in annual changes (Seater, 1981).[40] Dwyer (1982) also concludes that the par value of debt is an adequate measure of government debt.

Kormendi (1983) estimates the consumption function in Equation 4.37 with the market value of government debt for the United States.[41] This study extends the estimation to the par value of government debt.[42] In this exercise, two sets of replications are attempted, one at the par value of total government debt ($GB_t = PV$) and the other at market value of government debt, except the saving bonds which are considered at the par value ($GB_t = MVPVA$). The non-availability of the series on market value of government debt beyond 1976 restricts our period of estimation and comparison to 1931–76.

The results are presented in Table 4.8.[43] In Columns 4 and 5, the results are comparable with Column 3, where only market value of debt is used. Similar

---

38 The market value of saving bonds, in the absence of any price quotations, is computed notionally in the same proportion as the relation between the par value and market value of government debt which is traded in the market (Seater, 1981). The share of saving bonds in total government debt is nearly 6 per cent now as compared with 20 per cent in 1970s.

39 The rational consumer with complete information set and perfect foresight would have anticipated the future and then bought the saving bond at its capitalised price. This argument can be extended to the government bonds also but may be with a slightly weaker strength as regular price quotations on these are available.

40 Refer 4.4.1.1(b) for a detailed discussion.

41 The market value series has been taken from seater (1981).

42 The par value of debt that we have considered is equivalent to that considered by Seater (1981) for which he has constructed the market value series. This is the net debt held by the public, net of any holdings by the Federal Reserve System, Federal Agencies and Trust Funds.

43 In estimating Equation 4.37, it may be recalled, Kormendi (1983) tests the hypothesis that the coefficients of taxes, retained earnings and government interest payments and government debt are all equal to zero ($\beta_5 = \beta_6 = \beta_7 = \beta_8 = 0$) and the coefficient of government spending is negative, $\beta_2 < 0$.

results emerge for the post-war period 1947–76 (Columns 6 through 8) and the period 1931–76, excluding the war years (Columns 9 through 11).

Table 4.8: Examining the issue of par and market value of debt

Period	H_0:R.E. expected sign	1931–76	1931–76	1931–76	1947–76	1947–76	1947–76	1931–40 /47–76	1931–40 /47–76	1931–40 /47–76
GB_t		MV	MVPVA	PV	MV	MVPVA	PV	MV	MVPVA	PV
1	2	3	4	5	6	7	8	9	10	11
		*	*	*	*	*	*	*	*	*
Cons.		18.43 (1.3)	18.13 (1.3)	17.77 (1.2)	53.40 (1.8)	52.57 (1.9)	55.74 (1.8)	14.52 (0.8)	14.40 (0.8)	14.71 (0.8)
Y_t		0.32 (7.9)	0.32 (8.0)	0.30 (7.7)	0.21 (2.7)	0.22 (2.7)	0.20 (2.4)	0.31 (7.2)	0.31 (7.3)	0.31 (7.2)
Y_{t-1}		0.06 (2.8)	0.07 (2.9)	0.06 (2.7)	0.03 (0.8)	0.03 (0.8)	0.02 (0.4)	0.05 (1.9)	0.05 (1.9)	0.05 (1.9)
G_t	<0	-0.27 (12.6)	-0.27 (12.7)	-0.26 (12.3)	-0.14 (1.6)	-0.15 (1.7)	-0.14 (1.5)	-0.16 (2.7)	-0.16 (2.7)	-0.16 (2.6)
W_t	>0	0.02 (2.7)	0.02 (2.6)	0.02 (2.7)	0.02 (1.7)	0.02 (1.6)	0.02 (1.9)	0.02 (3.0)	0.02 (3.0)	0.02 (3.0)
TR_t		0.60 (3.7)	0.61 (3.7)	0.64 (3.8)	0.44 (1.9)	0.46 (1.9)	0.40 (1.6)	0.56 (3.3)	0.57 (3.4)	0.57 (3.4)
T_t	=0	0.02 (0.3)	0.02 (0.3)	0.03 (0.3)	0.09 (0.7)	0.09 (0.7)	0.09 (0.7)	-0.02 (0.2)	-0.02 (0.3)	-0.02 (0.3)
RE_t	=0	0.03 (0.2)	0.03 (0.2)	0.03 (0.2)	0.13 (0.8)	0.13 (0.8)	0.13 (0.8)	0.06 (0.5)	0.06 (0.5)	0.06 (0.5)
$GINT_t$	=0	1.47 (1.6)	1.59 (1.7)	2.25 (2.0)	1.84 (1.6)	1.87 (1.6)	1.86 (1.4)	1.30 (1.3)	1.32 (1.3)	1.44 (1.3)
D_t	=0	-0.06 (2.8)	-0.06 (2.9)	-0.06 (2.6)	-0.02 (0.5)	-0.02 (0.6)	-0.01 (0.1)	-0.01 (0.8)	-0.02 (0.8)	-0.02 (0.7)
R^2-Adj.		0.85	0.85	0.85	0.74	0.75	0.74	0.87	0.87	0.86
SEE		50.07	49.92	50.34	53.13	53.04	53.42	49.51	49.47	49.70
F-stat		0.91	1.03	1.36	1.08	1.10	0.90	0.64	0.65	0.69
DW		1.90	1.91	1.93	2.02	2.02	2.04	1.92	1.92	1.93

The dependent variable is private consumption expenditure. Y_t is net national product, G_t is government expenditure on goods and services, W_t is private wealth, TR_t is transfer payments, T_t is current taxation, RE_t is corporate retained earnings, $GINT_t$ is net interest payments by government omits outstanding debt, and D_t is stock of government debt. The three measures of government debt (GB_t) are MV = Market value of government debt. $MVPVA$ = Market value of government debt except that of saving bonds which are at par value. PV = Par value of government debt.

H_0: R.E. is the null hypothesis under the Ricardian Equivalence Hypothesis. * Corrected for autocorrelation using the Cochrane-Orcutt method. The *t-statistics* are shown in parentheses. The *F-statistics* tests for $T_t = RE_t = GINT_t = 0$.

Source: Kormendi (1983) and author's compilation and calculation.

The above results imply that the consumption equation is not sensitive to the par or market value of debt series. The results of our replications with par values are similar to that of Barth, Iden and Russek (1986).[44]

The results in Table 4.8 also yield another interesting conclusion. The coefficient of government spending is always negative, but significant over long duration and insignificant over short duration specifications (1947–76). The government debt variable is always negative. It is generally insignificant except for the period 1931–76, inclusive of the war years. The results of the Equation 4.37 are thus sensitive to the time period, irrespective of which debt series – par or market value is used.[45]

4.6. Testing for Ricardian Equivalence Hypothesis – The model developed in this study

The exercise on replication in the previous section and the critical review of literature in Section 4.4 reveals the lack of consistent and appropriate model to test for the Ricardian Equivalence Hypothesis. This section empirically tests the model developed in Section 4.3, on the United States economy before its application to India. This application to the United States economy, for which exhaustive data is available, is to test for the robustness of the model. The model is also estimated for the various period specifications and its robustness examined for the par and market value of debt.

4.6.1. The model specifications

In Section 4.3, a three equation model was developed. It was discussed that consumption follows a random walk, given the permanent income hypothesis under rational expectations. Therefore, in such a consumption function the coefficient of the government debt variable should be insignificant. The consumption equation (derived in Section 4.3) is as follows,

---

44 Barth, Iden and Russek attempt replications for the period 1931–81, 1931–83, 1949–83, 1949–82, and 1952–82, considering only the par values of government debt.

45 Barth, Iden and Russek (1986) also draw similar conclusions.

$$C_t = a_0 + a_1 C_{t-1} + a_2 Z_t^u + a_3 GB_t^u + a_4 GB_t^a + \mu_t \qquad \text{Equation 4.41}$$

where, C is consumption expenditure, Z is the change in private sector wealth other than government bonds, and GB is government debt held by the public at the beginning of the period. The superscript 'u' and 'a' refer to the unanticipated and the anticipated component of the change in the variables, respectively. It is hypothesised that in such a consumption specification, the coefficient of government debt, both anticipated and unanticipated, should be insignificant to constitute support for the Ricardian Equivalence Hypothesis. This result would imply a strong case of debt-neutrality. The insignificant coefficient of anticipated change in government debt, $(a_4 = 0)$, implies that the rational consumer is indifferent to changes in debt and therefore makes no change in its consumption pattern. In case a_4 is significantly positive, then it implies that the consumer perceives the increase in government debt as an increase in wealth, while if it is significantly negative then it implies that the consumer is cautious and uncertain of the future effects of government debt.[46]

Similar argument also follows for the unanticipated change in government debt. As has been argued earlier in subsection 4.3.2 (Chapter 4), the unanticipated change in disposable income, due to the unanticipated change in the bond holdings, will be equal to the interest payments on these unanticipated bonds, and therefore the consumption pattern will not be affected. Therefore, in the estimation of Equation 4.41, unanticipated change in government debt is also expected to be insignificant to favour the Ricardian Equivalence Hypothesis. In case the coefficient of one or both the components of government debt – anticipated and the unanticipated, is significant, it would imply that consumption behaviour does not support the Ricardian Equivalence Hypothesis.

The derivation of the unanticipated change in private wealth held at the beginning of the period can be explained as follows. It is assumed that the rational consumer has the complete set of information at time 't' and therefore the private holding of wealth is influenced by the private wealth held at 't-1'. The additional relevant information that the consumer gathers in period 't-1' that influences the decision to invest in private wealth is approximated by the change in real interest rate and the change in real per capita income. Thus, it is hypothesised that the changes in the private holdings of current wealth are determined by the previous holding of wealth, changes in the interest rates and the income of the consumer. The unanticipated changes in wealth are derived from the following equation,

---

46   Kormendi (1983) and Barro (1976).

$$\Delta W_t = \beta_0 + \beta_1 \Delta W_{t-1} + \beta_2 \Delta i_{t-1} + \beta_3 \Delta Y_{t-1} + \varepsilon_t \qquad \text{Equation 4.42}$$

where, W_t is real per capita private wealth in the beginning of the period,[47] i is the real interest rate measured in terms of corporate bond rate, Aaa (Moody's) and Y is the real per capita net national product. The error term (ε_t) from equation 4.42 is considered to represent the unanticipated change in wealth (Z^u_t).[48]

The evolution of government debt held by the public in the beginning of the period can be explained as follows. The changes in interest rates and any additional information on income generated in period 't-1' may prompt revision in the formation of expectations for the future in period 't'. In addition, the rational consumer can be expected to analyse government finances to form expectations on current deficit and supply of government bonds. This additional information is sought to be captured in empirical estimation by including taxes in the equation. The anticipated and the unanticipated changes in government debt held by public are estimated on the basis of the following equation,

$$\Delta GB_t = \lambda_0 + \lambda_1 \Delta GB_{t-1} + \lambda_2 \Delta TX_{t-1} + \lambda_3 \Delta i_{t-1} + \lambda_4 \Delta Y_{t-1} + v_t \qquad \text{Equation 4.43}$$

where, GB_t is the real per capita total government debt held by public at the beginning of the period, TX is the real per capita total government taxes, i is the real interest rate measured in terms of corporate bond rate, Aaa (Moody's) and Y is the real per capita net national product. The residual term in the equation (v_t) is considered to represent the unanticipated changes in government debt held by the public (GB^u_t) while the anticipated changes in government debt (GB^a_t) are then derived as $GB^a_t = GB_t - GB^u_t$.

---

47 As a measure of private wealth, the stock of residential plus non-residential fixed capital plus an estimate of the stock of human capital is used. The wealth series was computed from the stock of private national wealth from Goldsmith (1956), and updated from the *Historical Statistics of the United States, Colonial Times to 1970*, till 1969. The data for the period 1970 onwards is computed from 'Survey of Current Business', various issues. The data on human capital was collected from Kendrick (1976). The complete wealth series, inclusive of human capital was extended following the procedure in Barth, Iden and Russek (1986) and Kormendi and Meguire (1986, 1990).

48 The use of generated regressors in the equation are considered appropriate following Pagan (1984). Pagan argues that the use of such generated regressors in most two-step estimators are consistent, efficient and provide valid inferences. This especially holds when only unlagged residuals are present in the regression.

4.6.2. Data sources and the period of the empirical estimation for the united states

The data used in this section has been collected from the *National Income and Product Accounts* of the United States, 1929–88 (NIPA), *Economic Report of the President* (ERP), *Survey of Current Business* (SCB) and *Statistical Abstract of the United States*. The dependent variable is the real per capita consumption expenditure. This study has calculated consumer expenditure on non-durables and services plus an imputed flow from the Bureau of Economic Analysis (BEA) stock of consumer durables.[49] The other relevant variables in the equation are also in real per capita terms.[50] The model represented in the equation system 4.41 to 4.43 is estimated for the United States, using annual data for the period 1930–93.

4.6.3. Empirical results

4.6.3.1. Stationarity of the data series

The data series in the regression are required to be stationary. The results presented in Table 4.9 show that all the series are $I(1)$. The Augmented Dickey-Fuller test results show that most of the series are stationary in first differences at 1 per cent level of significance. Therefore, OLS regression in first differences has been used to estimate the Equations 4.41 to 4.43.

Table 4.9: Testing for unit roots – Augmented Dickey-Fuller test

Period	1931–76				1931–93			
Model tested	C No T	C and T	C No T	C and T	C No T	C and T	C No T	C and T
Variables	Levels		First differences		Levels		First differences	
1	2	3	4	5	6	7	8	9
CE	2.1 (1)	-0.1 (1)	-4.3* (0)	-5.0* (0)	1.9 (2)	-1.3 (2)	-4.5* (1)	-5.2* (1)

Table continued

---

49 This practise is followed by Kormendi (1983), Barth, Iden and Russek (1986) and Kormendi and Meguire (1986 and 1990), as well as the Bureau of Economic Analysis (BEA), United States of America. Under this methodology, consumer expenditure on non-durables and services is added to 10 per cent of consumer expenditure on durables and 30 per cent of total net stock of durable goods owned by consumers to compute annual consumer expenditure.

50 The deflator used throughout this section is the implicit price deflator for the net national product.

Table 4.9: Testing for unit roots – Augmented Dickey-Fuller test

Period	1931–76				1931–93			
Model tested	C No T	C and T	C No T	C and T	C No T	C and T	C No T	C and T
Variables	Levels		First differences		Levels		First differences	
1	2	3	4	5	6	7	8	9
W	2.3 (1)	0.1 (1)	-3.3** (1)	-4.5* (1)	0.5 (1)	-1.9 (1)	-3.7* (1)	-3.6** (1)
i	-2.3 (3)	-2.5 (3)	-6.0* (1)	-5.9* (1)	-2.2 (3)	-2.9 (3)	-7.1* (2)	-7.0* (2)
Y	-1.3 (2)	-3.1 (2)	-4.4* (1)	-4.4* (1)	-1.2 (0)	-2.6 (0)	-5.3* (1)	-5.3* (1)
GBM	-2.4 (2)	-2.3 (2)	-4.0* (1)	-4.1** (1)				
GBP	-2.2 (2)	-2.1 (2)	-4.7* (1)	-4.7* (1)	-0.8 (2)	-1.3 (2)	-5.3* (1)	-5.3* (1)
TX	-0.6 (0)	2.2 (0)	-4.8* (1)	-4.8* (1)	-0.7 (0)	-2.8 (0)	-5.9* (0)	-5.8* (0)

C = Constant. T = Trend. CE is consumption expenditure, W is wealth, 'i' is interest rate, Y is net national product, GB is government debt, two measures of which are tested here - GBM is government debt at market value and GBP is government debt at par value, TX is government taxes. Figures in parentheses are the lag values chosen to ensure that the residuals are white noise.
* Significant at the level of 1 per cent. ** Significant at the level of 5 per cent.
Source: Author's compilation.

4.6.3.2. Estimating the wealth and government debt functions

The wealth and the government debt functions specified in the Equations 4.42 and 4.43 are estimated in the Tables 4.9 and 4.10, respectively. The two functions are estimated for the six period specifications – 1931–76, 1931–93, 1947–76, 1947–93, 1931–40/47–76 and 1931–40/47–93. The war years are abnormal years but crucial, and therefore a dummy variable has been used for the period 1941–46, when the war years are included in the estimation.

The wealth function shows that lagged wealth is significant in all the periods (Table 4.10). The real interest rate is not significant in all the cases, while income is significant in most cases except for the period after the war years (Columns 4 and 5). The dummy variable is significant in the equation (Columns 1 and 2).

Table 4.10: Estimating the wealth function

Period	1931–76	1931–93	1947–93	1947–76	1931–40\47–76	1931–40\47–93
1	2	3	4	5	6	7
Cons.	821.95	482.43	618.52	1278.10	383.31	74.19
	(3.0)	(2.0)	(2.2)	(3.7)	(1.4)	(0.3)
ΔW_{t-1}	0.53	0.64	0.63	0.41	0.64	0.71
	(4.3)	(6.8)	(6.0)	(2.8)	(5.7)	(8.2)
Δi_{t-1}	-8.98	-34.71	-74.35	-34.13	79.73	78.94
	(0.3)	(0.8)	(1.4)	(0.7)	(1.9)	(1.7)
ΔY_{t-1}	0.77	0.94	0.80	0.64	1.43	1.88
	(2.0)	(2.6)	(1.7)	(1.3)	(2.6)	(3.7)
DUM	-1537.00	-1527.80				
	(2.5)	(2.3)				
R^2-Adj	0.46	0.52	0.48	0.32	0.52	0.59
SEE	1258.80	1389.40	1447.80	1218.60	1114.90	1262.10
h-stat	0.66	1.47	1.76	0.96	-1.53	-0.28
LM	2.26	0.17	0.04	4.01	5.07	0.30

The dependent variable is wealth, W, in first differences. 'i' is interest rate, Y is net national product, DUM is dummy, used for the war period, 1941–46.

LM is the Jarque-Bera Asymptotic LM normality Test to test for the normality of the residuals.

Source: Author's compilation.

In the estimation of the debt equation, as the data on the market value of government debt is available till 1976, this variable has been restricted to some regressions.[51] The regressions for the period 1931–76 and 1947–76 are attempted for both the market and the par value of government debt. The other set of results for the longer period, 1931–93 and 1947–93 are restricted to the par value of the government debt. The results of estimating Equation 4.43 are presented in Table 4.11. The results are robust, and the coefficients of the variables are significant in all the estimations that include the war period (Columns 2–4) or pertain to the post-war period (Columns 5–7). The empirical results of the debt function for the period excluding the six war years, consistently show non-normal residuals as indicated by the Jarque-Bera asymptotic LM normality test (Columns 8, 9 and

---

51　The series on market value of government debt has been constructed by Seater (1981). This series has been used in many studies: Kormendi (1982), Seater and Mariano (1985), Kormendi and Meguire (1986 and 1990) and Barth, Iden and Russek (1986).

10). As the residuals from these equations are important variables in estimating the consumption function in Equation 4.41, this sample period specification has, therefore, been excluded from the final estimation.

Table 4.11: Estimating the government debt function

Period	1931–76	1931–76	1931–93	1947–93	1947–76	1947–76	1931-40 \47–76	1931–40 \47–76	1931–40 \47–93
	GBM	GBP	GBP	GBP	GBM	GBP	GBM	GBP	GBP
1	2	3	4	5	6	7	8	9	10
Cons.	-84.57	-75.21	-14.44	3.47	-101.22	-15.71	-16.94	-2.28	68.60
	(1.2)	(1.2)	(0.3)	(0.1)	(1.3)	(0.3)	(0.1)	(0.0)	(1.0)
ΔGB_{t-1}	0.52	0.57	0.64	0.94	0.56	0.89	0.344	0.47	0.74
	(4.7)	(5.7)	(7.8)	(12.0)	(2.9)	(6.6)	(1.6)	(2.3)	(5.7)
Δi_{t-1}	53.92	47.37	55.75	100.83	64.17	91.22	11.09	15.42	35.12
	(4.0)	(4.1)	(5.2)	(9.6)	(2.7)	(6.2)	(0.4)	(0.7)	(2.1)
ΔY_{t-1}	0.81	0.80	0.72	0.31	1.02	0.46	0.01	-0.15	-0.06
	(4.3)	(4.7)	(4.8)	(2.1)	(3.6)	(2.5)	(0.0)	(0.5)	(0.2)
ΔTX_{t-1}	-1.14	-0.97	-1.03	-0.80	-1.96	-0.90	-1.15	-0.59	-0.72
	(2.2)	(2.1)	(2.5)	(2.4)	(3.1)	(2.2)	(1.4)	(0.9)	(1.3)
DUM		461.74	288.76	238.32					
		(1.9)	(1.3)	(1.3)					
R^2-Adj	0.75	0.78	0.75	0.84	0.65	0.83	0.04	0.10	0.36
SEE	397.45	358.64	346.46	214.15	343.96	214.94	533.50	453.90	401.28
h-stat	0.40	1.79	2.55	0.58	-	0.58	-	-	-1.97
LM	2.03	1.35	2.25	1.11	1.63	3.45	493.16	1043.01	1967.71

The dependent variable is government debt (GB) in first differences, two measures of which are used here - GBM is government debt at market value and GBP is government debt at par value, 'i' is interest rate, Y is net national product, TX is taxes and DUM is dummy, used for the war period, 1941–46. LM is the Jarque-Bera Asymptotic LM normality Test to test for the normality of the residuals.
Source: Author's compilation.

Finally, in Table 4.12, the anticipated and unanticipated components of the wealth and government debt are investigated for stationarity. The ADF test reveals that such components, computed from the Equations 4.42 and 4.43, the estimates of which are presented in Tables 4.10 and 4.11, are stationary at 1 per cent level of significance.

Table 4.12: Testing for stationarity in the anticipated and the unanticipated components of wealth and government debt – Augmented Dickey-Fuller test

Period	1931–76		1931–93	
Model Tested	C No T	C and T	C No T	C and T
Variables	First Differences		First Differences	
1	4	5	8	9
W^u	-6.3*(0)	-6.4*(0)	-6.8*(0)	-6.8*(0)
GBM^u	-6.8*(0)	-6.8*(0)		
GBM^a	-4.2*(1)	-4.3*(1)		
GBP^u	-5.8*(0)	-5.8*(0)	-6.4*(0)	-6.9*(0)
GBP^a	-4.4*(1)	-4.5*(1)	-5.4*(1)	-5.3*(1)

C = Constant. T = Trend. W is the wealth, GB is government debt, two measures of which are used here - GBM is government debt at market value and GBP is government debt at par value, The superscript 'a' and 'u' refer to the anticipated and the unanticipated components and are computed from the Equations 4.42 and 4.43 which are in first differences and the estimates of which are presented in Tables 4.10 and 4.11.

Figures in parentheses are the Lag values chosen to ensure that the residuals are white noise. * Significant at the level of 1 per cent.

Source: Author's compilation.

4.6.3.3. Estimating the consumption function for the Ricardian equivalence

The consumption function, testing for the Ricardian equivalence, is estimated for the following four period omitting – 1931–93, 1931–76, 1947–76 and 1947–93. The period excluding the war period has been excluded as the results derived from the estimation of the debt function are not robust. The data on market value of government debt of the United States is available till 1976. Therefore, the use of this series is restricted to only two period specifications – 1931–76 and 1947–76.

The empirical estimates of Equation 4.41 are presented in Table 4.13. All the estimates in the table suffer from serial correlation as shown by the low values of DW statistics. Therefore, the results cannot be confidently analysed.[52]

---

52 The presence of serial correlation in pure permanent income hypothesis can be expected (Blinder and Deaton, 1985, 478) but under the derivation of rational expectations, it is a cause of concern.

Table 4.13: Test for Ricardian equivalence and consumption –
The model developed in this study

Period	Ho:R.E. expected sign	1931–93 GBP	1931–76 GBP	1931–76 GBM	1947–93 GBP	1947–76 GBP	1947–76 GBM
Debt							
1	2	3	4	5	6	7	8
Cons.		161.29 (11.5)	157.17 (9.2)	159.34 (9.1)	177.30 (12.6)	185.67 (10.7)	190.28 (10.4)
GB^a	=0	0.13 (4.5)	0.09 (2.8)	0.09 (2.7)	0.15 (4.9)	0.12 (3.3)	0.12 (3.3)
GB^u	=0	-0.04 (1.0)	-0.05 (1.1)	-0.03 (0.7)	0.06 (0.8)	0.16 (1.9)	0.07 (1.4)
W^u	=0	0.02 (1.8)	0.02 (1.3)	0.01 (0.8)	0.03 (2.5)	0.03 (2.1)	0.03 (2.1)
DUM		-167.68 (2.9)	-112.13 (1.8)	-119.26 (1.8)			
R^2-Adj		0.24	0.11	0.09	0.32	0.32	0.27
SEE		103.44	101.80	103.03	96.68	86.92	89.81
DW		1.26	1.32	1.21	1.11	1.20	1.21
Q		15.67	12.76	15.73	13.69	11.12	9.27
LM		0.66	0.23	0.41	0.95	1.31	0.80
F-stat		11.06*	4.55**	3.98**	12.02*	7.45*	6.15*

The dependent variable is consumption expenditure in first differences. W is the wealth series, GB refers to the government debt, two measures of which are used - GBP is par value of government debt and GBM is market value of government debt. The superscript 'a' and 'u' refer to the anticipated and the unanticipated components and are computed from the Equations 4.42 and 4.43 which are in first differences and the estimates of which are presented in Tables 4.10 and 4.11.

H_o: R.E. refers to the Null Hypothesis under the Ricardian equivalence. The *t-statistics* are shown in parentheses. Q is the Box-Pierce-Ljung statistic to test for any autocorrelation in the residuals. LM is the Jarque-Bera Asymptotic LM Normality Test to test for the normality of the residuals. The *F-statistics* tests for $GB^a = GB^u = 0$. * Significant at the level of 1 per cent. ** Significant at the level of 5 per cent

Source: Author's compilation.

The presence of serial correlation signifies a misspecified specification. Therefore, an attempt is made to respecify the equation with the lagged consumption in the regression. The inclusion of lagged consumption in the equation improves the results and provides robust estimation (Table 4.14).

The results show that lagged consumption is significant in all the cases. The significant changes in lagged consumption are consistent with the simple model of habit formation (Deaton, 1987, 1992).[53] Deaton (1987) shows that the consumption model with habit formation is consistent with data. This result therefore rejects the joint hypothesis of permanent income hypothesis under rational expectations.[54]

In Table 4.14 (Column 3), the results for the period 1931–93, indicate that the coefficient of the anticipated government debt is significant and the unanticipated government debt is insignificant. The results for other periods (1931–76, 1947–76, and 1947–93) presented in Columns 4 through 8 are consistently similar.

Table 4.14: Test for Ricardian equivalence and consumption – The modified model

Period	Ho:R.E. expected sign	1931–93	1931–76	1931–76	1947–93	1947–76	1947–76
Debt		GBP	GBP	GBM	GBP	GBP	GBM
1	2	3	4	5	6	7	8
Cons.		97.03 (4.8)	100.95 (4.2)	103.79 (4.5)	105.33 (4.4)	125.25 (4.4)	131.47 (4.5)
C_{t-1}		0.41 (4.0)	0.41 (3.0)	0.41 (3.3)	0.40 (3.6)	0.38 (2.6)	0.37 (2.5)
GB^a	=0	0.10 (3.6)	0.08 (2.5)	0.08 (2.6)	0.13 (4.6)	0.12 (3.7)	0.12 (3.7)
GB^u	=0	0.02 (0.6)	0.03 (0.5)	0.03 (0.6)	0.10 (1.4)	0.17 (2.3)	0.07 (1.5)
W^u	=0	0.01 (1.3)	0.01 (0.6)	0.01 (0.6)	0.02 (2.1)	0.03 (1.9)	0.03 (2.0)

Table continued

---

53 These results are contradictory to the permanent income hypothesis under rational expectations, where only surprises are expected to be significant to current consumption. However, subsequent and more detailed analysis has led to the view that aggregate consumption is responsive to anticipated changes in income (Flavin, 1981; Hayashi, 1982; Hansen and Singleton, 1982; Bean, 1986; and Blinder and Deaton, 1985). Deaton (1985) argues that the smoothness of consumption is consistent with the model of habit formation. The assumption of habit formation is inconsistent with the assumption that utility function is intertemporally additive and therefore additivity rules out habit formation. Mankiw (1982), Muellbauer (1985) and Hayashi (1985a) yield similar conclusions.

54 Sargent (1978) and Flavin (1981 and 1985) are some of the prominent studies which yield similar results.

Table 4.14: Test for Ricardian equivalence and consumption – The modified model

Period	Ho:R.E. expected sign	1931–93	1931–76	1931–76	1947–93	1947–76	1947–76
Debt		GBP	GBP	GBM	GBP	GBP	GBM
1	2	3	4	5	6	7	8
DUM		-116.74 (2.3)	-91.75 (1.6)	-104.30 (1.7)			
R^2-Adj		0.40	0.27	0.28	0.47	0.44	0.39
SEE		91.76	92.61	92.17	85.67	78.65	82.19
h-stat		0.53	-0.64	-0.22	1.27	0.51	0.141
LM		1.03	0.18	0.26	3.39	0.41	2.63
F-stat		6.830*	3.23***	3.44**	11.31*	9.59*	7.73*

The dependent variable is consumption expenditure, C, in first differences. GB refers to the government debt, two measures of which are used - GBP is par value of government debt and GBM is market value of government debt, W is the wealth series. The superscript 'a' and 'u' refer to the anticipated and the unanticipated components and are computed from the Equations 4.42 and 4.43 which are in first differences and the estimates of which are presented in Tables 4.10 and 4.11.

H_o: R.E. refers to the null hypothesis under the Ricardian equivalence. The *t-statistics* are shown in parenthesis. *LM* is the Jarque-Bera Asymptotic LM Normality Test to test for the normality of the residuals. The *F-statistics* tests for $GB^a = GB^u = 0$. * Significant at the level of 1 per cent. ** Significant at the level of 5 per cent.

*** Significant at the level of 10 per cent.

Source: Author's compilation.

In the equation with the par value of debt for the period 1947–76 (Column 7), the coefficient of the unanticipated component of government debt is also significant. The results are, however, not sensitive to the use of the par or the market value of government debt.[55] The joint hypothesis that the coefficients of the anticipated and unanticipated government debt are insignificant is rejected in all the sample periods, including the war period or after the war period. The results contradict the Ricardian Equivalence Hypothesis.

Thus, the conclusion emerges that given the appropriate specification of the consumption function, the United States economy does not exhibit Ricardian behaviour. This conclusion is valid even if the debt is on par value or market value, and for different period specifications. In addition, the joint hypothesis of permanent income hypothesis under rational expectations as derived by Hall (1978) is rejected.

---

55 This strengthens the argument presented in Section 4.5.2, Chapter 4.

4.7. Conclusions

In this chapter, it has been argued that the consistent way to test for the Ricardian Equivalence Hypothesis is to begin with an appropriate theoretical consumption model. Ricardian equivalence inherently implies an underlying assumption of rational expectations in the consumption behaviour. Therefore, permanent income hypothesis incorporating rational expectations is considered to be an appropriate consumption function to test for the Ricardian Equivalence Hypothesis. Having established the rationale, a model is then derived, from the consumption function which follows a random walk, to test for the Ricardian equivalence. In the specification of the model the role of rational expectations is stressed and the relevant variables are decomposed into the anticipated and the unanticipated components.

In the section on review of literature, it is argued that a large number of studies testing the Ricardian Equivalence Hypothesis suffer from measurement and methodological problems. These involve complex issues like data specification, identification, simultaneity, treatment of expectations and the choice of the form of equation.

In the literature on Ricardian equivalence, it emerges that most of the studies have been conducted for the United States. Of a large number of these studies, nine follow the permanent income model incorporating the rational expectations. The results of five studies, amongst these, clearly support Ricardian equivalence while only two refute it. The results of the other two are mixed/inconclusive. Thus, the empirical evidence is strongly in favour of the Ricardian Hypothesis.

The result of the experiment, in this chapter, to replicate some of the major studies, given a common data set, indicates that the conclusions from these studies are sensitive to the sample period specification. It is also argued that these models are not appropriately specified and are not consistent with the permanent income hypothesis under rational expectations. In addition, the issue of par and market value of debt is examined. In the empirical estimation, the results are not sensitive between the two series.

Finally, empirical estimates of the model developed in this study are presented for the United States economy. The empirical estimation rejects the joint hypothesis of permanent income under rational expectations. The consumption pattern is consistent with the model of habit formation. Finally, the results do not support the Ricardian Equivalence Hypothesis. The estimates are however robust to the alternative sample period specifications or to the use of par and market value of government debt. Thus, it can be concluded that given an appropriate consumption function, the empirical evidence does not support the Ricardian Equivalence Hypothesis in the United States.

5

Ricardian Equivalence and Consumption in India

In this chapter, the empirical results of the model that has been developed in the previous chapter, incorporating the Ricardian Equivalence Hypothesis in the permanent income specification under rational expectations is presented. The model is empirically estimated and its robustness is examined in the context of India.

This chapter consists of five sections. The few empirical studies on domestic debt and consumption in India are briefly discussed in Section 5.1. In Section 5.2, the model to be estimated is briefly discussed in the context of India. This is followed by a section on data specifications and definitions used in the estimation. The empirical results are presented in Section 5.4. Finally, the conclusions follow in Section 5.5.

5.1. Review of literature of empirical studies on Ricardian equivalence and consumption in India

In India, five studies on domestic debt and consumption have been conducted. Two studies reject Ricardian equivalence, while two other yield mixed results. Ricardian equivalence is supported by only one study (Table 5.1). Amongst these, three studies (Study No. 3, 4 and 5 in the Statement) follow the models which have been developed earlier and empirically estimated for the United States. The limitations of these basic models have been critically discussed in detail in the previous chapter (Section 4.4.1). In the other two studies (Study No. 1 and 2), the equation specified and estimated appears to be *ad hoc*.

In all the five studies, problems of data availability, specification and estimation emerge. The most important of these is the use of the data in levels, and the definition of the income and the consumption variables. The data series on macro aggregates are generally non-stationary at levels. Hence, the use of data in levels could yield spurious results. In the case of the income variable, as discussed by Kormendi (1983), the appropriate definition would be the national income, and not private income (Study No. 1) or disposable income (Study No. 5). In the case of the consumption variable, the appropriate definition should include some component of the final consumption expenditure on durable goods. In none of these studies such a computation is attempted and either total consumption expenditure (Study No. 1 to 5) or only non-durable consumption expenditure (Study No. 5) is used in the regressions.

Thus, the existing empirical studies on Ricardian equivalence in India are few. These studies suffer from problems of misspecification of the model and data definitions. The conclusions emerging from such studies, therefore, need to be cautiously interpreted.

5.2. Testing for Ricardian equivalence under permanent income: Hypothesis incorporating rational expectations

In this section, the model developed in Chapter 4, is estimated for India. The three major equations of the model for such estimation are briefly discussed in the context of India.

In the previous chapter, it was derived that the permanent income hypothesis under rational expectations yields a consumption function that follows a random walk.[1] Therefore, in such a consumption function the coefficient of the government debt variable should be insignificant. The equation is as follows

$$\Delta C_t = a_0 + a_1 GB^a_t + a_2 GB^u_t + a_3 Z^u_t + \mu_t \qquad \text{Equation 5.1}$$

where, C is consumption expenditure, GB is government debt held by the public at the beginning of the period, and Z is the private sector wealth at the beginning of the period. The superscript 'u' and 'a' refer to the unanticipated and the anticipated components of the change in the variables, respectively. The changes in private sector wealth and the government bonds are each derived from different equations, specified in first differences.

The derivation of the unanticipated change in private wealth can be explained as follows. It is assumed that the rational consumer at any time 't' has a complete set of information and, therefore, the private holding of wealth may be influenced by income, interest rates and any other relevant additional information. The unanticipated changes in wealth are derived from the following equation,

$$\Delta W_t = \beta_0 + \beta_1 \Delta Y_{t-1} + \beta_2 \Delta i_{t-1} + \beta_3 \Delta V_{t-1} + \varepsilon_t \qquad \text{Equation 5.2}$$

---

1   Section 4.3, Chapter 4.

Table 5.1: Empirical studies on Ricardian Equivalence Hypothesis and consumption in India

Study and year	Data specifications	Model followed	Dependent variable	Independent variables	Technique employed	Conclusion
1	2	3	4	5	6	7
1. Gopalakrishnan (1989)	1961–81, Annual	None	C	PY, PYT, G, PD	OLS, levels	Supports Ricardian equivalence
2. Gopalakrishnan (1991)	1961–87, Annual	None	C	Y, G, T^*, D	OLS, differences	Mixed
3. Gupta (1992)	1960–85, Annual	Buiter and Tobin (1980); Aschaer (1985)	C	YP, YT, GP, GT, T, G, DF	OLS, levels	Rejects Ricardian equivalence
4. Ghatak and Ghatak (1993)	1950–86, Annual	Buiter and Tobin (1980); Kormendi (1983); Boskin (1985)	C	Y, G, T	Cointegration, differences	Mixed
5. Mohanty (1995)	1961–90 (C) and 1968–90 (CND), Annual	Modigliani and Sterling (1986); Modigliani and Jappelli (1987)	C, CND	$Y, PD, W, DF, i, YR.$	2SLS, levels	Rejects Ricardian equivalence

Key:

Dependent variables – C: Total private consumption; CND: Private consumption of non-durable goods.

Independent variables

D	Domestic debt	PD	Public debt	
DF	Budget deficit	PY	Private income	W Wealth
G	Government expenditure	PYT	Private transitory income	Y Income
GP	Permanent government expenditure	T	Taxes	YP Permanent income
GT	Transitory government expenditure	T^*	Taxes net of transfers	YR Ratio of non-agricultural income to agricultural income
i	Interest payments to domestic residents			YT Transitory income

Source: Author's compilation.

where, W_t is real per capita private wealth in the beginning of the period, i is the interest rate, Y is the income and V is a vector of any other information that may be available to the consumer. The error term (ε_t) from Equation 5.2 is considered to represent the unanticipated change in wealth (Z^u_t).

The income variable is expected to be significant in the wealth equation. In India, as the interest rates are administered and regulated, these may not be important for the formation of expectations.[2] The formation of expectations can be influenced by the change in the government expenditure, particularly when huge investment expenditures are being regularly incurred by the government for economic development.

The anticipated and the unanticipated changes in government debt held by the public are estimated on the basis of the following equation,

$$\Delta GB_t = \lambda_0 + \lambda_1 \Delta Y_{t-1} + \lambda_2 \Delta i_{t-1} + \lambda_3 \Delta V_{t-1} + \lambda_4 \Delta GB_{t-1} + v_t \qquad \text{Equation 5.3}$$

where GB_t is domestic debt held by the public in the beginning of the period. The residual term in the equation (v_t) is considered to represent the unanticipated changes in government debt held by the public (GB^u_t) while the anticipated changes in government debt (GB^a_t) are then derived as $GB^a_t = GB_t - GB^u_t$.

The variables in Equation 5.3 can be specified and explained as follows. In the case of privately held government debt, the changes in interest rates and any additional information on income may prompt revision in the formation of expectations for the future. In the context of India, where most of domestic debt is held by the captive market or is in the form of committed savings like the provident funds, the major investment determinant is expected to be only the income variable. In addition, the change in the previous period holding is also important, given the ownership pattern of government debt. In view of the administered interest rates and lack of debt instruments in the market, interest rate is not expected to be significant in the equation. However, the short term yield rate, given the economic uncertainties in the face of economic development, may be informative and therefore preferable to the long term yield rate. Further, government expenditure may be considered to provide some additional information.

---

2 The insignificance of the interest rates in the money demand function has been emphasised in many studies in India. Detail discussion on the interest rates and money demand function is presented in Chapter 6, Section 6.1.1.3.

It is hypothised that given the permanent income hypothesis under rational expectations, consumption follows a random walk and only surprises can influence the current consumption.[3] Therefore, in such a consumption specification, as argued in subsection 4.3.2 (Chapter 4), the coefficient of government debt, both anticipated and unanticipated, should be insignificant ($a_1 = a_2 = 0$ in Equation 5.1) to constitute support for the Ricardian Equivalence Hypothesis.

5.3. Issues pertaining to data specifications and the period of estimation

The data used in the empirical work has been collected from the National Accounts Statistics, Central Statistical Organisation (CSO), Government of India,[4] and various publications of RBI, especially the *Annual Reports* and the *Report on Currency and Finance*.

The dependent variable is the real per capita private final consumption expenditure in the empirical estimation. The total private final consumption expenditure (CT) is decomposed into durable goods (CD), semi-durable goods (CSD), non-durable goods (CND) and services (CS).[5] In the estimation, apart from using CT and CND, three more consumption measures are computed. These are (a) consumption expenditure on non-durables and services, $CNDS$ (= $CND+CS$); (b) consumption expenditure on semi-durables, non-durables and services, $CNDT$ (= $CSD+CND+CS$); and (c) consumption expenditure incorporating some component of current purchases of durable goods, CDT (= $0.3*CD+CSD+CND+CS$). The proportion of current purchases of durable goods in CDT at 30 per cent is based on the following consideration. In the United States, Bureau of Economic Analysis uses 10 per cent of current expenditure on durable goods and 30 per cent of total net stock of durable goods owned by consumers, to

---

3 Permanent Income Hypothesis in India is empirically supported by Gopalakrishnan (1989) for the period 1960–61 to 1980–-81. Laumas and Laumas (1976) find no support for a loose variant of the permanent income hypothesis during the period 1929–60 while Bhalla (1980) finds mixed support on the basis of the household panel data for rural India, 1968–-69 to 1970–-71.

4 The data on consumption expenditure and its various components was specially received from the Central Statistical Organisation, Government of India.

5 The share of CD, CSD, CND and CS in the total consumption expenditure changed from 1.3 per cent, 10.2 per cent, 70.4 per cent and 18.1 per cent, in 1970–71 to from 3.2 per cent, 14.1 per cent, 62.5 per cent and 20.2 per cent, in 1994–95 respectively.

compute the annual consumption flow measure.[6] In India, in the absence of the series on net stock of durable goods owned by the consumers, the rate of 30 per cent of annual purchases is considered appropriate to compute a flow measure.

In the empirical estimation, total private final consumption expenditure (CT) was tested separately, considering that consumption expenditure on durable goods also follow a random walk (Mankiw, 1982).[7] The other reason pertains to the definition of durable goods. In the United States, for which most of the studies have been conducted,[8] durable goods refer to those commodities that have an average life of at least three years.[9] On the other hand, in India, consumer durables refer to those goods which have an expected lifetime of considerably more than one year.[10]

There has been a revision in the estimation of the series on consumption expenditure on consumer durables since 1980–81.[11] Therefore, a dummy has been used in the regressions which use total consumption expenditure (CT) or some component of consumption expenditure on durable goods (CDT).

The other issue pertains to the debt variable. The data on domestic debt in India is available only on the par value and not on the market value. As already discussed in detail in the previous chapter this should not cause any ambiguity in the results, given a robust underlying consumption model.[12] In addition, in the case of India, where the interest rates have been highly regulated in the economy, the divergence between the two values cannot be expected to be significant. In fact, even for the United States, where the market related interest rates prevail, the two series are closely related.[13]

The interest rate series, used in the estimation of the wealth and debt functions, is the minimum redemption yield on the short term (one to five years) central government securities (YD_{St}). This is considered to be an appropriate proxy for the yield pattern on government securities in the absence of any data on yield pattern of total government securities, inclusive of the state governments. However, the

---

6   This practise is followed by Kormendi (1983), Kormendi and Meguire (1986 and 1990), and Barth, Iden and Russek (1986).
7   However, Hall (1978) only considers consumer expenditure on non-durables goods and services.
8   Refer Section 4.4, Chapter 4.
9   Bureau of Economic Analysis (1993), M-6.
10 Central Statistical Organisation (1989), 341.
11 Central Statistical Organistaion (1989), 205.
12 Section 4.5.2, Chapter 4.
13 Section 4.4.1.1.2, Chapter 4.

yield pattern on central and state government securities are closely related. Also, as the central government securities are more popular, the yield pattern on these can be considered as an appropriate representative for the returns on the other government securities as well.

The official data series on wealth is available in the form of net stock of capital goods held in the private sector (private corporate and household) from 1981 onwards.[14] In the absence of any other comprehensive series, a wealth series has been constructed for the earlier years using the annual data on net capital formation in the private sector (Data Appendix). In the case of the government expenditure on goods and services, the data on total government purchases is not available for India. The available data series pertains to government final consumption expenditure on goods and services consisting of the purchases of the non-durable goods and services by the government and expenditure incurred on durable goods for defence purposes.[15]

The NNP deflator is used to compute the series at constant prices in cases where they are available only at current prices. All the relevant variables used in the estimation of the equations are in real per capita terms. The detail computation of data series used in the analysis is presented in the Data Appendix.

The revised data series on components of consumption expenditure are available from 1970–71 to 1994–95 only on an annual basis. In view of the above limitations of the data availability on consumption expenditure, the estimation is restricted to the annual series for the period 1971–95.

5.4. Empirical results

In this section, the empirical results are presented. Firstly, the wealth and debt functions are estimated. The anticipated and the unanticipated components of the wealth and debt series are computed which are then used in the consumption function to test for the Ricardian Equivalence Hypothesis.

5.4.1. Estimating the anticipated and the unanticipated components of domestic debt and wealth

5.4.1.1: Stationarity of the data series

In the estimation of the debt and the wealth functions, the data series are required

---

14 This information has been specially verified from the Central Statistical Organisation, Government of India.

15 Central Statistical Organistaion (1989), 27.

to be stationary. In Table 5.2, the results of the unit roots test, following the augmented Dickey-Fuller testing procedure, are presented. The data series used in the estimation are $I(1)$.

Table 5.2: Testing for unit roots – Augmented Dickey-Fuller test (1971–95)

Variables	Levels	Levels	Differences	Differences
	C	C and T	C	C and T
1	2	3	4	5
CT	0.6(1)	-3.0(1)	-5.5(1)*	-5.4(1)*
CND	0.2(2)	-2.7(2)	-7.3(1)*	-7.0(1)*
CNDT	0.2(1)	-2.7(2)	-5.9(1)*	-5.7(1)*
CNDS	0.9(2)	-3.1(2)	-6.4(1)*	-6.9(1)*
CDT	0.2(2)	-2.6(2)	-5.7(1)*	-5.7(1)*
W	0.2(0)	-1.3(0)	-4.0(0)*	-3.9(0)**
Y	0.5(0)	-2.5(0)	-5.3(0)*	-5.6(0)*
i	-2.1(2)	-2.1(2)	-7.0(1)*	-6.7(1)*
GS	0.9(0)	2.7(0)	-4.0(0)*	-3.7(0)**
GB	2.6(0)	-1.8(0)	-2.7(1)***	-4.2(1)**

C = Constant. T = Trend. CT is total consumption, CDT is consumption with some component of durable good, CNDT is consumption of semi durables, non-durables and services, CNDS is consumption of non-durables and services, CND is consumption of non-durables, W is wealth, Y is net national product, i is interest rate, GS is government expenditure, GB is government debt.

Figures in parenthesis are the lag values chosen to ensure that the residuals are white noise.
* Significant at the level of 1 per cent. ** Significant at the level of 5 per cent. *** Significant at the level of 10 per cent.

Source: Author's compilation.

5.4.1.2. Estimating the wealth and domestic debt functions

The empirical estimates of the Equations 5.2 and 5.3, are presented in Table 5.3. In the case of the private sector wealth (Column 2) the empirical results substantiate the theoretical arguments. The interest rate is insignificant in the regression, while the income and the government expenditure are significant. An attempt to estimate the equation with other interest rates or with the series on gold prices, as personal holdings of gold are psychologically important for the Indian households, did not lead to any qualitative difference in the equation. Therefore, the interest rate variable is dropped from the equation and the equation with the income and government expenditure is retained for the estimation of the unanticipated component of private sector wealth (Column 3).

Table 5.3. Estimating the wealth and the domestic debt functions (1971–95)

1	Wealth function		Domestic debt function		
	2	3	4	5	6
Cons.	84.33	86.22	12.21	9.87	12.88
	(10.6)	(11.6)	(1.3)	(1.1)	(1.5)
ΔY_{t-1}	0.19	0.15	0.01	0.13	0.13
	(1.8)	(1.8)	(0.0)	(1.2)	(1.3)
ΔGS_{t-1}	-1.65	-1.67	0.77	1.1	
	(2.3)	(2.4)	(0.7)	(1.1)	
Δi_{t-1}	-0.87		1.81		
	(0.7)		(1.2)		
ΔGB_{t-1}			0.57	0.42	0.57
			(2.0)	(1.6)	(2.7)
R^2-Adj	0.15	0.17	0.36	0.35	0.34
SEE	26.54	26.25	30.33	30.66	30.90
DW	1.81	1.83	2.08	1.77	1.71
h-stat	-	-	!	!	!
CHI-SQ	5.05	5.17	-	-	-
LM	0.59	0.29	0.11	1.22	0.72

The dependent variable, in first differences, is wealth, W_p, in Columns 2 and 3, and domestic debt, GB_p, in Columns 4, 5 and 6. Y is net national product, i is interest rate, GS is government expenditure. The variables are specified in first differences. Figures in parenthesis are the *t-values*. ! Cannot be computed. CHI-SQ statistic is the Box-Pierce statistic for a test that the residual autocorrelations are jointly zero when there are no lagged dependent variables. The LM is the Jarque-Bera Asymptotic LM Normality test to test for the normality of the residuals.

Source: Author's compilation.

Similarly, privately held domestic debt is explained by the changes in the levels of income, government expenditure, interest rate and lagged domestic debt held by the public. In the estimation, only the lagged dependent variable is significant (Column 4). Given the theoretical basis, the insignificance of the interest rate is expected.[16] In the next regression, the interest rate is omitted and no variable is

---

16   The short term yield rate on government securities is insignificant in the regression (Column 4). The exercise with the long-term yield rate did not make any qualitative difference in the equation. The yield rates are not significant due to the existence of the captive market. In the captive market, investments in government bonds are made statutorily, and yield rates may not play an important role.

significant (Column 5). The estimation of the regression without the income variable, but including the interest rate yields a high *h-statistics* suggesting the presence of misspecification error.[17] Finally, the equation is re-estimated without the government expenditure and the lagged dependent variable is significant again (Column 6). The *t-ratio* of the income variable also improves, though marginally. This equation for different time period specification yields consistent results. In view of the economic situation in India, and the nature of the ownership pattern of domestic debt, this estimation is considered appropriate theoretically. Therefore, it is used in the computation of the anticipated and the unanticipated components of domestic debt.

5.4.2. Estimating the consumption function for the Ricardian Equivalence Hypothesis

5.4.2.1. Stationarity of the components of domestic debt and wealth

The results of the test for stationarity of the anticipated component of domestic debt, and the unanticipated component of domestic debt and wealth, are presented in Table 5.4. The generated variables are computed from the equation in first differences and are stationary, following the results of the augmented Dickey-Fuller Test.

Table 5.4: Testing for stationarity in the anticipated and the unanticipated components of domestic debt and the unanticipated component of wealth-augmented Dickey-Fuller Test (1971–95)

Variables	First differences	First differences
	C	C and T
1	2	3
GB^A	-3.9(1)**	-4.0(0)**
GB^U	-4.4(0)*	-4.5(0)*
W^U	-4.6(0)*	-4.5(0)*

C = Constant. T = Trend. GB is domestic debt, W is the private sector wealth, the superscripts 'a' and 'u' refer to the anticipated and unanticipated values, computed on the basis of the estimations, in first differences, presented in Table 5.3.

Figures in parenthesis are the lag values chosen to ensure that the residuals are white noise.
* Significant at the level of 1 per cent. ** Significant at the level of 5 per cent.

Source: Author's compilation.

---

17 The regression is not reported in the table.

Table 5.5: Empirical results of the estimation of Ricardian equivalence and consumption– The model developed in this study (1971–95)

	H_o:R.E. expected Sign	Consumption expenditure				
		CT	CDT	CNDT	CNDS	CND
1	2	3	4	5	6	7
Cons.		23.17	22.62	31.83	22.58	21.49
		(2.0)	(2.0)	(2.8)	(2.1)	(2.0)
GB^a_t	=0	-0.43	-0.44	-0.21	-0.11	-0.26
		(1.6)	(1.6)	(0.8)	(0.4)	(1.1)
GB^u_t	=0	0.56	0.54	0.68	0.58	0.52
		(2.6)	(2.5)	(3.1)	(2.8)	(2.5)
W^u_t		-0.18	-0.15	-0.15	-0.02	-0.02
		(0.7)	(0.6)	(0.6)	(0.1)	(0.1)
DUMMY		29.72	28.77			
		(2.1)	(2.1)			
R^2-Adj		0.40	0.38	0.27	0.19	0.17
SEE		28.22	28.40	30.64	29.27	28.74
DW		1.83	1.86	1.92	1.95	1.99
CHI-SQ.		3.90	4.04	3.99	5.42	5.77
LM		0.76	0.79	0.09	0.56	0.83
F-stat		5.35**	5.14**	5.14**	3.89**	3.71**

The dependent variable, in first differences, is consumption expenditure - CT is total consumption, CDT is consumption with some component of durable goods, CNDT is consumption of semi durables, non-durables and services, CNDS is consumption of non-durables and services, and CND is consumption of non-durables. GB is government debt and W is wealth. The superscripts 'a' and 'u' refer to the anticipated and unanticipated values, computed on the basis of the estimations, in first differences, presented in Table 5.3.

H_o: R.E. Expected Sign under the Null Hypothesis of Ricardian Equivalence.

The *t-statistics* are shown in parentheses. CHI-SQ statistic is the Box-Pierce statistic for a test that the residuals autocorrelations are jointly zero when there are no lagged dependent variables. The LM is the Jarque-Bera Asymptotic LM Normality test to test for the normality of the residuals. F-statistics tests for $GB^a_t = GB^u_t = 0$.

** Significant at the level of 5 per cent.

Source: Author's compilation.

5.4.2.2. Testing Ricardian Equivalence Hypothesis for India

The empirical results of estimating Equation 5.1 are presented in Table 5.5. In the case of the total final private consumption expenditure (Column 3) and its components (Columns 4–7), the results are consistently similar. The coefficient of the anticipated domestic debt is insignificant but that of the unanticipated component is significant. The joint hypothesis that the coefficients of the two component are insignificant ($\alpha_1 = \alpha_2 = 0$) is rejected in all the cases at the 5 per cent level of significance. Thus, the results do not support the Ricardian Equivalence Hypothesis.

The rejection of the Ricardian equivalence result in India can be due to many reasons, the important ones being (*a*) presence of imperfect capital market, and (*b*) presence of regulated interest rates.

In an attempt to test for the robustness of the results, this study has experimented with Equation 5.1, by including the lagged changes in consumption, thereby, testing for the hypothesis of habit formation. It is hypothesised that if the coefficient of lagged consumption is significant then the permanent income hypothesis under rational expectations is rejected. The results of our experiment are presented in Table 5.6. The coefficient of lagged consumption is insignificant in all the equations. Hence, the hypothesis of habit formation does not find support in India.

Table 5.6: Testing the robustness of results of Ricardian equivalence in India, 1971–95

	H_0:R.E. Expected sign	Consumption expenditure				
		CT	CDT	CNDT	CNDS	CND
1	2	3	4	5	6	7
Cons.		21.85	21.26	29.89	20.57	19.34
		(1.8)	(1.7)	(2.5)	(1.8)	(1.7)
C_{t-1}@		-0.22	-0.23	-0.29	-0.31	-0.30
		(0.9)	(1.0)	(1.1)	(1.2)	(1.3)
GB^a_t	=0	-0.19	0.19	0.07	0.14	-0.07
		(0.5)	(0.5)	(0.2)	(0.4)	(0.2)
GB^u_t	=0	0.56	0.55	0.66	0.55	0.48
		(2.5)	(2.5)	(3.0)	(2.6)	(2.4)

Table continued

Table 5.6: Testing the robustness of results of Ricardian equivalence in India, 1971–95

	H_0:R.E. Expected sign	Consumption expenditure				
		CT	CDT	CNDT	CNDS	CND
1	2	3	4	5	6	7
Z^u_t		-0.22	-0.20	-0.20	-0.08	-0.07
		(0.9)	(0.8)	(0.8)	(0.3)	(0.3)
DUMMY		27.44	26.23			
		(1.9)	(1.8)			
	·					
R^2-Adj		0.38	0.36	0.28	0.20	0.19
SEE		29.11	29.196	30.83	28.99	28.38
h-stat		!	!	!	!	!
LM		0.19	0.23	0.76	1.32	1.38
F-stat		3.54***	3.30***	4.54**	3.61**	2.76***

The dependent variable, in first differences, is consumption expenditure - CT is total consumption, CDT is consumption with some component of durable goods, CNDT is consumption of semi durables, non-durables and services, CNDS is consumption of non-durables and services, and CND is consumption of non-durables. GB is government debt and W is wealth. The superscripts 'a' and 'u' refer to the anticipated and unanticipated values, computed on the basis of the estimations, in first differences, presented in Table 5.3. @ Lag value of the respective measure of consumption.

H_0: R.E. Expected sign under the null hypothesis of Ricardian equivalence.

The *t-statistics* are shown in parentheses.! cannot be computed. The *LM* is the Jarque-Bera Asymptotic LM Normality test to test for the normality of the residuals. F-statistics tests for GB^a_t = GB^u_t = 0. ** Significant at the level of 5 per cent. *** Significant at the level of 10 per cent.

Source: Author's compilation.

The coefficients of the unanticipated component of domestic debt in all the regressions are similar to the results presented in Table 5.5. The anticipated component of domestic debt continues to be insignificant, while the coefficient of the unanticipated component of domestic debt is significant. Thus, the results imply the rejection of Ricardian equivalence in India.

5.5. Conclusions

It can be concluded on the basis of the empirical results that given the appropriate specification of the consumption function, the consumers in India do not exhibit Ricardian behaviour. This result is robust for different components of the private final consumption expenditure. Thus, given the permanent income specification under rational expectations, the private sector consumption pattern in India does not exhibit Ricardian behaviour. Total consumption expenditure, including expenditure on durable goods, yields similar results as the consumption expenditure on non-durables and services. In the Indian context, permanent income hypothesis under rational expectations holds. The data rejects the alternate hypothesis of habit formation.

Appendix 5.1

Data specification and construction

The primary data series are

- NY_t Net National Product (market prices) at 1980–81 prices.
- NGS_t Government Final Consumption Expenditure on goods and services at 1980–81 prices.
- NCT_t Total Private Final Consumption Expenditure at 1980–81 prices.
- NCD_t Private Final Consumption Expenditure on Durable Goods at 1980–81 prices.
- $NCSD_t$ Private Final Consumption Expenditure on Semi-durable Goods at 1980–81 prices.
- $NCND_t$ Private Final Consumption Expenditure on Non-Durable Goods at 1980–81 prices.
- NCS_t Private Final Consumption Expenditure on Services at 1980–81 prices.
- NGB_t Domestic debt held by the public in the beginning of the period.
- NSP_t Net Capital Stock in the private sector at real prices for the period 1980–81 to 1993–1994.
- $NCCF_t$ Net Capital Formation in the private sector at current prices for the period 1970–71 to 1979–80.
- $NTCF_t$ Net total capital Formation at current prices for the period 1970–71 to 1979–80.

$NTCRF_t$ Net Total Capital Formation at real prices for the period 1970–71 to 1979–80.

NYD_{St} Redemption Yield on short term (for one to five years) Central Government Securities (minimum of the range).

POP_t Population of India (mid-year).

DEF_t Implicit Price Deflator for net national product at market prices.

The following transformations were done to generate the variables used in the empirical estimation

$Y_t = NY_t/POP_t$

$GS_t = NGS_t/POP_t$

$CT_t = NCT_t/POP_t$

$CD_t = NCD_t/POP_t$

$CSD_t = NCSD_t/POP_t$

$CND_t = NCND_t/POP_t$

$CS_t = NCS_t/POP_t$

$CDT_t = 0.3*CD_t + CSD_t + CND_t + CS_t$

$CNDT_t = CSD_t + CND_t + CS_t$

$CNDS_t = CND_t + CS_t$

$YD_{St} = NYD_{St} - INF_t$

$INF_t = [DEF_t - DEF_{t-1}]/DEF_{t-1}]$

$GB_t = NGB_t/[(0.5*DEF_{t-1}*POP_{t-1}) + (0.5*DEF_t*POP_t)]$

$W_t = NW_t/[(0.5*POP_{t-1}) + (0.5*POP_t)]$

$NW_t = NSP_t (1982 - 1995)$

$NW_t = NSP_{t+1} - NCF_t (1970 - 1981)$

$NCF_t = NCCF_t*100/DCF_t$

$DCF_t = NTCF_t/NTCRF_t$

6

Monetisation of Debt in India

In India, the rising public debt has been supported by the central bank, the RBI. This trend has specially been followed since 1971. The rise in the support of the government debt by RBI has implications for the rising net-RBI credit to the government and consequently reserve money, money supply and the price level. This aspect of the rising monetised debt and its relationship with the price level has not been investigated earlier in the empirical work. The relationship between the monetised debt and the price level, and the monetary aggregates is investigated in this chapter.

In Section 6.1, an analytical model is discussed wherein the rising importance of monetised debt in the context of a small open economy is analysed. The implications derived from the Mundell-Fleming model suggest a close relationship between monetary aggregates and the price level in India. The rising trend in monetised debt and its relationship with other monetary aggregates is discussed in Section 6.2. The concept of Granger causality is briefly discussed in the next section. A brief critical review of the empirical literature on causality between the monetary aggregates and prices in India is presented in Section 6.4. The data base and the methodological issues for the causality test are discussed in Section 6.5 followed by a section on empirical results. Finally, the conclusions are presented in Section 6.7.

6.1. The analytical framework

In this section, an analytical framework on the implications of the rising monetised debt is developed. A brief review of the economic conditions prevailing in India during the period of the study is presented. This is followed by a discussion on the open economy model and the implications emerging therefrom.

6.1.1. The prevalent economic situation in India

The Indian economy has passed through a period of transition in the last five decades. The economic condition has changed especially since July 1991 when the current liberalisation measures were initiated. Therefore, a brief overview of the prevalent economic situation during the period, 1951 to 1995, relevant to the analysis of the open economy model, is presented in this subsection. The major relevant areas focussed in discussion are the exchange rate, capital mobility and trade restrictions, and interest rate and demand for money.

6.1.1.1. Exchange rate in India

India had been following a fixed exchange rate from 1947 till 1975 with its currency pegged to the pound sterling. During this period, major revisions in the exchange rate were made in June 1966, July 1972 and July 1975.[1] In view of instability in the exchange rate of the pound sterling during the early 1970's, the Indian rupee was delinked from the pound sterling with effect from 25 September 1975 and its value began to be determined with reference to a basket of currencies. Since then, the exchange rate of the rupee has been adjusted regularly on the basis of the weighted average of the exchange rate movements of the currencies of the major trading partners of India, with pound sterling serving as the intervention currency. Further, a downward adjustment of about 18 per cent in the external value of the rupee against the major currencies (US dollar, pound sterling, deutsche mark, Japanese yen and French franc) was effected in two steps on 1 and 3 July 1991.[2]

The exchange rate system in India was partially liberalised from 1 March 1992 with the introduction of partial convertibility of the rupee, followed by another round of liberalisation from 1 March 1993. Thus, the exchange rate in India, during this period has moved from the fixed exchange rate regime to the managed float. In addition, there have been regular adjustments in the exchange rate, apart from major revisions, which were necessitated from time to time, due to major problems of alignment with other currencies.[3]

6.1.1.2. Capital mobility in India and trade restrictions

In view of the need to conserve limited foreign exchange reserves for essential imports like petroleum goods, foodgrains and defence equipment, and also for the protection of the domestic industry, tariff barriers on imports have traditionally been high. This restrictive trade policy led to a limited growth in external trade. In addition, capital mobility has been strictly restricted and even the entry of multinationals in the country discouraged.

---

1   Since June 1966, regular adjustments were made in the exchange rates.
2   Ministry of Finance, Government of India (1992), 64.
3   Ministry of Finance, Government of India (1992), 64.

However, since 1991, gradual liberalisation has been attempted to integrate the domestic industry with the global economy. Consequently, trade barriers are being abolished, foreign investment is being encouraged and exchange control restrictions are being gradually removed. These liberalised policy measures have yet to yield results and therefore imperfect capital mobility still continues to prevail.

6.1.1.3. Interest rate and demand for money

The interest rate structure in India is closely monitored and all the interest rates are administered. In addition, the interest rates are sticky towards the lower end, to make financial resources available to the government (needed for investment purposes) at low cost.[4] There have been a large number of empirical studies investigating the demand for money function in India.[5] These studies conclude that real income is the predominant factor in explaining the demand for money. The demand for money is not found to be sensitive to interest rates in India, in view of the administered interest rate regime.[6] Rangarajan (1995) emphasises the stability of the money demand function in India.[7]

6.1.2. The open economy model for a small economy

In view of the discussion in the previous section, the Indian economy can be characterised by, (a) fixed exchange rate, rigidly till 1966 and with regular adjustments till 1975, and closely managed float since then; (b) high tariff barriers; (c) restrictive policies leading to imperfect capital mobility; and (d) administered interest rate regime. In this section, the open economy model is analysed in the context of fixed exchange rate with imperfect capital mobility.

The open economy model, applicable to a small open economy, has been developed by Mundell (1968) and Fleming (1962). This model is basically an

---

4   To illustrate, the discount rate on 91 day Treasury bills fixed at 4.6 per cent in 1974 continues to prevail so far. The discussion, in detail, is presented in Chapter 2 (Sections 2.2.1.1.3 and 2.2.1.2.1).

5   The important ones are Gujarati (1968), Gupta (1979), Brahmananda (1980), and Bhole (1985).

6   Report of the Committee to Review the Working of the Monetary System, Reserve Bank of India, (1985), 143.

7   The reserve money multiplier in India is predictable on a quarterly basis (Chitre, 1986). The demand for currency and deposits also show they are stable and can be behaviourally explained (RBI, 1985, 103,). Rangarajan and Singh (1984) conclude for the 1970s that reserve money and money stock in India are closely related.

open economy version of the traditional *IS-LM* model. The main equations of the Mundell-Fleming model are the following,

(a) $Y = E(r - \pi, Y) + CA(\varepsilon, Y)$ \hfill Equation 6.1

(b) $M/p = L(r, Y)$ \hfill Equation 6.2

(c) $BP = CA(\varepsilon, Y) + NCF(r - r^* - Ee)$ \hfill Equation 6.3

(d) $M = m.H$ \hfill Equation 6.4

where, Y is income, r is interest rate, π is expected inflation, ε is real exchange rate, M is nominal money, P is price level, BP is balance of payments, r^* is foreign interest rate, Ee is expected rate of change in domestic currency, and H is base (reserve) money. The real exchange rate can be defined as $\varepsilon = P/eP^*$, where, e is nominal exchange rate and P^* is foreign price level.

The first equation describes the goods market and expresses the *IS* curve relating the savings, investments, government expenditure and net exports. The second equation is the *LM* equation reflecting the money market equilibrium. The third equation reflects the relationship between the trade balance and the net capital inflow from abroad. Finally, the fourth equation is the money supply equation, where the money supply is endogenous and depends on the base money.

In the Equation 6.3, net capital flow is expressed as a function of the domestic interest rate, foreign interest rate and the expected rate of change in the domestic currency. In the case of India, domestic interest rates are controlled by the government and the monetary authority, while the world interest rate is given. In the fixed exchange rate regime, in the long run, the exchange rate is not expected to fluctuate. Therefore, Equation 6.3 would reduce to,

$BP = CA(\varepsilon, Y)$. \hfill Equation 6.3′

The equation system above (Equations 6.1, 6.2, 6.3′ and 6.4) is linearised around equilibrium. In the model, in the short run, the endogenous variables are Y, M, P and BP. The price level and expected inflation is assumed to be fixed ($P = \bar{P}$ and $\pi = \bar{\pi}$). Therefore, $dP = d\pi = 0$. Hence, in analysing the relationship between monetised debt and the price level, the discussion is focussed on the long run.

The endogenous variables, in the long run, in the model are: M, π, P and BP. Taking total differentials of the Equations 6.1, 6.2, 6.3′, and 6.4, it can be derived that

$dY = E_{r-\pi}(dr - d\pi) + E_Y dY + CA_\varepsilon d\varepsilon + CA_Y dY$ \hfill Equation 6.1′

$(1/p)dM - (M/p^2)dP = L_r dr + L_Y dY$ \hfill Equation 6.2′

$dBP = CA_\varepsilon d\varepsilon + CA_Y dY$ 　　　　　　　　　　　　　　Equation 6.3''

$dM = m.dH$ 　　　　　　　　　　　　　　　　　　　　Equation 6.4'

In the long run, under the fixed exchange rate regime, $d\pi = dBP = 0$ and the growth in output is equal to the natural rate of growth, therefore, $dY = dY^n = 0$, where Y^n is the natural rate of growth. Further, under the administered interest rate regime $dr = 0$. Substituting these values in the model, it can be derived that

$0 = CA_\varepsilon d\varepsilon$ 　　　　　　　　　　　　　　　　　　　　Equation 6.1''

$(1/p)dM - (M/p^2)dP = 0$ 　　　　　　　　　　　　　　Equation 6.2''

$0 = CA_\varepsilon d\varepsilon$ 　　　　　　　　　　　　　　　　　　　　Equation 6.3'''

$dM = m.dH$ 　　　　　　　　　　　　　　　　　　　　Equation 6.4''

Solving further, it can be derived that,

$(dM/M) = (dP/P)$ 　　　　　　　　　　　　　　　　Equation 6.5

or

$dP = (P/M)dM$ 　　　　　　　　　　　　　　　　　Equation 6.6

Equations 6.5 and 6.6 imply that changes in the price level are proportional to changes in the money supply. Further substitution of the value of dM from Equation 6.4'' gives,

$dP = (P/M)m.dH$ 　　　　　　　　　　　　　　　　Equation 6.7

Equation 6.7 relates changes in reserve money and the price level. An important component of reserve money is the monetised debt.

It has been emphasised by monetarists generally, and by Buchanan and Wagner (1977) especially, that a monetised deficit results in raising the price level. The central bank could be passively monetising the rising debt to hold down the interest rates on government securities. King and Plosser (1985) investigate the time series relationship between debt growth and seigniorage, and seigniorage and inflation, in the United States and 12 other developed countries, but find no positive correlation between the two.[8] For the developing countries, there are a very few studies analysing such a relationship. Buiter and Patel (1992) conclude that in India, seigniorage increases with the rate of inflation. Gupta (1992) concludes, on the basis of results from nine developing countries in Asia, that deficits and seigniorage are closely related.[9]

8 　These are the United States, the United Kingdom, France, Germany, Italy, Switzerland, Japan, Spain, Argentina, Brazil, Chile, Mexico and Korea.

9 　These are India, Indonesia, South Korea, Malaysia, Pakistan, Philippines, Singapore and Sri Lanka.

In this chapter, the relationship between the monetised debt and the price level, and that between the monetised debt and other monetary aggregates is investigated. The empirical analysis is further extended to investigate the relationship between various monetary aggregates and the price level. In India, some empirical studies have established the relationship between money supply and prices. The hypotheses being investigated is that the rise in monetised debt is a major cause of growth in the monetary aggregates and the price level. The hypothesis, to be empirically examined in Section 6.6, can be specified as follows, where, '→' indicates the hypothised direction of causation:

(a) Monetised debt → Reserve Money

(b) Monetised debt → Money supply

(c) Monetised debt → Prices

(d) Reserve Money → Money Supply

(e) Reserve Money → Prices

(f) Money Supply → Prices

6.2. Importance of monetised debt in relation to the monetary aggregates and the price level

In this section, the rising trend of monetisation of debt and its importance to other monetary aggregates is established. The monetisation of debt has regularly been used as a substitute for other fiscal instruments during wars, famines\floods, and other external shocks. The increasing use of monetisation of debt has led to the rise in the money supply and prices.

6.2.1. Monetised debt as an important component of the reserve money

In the previous section, it was derived that the open economy model implies a correlation in changes between the monetary base and prices. In this subsection, the sources of the reserve (base) money are presented. The rising importance of monetised debt in the composition of reserve money emerges in the discussion.

Monetisation of Debt in India 151

In India, the main sources of reserve money are net RBI credit to government (NRBIG),[10] RBI credit to banks,[11] RBI credit to the commercial sector,[12] net foreign exchange assets of the RBI,[13] government's currency liabilities to the public,[14] and net non-monetary liabilities of RBI.[15] The most important of these sources is net RBI credit to government which represents the domestic debt held by RBI, netted against any deposits of the Government held by it (Table 6.1). Hence, in analysing the impact of RBI's holdings of government debt, generally referred to as monetised debt, this measure is considered appropriate.[16]

---

10   RBI credit to government, both central and the state governments, specifically, comprises of following: (*i*) Rupee securities held in Issue Department; (*ii*) Treasury bills purchased and discounted; (*iii*) Investments in government securities (Total investment of Banking Department less investments other than government securities including foreign securities held in investment account); (*iv*) Rupee coins in Issue and Banking Departments; and (*v*) Loans and advances to state governments. Item (*iv*) needs further clarification. The RBI comes to acquire the government currency as the central government's agent for distribution of currency to the public as well as a backing against its own currency. The government currency appears as an asset in the balance sheet of RBI. The amount of this component is very small and the inherent nature of this component reveals that there are not many short-term variations. The rupee coins held in Issue Department of RBI, where most of these are held, as a percentage of net RBI credit to government declined from 11.8 per cent in 1951 to 6.3 per cent in 1961, 1.4 per cent in 1971, 0.4 per cent in 1981, and negligible amount in 1991. Thus, it is a insignificant component.

11   Against security of government bonds, usance bills, or promissory notes and through the purchase or rediscounting of bills.

12   Aggregate of the RBI's investments in shares/bonds of financial institutions, loans and advances to financial institutions, and internal bills purchased and discounted.

13   The gross foreign exchange assets of the RBI comprise (*i*) gold coin and bullion; (*ii*) foreign securities including those held in investment account; and (*iii*) balances held abroad. The foreign exchange liabilities represented by the IMF Account No. 1 less the portion of India's IMF quota subscription and some other payments in rupees are subtracted from this balance to arrive at net foreign exchange assets of the RBI.

14   Comprises one-rupee notes and coins and small coins. The government directly controls only the total issue of its currency but within narrow limits.

15   Consists of owned funds of the RBI held in various forms as reserves, contributions to national funds and compulsory deposits of the public. The net non-monetary liabilities imply the excess of non-monetary liabilities over other assets. These other assets refer to advances to certain commercial banks under special arrangements in respect of their investments abroad apart from traditional items like premises, fixtures, etc.

16   An important advantage of using this series is its availability from 1951. In contrast, data on ownership pattern of public debt, discussed in Chapter 2, is based on surveys and is available on a consistent basis from 1959.

Table 6.1: Sources of reserve money

(per cent)

Year (end-March)	RBI's credit to the			Net foreign exchange assets of RBI	Govt.'s currency liability to the public	Net non-monetary liabilities of RBI	Total (2+3+4+ 5+ 6-7)
	Govt. (net)@	Banks	Comm. Sect.				
1	2	3	4	5	6	7	8
1951	30.96	3.90	0.07	58.97	16.19	10.07	100.00
1961	84.95	8.33	0.40	8.28	9.23	11.20	100.00
1971	79.08	14.02	2.60	11.18	7.98	14.85	100.00
1981	81.08	6.73	9.06	25.07	3.29	25.24	100.00
1991	101.22	11.40	7.22	9.09	1.85	30.78	100.00
1995	59.95	7.96	3.89	44.14	1.41	17.34	100.00

@ Refers to the monetised debt. Comm. Sect. refers to the commercial sector.

Source: RBI.

The growth in reserve money is closely related to the increase in monetised debt (Figure 6.1). The sudden spurt in monetised debt during 1955 to 1957 was due to lack of public support for the government's market borrowing programme as a result of slack money market conditions, which consequently had to be supported by the RBI. The financial resources were required for investment purposes by the government.[17] The spurts in 1962–63 and 1965–66 were due to the war expenditure with China and Pakistan, respectively. The other big spurt in monetised debt during 1971–73 is due to the war with Pakistan and the influx of refugees from Bangladesh in 1971.[18] The increase in monetised debt during 1979–81 is result of the expansionary fiscal policy during 1977 and 1978. In 1979, national income, at real prices, declined by 5.3 per cent while agriculture and industrial production declined by 15.5 per cent (due to drought) and 1.4 per cent, respectively. In view of the decline in production, but increased expenditure on drought and natural calamities' relief and certain committed expenditures, and decline in external aid, increasing reliance was placed on net RBI credit to

---

17 Monetised deficit accounted for 24.4 per cent of total plan outlay in the Second Five Year Plan (1956–61).

18 The number of refugees from Bangladesh had reached ten million by December 1971. 7 million of these were housed in government camps (Ministry of Finance, Government of India ,1972, 44).

government. The increase in monetised debt, consistently since 1985, was due to increased relief expenditure on agriculture in the form of subsidy (food and fertiliser), because of a negative growth rate in the agriculture sector during 1984–85, 1986–88, and 1991–92.

Figure 6.1: Monetised debt and reserve money: Annual growth, (1952-95)

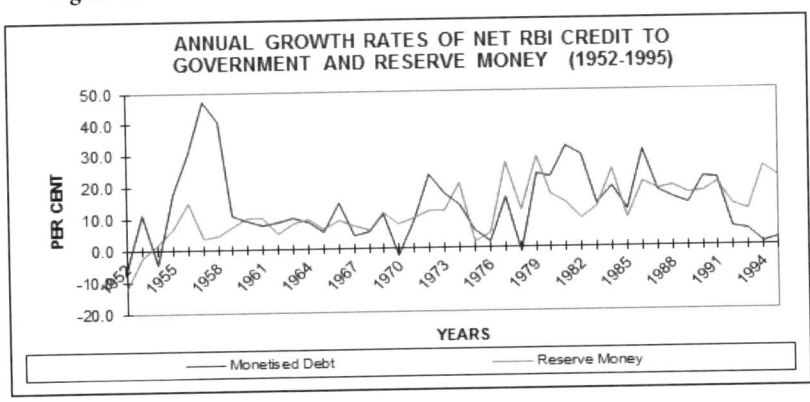

Source: RBI.

Since 1991, a concerted effort was made by the government to control the rise in net RBI credit to government. These steps included offering market related returns on Treasury bills, and government securities, and conducting active open market operations. The increase in reserve money since the early 90s, in a divergent trend from monetised debt, is due to increase in the foreign exchange reserves, firstly, as a result of rise in foreign aid from the IMF and the World Bank,[19] and secondly, due to opening up of the Indian economy and consequent inflow of foreign investment.

6.2.2. Monetised debt, money supply and prices

The money stock measures generally used in India are the narrow (M1)[20] and broad money (M3).[21] The relationship in annual growth rate of monetised debt,

---

19 External debt owed to the IMF increased from US $ 1.5 billion at end of March 1990 to $ 4.3 billion at end of March 1995. Similarly, external debt under multilateral arrangements increased from US $ 18.4 billion to $ 26.1 billion over the similar period, respectively.

20 Narrow money consists of (*i*) currency notes and coins with the public (excluding cash on hand of all banks); (*ii*) demand deposits (excluding interbank deposits) of all commercial and cooperative banks; and (*iii*) other deposits held with RBI.

21 Broad Money consists of (*i*) M1; and (*ii*) time deposits of all commercial and cooperative banks (excluding inter-bank time deposits).

reserve money and money supply are presented in Figures 6.2 and 6.3. These two figures exhibit a close relationship between monetised debt and reserve money, and the two measures of money supply.[22]

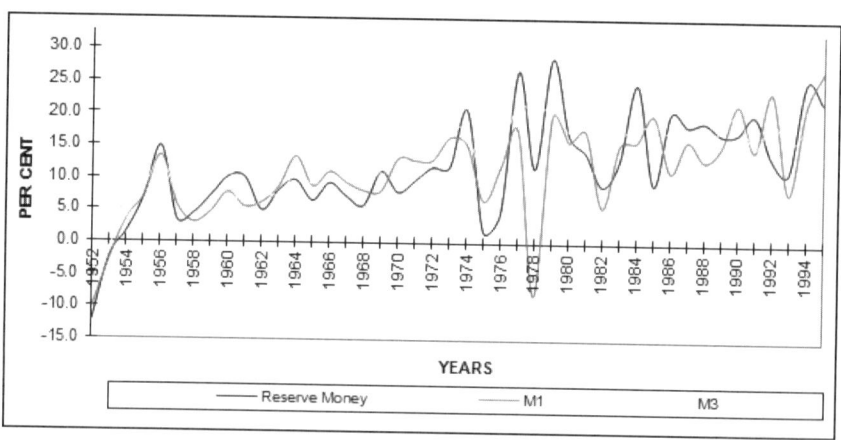

Figure 6.2: Monetised debt and money supply: Annual growth (1952–95)

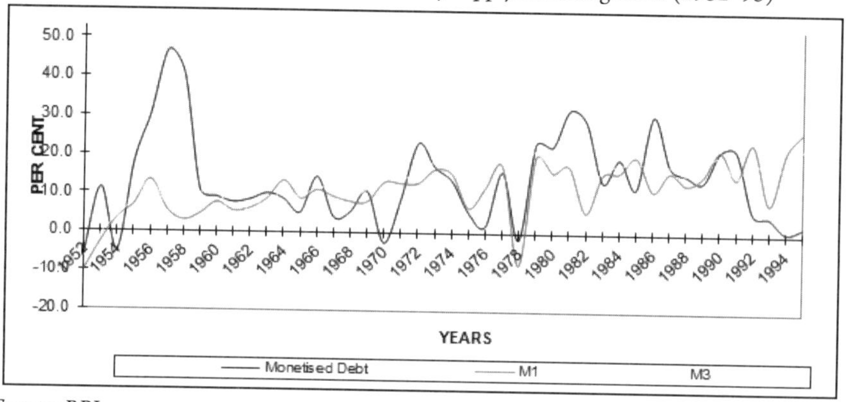

Source: RBI.

Figure 6.3: Reserve money and money supply: Annual growth (1952–95)

Source: RBI.

The dip in the M3 series at 1961 and the M1 series at 1978, in Figure 6.2, is due to revision in the concept, definition and compilation of money supply in India.[23] In case of the M1 series, cause of the substantial decline is the revision

---

22 Rangarajan and Singh (1984) conclude for the 1970s that reserve money and money stock are closely related in India.

23 Reports of the Working Group on Money Supply in India, 1961 and 1977.

in definition of the demand and time liabilities of the saving deposits.[24] Demand deposits constitute a part of narrow money while time deposits are included in broad money. Consequently, the banks, on various dates, starting from January 1978 to January 1981, but mainly in 1980 (April to June),[25] began to classify a large proportion of their savings deposits as time deposits and a lower proportion as demand liabilities.[26]

The role of monetised debt in relation to various money supply measures is presented in Table 6.2. The importance of borrowing by the government from the RBI is revealed from the monetary ratios as well as the incremental ratios (ratio of change in the two variables). In a number of years, change in monetised debt has been causing a one-to-one change in the monetary aggregates, especially reserve money and narrow money (Bhalla, 1981b; Minhas, 1987). The measures to sterilise the expansionary effect of rising monetised debt were being fully exploited. The cash reserve ratio rose from 3 per cent in 1973 to nearly 15 per cent (effectively) in 1984,[27] where it has been since then.[28] The statutory liquidity ratio[29] for the commercial banks rose from 26 per cent in 1970 to 30 per cent in 1973 and further to 35 per cent in 1984 and 38.5 per cent in 1991. Since 1991, this has recorded a decline and is estimated at 29.5 per cent in 1995.[30]

---

24 Till March 1978, there was no uniformity in classification of savings deposits. The banks determined the demand component of their savings deposits on the basis of the maximum amount a depositor could withdraw. Banks were advised by RBI to follow a uniform pattern in October 1977.
25 This pertains to the first quarter of fiscal year 1980–81. In India, as mentioned in Chapter 2, a fiscal year pertains to the period 1 April to 31 March.
26 RBI (1981), 86, and RBI (1991), 246.
27 Ministry of Finance, Government of India (1990), 103.
28 Cash reserve ratio was reduced to 14 per cent in 1993 but raised again to 15 per cent in 1994.
29 Applicable to net demand and time liabilities.
30 Ministry of Finance, Government of India (1995), 45.

Table 6.2: Monetary ratios

Year (end-March)	Monetary ratios			Incremental monetary ratios		
	RM/MD	M1/MD	M3/MD	RM/MD	M1/MD	M3/MD
1	2	3	4	5	6	7
1952	3.02	4.18	4.92	6.67	7.56	5.56
1961	1.18	1.51	2.09	1.50	1.10	0.60
1971	1.26	1.94	2.89	1.38	2.73	4.50
1981	1.23	1.54	3.66	0.63	0.94	2.43
1991	0.99	1.05	2.99	0.93	0.75	2.21
1995	1.67	1.89	5.23	14.05	18.68	44.26

Incremental monetary ratios refer to the ratio of change in the two variables.
RM is reserve money, MD is the monetised debt, M1 is narrow money and M3 is broad money
Source: RBI.

In India, many studies have emphasised the applicability of monetarist theory to India, whereby a rise in the money supply directly affects the price level.[31] Figures 6.4 and 6.5 show a close relationship between these variables.

Figure 6.4: Monetised debt, reserve money and prices: Annual growth (1952–95)

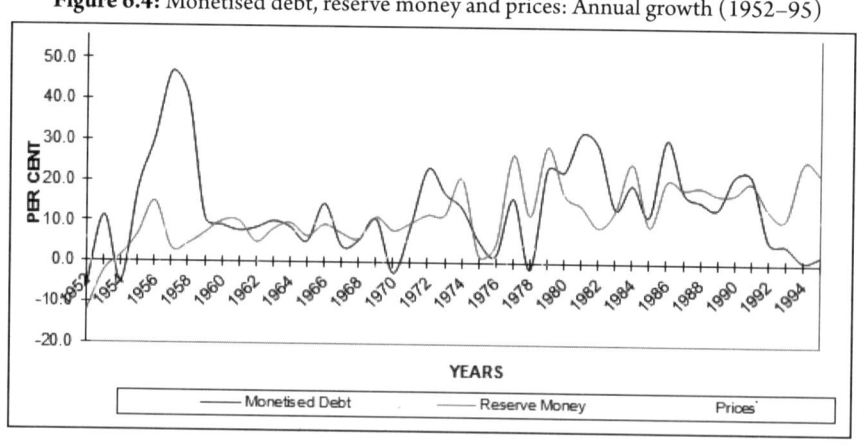

Source: RBI.

---

31 Brahmananda (1974, 1977), Bhalla (1981b), RBI (1985) and Minhas (1987).

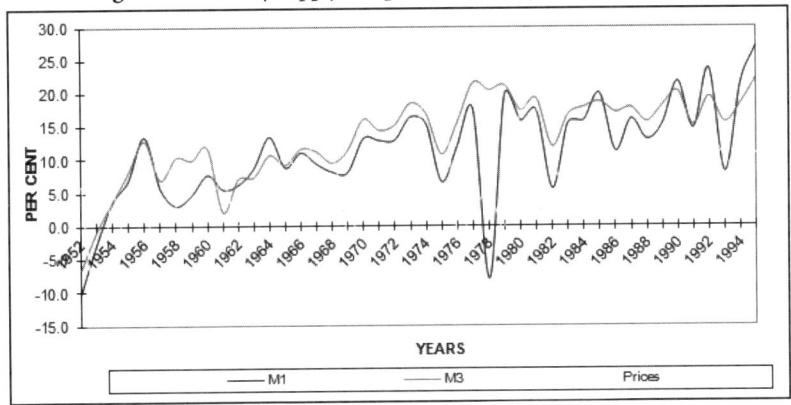

Figure 6.5: Money supply and prices: Annual growth (1952–95)

Source: RBI.

The spurts in the price level during the period can be explained in terms of external shocks to the economy as well as to the imbalance between the growth in the monetary variables and in the real sector. The spurt in prices during 1957 is due to high investment, low savings, expansionary fiscal policy and monetary policy followed in 1956 and 1957. The continuous high rate of growth in the price level during 1962 to 1968 is due to many reasons – war (1962, 1965 and 1966); devaluation of the currency by 36.5 per cent in June 1966, causing a rise in prices of imported goods; droughts (1962, 1965 and 1966); and decontrol of prices of many commodities between 1963 and 1966; increase in monetised debt in 1962, 1963 and 1966; increase in M1 and M3 during 1961–64 and in 1966.

The increase in the price level during 1971–75 has also been due to several reasons. The important ones being the war with Pakistan in December 1971, droughts in certain parts of India and floods in certain others in 1971, followed by consecutive droughts in 1972 and 1973. The rise in monetised debt during 1970–72 and in money supply during 1969–73 are important causes of rise in price level. The oil price hike by OPEC during 1973–75 also had an impact on general prices in India during the period.[32] The decline in prices in 1976 was due to strict and determined action against hoarding and blackmarketing initiated by

---

32 The unit value index of imports of petroleum crude increased from 135 in 1973 to 736 in 1975 and 829 in 1976, while the quantum index rose from 198 to 239 and 234, during the similar period, respectively. The impact on the general domestic prices can be captured from the movements in the wholesale price index of the group 'petroleum crude and natural gas.' The Wholesale Price Index (Base 1970-71=100) of this group increased from 142 in 1973 to 687 in 1975 and 700 in 1976.

the government, in view of the deteriorating economic situation in the country and tightening of the monetary policy. Figures 6.4 and 6.5 show that the growth in monetised debt and money supply declined in the period preceding the decline in the price level. The price rise since 1979 is again due to a number of reasons – the expansionary monetary and fiscal policy in 1978 and 1979; the drought of 1979, causing a decline in hydro generation, agriculture and industrial production; and a rise in prices of petroleum goods in 1979.

Thus, in this section, the importance of monetised debt in India is discussed. The government had to increasingly resort to monetisation of debt due to wars and drought conditions during this period which led to increase in money supply and prices.

6.3. The concept and test of Granger causality in economics

In this section, a brief discussion on the concept of Granger causality in economics is presented. This is followed by a brief description of the Granger causality test used in the empirical estimation of the hypothesis discussed in section 6.1.

6.3.1: The concept of Granger causality in economics

The concept of causality in economics was formalised by Granger (1969), who built on the earlier work of Wiener (1956). The definition of causality given by Granger is purely statistical and is not an acceptable definition of causation for most philosophers of science (Bunge, 1959). Rather Granger's definition refers to the more limited concept of predicability[33] and this limitation is acknowledged and recognised by use of the term 'Granger causality' in econometrics. The present work, refers to causality in the Grangerian sense.

6.3.2: Tests of Granger causality in economics

There are various tests popularly employed to test for Granger causality in economics. These tests, surveyed in Pierce and Haugh (1977), can be basically categorised into three groups: cross-correlation tests, cross-spectral tests and the direct tests. In case of direct tests, the three popular tests are given by Granger (1969), Sims (1972) and Geweke (1982).[34]

---

33 Granger (1969) causality is based on two important axioms (i) The past and present may cause the future but the future cannot predict the past; and (ii) all causal relationships remain invariant in direction through time.

34 Geweke's test can be considered as a modified Sims' test, where the lagged values of the dependent variable are included in the equation to correct for serial correlation.

It is difficult to rank these tests in terms of their statistical properties as concluded by Guilkey and Salemi (1982), Nelson and Schwert (1982), and Geweke, Meese and Dent (1983). Feige and Pearce (1979) show that results of causality tests are sensitive to the use of filters applied to make the series stationary, and that different causality tests yield different conclusions. However, Guilkey and Salemi (1982) suggest that Granger's test is superior to the Sims' test, because of its computational simplicity and a smaller loss of degrees of freedom. Geweke, Meese and Dent (1983) show different results are derived on the basis of different test statistics employed. Roberts and Nord (1985) argue that the results are sensitive to the functional form specification in a Sims' type of test. Thornton and Batten (1985) conclude that causality tests are sensitive to the lag length.

6.3.2.1. Granger's test

This test is based on the procedure, not actually suggested but implicitly contained, in Granger (1969). This test is simple and therefore extensively used in empirical literature. The test can be briefly explained as follows. Let X_t and Y_t be two stationary time series. The test then can be explained by the following model,

$$X_t = \sum_{j=1}^{m} \alpha_j X_{t-j} + \sum_{j=1}^{m} \beta_j Y_{t-j} + \varepsilon_t$$

$$Y_t = \sum_{j=1}^{m} \delta_j X_{t-j} + \sum_{j=1}^{m} \lambda_j Y_{t-j} + \eta_t$$

Equation 6.16

where, the error terms, ε_t and η_t are assumed to be uncorrelated. The lag term, m, is assumed to be finite and shorter than the time series. The test is sensitive to the lag length but Hsiao (1981) suggests a simple method to select the lag length (discussed in the next subsection).

The definition of causality would imply that Y_t is causing X_t ($Y_t \rightarrow X_t$), if some β_j is significant. Similarly, X_t is causing Y_t ($X_t \rightarrow Y_t$), if some δ_j is not insignificant. If both events occur, then feedback relationship exists between the two variables ($X_t \leftrightarrow Y_t$).

6.3.2.1.1. Selection of lag length for Granger test

The selection of the appropriate lag length of the variables in the equation is important for the Granger test as it is sensitive to the lag length. Hsiao (1981) suggests a solution to the lag selection problem through the use of Final Prediction Error (FPE) of Akaike (1969). Hsiao argues that the method of FPE is robust as it balances the risk arising out of a bias when a lower order is selected and the risk due to increase in variance when higher order is selected. This selection procedure allows a variable to depend on a subset of variables under consideration and allows each variable to enter the equation with a different lag. Thornton and Batten (1985) examine three different methods of lag selection for causality tests. These methods are the Hsiao's (1981) FPE procedure, the Bayesian estimation criterion outlined by Geweke and Meese (1981), and the technique suggested by Pagano and Hartley (1981). Thornton and Batten conclude that the FPE criterion performs well in the selection of an appropriate model.

6.4. Review of literature on causality between monetary aggregates and price level in India

There have been a large number of empirical studies analysing the relationship between two variables since the Granger's (1969) and Sims' (1972) papers on causality. The causal relationships investigated include that between money and prices, wages and prices, monetary aggregates, interest rates and stock prices, exchange rates and money supply, and money and income. Feige and Pearce (1976 and 1979) provide a brief survey on empirical work on these causality tests.

In India, no study has analysed the causal relationship between monetised debt and prices, and between monetised debt and other monetary aggregates. The major empirical work on Granger causality between money supply and prices is summarised in Table 6.3. These studies have used various methods of causality. The data employed in the estimation has also varied between monthly, quarterly and annual series. The results consistently support the hypothesis that direction of causality flows from money supply to prices.

In most of the empirical work that has been attempted in India on direction of causality between monetary aggregates and prices, the time series employed has only been for about two decades (exceptions are Biswas and Saunders, 1990; and Jadhav, 1994). The period of two decades is comparatively short for such an analysis, firstly, to capture the long term trend in these variables, and secondly, due to limitations of a small sample size. To increase the number of observations, many studies have resorted to the monthly data. In case of a developing country like India, where forces of demand and supply are not market-operated due to demand constraints and supply bottlenecks, monthly data may not be appropriate[35]

---
35   Rangarajan and Singh (1984).

Therefore, annual or quarterly data is considered appropriate for analysis in the Indian context.

Table 6.3: Important empirical studies on causality between the monetary aggregates and the price level in India

S. No	Study and year	Data specification	Causality test employed	Variables	Conclusions
1	Bhalla (1981b)	Quarterly, 1956–76	Granger's, Sims' and Cross-correlation test	M1 and CPI	M1→CPI
2	Ramachandra (1983)	Annual, 1951–71	Sims' test	M1 and ID	M1→ID
3	Sharma (1984)	Quarterly, 1962–80	Sims' test	M1, M3 and WPI	M1→WPI; M3↔WPI
4	Bhattacharya and Sharma (1985)	Monthly, 1960–83	Cross-correlation test	M1 and WPI	M1→WPI (1960–78) WPI→M1 (1978–83)
5	Nachane and Nadkarni (1985)	Quarterly, 1960–82	Sims', McClave-Hsiao, cross-correlation, and transfer function tests	M1, M3, H and WPI	WPI→H ; H→M1 H→M3 M1→WPI; M3→WPI
6	Ray and Namboodri (1988)	Monthly, 1971–86	Cross-correlation test	M3, H and WPI	M3←|→H ; M3⇔H M3←|→WPI; M3⇐|⇒WPI
7	Singh (1989)	Quarterly, 1971–87	Granger's and Sims' test	M3 and WPI	M3↔WPI

Table continued

Table 6.3: Important empirical studies on causality between the monetary aggregates and the price level in India

S. No	Study and year	Data specification	Causality test employed	Variables	Conclusions
8	Biswas and Saunders (1990)	Quarterly, 1957–86	Granger's test	H, M1, M2, CPI and WPI	H↔CPI; H↔WPI M1↔CPI; M1↔WPI M3↔CPI; M3↔WPI
9	Jadhav (1994)	Annual, 1956–88	Granger's and Sims' test	M3 and ID	M3→ID

'→' refers to direction of causality, '⇒' refers to direction of instantaneous causality, '↔' refers to causal feedback, '⇔' refers to instantaneous causal feedback, '←|→' refers to lack of causal relationship, '⇐|⇒' refers to lack of instantaneous causal relationship.

Key: ID = Income Deflator; H = Monetary Base; M1 = Narrow Money; M3 = Broad Money; WPI = Wholesale Price Index; CPI = Consumer Price Index.

Source: Author's compilation.

The study by Nadkarni and Nachane (1985) is robust in statistical techniques and in use of quarterly data series, but the period of study is limited to 1960–82. Biswas and Saunders (1990) determine the lag length on basis of the FPE criterion and use quarterly data for the period 1956–86. But both these studies suffer from two major problems. Firstly, in India, the major problem of the large monetisation of debt began in the early 1970s and peaked in the early 1990s which is not captured in these studies. Secondly, and more importantly, the data base of the monetary aggregates has undergone two major changes, first in 1961 and the other during 1977–81. These two studies only provide summary results and do not give the coefficients of the variables nor mention about the behaviour of the residuals or of the adjustments made to the series to attain normality in the residuals.[36] Jadhav (1994) uses annual data for the period 1956–88 and fixes the lag lengths arbitrarily. Hence, given that causality tests are sensitive to lag length, these results cannot be considered reliable.

In India, there have been few attempts to study the relationship between reserve money and prices. Nadkarni and Nachane (1985) conclude that causality runs from prices to reserve money. Biswas and Saunders (1990), using Granger's test for two periods, 1956–86 and 1962–80, report a feedback relationship between the variables.

---

36 In the empirical work attempted here, both series on money supply show an outlier at the point of revision in the data. This is discussed in Section 6.5.2.2.

6.5. Data base and the methodological issues pertaining to empirical estimation

In this section, the data base of the study is discussed. This is followed by a discussion on the methodological issues pertaining to stationarity of data and selection of lag length.

6.5.1. Data base employed in empirical estimation

The period of reference for this study is 1951–95 for the annual and 1971–95 for the quarterly series. The annual data for the period 1971–95 is available in different publications of RBI. The data for the period 1951–70 has been collected and generated through various published sources of the RBI and the Government of India. The reason for restricting the use of quarterly series to 1971–95 is the non-availability of consistent data on money supply prior to this period.

The data series used are narrow ($M1$) and broad money ($M3$), reserve money (RM), net RBI credit to government as monetised debt (MD), and the wholesale price index (P). It is important to mention here that there has been a revision in the concept of money supply in India in 1961 and 1977, consequent to the suggestions made by the two Reports of the Working Group on Money Supply in India, respectively.[37] The available annual series for the period 1951 to 1970 on narrow money and broad money already incorporated the revision suggested by the First Report. The Report of 1977 (Second Group) was very important for this study, as the revision in the concept and compilation of data series on money supply was carried out for the period 1970 onwards. However, the Report itself contains revised series from 1970 to 1976 on annual and monthly basis (March 1970 to September 1976). As a result, revised annual data since 1970–71 is available on a consistent basis, but for the previous years, the old data series on the two measures of money supply, which were broadly similar to the new, have been used.[38] The revision in the compilation process was carried out by the reporting banks during 1978 to 1981. However, in the empirical section, equations have been separately estimated, where ever suggested by the Chow test, for the shorter annual period 1971–95.

---

37 RBI (1961 and 1971).

38 Prior to this revision, two money stock measures were available in India– money supply with the public and the aggregate monetary resources. These two measures were similar to the new measures of $M1$ and $M3$, respectively. For example, money supply with the public for financial year ending 1970 was placed at ₹ 63.4 billion while figures for $M1$ were ₹ 65.4 billion. Similarly, aggregate monetary resources for the similar period were placed at ₹ 93.4 billion while $M3$ amounted to ₹ 96.4 billion.

The quarterly series has been constructed from monthly data. The monthly data from April 1970 to October 1975 has been collected from the above mentioned Second Report.[39] The data for the period November 1975 to March 1978 has been collected from various monthly bulletins of the RBI. The data for the period April 1978 to March 1995 has been collected from annual publications of the RBI. The monthly data was deseasonalised using the Census X-11 method before computing their quarterly averages.

6.5.2. Methodological issues

In this subsection, two important issues pertaining to stationarity of time series data used in causality test, and selection of appropriate lags by the FPE criterion are discussed.

6.5.2.1. Stationarity of time series data

The data series to be used for estimation of the causality test are required to be in covariance stationary form. There are various methods to achieve stationarity in data, most popular being the use of *ad hoc* filters (Sims, 1972) and differencing of time series. To test for stationarity of the series, the concept of unit roots has been used (Table 6.4). The results reveal that first differences of data series in logs are stationary. Generally, the data series are stationary at the significant level of one per cent, but the annual data series for the period 1951–95 for monetised debt and broad money, are stationary at the 5 per cent level of significance.

Table 6.4: Testing for stationarity of the series – The unit roots-augmented Dickey-Fuller test

Variables	Levels		First differences	
	C	C and T	C	C and T
1	2	3	4	5
A. Annual: 1951–95				
MD	-0.92(1)	-2.37(1)	-3.96(0)*	-3.96(0)**
RM	4.29(1)	-0.33(1)	-4.77(0)*	-7.48(0)*
MI	4.63(1)	0.12(1)	-5.35(0)*	-8.24(0)*
M3	3.09(1)	-1.66(1)	-2.98(0)**	-4.85(0)*
P	0.87(1)	-3.11(1)	-4.61(0)*	-5.02(0)*
B. Quarterly: 1971–95				
MD	-0.57(3)	-1.44(3)	-7.34(0)*	-7.35(0)*
RM	1.29(3)	-2.44(3)	-8.49(0)*	-8.75(0)*
MI	1.10(2)	-1.32(2)	-7.98(0)*	-8.09(0)*

Table continued

---

39 RBI (1977), 46–63.

Table 6.4: Testing for stationarity of the series – The unit roots-augmented Dickey-Fuller test

Variables	Levels		First differences	
	C	C and T	C	C and T
1	2	3	4	5
M3	0.53(2)	-2.78(2)	-7.04(0)*	-7.00(0)*
P	-0.47(0)	-1.81(0)	-5.27(0)*	-5.24(0)*

C = Constant. T = Trend. MD is monetised debt, RM is reserve money, M1 is narrow money, M3 is broad money and P is price level.

Figures in parenthesis are lag values chosen to ensure that the residuals are white noise. * Significant at 1 per cent. ** Significant at 5 per cent.

Source: Author's compilation.

6.5.2.2. Selection of lag lengths

In the empirical work, lag length for each variable[40] has been determined by the FPE criterion.[41] The following sequential procedure, suggested by Hsiao (1981), was employed to select the lags for a two variable (x, y) case: (i) Treat y as a one-dimensional autoregressive process and compute its FPE with the maximum order of lags varying from 1 to p. Choose the order which yields the minimum FPE, say n; (ii) treat y as a controlled variable with the order pre-specified to be n, and treat x as the manipulated variable. Compute the FPE of y by varying the order of lags of the manipulated variable, x, from 1 to p. Choose the order which yields the minimum FPE, say m; (iii) the smallest FPE's of the above two steps are compared. If the FPE of step (i) is less than that of step (ii) then a one-dimensional autoregressive representation of the controlled variable is used. If the converse holds then the lag lengths of the two variables in the equation for predicting y, is n for y and m for x; and (iv) the above delineated steps are repeated for the x process, treating y as the manipulated variable.

The maximum lag length with which this study explored the FPE's is five years in case of the annual data, and 20 quarters for the quarterly data, for autoregressive lag as well as for lag of the manipulated variable.[42] The minimum FPE's in each series are highlighted in Table 6.5.

---

40   In view of some limitations of the FPE criterion, as mentioned by Schwarz (1978) and Hannan and Quinn (1979), experiments were made, in this study, in the initial stages with Akaike (1974) and Hannan and Quinn (1979) criteria in addition to the FPE. The preliminary analysis showed that all three criteria determine the same order of lag.

41   Refer Section 6.3.2.1.1.

42   In the Indian context, generally 12 lags are specified for quarterly series. In case of annual series, Ramachandra (1983) arbitrarily selects 1 lag while Jadhav (1994) chooses 6 lags. Given the nature of Indian data, it was considered appropriate to explore with 5 annual lags and therefore 20 quarterly lags.

Table 6.5: FPE of autoregressive process for the variables

Lags	Annual – 1951–95 FPE×10⁻⁴					Quarterly – 1971–95 FPE×10⁻⁴				
	MD	RM	M1	M3	P	MD	RM	M1	M3	P
1	2	3	4	5	6	7	8	9	10	11
1	**13.232**	6.903	7.201	1.914	5.353	3.277	0.673	**1.918**	**0.120**	0.529
2	13.931	6.813	7.151	1.756	5.339	3.336	**0.660**	1.969	0.121	0.537
3	13.432	6.402	6.918	1.772	5.620	3.392	0.661	1.939	0.124	0.541
4	14.063	6.544	**6.281**	**1.664**	**5.336**	2.831	0.674	1.986	0.125	0.553
5	14.339	**5.776**	6.479	1.753	5.589	2.645	0.688	2.018	0.125	0.556
6						2.703	0.706	2.071	0.128	0.530
7						2.668	0.724	2.126	0.129	0.539
8						2.664	0.733	2.172	0.130	0.524
9						2.701	0.726	2.209	0.133	0.535
10						**2.533**	0.744	2.268	0.134	0.546
11						2.543	0.763	2.328	0.136	0.561
12						2.597	0.783	2.388	0.129	0.576
13						2.639	0.794	2.452	0.132	0.548
14						2.709	0.756	2.518	0.125	0.523
15						2.761	0.776	2.554	0.128	0.532
16						2.798	0.787	2.610	0.126	0.535
17						2.862	0.808	2.678	0.127	0.545
18						2.896	0.814	2.751	0.129	**0.517**
19						2.974	0.836	2.824	0.132	0.531
20						2.958	0.849	2.895	0.132	0.533

MD is monetised debt, RM is reserve money, M1 is narrow money, M3 is broad money and P is price level.

Source: Author's compilation.

Hsiao (1981) suggests that no further residual analysis is required as FPE formula is derived under the assumption that residuals are white noise.[43] However, in the specification tested here, annual series of money supply, M1 and M3, and quarterly series of M1, exhibit abnormality in the residuals (Columns 4 and 6 in Table 6.6, and Column 4 in Table 6.7). To correct this abnormality, the procedure for selection of lag length was investigated. The lag lengths selected using the Schwarz (1978) and the Akaike (1974) information criteria reveal similar abnormality in the residuals. The residual plots of the two time series exhibit an outlier at 1978 for annual series on M1, at 1961 for annual series on M3, and at first quarter of 1980[44] for quarterly series on M1. These outliers are easily explainable

---

43 Footnote 5, 95.
44 Refers to fiscal year 1980–81 and therefore the outlier is at April–June 1980.

in terms of the revisions in the concept and definition of the money supply in India at these data points.[45] An attempt to correct these outliers with a dummy yields good results (Columns 5 and 7 in Table 6.6, and Column 5 in Table 6.7).

Table 6.6: Autoregressive equations of variables for 1951–95, annual

Coefficient on lag	Variable						
	MD	RM	M1	M1*	M3	M3**	P
1	2	3	4	5	6	7	8
(-1)	0.505	0.081	-0.049	0.060	0.371	0.385	0.282
	(3.6)	(0.5)	(0.3)	(0.5)	(2.3)	(2.8)	(1.8)
(-2)		0.069	0.149	0.145	0.182	0.151	-0.232
		(0.4)	(0.9)	(1.2)	(1.1)	(1.0)	(1.5)
(-3)		0.191	0.269	0.147	0.022	0.049	0.106
		(1.1)	(1.6)	(1.2)	(0.1)	(0.3)	(0.7)
(-4)		0.052	0.379	0.453	0.296	0.232	-0.245
		(0.3)	(2.3)	(3.6)	(2.0)	(1.8)	(1.9)
(-5)		0.349					
		(2.5)					
Constant	0.025	0.018	0.016	0.016	0.010	0.013	0.034
	(2.6)	(1.6)	(1.2)	(1.6)	(1.3)	(2.2)	(4.5)
Dummy				-0.096*		-0.038**	
				(5.1)		(3.5)	
FPE×10^{-4}	13.232	5.776	6.281	3.700	1.664	1.275	5.336
R^2-Adj.	0.241	0.271	0.172	0.523	0.561	0.671	0.076
SSE	0.046	0.016	0.019	0.010	0.005	0.003	0.016
h stat	-1.357	-0.324	!	1.005	**3.986**	-0.556	1.739
LM Test	-0.993	0.459	**41.591**	0.174	**10.961**	2.954	0.805
Chow Test	0.311	2.686	0.790	1.962	1.757	-1.251	0.507
G-Q Test	0.860	0.698	0.150	0.017	2.415	0.366	4.140
F-stat	13.034	3.825	2.973	9.333	13.149	16.521	1.782

MD is monetised debt, *RM* is reserve money, *M1* is narrow money, *M3* is broad money and *P* is price level. '-' refers to the lag values.! cannot be computed.

Figures in parentheses are the *t-values*. *LM Test* is the Jarque-Bera asymptotic LM normality test for the residuals. *Chow Test* at 1971 with 21 and 18 degrees of freedom. *G-Q* is the Goldfeld-Quandt Test at 1971 with 10 and 7 degrees of freedom. * Dummy at year 1978. ** Dummy at year 1961.

Source: Author's compilation.

---

45 Refer section 6.2.2.

Table 6.7: Autoregressive equations of variables for 1971–95, quarterly

Coeffici-ent on lag	Variable					
	MD	RM	M1	M1*	M3	P
1	2	3	4	5	6	7
(-1)	0.267 (2.3)	-0.136 (1.2)	0.175 (1.6)	0.111 (1.9)	0.201 (1.9)	0.137 (1.1)
(-2)	0.171 (1.4)	0.201 (1.9)				0.147 (1.2)
(-3)	-0.006 (0.1)					0.256 (2.0)
(-4)	0.327 (2.5)					-0.032 (0.2)
(-5)	-0.387 (2.8)					-0.107 (0.8)
(-6)	0.141 (1.0)					-0.219 (1.8)
(-7)	0.228 (1.7)					-0.251 (2.1)
(-8)	0.242 (1.8)					0.082 (0.7)
(-9)	-0.061 (0.4)					0.054 (0.4)
(-10)	-0.336 (2.5)					-0.044 (0.4)
(-11)						0.025 (0.2)
(-12)						0.139 (1.1)
(-13)						-0.168 (1.4)
(-14)						-0.268 (2.2)
(-15)						-0.096 (0.7)
(-16)						0.219 (1.8)
(-17)						0.018 (0.2)
(-18)						-0.253 (2.2)
Cons.	0.006 (1.8)	0.016 (5.6)	0.012 (5.4)	0.014 (12.1)	0.014 (7.1)	0.011 (3.6)
Dum*				-0.102 (13.9)		
FPE×10⁻⁴	2.533	0.660	1.918	0.541	0.120	0.517
R²-Adj.	0.345	0.044	0.020	0.726	0.030	0.294
SSE	0.014	0.004	0.014	0.003	0.001	0.002
h stat	-	0.047	-0.255	-0.049	-0.629	!
LM	5.169	0.142	**4574.182**	6.147	0.138	1.461
F-stat	5.014	2.753	2.402	101.978	3.337	2.766

MD is monetised debt, *RM* is reserve money, *M1* is narrow money, *M3* is broad money and *P* is price level. '-' refers to the lag values. ! cannot be computed.

Figures in parentheses are the *t-values*. *LM* Test is the Jarque-Bera asymptotic LM normality test for the residuals. * Dummy at Quarter 1, 1980 (fiscal year 1980-81).

Source: Author's compilation.

The lag lengths of the independent (manipulated) variable that enter the equation, determined by the FPE criterion, are presented in Table 6.8. In some cases, the FPE of the equation, including the manipulated variable, is more than that derived from the respective autoregressive equation of the controlled variable. Hsiao (1981) suggests that in such cases the autoregressive representation of only the controlled variable is appropriate. However, in this analysis, in all such cases, coefficients of the manipulated variable are insignificant, supporting Hsiao's hypothesis (such cases are marked by '$' in Table 6.8 and Appendix Tables A1 to A9).

Table 6.8: Minimum FPE and the optimal lag structures of the variables

Dependent variable	Annual 1951–95				Quarterly 1971–95			
	Auto-lags	Independent variable (IV)	Lags IV	FPE×10⁻⁴	Auto-lags	Independent variable (IV)	Lags IV	FPE×10⁻⁴
1	2	3	4	5	6	7	8	9
MD	1	RM	4	10.793	10	RM	19	2.106
MD	1	M1	4	13.490$	10	M1	11	2.426
MD	1	M3	4	13.424$	10	M3	5	2.318
MD	1	P	3	12.536	10	P	3	2.573$
RM	5	MD	1	5.712	2	MD	1	0.588
RM	5	M1	4	5.815$	2	M1	2	0.607
RM	5	M3	1	4.914	2	M3	14	0.581
RM	5	P	1	3.702	2	P	1	0.676$
M1*	4	MD	4	3.276	1	MD	1	0.553$
M1*	4	RM	1	3.092	1	RM	1	0.554$
M1*	4	P	5	3.303	1	P	1	0.550$
M3**	4	MD	1	1.234	1	MD	2	0.106
M3**	4	RM	3	1.284$	1	RM	1	0.120
M3**	4	P	4	1.011	1	P	1	0.123$
P	4	MD	1	5.584$	18	MD	1	0.526$
P	4	RM	1	3.561	18	RM	3	0.488
P	4	M1	1	3.714	18	M1	13	0.413
P	4	M3	2	3.611	18	M3	6	0.439

MD is monetised debt, RM is reserve money, M1 is narrow money, M3 is broad money and P is price level. FPE refers to the Final Prediction Error. IV refers to the independent variable. * Includes a dummy for the year 1978 (annual series) and the first quarter of 1980 (quarterly series). ** Includes a dummy for the year 1961 (annual series). $ FPE in this equation is greater than the FPE derived from the respective autoregressive equation of the dependent variable presented in Tables 6.5 to 6.7.

Source: Author's compilation.

6.6. Empirical results on direction of causality

In this section, results of the causality test for the two period subsets, 1951–1995 (annual) and 1971–95 (quarterly), are presented. In some cases, the sum of the coefficients of the manipulated variable in the regression is negative and therefore are being considered counter-intuitive, (marked by an asterisk '@@' in Tables

6.9–6.18). In all such cases, though even if the F-test establishes the significance of the coefficients in the equation, these results are not considered as supporting the hypothesis of the direction of causality.

The empirical results are presented in the following pattern. First, the relationship between monetised debt and the monetary aggregates, and the price level is investigated (Tables 6.9–6.12). Then, the results exploring the relationship between reserve money and money supply, and the price level are presented (Table 6.13–6.15). Finally, the relationship between the two series of money and the price level is explored (Tables 6.16 and 6.17).

In Table 6.9, the causal relationship between monetised debt and reserve money is investigated. The results for the annual and quarterly series show that the rise in monetised debt is caused by the rise in reserve money. In Tables 6.10 and 6.11, the causal relationship between money supply and the monetised debt is explored. The results reveal that the rise in monetised debt has been caused by the rise in money supply during 1971–95 (quarterly series). The annual data series for the period 1951–95 do not exhibit any relationship between the growth in monetised debt and money supply. Finally, the results in Table 6.12 show that the growth in monetised debt and price level is not causally related.

Table 6.9: Granger causality test: Monetised debt (MD) and reserve money (RM)

Coefficient on lag of	No. of lags	Annual 1951–95				Quarterly 1971–95			
		Dependent Variable							
		MD		RM		MD		RM [@@]	
1	2	3		4		5		6	
MD	(-1)	0.514	(4.1)	-0.150	(1.4)	0.086	(0.6)	-0.158	(3.3)
	(-2)					0.075	(0.5)		
	(-3)					0.188	(1.3)		
	(-4)					0.271	(1.7)		
	(-5)					-0.332	(2.1)		
	(-6)					0.264	(1.7)		
	(-7)					0.274	(1.9)		
	(-8)					0.275	(1.9)		
	(-9)					0.106	(0.7)		
	(-10)					-0.259	(1.8)		
RM	(-1)	-0.066	(0.3)	0.119	(0.8)	-0.090	(0.3)	-0.057	(0.5)
	(-2)	0.727	(3.3)	0.085	(0.5)	0.342	(1.4)	0.199	(1.9)

Table continued

Table 6.9: Granger causality test: Monetised debt (MD) and reserve money (RM)

Coefficient on lag of	No. of lags	Annual 1951–95				Quarterly 1971–95			
		Dependent Variable							
		MD		RM		MD		RM @@	
1	2	3		4		5		6	
	(-3)	0.040	(0.2)	0.283	(1.7)	-0.071	(0.3)		
	(-4)	-0.588	(2.8)	0.072	(0.4)	0.284	(1.2)		
	(-5)			0.242	(1.6)	0.503	(2.1)		
	(-6)					0.233	(1.0)		
	(-7)					0.463	(1.9)		
	(-8)					-0.109	(0.4)		
	(-9)					-0.236	(0.9)		
	(-10)					-0.601	(2.6)		
	(-11)					-0.129	(0.5)		
	(-12)					0.338	(1.4)		
	(-13)					0.174	(0.7)		
	(-14)					-0.339	(1.4)		
	(-15)					-0.099	(0.4)		
	(-16)					-0.183	(0.7)		
	(-17)					0.303	(1.2)		
	(-18)					-0.317	(1.4)		
	(-19)					-0.372	(1.7)		
Constant		0.019	(1.2)	0.023	(2.0)	-0.002	(0.1)	0.017	(6.2)
R^2-Adj.		0.436		0.295		0.552		0.159	
SSE		0.031		0.015		0.007		0.004	
h stat		-1.166		-0.254		!		-1.041	
LM Test		0.754		0.001		3.235		0.658	
Chow Test		1.380		2.852					
G-Q Test		1.414		0.998					
F-stat		6.864		3.646		4.238		5.789	
F-stat@		4.195*		2.111		2.607*		11.109*	

'-' refers to the lag values. ! cannot be computed. @@ The sum of the coefficients of the independent variable in the equation are counter-intuitive.

Figures in parentheses are the *t-values*. *LM* Test is the Jarque-Bera asymptotic LM normality test for the residuals. *Chow* Test at 1971 with 21 and 18 degrees of freedom. *G-Q* is the Goldfeld-Quandt Test at 1971 with 10 and 7 degrees of freedom. *F-stat@* tests for the values of the independent variable. * Significant at 1 per cent.

Source: Author's compilation.

Table 6.10: Granger causality test: Monetised debt (MD) and narrow money (M1)

Coefficient on lag of	No. of lags	Annual – 1951–95				Quarterly – 1971–95			
		Dependent Variable							
		MD$		M1@@		MD		M1$	
1	2	3		4		5		6	
MD	(-1)	0.417	(2.9)	0.034	(0.4)	0.275	(2.3)	-0.023	(0.5)
	(-2)			-0.120	(1.4)	0.215	(1.6)		
	(-3)			-0.184	(2.2)	-0.038	(0.3)		
	(-4)			0.105	(1.4)	0.466	(3.2)		
	(-5)					-0.441	(2.8)		
	(-6)					0.115	(0.7)		
	(-7)					0.325	(2.2)		
	(-8)					0.195	(1.2)		
	(-9)					0.082	(0.5)		
	(-10)					-0.562	(3.6)		
M1	(-1)	0.201	(0.8)	-0.009	(0.1)	0.045	(0.3)	0.105	(1.7)
	(-2)	0.153	(0.6)	0.137	(1.2)	-0.284	(1.8)		
	(-3)	-0.223	(0.9)	0.241	(2.0)	0.411	(2.6)		
	(-4)	-0.571	(2.3)	0.496	(4.1)	-0.045	(0.2)		
	(-5)					-0.037	(0.2)		
	(-6)					0.085	(0.5)		
	(-7)					0.127	(0.8)		
	(-8)					0.117	(0.7)		
	(-9)					-0.208	(1.4)		
	(-10)					-0.253	(1.9)		
	(-11)					0.311	(2.3)		
Constant		0.050	(2.4)	0.023	(2.2)	0.001	(0.2)	0.015	(10.1)
Dummy				-0.106	(6.1)			-0.101	(12.9)
R^2-Adj.		0.294		0.612		0.443		0.724	
SSE		0.039		0.008		0.010		0.004	
h-stat		-0.840		0.587		!		-0.153	
LM Test		0.878		0.509		5.128		7.439	
Chow Test		1.479		1.846					
G-Q Test		0.950		0.038					
F-stat		4.170		7.665		3.879		67.362	
F-stat@		1.705		2.896**		2.049**		0.235	

$ Final Prediction Error (FPE) in this equation is more than that in the autoregressive equation of the dependent variable. Includes a *Dummy* for M1 at 1978 (annual series) and for first quarter of 1980 (quarterly series). @@ The sum of the coefficients of the independent variable in the equation are counter-intuitive. '-' refers to the lag values. ! cannot be computed.

Figures in parentheses are the *t-values*. *LM Test* is the Jarque-Bera asymptotic LM normality test for the residuals. *Chow* Test at 1971 with 21 and 18 degrees of freedom. *G-Q* is the Goldfeld-Quandt Test at 1971 with 10 and 7 degrees of freedom. *F-stat@* tests for the values of the independent variable. ** Significant at 5 per cent.

Source: Author's compilation.

Table 6.11: Granger causality test: Monetised debt (MD) and broad money (M3)

Coefficient on lag of	No. of lags	Annual 1951–95				Quarterly 1970–1995			
		Dependent Variable							
		MD$		M3		MD		M3@@	
1	2	3		4		5		6	
MD	(-1)	0.458	(3.3)	-0.070	(1.7)	0.126	(1.0)	-0.037	(1.8)
	(-2)					0.094	(0.8)	-0.059	(2.8)
	(-3)					-0.017	(0.1)		
	(-4)					0.421	(3.3)		
	(-5)					-0.265	(1.9)		
	(-6)					0.212	(1.5)		
	(-7)					0.275	(2.1)		
	(-8)					0.211	(1.7)		
	(-9)					-0.029	(0.2)		
	(-10)					-0.250	(1.9)		
M3	(-1)	0.453	(1.0)	0.366	(2.7)	-0.297	(0.5)	0.110	(1.0)
	(-2)	0.553	(1.1)	0.185	(1.3)	0.430	(0.8)		
	(-3)	0.179	(0.3)	0.078	(0.5)	0.585	(1.1)		
	(-4)	-0.934	(2.2)	0.199	(1.6)	0.739	(1.4)		
	(-5)					1.358	(2.7)		
Constant		0.011	(0.5)	0.017	(2.6)	-0.047	(2.2)	0.017	(8.5)
Dummy				-0.039	(3.7)				
R^2-Adj.		0.298		0.688		0.433		0.169	
SSE		0.038		0.003		0.012		0.001	
h - stat		-1.960		-1.229		!		1.139	
LM Test		1.175		2.075		2.404		0.198	
Chow Test		0.693		-1.029					
G-Q Test		0.926		0.399					
F-stat		4.226		15.013		4.878		6.150	
F-stat@		1.757		2.847		3.048**		7.277*	

$ Final Prediction Error (FPE) in this equation is more than that in the autoregressive equation of the dependent variable. Includes a *Dummy* for M3 at 1961 (annual series). @@ The sum of the coefficients of the independent variable in the equation are counter-intuitive. '-' refers to the lag values. ! cannot be computed.

Figures in parentheses are the *t-values*. *LM* Test is the Jarque-Bera asymptotic LM normality test for the residuals. *Chow Test* at 1971 with 21 and 18 degrees of freedom. *G-Q* is the Goldfeld-Quandt Test at 1971 with 10 and 7 degrees of freedom. *F-stat@* tests for the significance of the coefficients of the independent variable. * Significant at 1 per cent. ** Significant at 5 per cent.

Source: Author's compilation.

Table 6.12: Granger causality test: Monetised debt (MD) and prices (P)

Coefficient on lag of	No. of lags	Annual 1951–95				Quarterly 1970–95			
		Dependent Variable							
		MD@@		P$		MD$		P$	
1	2	3		4		5		6	
MD	(-1)	0.373	(2.6)	0.050	(0.4)	0.228	(1.9)	0.041	(0.8)
	(-2)					0.166	(1.3)		
	(-3)					-0.029	(0.2)		
	(-4)					0.288	(2.2)		
	(-5)					-0.362	(2.6)		
	(-6)					0.159	(1.1)		
	(-7)					0.232	(1.8)		
	(-8)					0.218	(1.6)		
	(-9)					-0.056	(0.4)		
	(-10)					-0.324	(2.3)		
P	(-1)	-0.129	(0.5)	0.279	(1.7)	-0.012	(0.1)	0.144	(1.1)
	(-2)	-0.311	(1.3)	-0.225	(1.4)	-0.021	(0.1)	0.161	(1.3)
	(-3)	-0.432	(1.8)	0.123	(0.7)	0.485	(1.9)	0.247	(1.9)
	(-4)			-0.215	(1.5)			-0.061	(0.4)
	(-5)							-0.102	(0.8)
	(-6)							0.212	(1.7)
	(-7)							-0.242	(2.0)
	(-8)							0.080	(0.7)
	(-9)							0.064	(0.5)
	(-10)							-0.036	(0.3)
	(-11)							0.041	(0.3)
	(-12)							0.132	(1.1)
	(-13)							-0.169	(1.4)
	(-14)							-0.260	(2.1)
	(-15)							-0.072	(0.6)
	(-16)							0.213	(1.7)
	(-17)							0.036	(0.3)
	(-18)							-0.247	(2.1)
Constant		0.059	(3.7)	0.030	(2.5)	0.004	(0.9)	0.011	(2.9)
R^2-Adj.		0.330		0.055		0.357		0.291	
SSE		0.038		0.016		0.014		0.002	
h stat		-0.507		!		!		!	
LM Test		1.063		0.870		4.965		1.938	

Table continued

Monetisation of Debt in India 175

Table 6.12: Granger causality test: Monetised debt (MD) and prices (P)

Coefficient on lag of	No. of lags	Annual 1951–95		Quarterly 1970–95	
		Dependent Variable			
		MD@@	P$	MD$	P$
1	2	3	4	5	6
Chow Test		1.525	0.388		
G-Q Test		1.117	4.105		
F-stat		5.668	1.439	4.251	2.640
F-stat@		2.636***	0.229	1.400	0.662

$ Final Prediction Error (FPE) in this equation is more than that in the autoregressive equation of the dependent variable. @@ The sum of the coefficients of the independent variable in the equation are counter-intuitive. '-' refers to the lag values. ! cannot be computed.

Figures in parentheses are the *t-values*. *LM* Test is the Jarque-Bera asymptotic LM normality test for the residuals. *Chow* Test at 1971 with 21 and 18 degrees of freedom. *G-Q* is the Goldfeld-Quandt Test at 1971 with 10 and 7 degrees of freedom. *F-stat@* tests for the significance of the coefficients of the independent variable. *** Significant at 10 per cent.

Source: Author's compilation.

The causal relationship between the two series of money supply and the reserve money is mixed. In the case of the annual series, the results reveal, that the rise in reserve money causes a rise in narrow money, while the quarterly data yields contrary conclusions (Table 6.13). In the case of the broad money, for annual data during 1951–95, direction of causality flows from rise in money supply to reserve money, while quarterly data shows no relationship during 1971–95 (Table 6.14). The direction of causality from the rise in reserve money to the price level is supported for the period 1951–95 (annual series) and 1971–95 (quarterly series) (Table 6.15).

Table 6.13: Granger causality test: Reserve money (RM) and narrow money (M1)

Coefficient on lag of	No. of lags	Annual – 1951–95				Quarterly – 1970–95			
		Dependent Variable							
		RM$		M1		RM		M1$	
1	2	3		4		5		6	
RM	(-1)	0.102	(0.5)	0.394	(2.9)	-0.222	(1.9)	0.035	(0.3)
	(-2)	0.202	(1.1)			0.224	(2.0)		
	(-3)	0.151	(0.8)						
	(-4)	-0.087	(0.4)						
	(-5)	0.307	(2.1)						
M1	(-1)	-0.174	(0.9)	-0.147	(1.1)	0.201	(2.9)	0.102	(1.6)

Table continued

Table 6.13: Granger causality test: Reserve money (RM) and narrow money (M1)

Coefficient on lag of	No. of lags	Annual – 1951–95				Quarterly – 1970–95			
		Dependent Variable							
		RM$		M1		RM		M1$	
1	2	3		4		5		6	
	(-2)	-0.194	(1.0)	0.139	(1.2)	-0.104	(1.5)		
	(-3)	0.143	(0.7)	0.136	(1.2)				
	(-4)	0.379	(1.9)	0.378	(3.3)				
Constant		0.014	(1.1)	0.009	(1.1)	0.016	(5.7)	0.014	(7.3)
Dummy				-0.111	(6.2)			-0.101	(13.9)
R^2-Adj.		0.326		0.610		0.143		0.723	
SSE		0.013		0.008		0.004		0.004	
h stat		!		0.560		!		-0.169	
LM Test		0.031		0.891		0.073		6.189	
Chow Test		2.129		1.858					
G-Q Test		0.498		0.018					
F-stat		3.042		10.908		4.173		67.198	
F-stat@		1.673		8.366*		5.274*		0.104	

$ Final Prediction Error (FPE) in this equation is more than that in the autoregressive equation of the dependent variable. Includes a *Dummy* for M1 at 1978 (annual series) and at the first quarter of 1980 (quarterly series). '-' refers to the lag values.

! cannot be computed.

Figures in parentheses are the *t-values*. *LM* Test is the Jarque-Bera asymptotic LM normality test for the residuals. *Chow* Test at 1971 with 21 and 18 degrees of freedom. *G-Q* is the Goldfeld-Quandt Test at 1971 with 10 and 7 degrees of freedom. *F-stat@* tests for the significance of the coefficients of the independent variable. * Significant at 1 per cent.

Source: Author's compilation.

Table 6.14: Granger causality test: Reserve money (RM) and broad money (M3)

Coefficient on lag of	No. of lags	Annual – 1951–95				Quarterly – 1970–95			
		Dependent Variable							
		RM		M3$		RM@@		M3	
1	2	3		4		5		6	
RM	(-1)	-0.241	(1.3)	-0.079	(0.8)	-0.155	(1.2)	0.082	(1.5)
	(-2)	-0.052	(0.3)	-0.170	(1.6)	0.290	(2.1)		
	(-3)	0.136	(0.9)	0.184	(1.8)				
	(-4)	0.058	(0.4)						

Table continued

Table 6.14: Granger causality test: Reserve money (RM) and broad money (M3)

Coefficient on lag of	No. of lags	Annual – 1951–95				Quarterly – 1970–95			
		Dependent Variable							
		RM		M3$		RM@@		M3	
1	2	3		4		5		6	
	(-5)	0.235	(1.8)						
M3	(-1)	0.830	(2.7)	0.388	(2.5)	0.924	(3.0)	0.111	(0.9)
	(-2)			0.308	(1.7)	-1.071	(3.4)		
	(-3)			0.271	(1.5)	0.335	(1.2)		
	(-4)			0.251	(1.9)	-0.178	(0.7)		
	(-5)					0.113	(0.5)		
	(-6)					-0.124	(0.5)		
	(-7)					-0.157	(0.6)		
	(-8)					0.205	(0.8)		
	(-9)					-0.269	(1.0)		
	(-10)					-0.351	(1.3)		
	(-11)					0.964	(3.5)		
	(-12)					-0.731	(2.6)		
	(-13)					0.235	(0.8)		
	(-14)					-0.653	(2.6)		
Constant		-0.001	(0.1)	0.012	(2.0)	0.028	(2.1)	0.014	(7.3)
Dummy				-0.042	(3.9)				
R^2-Adj.		0.393		0.689		0.284		0.047	
SSE		0.013		0.003		0.003		0.001	
h stat		!		-1.985!!		!		!	
LM Test		2.034		2.168		1.005		0.494	
Chow Test		1.784		-0.498					
G-Q Test		0.481		0.264		.			
F-stat		5.105		11.557		2.883		2.877	
F-stat@		7.653*		1.652		2.772*		2.356	

$ Final Prediction Error (FPE) in this equation is more than that in the autoregressive equation of the dependent variable. Includes a *Dummy* for M3 at 1961 (annual series). @@ The sum of the coefficients of the independent variable in the equation are counter-intuitive. '-' refers to the lag values. ! cannot be computed.

Figures in parentheses are the *t-values*. *LM* Test is the Jarque-Bera asymptotic LM normality test for the residuals. *Chow* Test at 1971 with 21 and 18 degrees of freedom. *G-Q* is the Goldfeld-Quandt Test at 1971 with 10 and 7 degrees of freedom. *F-stat@* tests for the significance of the coefficients of the independent variable. !! The Lagrange Multiplier statistic for autocorrelation, which is a variant of Breusch and Pagan (1980) does not detect any autocorrelation in the residuals.

* Significant at 1 per cent.

Source: Author's compilation.

Table 6.15: Granger causality test: Reserve money (RM) and prices (P)

Coefficient on lag of	No. of lags	Annual 1951–95				Quarterly 1970–95			
		Dependent Variable							
		RM@@		P		RM$		P	
1	2	3		4		5		6	
RM	(-1)	-0.104	(0.8)	0.524	(4.3)	-0.133	(1.2)	0.216	(2.1)
	(-2)	0.383	(2.6)			0.216	(1.9)	0.064	(0.6)
	(-3)	0.232	(1.8)					-0.205	(1.9)
	(-4)	0.148	(1.1)						
	(-5)	0.402	(3.6)						
P	(-1)	-0.673	(4.5)	0.272	(2.1)	-0.055	(0.4)	0.142	(1.1)
	(-2)			-0.077	(0.6)			0.164	(1.4)
	(-3)			-0.025	(0.1)			0.218	(1.8)
	(-4)			-0.304	(2.9)			-0.018	(0.1)
	(-5)							-0.083	(0.7)
	(-6)							-0.213	(1.7)
	(-7)							-0.212	(1.8)
	(-8)							0.066	(0.6)
	(-9)							0.056	(0.4)
	(-10)							-0.048	(0.4)
	(-11)							0.001	(0.0)
	(-12)							0.089	(0.8)
	(-13)							-0.133	(1.1)
	(-14)							-0.231	(1.9)
	(-15)							-0.069	(0.6)
	(-16)							0.186	(1.5)
	(-17)							-0.023	(0.2)
	(-18)							-0.273	(2.3)
Constant		0.024	(2.6)	0.008	(0.9)	0.017	(5.5)	0.011	(2.0)
R^2-Adj.		0.543		0.397		0.034		0.355	
SSE		0.010		0.010		0.005		0.002	
h stat		0.953		-0.042		-0.097		!	
LM Test		1.326		1.237		0.168		1.204	
Chow Test		1.167		2.655					
G-Q Test		0.757		2.331					
F-stat		8.525		6.009		1.879		2.992	
F-stat@		20.643*		19.117*		0.191		2.802**	

$ Final Prediction Error (FPE) in this equation is more than that in the autoregressive equation of the dependent variable. @@ The sum of the coefficients of the independent variable in the equation are counter-intuitive.

'-' refers to the lag values. ! cannot be computed.

Figures in parentheses are the *t-values*. *LM* Test is the Jarque-Bera asymptotic LM normality test for the residuals. *Chow* Test at 1971 with 21 and 18 degrees of freedom. *G-Q* is the Goldfeld-Quandt Test at 1971 with 10 and 7 degrees of freedom. *F-stat@* tests for the significance of the coefficients of the independent variable. * Significant at 1 per cent. ** Significant at 5 per cent.

Source: Author's compilation.

Finally, the relationship between the two series of money supply and prices are presented in Tables 6.16 and 6.17. In the case of narrow money, the results reveal a feedback relationship with the price level for the period 1951–95, while for the period 1971–95, the results show that the rise in narrow money causes the price level to rise (Table 6.16). In the case of broad money, direction of causality is from the money supply to the price level (Table 6.17).

Table 6.16: Granger causality test: Narrow money (M1) and prices (P)

Coefficient on lag of	No. of lags	Annual 1951–95				Quarterly 1970–95			
		Dependent Variable							
		M1		P		M1$		P	
1	2	3		4		5		6	
M1	(-1)	0.062	(0.5)	0.515	(4.1)	0.111	(1.9)	-0.013	(0.2)
	(-2)	0.266	(1.9)					0.036	(0.7)
	(-3)	0.138	(0.9)					-0.119	(2.2)
	(-4)	0.357	(2.6)					0.017	(0.3)
	(-5)							-0.040	(0.7)
	(-6)							0.132	(2.3)
	(-7)							0.096	(1.6)
	(-8)							0.080	(1.3)
	(-9)							-0.052	(0.8)
	(-10)							0.051	(0.8)
	(-11)							-0.165	(2.7)
	(-12)							0.018	(0.3)
	(-13)							0.135	(2.2)
P	(-1)	-0.188	(1.2)	0.192	(1.4)	0.087	(0.8)	0.141	(1.0)
	(-2)	-0.118	(0.8)	-0.169	(1.3)			0.089	(0.7)
	(-3)	0.149	(0.9)	-0.048	(0.3)			0.498	(3.8)
	(-4)	0.118	(1.1)	-0.205	(1.9)			0.003	(0.0)
	(-5)	0.194	(1.9)					-0.008	(0.1)
	(-6)							-0.409	(3.1)
	(-7)							-0.313	(2.4)
	(-8)							-0.033	(0.2)
	(-9)							0.236	(1.8)
	(-10)							0.161	(1.2)
	(-11)							0.089	(0.7)
	(-12)							0.155	(1.3)
	(-13)							-0.331	(2.8)
	(-14)							-0.320	(2.8)
	(-15)							-0.144	(1.2)
	(-16)							0.385	(3.1)
	(-17)							0.034	(0.3)
	(-18)							-0.191	(1.7)

Table continued

Table 6.16: Granger causality test: Narrow money (M1) and prices (P)

Coefficient on lag of	No. of lags	Annual 1951–95				Quarterly 1970–95			
		Dependent Variable							
		M1		P		M1$		P	
1	2	3		4		5		6	
Constant		0.012	(1.4)	0.014	(1.6)	0.014	(9.2)	0.006	(1.2)
Dummy		-0.122	(6.0)			-0.103	(13.9)		
R^2-Adj.		0.617		0.371		0.725		0.504	
SSE		0.007		0.011		0.004		0.001	
h stat		-0.181		-0.137		-0.109		!	
LM Test		1.412		3.458		4.351		0.584	
Chow Test		0.512		3.155#					
G-Q Test		0.015		1.907					
F-stat		7.115		5.488		67.884		3.493	
F-stat@		2.614**	'-'	16.962*		0.652		2.884**	

$ Final Prediction Error (FPE) in this equation is more than that in the autoregressive equation of the dependent variable. Includes a *Dummy* for M1 at 1978 (annual series) and first quarter of 1980 (quarterly series). '-' refers to the lag values. ! cannot be computed. Figures in parentheses are the *t-values*. LM Test is the Jarque-Bera asymptotic LM normality test for the residuals. *Chow* Test at 1971 with 21 and 18 degrees of freedom. G-Q is the Goldfeld-Quandt Test at 1971 with 10 and 7 degrees of freedom. *F-stat@* tests for the significance of the coefficients of the independent variable. # The causality test for the shorter period of 1971-95, on annual basis, yields similar result for the direction of causality. * Significant at 1 per cent. ** Significant at 5 per cent.

Source: Author's compilation.

Table 6.17: Granger causality test: Broad money (M3) and prices (P)

Coefficient on lag of	No. of lags	Annual – 1951–95				Quarterly – 1970–95			
		Dependent Variable							
		M3		P		M3$		P	
1	2	3		4		5		6	
M3	(-1)	0.130	(0.9)	1.006	(4.1)	0.208	(1.9)	0.612	(2.5)
	(-2)	0.381	(2.5)	-0.389	(1.4)			-0.171	(0.7)
	(-3)	0.197	(1.1)					-0.503	(2.0)
	(-4)	0.050	(0.4)					0.136	(0.5)
	(-5)							-0.432	(1.7)
	(-6)							0.703	(2.7)
P	(-1)	-0.191	(2.4)	0.397	(2.6)	-0.042	(0.8)	0.116	(0.9)
	(-2)	0.026	(0.3)	-0.245	(2.0)			0.144	(1.2)
	(-3)	0.121	(1.5)	0.035	(0.2)			0.395	(3.1)
	(-4)	0.129	(2.2)	-0.395	(3.6)			-0.011	(0.1)
	(-5)							-0.188	(1.5)
	(-6)							-0.207	(1.7)
	(-7)							-0.288	(2.4)
	(-8)							0.085	(0.7)

Table continued

Table 6.17: Granger causality test: Broad money (M3) and prices (P)

Coefficient on lag of	No. of lags	Annual – 1951–95				Quarterly – 1970–95			
		Dependent Variable							
		M3		P		M3$		P	
1	2	3		4		5		6	
	(-9)							0.149	(1.3)
	(-10)							-0.092	(0.8)
	(-11)							0.016	(0.1)
	(-12)							0.280	(2.4)
	(-13)							-0.247	(2.0)
	(-14)							-0.242	(2.0)
	(-15)							-0.077	(0.6)
	(-16)							0.104	(0.8)
	(-17)							0.124	(1.0)
	(-18)							-0.266	(2.4)
Constant		0.015	(2.7)	0.001	(0.1)	0.015	(7.2)	0.004	(0.3)
Dummy		-0.044	(4.6)						
R²-Adj.		0.761		0.402		0.025		0.436	
SSE		0.002		0.010		0.001		0.002	
h stat		-1.845		-1.013		!		!	
LM Test		0.750		1.357		0.278		0.817	
Chow Test		-0.508		0.886					
G-Q Test		0.382		2.057					
F-stat		14.409		5.257		1.991		3.454	
F-stat@		4.074*		10.264*		0.660		3.432*	

$ Final Prediction Error (FPE) in this equation is more than that in the autoregressive equation of the dependent variable. Includes a *Dummy* for M3 (annual series) at 1961. '-' refers to the lag values. ! cannot be computed.

Figures in parentheses are the *t-values*. LM Test is the Jarque-Bera asymptotic LM normality test for the residuals. *Chow* Test at 1971 with 21 and 18 degrees of freedom. *G-Q* is the Goldfeld-Quandt Test at 1971 with 10 and 7 degrees of freedom. *F-stat@* tests for the significance of the coefficients of the independent variable. * Significant at 1 per cent.

Source: Author's compilation.

The summary results for the direction of causality for the annual and the quarterly series are presented in Table 6.18. In the case of the annual data for the period 1951–95, the summary results are presented in Column 5 (Table 6.18). The growth in monetised debt is neither related to prices nor money supply directly. The causal relationship is unidirectional from reserve money to monetised debt. The important result is that narrow ($M1$) and broad money ($M3$) show a feedback relationship with prices. Reserve money causes $M1$ and prices. $M3$ causes reserve money.

Table 6.18: Summary of conclusions: Test for Granger causality

S.No	Null hypothesis	Annual: 1951–95			Quarterly: 1971–95		
		F-Stat	p-value	Conclusion	F-Stat	p-value	Conclusion
1	2	3	4	5	6	7	8
1	RM→MD	4.20	0.00742	Yes	2.61	0.00393	Yes
2	MD→RM	2.11	0.15593	No	11.11	0.00135	Yes@@
3	M1→MD	1.71	0.17236	No	2.05	0.04053	Yes
4	MD→M1	2.89	0.03928	Yes@@	0.24	0.62880	No
5	M3→MD	1.76	0.16117	No	3.05	0.01607	Yes
6	MD→M3	2.85	0.10128	No	7.28	0.00131	Yes@@
7	P→MD	2.64	0.06542	Yes@@	1.40	0.25107	No
8	MD→P	0.23	0.63558	No	0.66	0.41897	No
9	M1→RM	1.67	0.18311	No	5.27	0.00729	Yes
10	RM→M1	8.37	0.00682	Yes	0.10	0.74727	No
11	M3→RM	7.65	0.00934	Yes	2.77	0.00316	Yes@@
12	RM→M3	1.65	0.19834	No	2.36	0.12909	No
13	P→RM	20.64	0.00007	Yes@@	0.19	0.66320	No
14	RM→P	19.12	0.00012	Yes	2.80	0.04828	Yes
15	P→M1	2.61	0.04624	Yes	0.65	0.42187	No
16	M1→P	16.96	0.00024	Yes	2.88	0.00419	Yes
17	P→M3	4.07	0.00967	Yes	0.66	0.41915	No
18	M3→P	10.26	0.00036	Yes	3.43	0.00626	Yes

MD is monetised debt, RM is reserve money, M1 is narrow money, M3 is broad money and P is price level. '→' refers to the direction of causal relationship. F-statistics is for the significance of the coefficients of the independent variable in the regression. p-value refers to the probability of the F-statistic. @@ The sum of the coefficients of the independent variable in the equation are counter-intuitive.

Source : Tables 6.9 to 6.17.

Source: Author's compilation.

In case of quarterly data, for the period 1971–95 (Column 8, Table 6.18), a rise in the money supply (both narrow and broad) as well as reserve money leads to a rise in price level. The results also reveal that growth in narrow money causes reserve money to rise. The rise in monetised debt is caused by a rise in reserve money and the money supply.

The results derived above are consistent with other empirical work in India. The hypothesis that growth in money supply leads to a rise in price level is also supported by Bhalla (1981b), Ramachandra (1983), Sharma (1984), Bhattacharya and Sharma (1985), Nachane and Nadkarni (1985), and Jadhav (1994). The feedback relationship between money supply and prices is also reported by Sharma (1984), Singh (1989) and Biswas and Saunders (1990). The result that reserve money causes narrow money is also supported by the results of Nachane and Nadkarni (1985).

6.7. Conclusions

The Indian economy is characterised by administered interest rates, managed exchange rates and high tariff barriers. In addition, monetised debt which is an important component of reserve money has been increasing in India, especially since the early 1970s. The open economy model implies, for the given economic condition in India, a relationship between monetary aggregates and the price level. Therefore, to examine this hypothesis, empirical tests to establish the direction of causality were conducted in this chapter.

The causal relationship between monetised debt and prices, and between monetised debt and monetary aggregates was estimated. No direct relationship between monetised debt and the price level is established. Rather, the results show that monetised debt rises due to the rise in reserve money and the money supply. The majority of causality results emerging from the Granger test for different periods substantiate the hypothesis of a causal relationship between reserve money, money supply and prices. Thus, for the annual data for the period 1951–95, the results show a feedback relationship between an increase in the money supply and prices. The rise in reserve money leads to a rise in monetised debt, narrow money and prices. The results from quarterly data for the period 1971–95, support the major conclusions for the overall period. The monetary aggregates lead to changes in the price level. Thus, the results generally support the hypothesis that direction of causality flows from money supply to prices.

7

Domestic Debt and Economic Growth in India

In India, domestic debt has been incurred with the main objective of enhancing planned investment for economic development. The rising trend in securing financial resources through public borrowing has specially been steep since the early-80s. In this chapter, the relationship between domestic debt and economic growth in India is explored.

In the literature, there are two views on the relationship between domestic debt and growth which are discussed in Section 7.1. On the basis of the theoretical discussion, a testable hypothesis is also formulated in this section to test the relationship between domestic debt and economic growth. This is followed by a brief review of the empirical literature. In section 7.3, trends in domestic debt and growth, and related issues of tax revenue and government expenditure are discussed. The econometric tests to investigate the relationship between two macro series are briefly mentioned in Section 7.4. The discussion on the data base and the methodological issues pertaining to empirical estimation is presented in Section 7.5. The empirical results are discussed in Sections 7.6 and 7.7. Finally, conclusions are presented.

7.1. Theoretical issues on domestic debt and economic growth

In this section, a discussion on the theoretical issues on domestic debt and its relation with economic growth is presented. The two views of domestic debt and growth, prevalent in literature, are discussed followed by a brief discussion on domestic debt and developing economies, with special reference to India. Finally, on the basis of the theoretical discussion, a hypothesis is formulated which is then empirically estimated later in the chapter.

7.1.1. The two views on government debt and economic growth

The impact of domestic debt on economic growth can be analysed in the context of two opposite views – traditional and the Ricardian.

7.1.1.1. The traditional view

In the traditional view, an increase in government debt, is a burden on the economy. In the short run, in view of the increase in government debt, the consumer would consider himself to be wealthier and therefore would resort to higher spending. The increased demand of goods and services, in view of sticky prices in the short run, will raise output and employment. As the marginal propensity to consume is higher than the marginal propensity to save, the increase in private savings, falls short of the government dis-saving. The real interest rate would rise in the economy encouraging capital inflow from abroad.[1] In the long run, the higher interest rate would discourage investment and thus crowd out private investment. The lower domestic savings mean a smaller capital stock. The inflow from abroad would result in greater foreign debt. The greater demand of domestic currency would also result in the loss of competitiveness of the domestic firms in the international markets. The higher aggregate demand results in a higher price level which adjusts over time and the economy returns to the natural rate of output. The lower investment eventually leads to a lower steady state capital stock and a lower level of output. Therefore, the overall impact, considering the long run period, would be a smaller total output and eventually lower consumption and reduced economic welfare. This is also referred to as the burden of the public debt, as each generation burdens the next, by leaving behind a smaller aggregate stock of capital (Metzler, 1951; Modigliani, 1961; Ferguson, 1964; Patinkin, 1989).

7.1.1.2. The Ricardian view

In the Ricardian view, government debt is considered equivalent to the future taxes (Barro, 1974, 1977). Considering that the consumers are rational and forward-looking, then the discounted sum of future taxes is equivalent to the current deficit. Thus, the shift between taxes and deficits do not generate aggregate wealth effects. The increase in government debt does not affect consumption. The rational

---

1   The economic logic of domestic debt in the Keynesian setting, applicable in the short run, is slightly different. Given a situation of 'excess supply' and a state of 'under-production', an expansion in aggregate demand would lead to increase in output, price level and the rate of return. This would imply that current and the future generation would be better off due to debt financing. Blinder and Solow (1973) and Tobin and Buiter (1980) argue that debt-financed government expenditure is expansionary in the Keynesian sense and even when output is supply constrained. However, the Keynesian view is no longer considered strong in view of the inconsistency of Keynesian economics with the competitive market economy and the optimising behaviour of rational economic agents, and its lack of micro-foundations.

consumer facing current deficits, saves for the future hike in taxes and therefore total savings in the economy are not affected – a decrease in government dis-saving is matched by increase in private savings. In view of the unchanged total savings, investment and interest rates are also unaffected and so also the national income.

Buchanan (1958) suggests that the incurrence of domestic debt results in the postponement of tax liability from the current to the future generations. This shift from current to future taxation could imply a shifting of tax burden from the current to future generations. Barro (1978a) argues that the shift from current to future taxation implied by debt issue does not involve a burden on later generations due to the phenomenon of operative intergenerational transfers.[2] The assumption of infinite lives and other assumptions, like the timing of taxation, public debt and capitalised future taxes are perfect substitutes, and the imperfections in the capital market, are discussed earlier in detail, in Chapter 3.[3]

Thus, to summarise, the traditional view implies that domestic debt reduces capital accumulation and growth in the long run. On the contrary, Ricardian Equivalence Hypothesis suggests that domestic debt does not affect macro aggregates and economic growth.

7.1.2. Domestic debt and growth in a developing economy with special reference to India

In India, the growth of domestic debt has been considered favourable in sharp contrast to the prevailing economic theories. Rao (1953)[4] argues that the purpose, and therefore, the effect of deficit financing undertaken in the industrialised countries is different from that in the underdeveloped countries. The developed countries may suffer from under-employed resources and under-utilised labour, necessitating the use of deficit financing to generate demand and stimulate the economy to full employment. But, in an underdeveloped economy like India, there exist insufficient equipment and utilisable resources, and high unemployment and disguised employment. The object of deficit financing in an underdeveloped country is to increase capital formation and thereby make efficient use of the available labour force.

In India, deficit financing is incurred to raise investment which is expected to increase the productivity or output per worker and raise the national income. In a

---

2 Pages 570–71.

3 Sections 3.3 to 3.7.

4 Pages 2–14 and 32–35.

Domestic Debt and Economic Growth in India

poor country like India, the private sector may not be able to provide the necessary investment for economic development. In such a situation, the government has to invest in core sectors to ensure capital formation. In the initial stages, due to the gestation period, the investment may not immediately occur and a gap between voluntary savings and investment may emerge. This gap is covered by forced savings produced through a rise in prices. Once economic development gets going vigorously, with capital formation and national income rising, then voluntary savings and investments increase that close this gap. It is argued that if deficit financing is appropriately managed[5] then the price level would not become inflationary, though a positive rate of inflation would emerge. This positive rate of inflation was also considered healthy for economic growth.[6]

Brahmananda (1980)[7] argues that the conditions are more conducive to development directed deficit financing in a country like India, than in developed countries.[8] But Brahmananda further argues that in the context of a planned

---

5   Appropriate management would require to consider the following: (a) scale on which investment is undertaken; (b) import and export elasticities; (c) purpose for which deficit financing is used; (d) gestation period; (e) wage rigidity; (f) effectiveness of the investment undertaken to bring about an increased flow of consumable output and the period taken for this flow to emerge; and (g) measures to keep the price level down.

6   Bernstein and Patel (1953) argue that the model as discussed by Rao (1953) is too simplistic and is possible only in an ideal case. This process of development through deficit financing generally results in an increased monetary dependence and inflationary pressures in the developing countries. They suggest, on the other hand, that the underdeveloped countries should depend on foreign assistance and capital to enhance investment as well as to maintain monetary stability. Tanzi and Blejer (1988) argue that developing countries are not able to finance a large portion of their expenditure through domestic debt and therefore have to resort to external debt which then has varied implications for economic development.

7   Pages 231–36.

8   The arguments are as follows: (a) In India, the proportion of currency to money supply is higher than in developed countries. Therefore, the money-supply augmenting effect is lower than the developed countries; (b) As currency has a lower income-velocity than bank money, the demand-boost effect of deficit financing is less than in developed countries; (c) As diverse financial intermediaries, have not yet developed in India, the liquidity effect of deficit financing is less than in developed countries; (d) As the Indian Economy has a planned pattern of investments and as the pace of private investment in fixed assets is largely regulated by industrial licensing, exchange allocation and capital issues control, India is in a better position to choke down accelerative investments, particularly in an undesirable direction, than is a developed economy; (e) As the Indian economy has a surplus of ordinary, unskilled labour, and also of trained and professional manpower, it should be possible to carry through productive investments without facing labour and skill shortages; (f) Prevalence of wage rigidity in India.

economy which is augmenting its growth potential year by year, deficit financing may not necessarily be inflationary but may actually result in increased production, higher efficiency in production technology, and therefore, a decline in prices.

The Report by RBI (1985) also suggests a similar role for deficit financing in India.[9] It is also theorised that the growth rate in the economy depends on the capital-output ratio, the rate of saving, investment priorities, efficiency of utilisation of existing capacity, technological factors, investment climate and a host of other factors. The government also holds a similar rationale for the role of domestic debt in India. The twin objectives of development planning that are pursued by the government are the economic growth with price stability.

Minhas (1987) argues that debt and growth are not related in India and that the Keynesian pump-priming track, advocated by the government, is not applicable to the Indian conditions. The pump-priming is to stimulate demand to coax out much larger output supplies which the existing, but temporarily idle, machines and plants had been producing. In India there is no such excess, but unutilised, capacity in plants and machinery exists, though the prevalent inefficient use of production facilities in Indian industry is a different issue. The other argument that deficit financing leads to the use of surplus labour for capital formation is also not applicable in India, according to Minhas. The domestic debt in India is being incurred for current expenditure rather than for investment purposes. Hence, the additional expenditure attributed to deficit financing does not lead to additional output but simply results in the build up of inflationary pressure.

Minhas has succinctly mentioned the fallacy in the policy being pursued by the government. Planning in India, which began in 1951, carried the strong imprint of Keynesian Economics. Hence, the emphasis on deficit financing and the concept of pump-priming. The Keynesian model of pump-priming is a short term model and therefore its application to the theory of economic growth may not be useful. Moreover, Keynesian economics does not provide a convincing description of the competitive market economy. It also lacks micro-foundations and is inconsistent with the optimising behaviour of rational economic agents. Therefore, the two views on the relationship between domestic debt and economic growth discussed in the earlier two subsections is considered appropriate and applicable even for the underdeveloped countries like India.

7.1.3. Formulation of the testable hypothesis

The hypothesis that can be tested empirically is discussed in this subsection. The

---

9   Pages 141–50 and 213–28.

effect of debt on some of the macro aggregates has been a focus of discussion in the last three chapters (debt and consumption in Chapters 4 and 5, and monetisation of debt and the price level in Chapter 6). In the present chapter, the relationship between economic growth and domestic debt is directly investigated. Therefore, the testable hypothesis focuses on these two economic series.

The long-term relationship between debt and growth is explored using the concept of cointegration. The concept of cointegration is fundamental to the understanding of the long-run relationships amongst the economic time series (Granger, 1988). If the two variables are cointegrated, they must obey an equilibrium relationship in the long run though they may drift apart in the short run. Thus, there is a steady-state relationship between the variables.[10] Further, Granger (1988) observes that cointegration is present if the two series are causally related and that causality is concerned with short-run forecastability. Therefore, the investigation is extended to study the causal relationship between debt and growth using the Granger causality tests.

Finally, the empirical analysis is extended to decompose domestic debt into the unanticipated component to explore the causal relationship, using the Granger causality test, between unanticipated component of debt and economic growth. The decomposition of domestic debt into the unanticipated component is done, broadly following the rational expectation approach (Barro, 1978b, 1980; Kormendi, 1984). The autoregressive equation for the domestic debt variable, with the lags selected on the basis of the minimum Final Prediction Error (Hsiao, 1981), is estimated. The error term of this equation has been assumed to represent the unanticipated component of domestic debt which is then used in the usual procedure to estimate Granger causality.

Thus, the hypothesis is framed as follows. If the results show that domestic debt, including the unanticipated component, and growth are correlated, it would imply support for the traditional approach. The contrary results would imply that Ricardian equivalence holds in India.

7.2. Brief review of empirical literature

In the empirical literature, there are a large number of studies which investigate the relationship between domestic debt and macro variables. These have generally

---

10 In the Indian context, though planned development was initiated in 1951, the consistent data on ownership pattern of domestic debt is available from 1959 till 1995. The time series with 37 annual observations is relatively short, but despite this limitation, cointegration tests are performed in the empirical section.

been discussed in the earlier chapters,[11] but only two studies (Barro, 1980 and Kormendi, 1984) have directly investigated the effects of domestic debt on economic growth. These two studies are briefly discussed and critically evaluated.

Barro (1980), formulates the following equation to establish the relationship between the unanticipated component of domestic debt and growth:

$$\log(Y_t) = a_0 + a_1 t + a_2 DMR_t + a_3 DMR_{t-1} + a_4 \log(G_t) + a_5 DBR_{t-1} \quad \text{Equation 7.1}$$

where, Y is output, t is the time trend, G is real federal purchases, DMR and DBR are the unanticipated components of money and debt growth which are the residuals drawn from Equations 7.2 and 7.3, respectively.

The unanticipated money growth rate of the M1 definition of the money stock is derived from the following equation in Barro (1981c):[12]

$$DM_t = a_0 + a_1 DM_{t-1} + a_2 DM_{t-2} + a_3 FEDV_t + a_4 \log[U/(1-U)]_{t-1} \quad \text{Equation 7.2}$$

where, M_t is an annual average of the M1, $DM_t = \log(M_t/M_{t-1})$, $FEDV_t = \log(FED_t) - [\log(FED)]_t^*$, FED is real federal expenditure and $\log(FED)^*$ is an exponentially declining distributed lag of the $\log(FED)$, and U is the annual average unemployment rate in the total labour force.

The unanticipated component of the domestic debt is derived from the following equation:

$$DB_t = a_0 + a_1 \pi_t^e + a_2 \left[P_t(FED_t - \overline{FED}_t)/\overline{B}_t\right] + a_3 (P_t \overline{FED}_t/\overline{B}_t) \log(Y_t/\overline{Y}_t) \quad \text{Equation 7.3}$$

where, $BD_t = \log(B_t/B_{t-1})$, B_t is the end-of-year stock of par value, interest-bearing public debt, excluding holdings of the Federal Reserve and federal agencies and

---

11   These have been discussed in Chapter 3 (general introduction on relationship between domestic debt and economic variables), Chapters 4 and 5 (domestic debt and consumption), and Chapter 6 (monetisation of domestic debt and price level). In addition, the following empirical work is also important. Barro (1978b), Niskanen (1978), Dwyer (1982) and Protopapadakis and Siegel (1987) find that deficits do not have any significant effects on the money supply or the inflation rate. McCallum (1984) concludes that positive government budget deficit can be maintained permanently and without inflation if it is financed by the issue of bonds rather than money. Levy (1981), Hamburger and Zwick (1981), Allen and Smith (1983) conclude that monetary base is expanded in response to government debt and support the hypothesis that deficits are inflationary.

Sargent and Wallace (1981) demonstrate theoretically that debt creation is inflationary. Barro (1979) concludes that debt-income ratio does not have a target value but rather moves randomly. Barro (1987) does not detect any clear relationship between budget deficits and interest rates. Barro (1989b and 1989c) argues that the shift between taxes and deficits do not matter for the interest rates and the output in the economy.

12   Page 140.

trust funds, $\bar{B}_t = \sqrt{B_t \cdot B_{t-1}}$, P_t is the GNP deflator, $\pi_t^e = E[\log(P_{t+1})] - \log(P_t)$ is an anticipated inflation rate constrained to equal the theoretical value of unity,[13] FED_t.

$\overline{FED}_t$ is real federal expenditure relative to normal, where the latter is based on a distributed lag of current and past actual values, and $\log(Y_t/\bar{Y}_t)$ is real GNP relative to its trend value $\bar{Y}_t$.

The coefficient of the variable, unanticipated growth of domestic debt, is significant in Equation 7.1, estimated on annual US data for the period 1949–77. Barro (1980a) concludes that the unanticipated component of domestic debt, or the debt shock, effects growth.

Pesaran (1982) criticises Barro on two major issues. Firstly, the theoretical considerations underlying the natural rate and the rational expectations model which form the basis of the Equation 7.1. Secondly, the method of decomposing the growth of money supply into its anticipated and unanticipated components, by assuming that the economic agents are able to perfectly predict the real growth of federal expenditure.[14] Most importantly, Pesaran (1987) shows that the inclusion of the current and lagged unanticipated effects in the equation has important implications for the asymptotic distribution of the estimators and the efficiency of the two-step estimators.[15] In the empirical work by Barro (1980), the Equation 7.1 and the price equation, are estimated in levels, and given the non-stationarity of the series, the results may not be robust.

In addition, the work attempted by Barro (1980) needs a sophisticated data set which may not be available for a developing country, and especially not for India, on a regular and reliable basis and therefore, its application becomes restricted. This is especially true for the variables like the unemployment rate and the interest

---

13 $E[\log(P_{t+1})]$ is a forecasted price level based on the following price equation derived in Barro (1978b, 564)

$\log(P_t) = a_0 + a_1 \log(M_t) + a_2 DMR_t + a_3 DMR_{t-1} + a_4 DMR_{t-2} + a_5 DMR_{t-3}$
$+ a_6 DMR_{t-4} + a_7 DMR_{t-5} + a_8 (G/y)_t + a_9 r_t + a_{10} t$ Equation FN 7.1

where, P_t is the GNP deflator, M_t is an annual average of the M1 definition of the money stock, DMR is the residual from the money equation (Equation 7.2 given in the text), G is the real federal purchases of goods and services, y is real GNP, r is the nominal interest rate, and t is the time trend.

14 The criticism by Pesaran (1982) is regarding the major issue of challenge to the Keynesian economics from the new classical macro-economics.

15 The models with the inclusion of the current and lagged unanticipated effects have been extensively analysed in literature (Leiderman, 1980; Attfield et al., 1981; Abel and Mishkin, 1983)

rate and to a lesser extent even to the series on money supply. Further, the interest rate variable may be fixed by the government or the monetary authority and market related interest rates may not be available for the economy. This is especially true for India and has been discussed in the previous chapter.[16]

The other empirical work investigating the relationship between domestic debt and growth is by Kormendi (1984). He estimates the following equation to explore evidence from a cross section of thirty four countries, about the relationship between debt and growth.

$$MY_j = a_0 + a_1 YI_j + a_2 SY_j + a_3 SM_j + a_4 MDY_j + a_5 MEY_j + a_6 MRY_j + \varepsilon_j \quad \text{Equation 7.4}$$

where, MY is the mean growth of per capita real gross domestic product YI is initial per capita real gross domestic product, SY is standard deviation of the growth of real gross domestic product, SM is the standard deviation of money supply growth, MDY is the mean ratio of deficits to income (gross domestic product), MEY is mean ratio of government expenditure to income, MRY is the mean ratio of the change in reserve money to income, and subscript 'j' refers to the country j.

Kormendi hypothesises that for the Ricardian equivalence proposition to hold, the coefficient on the variable MDY should be insignificant ($\alpha_4=0$). On the basis of the cross-country analysis for 34 countries, including the developed and the underdeveloped, for the period 1957–77, Kormendi concludes that Ricardian equivalence holds and that debt and growth are not related.

In the case of Kormendi (1984) a cross-section study of 34 countries cannot be expected to yield reliable results. The sample by Kormendi extends widely from the highly developed countries (the US, the UK, Japan and Australia) to the underdeveloped countries (Sri Lanka). The aggregation of such diverse group of economies may not yield a meaningful result. In addition, in Equation 7.4, the variable pertaining to deficit, reserve money, and expenditure, though scaled by income, may be influencing each other and therefore the coefficients may not be robust. In the absence of diagnostic tests provided with the empirical results, the conclusions to that extent are not strong.

7.3. Trends in domestic debt and economic growth in India

In this section, the trend in domestic debt and growth is presented. The rise in the domestic debt in India, according to the government, is to finance economic

---

16   Section 6.1.1.3, Chapter 6.

development through huge planned investment. The trend in the share of domestic debt in such development plans is also discussed. The main reasons for rising domestic debt are two – firstly, the inelasticity in the tax revenues, and secondly, the already high tax-income ratio.

The increase in growth of domestic debt has been generally higher than tax revenue. The domestic borrowing from the public[17] increased by 14.8 per cent during 1961–95 as compared with the growth of 14.7 per cent and 15.2 per cent in tax revenue and total expenditure, respectively.[18] Thus, the ratio of annual accruals of domestic debt from the public as a per cent of GDP increased more than two fold from 2.5 per cent in 1961 to 6.9 per cent in 1995, while tax revenue as a ratio of GDP increased from 8.9 per cent to 16.9 per cent. Chelliah (1991) argues, that domestic borrowing from the public have been used for financing the rising government expenditure other than the capital formation. The major cause of rise in the expenditure is due to the rising outlay on defence, interest payments, food subsidies and general administration. These represent broadly the non-developmental expenditure (NDE) incurred by the government.[19] The total tax revenue of the government (TTR) as a per cent of non-developmental expenditure has been declining sharply since 1981 while its proportion has been generally stable with regard to total expenditure (TE). On the contrary, the ratio of annual domestic borrowing from the public (ADBP) as a proportion of the two measures of expenditure has consistently been rising over the period (Figure 7.1). The higher proportion of taxes required to meet non-developmental expenditure imply increasing reliance on domestic borrowing to meet other expenditure, especially for development purposes.

---

17 Excludes the amount of domestic debt held within the government and by RBI.

18 Data on consistent basis pertaining to total expenditure and tax revenue is available only since 1961.

19 The other important items of non-developmental expenditure are tax collection charges, police, subsidy on controlled cloth, grants and loans to foreign countries, and famine relief (Government of India, 1995, S-41).

Figure 7.1: Annual accruals in domestic debt held by public (ADBP) and total tax revenue (TTR) of the government as percentage of total expenditure (TE) and non-developmental expenditure (NDE), (1961–95)

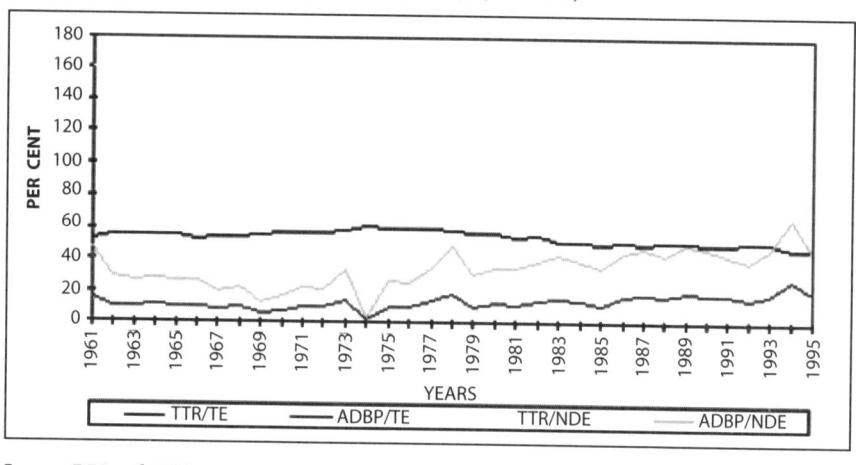

Source: RBI and GOI.

The growth pattern of domestic debt does not show any specific application of the tax smoothing principle in the Indian context. This is substantiated from the fact that the growth rate of domestic debt does not show any substantial increase during 1962–63,[20] 1965–66[21] and 1971–72,[22] the three years during which India had a war with its neighbours across its borders. In addition, since 1981 the rate of growth in domestic debt is consistently higher than the tax rate. Rather, in the Indian context, domestic debt is taken as a financial instrument, *per se*, and has consistently been used to meet the ever rising government expenditure. It has also been resorted to, whenever, for any reasons – political or economic, there is a shortfall of financial resources either from taxes or generated surpluses from public enterprises.

In India, domestic debt held by the public recorded a higher growth than gross domestic product. The ratio of domestic debt held by public as a percentage of GDP increased nearly two-fold from 24.5 per cent to 46.8 per cent over the period 1960–95. The growth in domestic debt held by public has been higher than that recorded by GDP during most of the years (Figure 7.2). The sharp increase in growth in domestic debt held by the public during 1973 is due to the increased

---

20 Government of India (1963), 5.
21 Government of India (1966), 1.
22 Government of India (1972), 1 and 44.

expenditure incurred on the refugees from Bangladesh,[23] consecutive droughts of 1972 and 1973 and deliberate efforts by the government to make good the short-falls in the Fourth Plan targets.[24]

The sharp dip in the trend growth rate of domestic debt held by public in 1974[25] needs to be explained. In 1974, the economy was still recovering from the war with Pakistan in December 1971 and the related refugee problem from Bangladesh, and the severe consecutive droughts recorded in 1972 and 1973. In addition, international prices of non-ferrous metals rose in 1973, substantial increases in the administered prices of iron and steel items in September-October, 1973 were made,[26] and finally the oil-price shock had its impact in India from October-November, 1973.[27] These factors resulted in the increase in the price level. The wholesale price index (WPI) increased by 26 per cent between December, 1972 and December, 1973. This was in addition to the increase of 14 per cent between December 1971 and December 1972.[28] It was due to these economic reasons that the growth in public subscription to the government borrowing program suffered a sharp decline during the year.

Figure 7.2. Domestic debt held by the public (DDP) and GDP – Annual growth (1960–95)

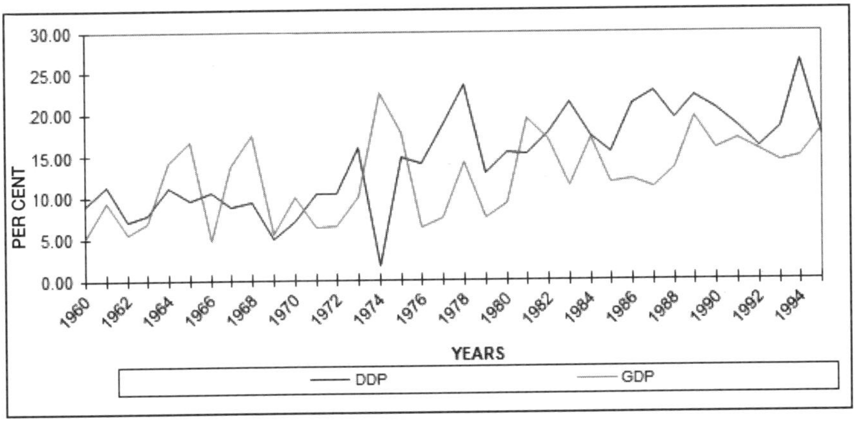

Source: RBI and GOI.

---

23   The number of refugees from Bangladesh had reached 10 million by December 1971 and 70 per cent of these were housed in government camps (Government of India, 1972, 44).
24   Government of India (1973), 1–2 and 45–53, and Government of India (1974), 1. Fourth plan refers to the fourth development plan in the series which started from 1951.
25   Pertains to financial year 1973–74.
26   Government of India (1974), 3.
27   Government of India (1974), 23.
28   Government of India (1974), 1.

The growth rate in the domestic debt held by public has been specially high in 1978. This is for political reasons.[29] The political uncertainty in the country led to the increase in domestic debt to meet the financial obligations at the cost of raising the tax rates. The annual growth in financial resources mobilised through domestic debt held by public increased from 18.7 per cent in 1977 to 23.5 per cent in 1978, while the annual increase in the tax collection declined from 10.3 per cent in 1977 to 7.3 per cent in 1978.

The high growth in domestic debt held by public since 1981 is due to the robust performance of the economy and the increasing reliance of the government on domestic debt. The high growth rate in 1994 is specially sharp due to unprecedented scale of open market operations conducted by tRBI to sterilise the increasing liquidity due to rising foreign exchange reserves during the year[30] and the shortfall in tax collection.[31] In addition, the increasing popularity of the new instruments, like 91-day Treasury bills, repos transactions, conversion of Treasury bills into dated securities and zero coupon bonds, attracted investors from the market.[32]

The increasing reliance on domestic borrowing and rising domestic debt, as emphasised earlier, has been justified by the government on the rationale of financing economic development. The country's economic development is being planned through the five year plans initiated in 1951. The initial high external borrowing have not been available since the fourth plan (1969–74) and since then, increasing reliance has been placed on domestic borrowing rather than on generated financial resources through taxation or surpluses from the public sector. In the eighth plan, the emphasis is to reduce the increasing dependence on borrowing witnessed in the seventh plan and the annual plan (1990–92). The share of the public sector has been rising over the planning period. The annual growth in GDP originating in the public sector has been more than that in the private sector (Figure 7.3).

---

29 Government of India (1979), 28.
30 RBI (1994), 65.
31 The sharp deceleration in tax receipts was due to customs and excise duties because of the slow growth in imports and sluggish industrial recovery despite measures by the government to improve tax buoyancy (RBI, 1994, VIII-1 to VIII-4).
32 RBI (1994), VII-14 - VII-15 and VIII-16 - VIII-23.

Figure 7.3. Gross domestic product – public and the private sector – annual growth (1962–95)

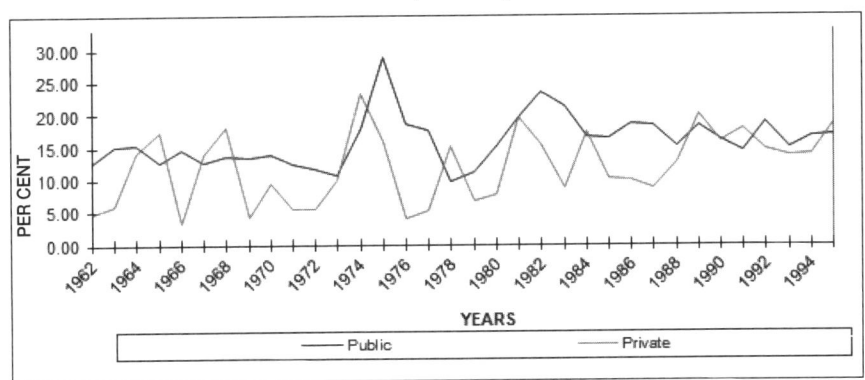

Source: GOI.

The data available since 1961 reveals that the share of GDP originating in the public sector increased from 10.0 per cent in 1961 to 27.3 per cent in 1995 (Table 7.1). In the case of the domestic capital formation, the role of public sector improved from 7.0 per cent in 1961 to 9.7 per cent in 1991 but has declined to 8.8 per cent in 1995.

Table 7.1. Role of public sector in national accounts aggregates (as per cent of GDP)

Years	GDP		Gross domestic capital formation	
*	Public sector	Private sector	Public sector	Private sector
1	2	3	4	5
1961	9.99	90.01	7.0	8.9
1971	13.84	86.16	6.5	10.6
1981	19.74	80.26	8.7	12.3
1991	26.18	73.82	9.7	15.5
1995	27.27	72.73	8.8	15.2

GDP at factor cost and gross domestic capital formation at current prices. * refers to the financial year.

Source: National Accounts Statistics, Government of India.

Source: Author's compilation.

7.4. Tests of cointegration and Granger causality

In the case of tests for cointegration, the Engle-Granger Cointegration Test has been employed, as suggested in Engle and Granger (1987). This test of cointegration is used in view of its simplicity to compute, and its wide-spread application in economic literature. The Engle-Granger test involves a two stage modelling strategy. In the first stage, the long run parameters are estimated by running a static regression in levels and testing for the null hypothesis of no cointegration by a Dickey-Fuller test for a unit root in the residuals, or by one of the other methods described in Engle and Granger (1987). If the residuals fail the test, the series do not have a cointegrating relationship. Otherwise, in the second stage, the residuals from the static regression are used as an error correction term in the dynamic, first-difference regression.

Thus, the static regression of the two series, x_t and y_t, which are $I(1)$, is run on levels,

$$y_t = a_0 + a_1 x_t + \varepsilon_t \qquad \text{Equation 7.5}$$

and then, the residuals ε_t are tested for stationarity. If x_t and y_t are not cointegrated, any linear combination of them will be non-stationary, and hence the residuals, ε_t, will be non-stationary. In the empirical section, the Engle-Granger Cointegration Test is used to investigate the long run relationship between domestic debt and growth.

The concept and tests of Granger causality are discussed in detail in the previous Chapter.[33] In this chapter, once again, the causality test suggested by Granger (1969) is estimated. In the empirical Sections 7.5 to 7.7, the concept of Granger causality is used to determine the direction of causality between domestic debt and economic growth.

7.5. Data base and methodological issues pertaining to empirical estimation

In this section, data base of the study is discussed. This is followed by a brief discussion on the methodological issues pertaining to stationarity of data and selection of the lag length.

7.5.1. Data base employed in empirical estimation

The two data series, which have been used in the empirical estimation, are the income variable and the domestic debt. The income variable used to represent the growth in the domestic economy is the real gross domestic product at factor cost at 1980–81 prices. The series on domestic debt is the par value of domestic debt held by public, excluding debt held within the government and RBI. The debt series is deflated using the GDP deflator (base 1980–81). The two data series used in empirical estimation are specified in logs.

---

33   Section 6.3, Chapter 6.

The period for this study is 1959–95 due to the consistent availability of data on the ownership pattern of domestic debt held by the public only from 1959 onwards. The annual data on domestic debt for the period is available in different publications of RBI – both annual and monthly. The data has been collected and compiled through such published sources of the Bank. The annual data on gross domestic product is available in different publications of the Government of India. The data on quarterly basis on gross domestic product is not available for India. Therefore, the study is based on the annual series.

7.5.2. Methodological issues

In this subsection, two important issues pertaining to stationarity of time series data used in causality test, and selection of appropriate lags by the FPE criterion are discussed.

7.5.2.1. Stationarity of time series data

The data series to be used for estimation of the causality test are required to be in covariance stationary form. There are various methods to achieve stationarity in data, most popular being the use of *ad hoc* filters (Sims, 1972) and differencing of the time series. To test for stationarity of the series, we have used the concept of unit roots (Table 7.2). The results reveal that first differences of the two data series in logs are stationary. The data series on GDP is stationary at the significance level of 1 per cent but the data series of domestic debt held by the public is stationary at the 1 and 5 per cent level of significance, with trend, and without trend in the equation, respectively.

Table 7.2: Testing for stationarity of domestic debt and GDP – The unit roots-augmented Dickey-Fuller test

Variables	Levels		First Differences	
	C	C and T	C	C and T
1	2	3	4	5
DDP	1.57 (2)	-2.04 (2)	-3.56 (1)**	-4.62 (1)*
GDP	1.45 (1)	-1.24 (1)	-5.03 (1)*	-5.69 (1)*

C = Constant. T = Trend. *DDP* is domestic debt held by the public. *GDP* is gross domestic product. Figures in parenthesis are lag values chosen to ensure that the residuals are white noise. * Significant at 1 per cent. ** Significant at 5 per cent.

Source: Author's compilation.

7.5.2.2. Selection of lag lengths

In the empirical work, the lag length for each variable has been determined by the final prediction error (FPE) criterion.[34] The selection procedure has been discussed in detail in the previous chapter.[35] To briefly mention, the sequential procedure, suggested by Hsiao (1981), was employed to select the lags in a two variable (x, y) case. The maximum lag length with which we explored the FPE's is five years for autoregressive lag as well as for lag of the manipulated variable.[36] The minimum FPE's in each series are highlighted in Table 7.3.

Table 7.3: FPE of autoregressive process for domestic debt and GDP

No. of lags	Annual - 1959 - 95 $FPE \times 10^{-4}$	
	DDP	GDP
1	2	3
1	**7.047**	**2.442**
2	7.174	2.497
3	7.622	2.659
4	8.111	2.681
5	8.009	2.860

DDP is domestic debt held by the public. *GDP* is gross domestic product.
Source: Author's compilation.

Hsiao (1981) suggests that no further residual analysis is required as the FPE formula is derived under the assumption that residuals are white noise.[37] However, in the specification tested here, domestic debt held by the public exhibits abnormality in the residuals (Column 2, Table 7.4). The residual plots of the time series exhibit an outlier at 1974. This outlier is easily explainable in

---

34 In view of some limitations of the FPE criterion, as mentioned by Schwarz (1978) and Hannan and Quinn (1979), we experimented with Akaike (1974) Information Criterion, in addition to the FPE. Our analysis shows that the two criteria determine the same order of lag.

35 Sections 6.3.2.1.1 and 6.5.2.2, Chapter 6.

36 Given the nature of Indian data, it was considered appropriate to explore with five annual lags. In the empirical literature in India, mentioned in Chapter 6 (Section 6.5.2.2), selection of such a lag length is discussed.

37 Footnote 5, 95.

terms of unusual fall in the domestic debt held by the public in 1974.[38] An attempt to correct this outlier with a dummy yields good results (Column 3, Table 7.4).

Table 7.4: Autoregressive equations of domestic debt and GDP

Coefficient on variables	Dependent variables		
	DDP	DDP*	GDP
1	2	3	4
(-1)	0.426 (2.6)	0.409 (3.1)	-0.172 (1.0)
Constant	0.016 (2.5)	0.019 (3.8)	0.021 (4.9)
Dummy		-0.089* (4.4)	
FPE×10⁻⁴	7.047	4.472	2.442
R²-Adj.	0.156	0.480	-0.005
SSE	0.019	0.011	0.006
h stat	1.187	1.054	!
LM Test	**17.197**	0.939	4.338
Chow Test	0.698	-1.428	0.493
G-Q Test	2.714	0.626!!	1.041
F-stat	6.551	14.861	0.869

DDP is domestic debt held by the public. GDP is gross domestic product. * Dummy at year 1974. ':' refers to the lag values. ! cannot be computed.

Figures in parentheses are the *t-values*. *LM Test* is the Jarque-Bera asymptotic LM normality test for the residuals. *Chow Test* with 15 and 16 degrees of freedom. *G-Q* is the Goldfeld-Quandt Test with 13 and 14 (! 12 and 13) degrees of freedom.

Source: Author's compilation.

The lag lengths of the independent (manipulated) variable that enter the equation, determined by the FPE criterion, are presented in Table 7.5. In both cases, FPE of the equation, including the manipulated variable, is more than that derived from the respective autoregressive equation of the controlled variable. Hsiao (1981) suggests that in such cases the autoregressive representation of only the controlled variable is appropriate. However, in our analysis, in both

---

38 Refer section 7.3.

cases, coefficients of the manipulated variable are insignificant, supporting Hsiao's hypothesis (such cases are marked by '$' in Tables 7.5 and 7.7).

Table 7.5: Minimum FPE and the optimal lag structures of domestic debt and GDP

Dependent variable	Auto lags	Independent variable (IV)	Lags of IV	FPE×10⁻⁴
1	2	3	4	5
DDP*	1	GDP	1	4.774$
GDP	1	DDP	5	2.480$

FPE refers to the Final Prediction Error. *DDP* is domestic debt held by the public. *GDP* is gross domestic product. * Includes a dummy for the year 1974.
$ FPE in this equation is greater than the FPE derived from the respective autoregressive equation of the dependent variable presented in Table 7.4.
Source: Author's compilation.

7.6. Empirical results

The empirical results are presented in this section. First, the results on the Engle-Granger cointegration test are discussed followed by the Granger causality test.

7.6.1. Engle-Granger cointegration test

The increase in the domestic debt in India has largely been to encourage economic development and growth. In the short run, the two may not be showing a relationship and may drift apart due to various economic and political reasons. But in the long run, these two series should exhibit a close relationship.[39] Therefore, in the present subsection, we investigate the cointegration relationship between domestic debt and economic growth using the Engle-Granger cointegration test.

The two data series of domestic debt held by public, and GDP, are I(1) as examined in Table 7.2 (Section 7.5). Therefore, the two series can now be used for the cointegration test. The results of the Engle-Granger cointegration test[40] based on the Augmented Dicky-Fuller regression equation for the residuals reveal that the domestic debt held by the public and economic growth are not cointegrated(Table 7.6).[41] The Cointegrating Regression Durbin Watson

---

39   Though, the process of planned economic development started in India in 1951, the data availability, however, restricts our analysis to a slightly shorter period of 1959–95.
40   The test is run in Shazam.
41   The Engle-Granger test is criticised to be sensitive to the choice of the dependent variable in finite samples (Dickey, Jansen and Thornton, 1991). Therefore, we experimented with DDP as the dependent variable. The results are consistent with those reported in Table 7.6. The two series are not cointegrated.

(CRDW)[42] value is also low at 0.349, which further substantiates the absence of the cointegrating relationship between the two variables.

Table 7.6: Engle-Granger cointegration test for domestic debt and growth*

Regress and: GDP	Test statistic: T-Test@	R^2	DW
1	2	3	4
Equation 1	-1.99 (2)	0.970	0.349
Equation 2	-2.19 (2)	0.978	1.208

* The test is run in Shazam. The two cointegrating regression equations are:

Equation 1: $GDP_t = a_0 + a_1 DDP_t + \mu_t$

Equation 2: $GDP_t = a_0 + a_1 t + a_2 DDP_t + \mu_t$

where, GDP is gross domestic product, DDP is domestic debt held by the public, and t is the time trend. *Equation 1* is without trend and *Equation 2* is with trend. GDP and DDP are in levels. A test for no cointegration is given by a test for unit root in the estimated residuals, $\hat{\mu}_t$. The augmented Dickey-Fuller regression for the unit root is $\Delta\hat{\mu}_t = \beta_0 \hat{\mu}_{t-1} + \sum_{j=1}^{m} \beta_j \Delta\hat{\mu}_{t-j} + v\varepsilon_t$. Test statistics reported in the Table is a *t-ratio* for $\beta_0 = 0$ (the τ-test). @ T-test with no constant and no trend. Figures in parenthesis are lag values chosen on the basis of the *AIC* criteria.

Source: Author's compilation.

7.6.2. Granger causality results

The empirical estimations of the equations are presented in Table 7.7. The equations are robust and the sign of the sum of coefficients is appropriate. In the case of the equation with GDP as the dependent variable (Column 4, Table 7.7), the *h*-statistic is high, though the *LM* statistic, a variant of Breusch and Pagan (1980), does not detect any autocorrelation. However, the Cochrane-Orcutt correction for autocorrelation also yields a significant F-statistic, implying similarity in the results and the direction of causality.

The summary results are presented in Table 7.8. The results substantiate the conclusion derived from the Engle-Granger cointegration test. In the case of Granger causality, the results indicate that the domestic debt held by public and economic growth are not causally related. The result is similar to the conclusion derived by Kormendi (1984) from the sample of 34 countries.

---

42 Sargan and Bhargava (1983).

Table 7.7: Granger causality test – Domestic debt and growth

Coefficient on lag of	No. of lags	Dependent variable	
		DDP$	GDP$
1	2	3	4
DDP	(-1)	0.407 (2.8)	0.132 (1.2)
	(-2)		-0.191 (1.5)
	(-3)		0.268 (2.1)
	(-4)		-0.298 (2.2)
	(-5)		0.247 (2.1)
GDP	(-1)	0.007 (0.0)	-0.066 (0.3)
Constant		0.019 (3.0)	0.015 (2.7)
Dummy		-0.090 (4.1)	
R^2-Adj.		0.461	0.114
SSE		0.011	0.005
h stat		1.188	!
LM Test		0.965	2.481
Chow Test		-0.914	0.397
G-Q Test		0.702	1.657+
F-stat		9.554	1.644
F-stat@		0.001	1.776

DDP is domestic debt held by the public and GDP is gross domestic product. The variables are in first differences. '-' refers to the lag values. ! cannot be computed.

Figures in parentheses are the *t-values*. LM Test is the Jarque-Bera asymptotic LM normality test for the residuals. *Chow Test* with 15 and 16 degrees of freedom.

G-Q is the Goldfeld-Quandt Test with 11 and 12 (+ 8 and 9) degrees of freedom.

F-stat @ Test for the values of the independent variable. $ FPE in this equation is greater than the FPE derived from the respective autoregressive equation of the dependent variable presented in Table 7.4.

Source: Author's compilation.

Table 7.8: Summary of conclusions emerging from the Granger causality test for domestic debt and growth

S.No	Null hypothesis	F-stat	p-value	Conclusion
1	2	3	4	5
1	DDP→ GDP	0.001	0.98061	No
2	GDP→ DDP	1.776	0.15603	No

'→' refers to the direction of Granger Causality. *DDP* is domestic debt held by the public and *GDP* is gross domestic product. *F-stat* tests for the significance of the coefficients of the independent variable in the equation. *p-value* refers to the probability value of the F-stat.

Source: Author's compilation.

7.7. Unanticipated change in domestic debt and economic growth

In the empirical work, under rational expectations, unanticipated components of the fiscal variables can affect the real sector (Barro, 1980a). Extending the same logic, the relationship between the unanticipated component of domestic debt held by public and economic growth is analysed in this section, using the Granger causality test.

7.7.1. Determination of the unanticipated component of domestic debt held by public

The unanticipated component of domestic debt is derived as the error term of the autoregressive equation of the domestic debt held by public. The appropriate autoregressive equation of domestic debt is derived in Section 7.5, using the minimum FPE criterion (Column 3, Table 7.4). The equation is specified in first differences of the series in logs. The error term of this equation is being considered as the unanticipated component of domestic debt and is used in the estimation of the Granger causality tests. Given the following autoregressive representation of the domestic debt held by the public,[43]

$$DDP_t = a_0 + a_1 DDP_{t-1} + D + \varepsilon_t \qquad \text{Equation 7.6}$$

where, DDP_t is domestic debt held by the public, and D is dummy at 1974. DDU_t is the unanticipated component of domestic debt held by the public, derived as the residual (ε_t) from Equation 7.6.

---

43 Excluding debt held by the government or RBI.

7.7.2. Stationarity of the unanticipated domestic debt and other methodological issues

The unit root test for stationarity of the unanticipated domestic debt held by public (DDU) shows that the series is stationary (Table 7.9). The data series for GDP, as already discussed in Section 7.5, is stationary in first differences.

Table 7.9: Testing for stationarity of unanticipated domestic debt and GDP – The unit roots-augmented Dickey-Fuller test

Variables	Levels		First differences	
	C	C and T	C	C and T
1	2	3	4	5
DDU	-	-	-4.41 (1)*	-5.01 (1)*
GDP	1.45 (1)	-1.24 (1)	-5.03 (1)*	-5.69 (1)*

C = Constant. T = Trend. DDU is unanticipated domestic debt. GDP is gross domestic product. Figures in parenthesis are lag values chosen to ensure that the residuals are white noise. * Significant at 1 per cent.

Source: Author's compilation.

In the empirical work, lag length for each variable has been determined by the FPE criterion, as discussed in Section 7.5. The maximum lag length with which we explored the FPE's is five years, for autoregressive lag as well as for lag of the manipulated variable. The minimum FPE's in each series are highlighted in Table 7.10.

Table 7.10: FPE of autoregressive process for unanticipated domestic debt and GDP

No. of Lags	FPE×10⁻⁴	
	DDU	GDP
1	2	3
1	**7.178**	**2.442**
2	7.316	2.497
3	7.827	2.659
4	8.141	2.681
5	8.477	2.860

DDU is the unanticipated component of domestic debt and GDP is gross domestic product.

Source: Author's compilation.

The autoregressive lag structure of the unanticipated series, on the basis of the minimum FPE is same as that in the case of domestic debt. However, as in the case of domestic debt, the residuals are not white noise (Column 2, Table 7.11).

The residual plot reveals an outlier at 1974, explainable in terms of the unusual fall in the domestic debt held by the public.[44] This outlier is corrected with the use of a dummy (Column 3, Table 7.11).

Table 7.11: Autoregressive equations of unanticipated domestic debt and GDP

Coefficient on variables	Variables		
	DDU	DDU*	GDP
1	2	3	4
(-1)	0.097	0.089	-0.172
	(0.5)	(0.6)	(1.0)
Constant	0.000	0.003	0.021
	(0.0)	(0.7)	(4.9)
Dummy		-0.089*	
		(4.4)	
FPE×10⁻⁴	7.178	4.247	2.442
R^2-Adj.	-0.023	0.359	-0.005
SSE	0.019	0.011	0.006
h stat	!	1.034	!
LM Test	**18.865**	1.530	4.338
Chow Test	1.124	-1.276	0.493!!
G-Q Test	2.403	0.579#	1.041##
F-stat	0.296	9.991	0.869

DDU is the unanticipated component of domestic debt and *GDP* is gross domestic product. * Dummy at year 1974. '-' refers to the lag values. ! cannot be computed. Figures in parentheses are the *t-values*. *LM Test* is the Jarque-Bera asymptotic LM normality test for the residuals. *Chow Test* at with 15 and 18 (!! 15 and 16) degrees of freedom. *G-Q* is the Goldfeld-Quandt Test with 13 and 16 (# 12 and 15; ## 13 and 14) degrees of freedom.

Source: Author's compilation.

The lag lengths of the independent (manipulated) variable that enter the equation, determined by the FPE criterion, are presented in Table 7.12. In one case, the FPE of the equation including the manipulated variable is more than that derived from the respective autoregressive equation of the controlled variable (marked by '$' in Tables 7.12 and 7.13).

---

44   Refer to Section 7.3. The outlier at 1974 is also present in the original equation. In the present case, where the residuals from the original equation are being considered, the outlier can be expected. This is because the OLS averages out the deviations from the mean.

Table 7.12: Minimum FPE and the optimal lag structures of unanticipated domestic debt and GDP

Dependent variable	Auto lags	Independent variable (IV)	Lags of IV	FPE×10⁻⁴
1	2	3	4	5
DDU*	1	GDP	1	4.511$
GDP	1	DDU	5	2.343

FPE refers to the Final Prediction Error. *DDU* is the unanticipated domestic debt and *GDP* is gross domestic debt. * Includes a dummy for the year 1974. $ FPE in this equation is greater than the FPE derived from the respective autoregressive equation of the dependent variable presented in Tables 7.11.

Source: Author's compilation.

7.7.3. Empirical results of Granger causality test

The estimated equations are presented in Table 7.13. The equations are robust and yield results similar to those when domestic debt, as such, is considered. In case of Granger causality, the coefficients of the independent variable are insignificant in the regressions.

Table 7.13: Granger causality test – unanticipated domestic debt and GDP

Coefficient on lag of	No. of lags	Dependent variable	
		DDU$	GDP
1	2	3	4
DDU	(-1)	0.101 (0.6)	0.137 (1.2)
GDP	(-1)	-0.050 (0.2)	-0.261 (1.3)
Constant		0.004 (0.6)	0.023 (5.3)
Dummy		-0.090 (4.3)	
R^2-Adj.		0.338	0.010
SSE		0.011	0.006
h stat		1.569	!
LM Test		1.213	4.338
Chow Test		-0.613	0.752
G-Q Test		0.692	1.166+
F-stat		6.457	1.162
F-stat@		0.033	1.428

DDU is the unanticipated component of domestic debt and GDP is gross domestic product. *Dummy* for the year 1974. '-' refers to the lag values. ! cannot be computed.

Figures in parentheses are the *t-values*. *LM Test* is the Jarque-Bera asymptotic LM normality test for the residuals. *Chow Test* with 15 and 18 degrees of freedom. *G-Q* is the Goldfeld-Quandt Test with 11 and 14 (+12 and 15) degrees of freedom. *F-stat* @ tests for the values of the independent variable. $ FPE in this equation is greater than the FPE derived from the respective autoregressive equation of the dependent variable presented in Table 7.11.

Source: Author's compilation.

The summary results are presented in Table 7.14. The results substantiate the earlier conclusions derived in section 7.6. The Granger causality test indicates that there is no causal relationship between the unanticipated domestic debt and economic growth. Thus, the results are different from those derived by Barro (1980), where for the US, unanticipated debt effects growth.

Table 7.14: Summary of conclusions emerging from the Granger causality test – unanticipated domestic debt and GDP

S.No	Null hypothesis	F-stat	p-value	Conclusion
1	2	3	4	5
1	DDU→ GDP	0.033	0.85710	No
2	GDP → DDP	1.428	0.24145	No

'→' refers to the direction of Granger Causality. *DDU* is the unanticipated component of domestic debt held by the public and *GDP* is gross domestic product. *F-stat* tests for the significance of the coefficients of the independent variable in the equation. *p-value* refers to the probability value of the F-stat.

Source: Author's compilation.

7.8. Conclusions

In the economic literature, two views on the relationship between domestic debt and growth are prevalent. The first view considers debt to be a burden on future generations in the long run. The other view, popularly called as the Ricardian Equivalence Hypothesis, considers the effects of debt to be neutral to the economy. The empirical literature is scanty on the issue.

In India, since the beginning of planned development in 1951, government argued for a high reliance on domestic borrowing for investment purposes. However, the trend in the growth of debt shows that it has been used by the government as a substitute for the shortfall, due to economic or political reasons, in the tax revenue and the surpluses generated from the public sector. Therefore, the rise in the domestic debt has not necessarily been incurred only for investment purposes but has consistently been used as an instrument to appropriate financial resources to meet the rising current government expenditure.

The empirical tests have been conducted to investigate the relationship between domestic debt held by public and economic growth in India. Cointegration and the Granger causality tests based on more than three and a half decades of annual data, support the hypothesis of Ricardian equivalence in India. Finally, in consideration of the rational expectation hypothesis, the effect of unanticipated component of domestic debt on growth has also been investigated. The results of the Granger causality test show no relationship between the series.

8

Separation of Debt from Monetary Management

In India, traditionally, a large component of domestic government debt was incurred at low rates of interest, which was statutorily prescribed for subscription by the institutional investors. A substantial amount of domestic debt was also monetised. The fiscal domination of monetary policy left very little manoeuvrability for RBI to pursue a monetary policy conducive to the overall objective of development of financial markets, price stability and economic growth.

In most of the developed economies, borrowing by the government from the central bank is prohibited. Also, to help the central bank to focus on the objective of stabilising the price level, debt management function has been separated from monetary authority. In India too, the issue was debated in late 1990's and it was concluded that such separation would require well-developed financial markets to finance government fiscal deficit. Then, India still had an administered interest rate regime. In the last decade, due to financial sector reforms undertaken since 1991, markets have developed rapidly and last remnants of administered interest rates on small savings are now being dismantled. Also, the Fiscal Responsibility and Budget Management Act of 2003 included a clause restricting the Government from directly borrowing from the RBI from 1 April 2006 except through Ways and Means Advances (WMAs) to meet temporary mismatches in receipts and payments or under exceptional circumstances. Therefore, it is considered that the separation of debt from monetary management can be undertaken now in India.

The separation has many advantages. First, separation would help the financial markets to integrate further. It is essential that the government mobilise its financial resources entirely from the market to help evolve a market yield curve. The interest rate structure that would consequently emerge would reflect market expectations and would be conducive to financial market integration. The development of a focused and transparent debt management strategy could also ensure that funds are available to the government at competitive rates of interest that will lead to expenditure prioritisation and to fiscal discipline in budget making. Prudence in fiscal and debt management that prevents any dominance on the monetary policy will encourage higher investment and economic growth.

Historically, the debt crises of 1982 and the Asian Crisis of 1997 had led many countries to assign priority to public debt management and then, a number of countries chose to separate debt from monetary management. As developments in the government securities market became more sophisticated, a different institutional structure was considered to be better suited to achieve different monetary policy and debt management objectives. Globally, substantial movement of international capital flows, and domestically, demonetisation of select currency in India, have led to a focus on issues of central bank independence. In normal economic circumstances, the central bank operates at the short-end of the market and debt management on the long end to minimise cost of raising resources but in times of crisis, the operations can become blurred. A separation in responsibilities was considered a better solution that reduces the risk of policy conflicts in the central bank actions. Also, once the financial markets had developed, the role of the central bank in sustaining the markets was considered minimal. Therefore, in many of the OECD countries, separation of debt and monetary management had been undertaken in the 1990's.

In recent years, after the global crisis of 2008, the issue of separation of monetary policy, fiscal policy and debt management has re-emerged. In many countries, during the period of crisis, scope of fiscal policy was expanded and debt to GDP ratios increased significantly. Consequently, debt management, in general, became difficult, and coordination between monetary and debt management assumed significance.

This chapter discusses the basics of debt management and its separation in Section 8.1. Traditional viewpoints about separation of debt management are presented in Section 8.2. Section 8.3 presents the debate on separating debt from monetary policies, in the aftermath of recent crisis. In Section 8.4, other relevant issues like central banks' independence, coordination between debt management, monetary and fiscal policy, and present global debt management practices are discussed. Indian debt management practices, role of RBI and the debate about separation of debt management in India are discussed in Section 8,4. Finally conclusions are presented in Section 8.5.

8.1. Some basics of debt management

The main objective of debt management is to minimise the cost of borrowings over the medium to long run, consistent with a prudent degree of risk. To achieve this minimisation of cost, promotion and development of efficient primary and secondary market for government securities are also important complementary objectives for debt management. Hence, Public debt management can be explained as the process of executing a strategy for managing the government's debt – to raise the required amount of borrowings, pursue cost/risk objectives, and also meet any other goal that the government might have prescribed (IMF, 2003). This may be expressed as a numerical target for the stock composition of the debt referred to as the strategic benchmark. The policy instrument is medium to long-term debt, and the composition is managed through new debt issuance, as well as changing the composition of existing debt through swaps, debt buybacks and exchange offers (Togo, 2007).

The debt management strategy in a number of countries is formulated in the framework of asset-liability management, implying the application of a portfolio approach to government debt management. In the portfolio approach, the importance of debt management in stabilisation policy will depend on how substitutable different types of bonds are, and how the return on bonds varies with changes in other asset prices. If different types of bonds are not perfect substitutes, then changing the mix of bonds in the private sector's portfolio could affect relative asset yields, investment and economic activity (Bernanke and Gertler, 1999; Vickers, 1999). Empirical results are mixed on this relationship. For the US, Agell and Persson (1992) found a small effect while Hess (1998) reported a significant effect on asset yields from changes in the maturity mix of government securities for the UK.

The important issue in this context is the relationship between debt and monetary management. Debt management has an impact on monetary policy through asset prices, and on fiscal policy through interest payments.

8.2. Separate debt management office – a traditional view

Traditionally, since early 1980's there was a growing consensus among practitioners to treat debt management as a separate policy instrument from monetary policy until 2008. A number of countries with liberalised financial markets and high levels of government debt sought to adopt professional debt management techniques to save cost and to provide policy signals to the market (Giovannini, 1997). The benefits of separation of the two functions were basically conditional upon the level of financial development as argued by Blommestein and Turner (2012).

The trend started with New Zealand in the 1980s, with the government recognising the need for proper policy assignment and accountability framework for debt management to meet the fiscal targets set in the then adopted Fiscal Responsibility Act. In Europe, several countries that were heavily indebted in the late 1980s and early 1990s like Belgium, France, Ireland and Portugal, decentralised debt management to varying extent, in order to reduce the variability of debt service cost that could jeopardise the targets set by the Growth and Stabilisation Pact. In the UK, debt management responsibilities were taken out of the Bank of England in order to remove the perception of conflict of interest in conducting debt management and monetary operations (Togo, 2007).

A number of countries have chosen to open a separate debt management office to have a more focused debt management policy (Table–1; details of three country case study are presented in Annex 1). The location of the debt management office is also important and will depend on a number of considerations. The dispersal of debt management functions within different layers of government can lead to lack of coherent debt management policy and overall risk assessment, and therefore higher operational risk. Some OECD countries have opted for an autonomous debt management office to improve operational efficiency (Austria, Finland, Ireland, Portugal, Sweden, Germany, Hungary, and UK) while others, seeking a balance between public policy and financial management, have a separate office but operating under the Ministry of Finance (Australia, Belgium, Canada, France, Netherlands, New Zealand, Poland and USA). In Denmark, debt management is undertaken by a privately owned central bank (OECD, 2002). In the case of developing countries, Currie, Dethier and Togo (2003) argue that the separate office can be initially placed under the Ministry of Finance while Kalderen (1997) suggests that in countries where fiscal deficits were high and financial markets were underdeveloped, a separate debt management office may be unsuitable for overall policy effectiveness of debt management.

On the basis of the experience of OECD countries, Cassard and Folkerts-Landau (1997) observed that several reasons emerge that justify the separation of debt management – to preserve the integrity and independence of the central bank, to shield debt management from political interference, to ensure transparency and accountability, and to improve debt management by entrusting it to portfolio

Table 8.1: Location of debt management office in select countries

Country	Location of debt management office	Scope of debt management			Advisory Board
		Cash	Debt	Contingent	
1	2	3	4	5	6
1. Australia	Separate agency under Treasury since 1999	Yes	Yes	No	Yes
2. Brazil	Debt office under Treasury since 1988	Yes	Yes	No	No
3. Colombia	Debt office under Treasury since 1991	No	Yes	Yes	Yes
4. Denmark	Debt office in central bank since 1991	Yes	Yes	Yes	No
5. France	Separate agency under Treasury since 2001	Yes	Yes	No	Yes
6. Germany	Separate agency under Treasury since 2001	Yes	Yes	No	No
7. Ireland	Separate agency under Treasury since 1991	Yes	Yes	No	Yes
8. Italy	Debt agency under Treasury – 1997	Yes	Yes	No	Yes
9. Mexico	Separate office in Treasury	No	Yes	Yes	No
10. New Zealand	Separate office under Treasury since 1988	Yes	Yes	Yes	Yes
11. Poland	Debt office within Treasury since 1994	No	Yes	Yes	No
12. Portugal	Separate debt office under Treasury since 1996	Yes	Yes	Yes	Yes
13. Sweden	Separate debt office under Treasury since 1789	Yes	Yes	Yes	Yes
14. UK	Separate debt office under Treasury since 1997	Yes	Yes	No	Yes
15. USA	Debt office within Treasury	Yes	Yes	No	No
16. South Africa	Debt management office within Treasury	Yes	Yes	Yes	No

Source: Various government websites.

managers with expertise in modern risk management techniques. The separation of debt and monetary management positively affects expectations as it explicitly indicates to the market and credit rating agencies that monetary policy is also independent of debt management. In case the two are not separated, then debt management policy eventually becomes subservient to the monetary policy as the monetary authorities attempt to use debt instruments to strengthen monetary policy signals and to enhance the credibility of the central bank.

There could emerge a conflict between different economic policies of the government. The classic conflict between monetary and debt management policy relates to the fixation of interest rates. The conflict between fiscal policy and debt management relates to the choice of keeping debt servicing costs low over the short term or over the medium-long term. A separate debt management authority is a step removed from the political process of budget making and generally would not succumb to the political pressure to trade-off long term debt management goals with short-run budget goals (Alesina, Prati and Tabellini, 1990). A separation of these policies was expected to avoid such conflicts and improve policy credibility.

Again, in case the central bank conducts debt management policy, conflicting objectives may emerge. Should liquidity be tightened based on monetary conditions prevailing in the economy or should it be relaxed to ensure success of market borrowing program of the government? Another area of concern could be interest rates which are of prime importance to the central bank. The government will like to borrow at low costs while the central bank will consider monetary and financial stability more important. The central bank may be tempted to manipulate financial markets to reduce the interest rates at which government debt is issued (Cassard and Folkerts-Landau (1997). Taylor (1998) argued that the Accord between the Federal Reserve and the Treasury in 1951, which emancipated the Fed from assisting the Treasury in borrowings at low rates of interest, helped the Fed to focus on interest rates. Even if a separate department within the central bank conducts debt management, the market will still perceive that the debt management decisions are influenced by inside information on interest rates. In contrast, a separate authority on fiscal issues would be required to present a separate debt management report to the Parliament which will prompt better fiscal discipline, appropriate audit, and financial and management controls.

In an autonomous debt office, staffing pattern can be more professionally competent, and the operational environment is similar to that of a privately-run commercial enterprise that is required to manage a portfolio within the risk parameters. Illustratively, the ongoing developments in the financial markets, illustratively the derivative instruments, require specialised training to monitor mark-to-market positions, over-the-counter dealings and pricing by the debt management authority, which would require competent and qualified professionals.

Thus, the main advantages of having a separate and autonomous debt office are: (a) signal to the financial markets that the government assigns institutional importance to the function; (b) commitment to the financial markets and the political parties for a transparent and accountable debt management policy; and (c) avoidance, at least, of any political pressures aimed at short-term political gains.

8.3. Separate debt management office – post-crisis debate

In view of the financial crisis, in recent years, there has been a rethink on the issue of separation of debt management because of the following factors: (a) sharp increase in government deficit and debt, because of the fiscal stimulus in many countries (Table-2); (b) use of unconventional monetary policy in advanced countries involving large scale purchase of government securities of varying maturities; (c) imposition of new liquidity requirements resulting in higher demand of government securities; and (d) increase in foreign ownership of government debt.

According to the conventional mandate, central banks were expected to operate in the bills market or short end of the market while debt managers were expected to operate in the long end of the same government securities market. In the post crisis period, the boundary between debt management and monetary policy became blurred mainly because of fiscal domination and unconventional monetary policy. The floatation of bonds by the debt manager, given the uncertainty, was of shorter maturity and not long-term bonds. This also created confusion in the role of the central bank and debt manager (Bank of England, 2011).

Thus, the thrust of the recent debate is that under different and difficult macroeconomic situations, the lines between debt and monetary policy become blurred and hence the two functions should be brought under the same agency. In the UK, where the separation took place in 1998 there is a discussion but not in the US where the two functions had been separated in earlier 1951. Goodhart (2012) argues that under quantitative easing there is a possibility that policy of debt management can negate the policy of the central bank. When the debt ratios increase, as in the case of UK or Greece, the short term interest rates also become a matter of concern to the respective government. Obviously, then the monetary policy and debt management has to be closely coordinated. Therefore, according to Goodhart (2012) separation between debt management and monetary policy is not desired as the existing arrangements are already under stress. Earlier also, Goodhart (2010)[1] argued that the central banks should be encouraged to revert to their role of managing national debt because with rising debt levels, debt management cannot be treated as a routine function which can be delegated to a separate independent institution.

Table 8.2: General government gross debt of select countries

(Percent of GDP)

Country	2006	2008	2010	2012	2014	2016	2017*
1	2	3	4	5	6	7	8
Brazil	65.8	61.9	63.0	62.2	62.3	78.3	81.2
China	32.2	27.0	33.7	34.3	39.9	46.2	49.3
France	64.2	68.0	81.6	89.5	95.2	96.6	97.4
Germany	66.6	65.1	81.0	79.9	74.9	67.6	64.7
Greece	102.9	109.4	146.2	159.6	180.9	181.3	180.7
Iceland	29.3	67.1	88.1	92.5	82.4	53.2	45.9
India	77.1	74.5	67.5	69.1	68.6	69.5	67.8
Indonesia	35.8	30.3	24.5	23.0	24.7	27.9	28.2
Ireland	23.6	42.4	86.3	119.6	105.4	76.4	74.8
Japan	186.0	191.3	215.9	236.6	242.1	239.2	239.2
Mexico	37.8	42.8	42.2	43.2	49.5	58.1	57.2
Netherlands	47.4	54.5	59.3	66.4	67.9	62.6	59.7
Portugal	61.6	71.7	96.2	126.2	130.6	130.3	128.6
Russia	10.5	7.4	10.6	11.8	15.6	17.0	17.1
Singapore	85.1	95.3	97.0	105.7	97.9	112.0	112.0
Slovenia	26.0	21.6	38.2	53.9	80.9	78.9	77.7
South Africa	29.8	26.5	34.7	41.0	46.9	50.5	52.4
Spain	38.9	39.4	60.1	85.7	100.4	99.3	98.5
United Kingdom	42.5	50.2	76.0	85.1	88.1	89.2	89.0
United States	63.6	73.6	95.7	103.4	105.2	107.4	108.3

Note: * Projections

Source: Fiscal Monitor, IMF

---

1   Debt Management is again becoming a critical element in the overall conduct of policy, as evident from events in Greece. Debt management can no longer be viewed as a routine function which can be delegated to a separate, independent body. Instead such management lies at the cross-roads between monetary policy and fiscal policy.

Traditionally, the government debt managers were guided to pursue a cost minimization policy but these institutional arrangements and principles would not hold in times of macro stress. At a recent OECD global debt forum meeting it was concluded that the global crisis has led to blurring of lines between debt management and monetary policy. It was also noted that different mandates appeared of the two institutions sometimes to be in conflict. The minutes of the US Treasury borrowing advisory committee had also hinted at some tensions according to Blommestein and Turner (2012).

On the other hand, the Study Group (SG) commissioned by the Committee on the Global Financial System (Chairman: Paul Fisher, 2011), after an extensive research, observed that there was little evidence that existing arrangements' for operational independence of sovereign debt management and monetary policy had created material problems. The SG concluded that modifying this independent arrangement would rather be risky, and that the central banks would benefit by keeping abreast of debt management activities. However, as would be expected in a difficult economic situation, SG did not recommend separation of debt management out of those central banks` where debt management functions were still being conducted.

Recent experience shows that there is a need for close communication and coordination among the relevant agencies managing monetary policy and debt management, as stressed by SG. This conclusion was also consistent with the Stockholm Principles (2011), which stated that 'communication among debt managers and monetary, fiscal and financial regulatory authorities should be promoted, given greater inter linkages across objectives, yet with each agency maintaining independence and accountability for its respective role'.[2]

According to Togo (2007), policy coordination would imply some form of decision-making process that determines a consistent policy mix that would result in the type of society that citizens want their elected government to implement. Governments would therefore need to figure out the desired economic outcome, and determine the policy mix through policy coordination that most effectively achieves this outcome. However, this choice of policy mix may mean that fiscal space may be reduced in the future if debt servicing costs increase due to the realisation of risky events, or monetary policy needs to be tightened to reign in high inflation caused by lax monetary policy in earlier periods.

---

2   Stockholm Principles (2011) were promulgated by debt managers and central bankers from 33 advanced and emerging market economies.

While theoretical arguments can be made to justify recent departures from policy, the reality is that in the post-crisis world, objectives of the central bank are no longer limited to price stability. In the United States, the Federal Reserve has essentially adopted a quantitative employment target and nominal GDP targets. Financial stability is also a central bank responsibility, according to new global understanding. The dilution of central bank independence is because of multiple objectives like pursuit of GDP growth, job creation and financial stability.[3] Further, the need to establish priorities when there is trade-offs, clearly requires political decisions, which cannot be made by unelected officials alone. Moreover, by pushing interest rates towards zero, the current policy of quantitative easing has strong, often regressive, income effects which cannot be implemented without political patronage. Hence, the emerging consensus, in the post-crisis period is that central banks' decision-making should be subject to political control and that policymakers must accept that central-bank independence will continue to weaken over the years (Blejer, 2013).

According to Goodhart (2010), the separation of debt and monetary management in England took place when debt operations became simpler and standardised, falling into a routine pattern. But given the crisis, debt management can no longer be considered as routine which can be delegated to a separate and independent body. In the present situation, therefore, the need is to combine an overall fiscal strategy with high calibre market tactics. But, the above argument by Goodhart is contrary to following reasons explained by Bank of England (1995) for separating debt management from the monetary policy: (a) monetary policy decisions should be seen as separate from debt management policy; (b) to ensure that Debt Management Office (DMO) did not have advance access to other policy decisions; (c) to avoid possible conflicts which could undermine the achievement of debt management objective of minimising the cost of government financing; and (d) to create a clearer allocation of the responsibilities for debt management and monetary policy.[4]

There are other important developments which have been largely ignored.

---

[3] Initially, central-bank independence was based on two main arguments which no longer apply because of multiple objectives being assigned to a central bank. First, politicians can exploit expansionary monetary policy's positive short-run effects at election time, without regard for its long-run inflationary consequences. Second, central banks have a clear comparative advantage in dealing with monetary issues, and can therefore be trusted to pursue their targets independently.

[4] In fact this was a key factor in shaping the new arrangement.

First, the government issues government securities which are required as collateral for repo transactions between the central bank and the financial markets as well as during transactions amongst the market players. Therefore, the tenor and coupon rate of these bonds is of interest to the central bank. Second, the fact that debt management was separate from monetary management in the US and OECD, provided transparency to the rescue operations launched by many governments in face of the global crisis. Independence of operations and objectives, and close coordination between different agencies lent credibility to the government policies. Third, in case of conflict of interest, closer coordination between the agencies, and clear explanations of differences helped the financial markets to understand the dilemma facing regulatory and statutory agencies, resulting in more accountability and responsibility. Fourth, if the interest rates are market determined then fiscal discipline is imposed on the government that would restrict fiscal profligacy and populist competitiveness during periods of crisis and elections. This, in a way, creates a level playing field between the public and private sector, and probably restricts crowding out of private sector due to large borrowings by the government.

8.4 Other related issues

8.4.1. Central bank independence

The other major factor of separation of debt from monetary management was the argument of independence of a central bank. In the years until 2008, because of the great moderation and US Fed's victory over inflation in the 1980s,[5] substantial evidence had been advanced in theoretical and empirical literature to support the political and economic independence of the central bank (Grilli, Masciandaro and Tabellini, 1991). Bade and Parkins (1980) define political independence as the ability of the central bank to choose its policy without the influence of the fiscal authority while economic independence refers to the freedom to use its monetary policy instruments. In support of central bank independence, Kydland and Prescott (1977), Barro and Gordon (1983a and 1983b), Burdekin and Laney (1988), Eschweiler and Bordo (1993), and Grilli, Masciandaro and Tabellini (1991) argue that more independent central banks reduce rate of inflation, while

---

5 Fed Reserve's victory (Under Paul Volcker) over inflation in the US was institutionalised in legislation and practices that granted central bank greater autonomy and, in some cases, formal independence from long standing political constraints. Now many central banks could be trusted to do the right thing; and they delivered. (El-Erian, 2013).

Alesina and Summers (1993) conclude that such independence has no impact on real economic performance. Wagner (1998) argues that making a central bank independent lowers expectations pertaining to inflation of private sector that determine wage and price contracts, and thereby also expectations that impact exchange rates. Blinder (1997), and Bernanke and Mishkin (1997) suggest that policymakers should announce targets and that policy transparency to achieve those specific targets will enhance accountability while providing independence to the central bank.

Goodhart (1994) argued that it was easier for the principal to appoint an agent and prescribe a single, quantified, easily recognised, measured and understood outcome, which would facilitate monitoring and accountability. A number of countries had granted increased independence to the central banks to focus on the objective of price stability and inflation targeting (Blinder, 2004; Cukierman, 1992). Unlimited access to central bank credit on easy terms by the government not only restricts independence of the central bank, but also adversely affects financial position of the banking sector. Kopits and Symansky (1998) argue that a prohibition on central bank credit to the government removes an important source of inflationary pressure.

In some countries, where financial markets are not developed, the need to finance the deficit of the government restricts the independence of the central bank – automatic and unlimited access to central bank credit is resorted to, supposedly for the purpose of capital expenditure expected to lead to higher economic growth.[6] Independent central banks are able to restrict such accommodation of fiscal deficits depending on the needs of monetary policy (Demopoulos, Katsimbris and Miller, 1987; Burdekin and Laney, 1988). Rather, Grilli, Masciandaro and Tabellini (1991) and Carracedo and Dattels (1997) mentioned that in many countries, borrowing from the central bank is prohibited. Sundararajan, Dattels and Blommestein (1997) argued that a ceiling on central bank credit to government promotes monetary restraint and helps to establish central bank credibility and operational autonomy. In the Maastricht Treaty (1992), only indirect credit and that also at the discretion of the central bank is extended to the government. Although OECD countries impose no formal

---

6   Cukierman (1992) discusses some of the structural reasons that led to flow of credit from the central bank to the government and eventually erosion of its independence: (i) underdeveloped financial markets; (ii) inelastic supplies of funds with respect to real rate of interest; (iii) large outstanding domestic debt; and (iv) inelastic revenue and expenditure of the government with respect to income.

constraints on indirect central bank credit to government, nevertheless there are often informal constraints – open market operations can only be done for monetary policy reasons.

The transfer of profits of the central bank to the government also restricts the independence of the central bank and could also be inflationary, if these lead to higher expenditure (Table 8.3).[7] Historically, the need to impose limits on

Table 8.3: Select country practices relating to distribution of profit

Country	Distribution of profit
1	2
Euro system	Up to 20 per cent of its profit in any year subject to a limit equal to 100 per cent of the ECB's capital.
Germany	Net profit is transferred to the federal government after setting aside amount for statutory reserves.
Canada	Net revenue of the bank is remitted to the receiver general for Canada.
Portugal	Net profit for the year is distributed equally between allocation to reserves and the State.
UK	Profit of both Issue (entire) and Banking (some amount) departments is payable to the Treasury.
Sweden	Central Bank makes a dividend payment to the treasury.
Italy	Net profit for the year, after allocations to the ordinary reserve and extraordinary reserve accounts and distribution of dividend to shareholders, transferred to the State.
South Africa	Nine-tenths of the surplus of the bank is paid to the Government.
Brazil	Net profit after constitution or reversal of reserves is transferred to the national treasury.
Norway	A third of the capital in the transfer after provisions is transferred to the Treasury every year.
Russia	Transfers fund to the federal budget amounting to 80 per cent of its profits.
Japan	5 per cent of net income for the fiscal year is transferred to the legal reserves.
Korea	Voluntary reserves are transferred to the government's general revenue account.
Australia	Net profit including transfers to/from unrealised profits reserve earnings available for distribution, payable to the government.
Singapore	Yearly net profit including transfer of reserves from currency fund is paid to the government.
USA	Excess earnings on federal reserve notes are transferred to the US treasury.

Source: Various websites of central banks.

---

7   If debt management activity is also undertaken by the central bank, then the profits may be substantially large.

the government's ability to finance itself through seigniorage revenue was one of the major reasons to grant independence to the central bank (Swinburne and Castello-Branco, 1991). Therefore, Blommestein and Thunholm (1997), and Sundararajan and Dattels (1997) argue that such profits should be netted out against treasury debt to the central bank and the rest of the profits should be transferred to the government.[8] Robinson and Stella (1988) argue that if profits of the central bank go to the government, then conversely transfers from the government should cover losses. This would imply a combined balance sheet of the central bank and the government resulting in a continuous flow of seigniorage revenue to the government, which, however, would not be acceptable to an independent central bank.

In literature, independence of a central bank has to be contextual, and has four main dimensions – (a) statutory independent from state with respect to nomination, tenure and termination of Governor; (b) independence of monetary policy instrument, implying managing interest rate or liquidly; (c) independence of monetary policy objectives – inflation targeting, credit control, priority sector lending or any other objective which is stipulated by the government; and (d) financing of government deficit.

The science of central bank as well as its functions are still evolving. The evolution as always, has not been easy and has had its share of challenges. Historically, in 1900, there were hardly a dozen central banks and each had been created, initially, to dispense some specific function of the government, mainly to issue currency and coinage or manage foreign exchange reserves. Regulation and supervision of banks came later, and later still inflation targeting and fixation of interest rates. The concept of independent central bank evolved in advanced economies and finds its roots in the successful anti-inflationary policy of Paul Volcker in the USA during 1979–82.

8.4.2. Need for coordination

In each country, the economic situation, including the state of domestic financial markets and the degree of central bank independence, would play an important role in determining the range of activities to be handled by the debt manager and the level of coordination that is necessary. Monetary policy and debt management clearly have to be complementary to each other but debt management should not be considered a tool of monetary management nor should monetary policy

---

8   Blommestein and Thunholm (1977) suggest that another way to restrict the transfer of seigniorage to the government is to maintain the real value of reserves and capital.

be considered the objective of debt management (Bank of England, 1995). The industrial countries have generally separated the objective and accountability of debt and monetary management. In the case of the EMU, monetary policy is operated by ECB while national authorities conduct debt management. The sharing of adequate information between Treasuries, national central banks and the European Central Bank is a norm, and ensured for the purpose of liquidity management. The industrialised countries also ensure that debt manager and monetary authority coordinate their activities in financial markets to avoid operating at cross-purposes.

In the case of developing countries, coordination between fiscal, monetary and debt management functions is considered even more crucial, where financial markets are under-developed and forecasts of government revenues and expenditure are inaccurate. The financing options of the government are limited and cash requirements are uncertain, and this then limits the independence of the central bank. The issuance of government securities by a separate debt office needs to be closely coordinated with the open market operations undertaken by the central bank to ensure appropriate liquidity conditions in the market.

Therefore, the role of the central bank in public debt management, though separated, would continue to be crucial. As an issuing agency of government securities and regulator of government securities market, the central bank organises rules and procedures for selling and delivering securities and for collecting payments for the government. As a fiscal agent, the central bank makes and receives payments, including interest payments and servicing of principal. As adviser to the government and to the debt manager, it could provide policy inputs on the design of the debt program, mix of debt instruments and maturity profile of debt stock. These inputs will be useful in providing stability to the overall debt program, facilitating smooth functioning of the market, and providing a stable environment for the conduct of monetary policy.

Another important change is concurrently occurring in the monetary policy objectives, internationally. While theoretical arguments can be made to justify recent departures from policy, the reality is that in the post-crisis world, objectives of the central bank are no longer limited to price stability.

8.4.3. Salient features of a debt management office

The shift to a separate debt office can be strategised to be gradual. As suggested by Currie, Dethier and Togo (2003), initially all the debt management activities can be consolidated in one office under the Ministry of Finance and only then the issue of separation to an independent office can be considered. First, the internal debt management activities of the central and state governments could be shifted to the debt office followed by external debt. The shifting of cash management of the government in terms of WMA could follow next, and then the contingent liabilities (Magnusson, 1999b). The transfer of cash management activity implies that the forecast of the budgetary gap and liquidity management of the government is undertaken by the debt manager, while the central bank can concentrate on the daily management of liquidity in the market.

All the debt management activities, including short-term cash requirements, domestic and external market borrowings, small savings and contingent liabilities should eventually be assigned to a single debt agency, as in the case of UK. The placing of all contingent liabilities in the single debt office will facilitate the scrutiny of issuances, record keeping, risk assessment, pricing, audit and approval by the Parliament. This will help in better coordination of the debt management function, operational efficiency, risk assessment, accountability and responsibility. Finally, cash management of important government undertakings of the government like the railways, post (including collections under small savings) and telecommunications, pension and provident funds, and reserve funds and deposits could be transferred to the debt office if considered appropriate or else, these commercial undertakings/funds could benefit from the expert advice available within the government sector. The management of pension and provident funds could also benefit from the advice and experience of the debt management office during the period of transition while pension reforms are being undertaken.

The location and salient features of the debt management office differ across countries but generally the legal authority to borrow in the name of the central government rests with the Parliament. Also, limits on borrowing are generally prescribed and the trend is to include all types of government debt under a single agency. The details are presented in (Appendix 8.2).

The debt management office is generally provided with a sufficient degree of functional autonomy to fulfill its mandate without political pressure. Such autonomy is permitted along with the requirement that the debt management office be accountable, and transparent in its operations, procedures and results. The activities of the agency are supervised by a special advisory board, which provides guidance on strategic and technical issues to the chief executive who regularly monitors its activities and reports directly to the concerned authority. The constitution and functioning of the advisory board lends credibility to the operations, which is necessary for robust market expectations (Calvo, 1988; Diamond and Dybvig, 1983). The membership of the advisory board, to function in a transparent and effective manner is generally broad based, with representatives from the government, market, academia and the central bank.

The chief officer executes the operational aspects and the office is mainly organised to independently cover operational work, policy and planning, risk assessment, regulations and audit. The front office is responsible for resource mobilisation, executing transactions in financial markets, including management of auctions and other forms of borrowing, and all other funding operations, including guarantee operations, hedging, and derivative transactions of the government. The middle office undertakes risk analysis, prepares alternate debt scenarios and assesses the performance of debt managers against any strategic benchmarks. The back office handles the settlement of transactions and the maintenance of financial records and market information system (debt registry, disbursements, and debt-service payments).

8.4.4. Important role of the RBI

The key role in management of internal debt is played by the RBI which could conflict with its pursuit of the objectives of monetary policy. The monetary policy of the RBI aims to provide adequate liquidity to meet credit growth and support investment demand in the economy, while continuing to maintain a vigil on movements in the price level, and to prefer a soft and flexible interest rate environment within the framework of macro-economic stability.

The RBI is the regulator and supervisor of the financial system, including banks, and also of the money, government securities and foreign exchange markets. The RBI has to balance the needs of the markets (manage liquidity), government requirements (fiscal requirements), balance sheet of the banks (asset prices and interest rate movements) and general price level (growth of money supply). The RBI is also a significant contributor of profits to the Central Government (Table 8.4).[9]

---

9   Under Section 47 of the RBI Act, 1934, after making provisions for bad and doubtful debts, depreciation in assets, contribution to staff and superannuation fund and for all matters for which provision is made by or under the Act, the balance of the profit of the RBI are paid to the central government.

Table 8.4: Profits of RBI transferred to central government (per cent of GDP)

Year	Revenue receipts	Non-tax revenue receipts	Profits of RBI transferred to central government
1	2	3	4
1990–91	12.2	2.0	0.1
1991–92	12.7	2.4	0.2
1992–93	12.5	2.6	0.2
1993–94	11.3	2.5	0.2
1994–95	11.4	2.3	0.4
1995–96	11.7	2.3	0.3
1996–97	11.7	2.3	0.4
1997–98	12.1	2.4	0.4
1998–99	11.2	2.5	0.3
1999–00	12.1	2.6	0.5
2000–01	11.8	2.6	0.4
2001–02	11.6	2.9	0.4
2002–03	12.1	2.9	0.4
2003–04	12.5	2.7	0.2
2004–05	12.3	2.5	0.2
2005–06	12.4	2.1	0.2
2006–07	13.3	1.9	0.3
2007–08	14.4	2.1	0.3
2008–09	12.8	1.7	0.4
2009–10	11.9	1.8	0.3
2010–11	13.4	2.8	0.2
2011–12	12.0	1.4	0.2
2012–13	12.1	1.4	0.3
2013–14	12.2	1.8	0.5
2014–15	12.1*	1.6	0.5
2015–16	12.6*	1.9	0.5

Source: RBI.

In the RBI, the Department of Internal Debt Management (DIDM), set up

Separation of Debt from Monetary Management

in April 1992, undertakes the work relating to government securities, Treasury bills and cash management. DIDM is organised essentially as a separate debt management office with the essential units- primary market (borrowing and cash management of both central and state), policy and research, dealing room, MIS and regulation (of primary dealers). The Department of Government and Bank Accounts (DGBA) maintain the accounts of both the governments – central and state, on a daily basis. On external debt, Department of External Investment and Operations in RBI works as a front office along with MoF. The function of cash management of the central and state governments is also performed by DIDM and DGBA in RBI. The managerial structure of public debt management is presented in Table 8.5.

Table 8.5: Management of public debt in India

Major items	Appropriated by	Managed by	Fixation authority for/determination of		
			Amount	Maturity	Interest rate
1	2	3	4	5	6
Market loans	Centre	MOF, RBI	MOF	MOF, RBI	Market
	State	DOF, RBI	MOF	DOF, RBI	RBI, Market
Market bonds	Centre	RM, MOF, RBI	RM, MOF	RM	RM, MOF, RBI
	State	RD, DOF, RBI	RD, DOF	RD	RD
Treasury bills	Centre	MOF, RBI	MOF, RBI	MOF, RBI	Market
WMA	Centre	MOF, RBI	MOF, RBI	MOF, RBI	RBI
	State	DOF, RBI	RBI	RBI	RBI
Loans from Bk and FI	State	DOF	RD	RD	RD, DOF
Small savings	State	MOF, DOF	MOF, DOF	MOF	MOF
Provident funds	Centre	MOL, MOF	MOL, MOF	MOL	MOL
	State	MOL, DOF	DOF	MOL	MOL
Reserve funds/ deposits	Centre	RM, MOF	RM	RM	RM
	State	RD, DOF	RD	RD	RD

Table continued

Table 8.5: Management of public debt in India

Major items	Appropriated by	Managed by	Fixation authority for/determination of		
			Amount	Maturity	Interest rate
1	2	3	4	5	6
External debt	Centre	MOF, RBI	MOF	MOF	MOF
Contingent liabilities	Centre	RM, MOF	RM	RM	RM
	State	RD, DOF	RD	RD	RD

MOF – Ministry of Finance; DOF – Department of Finance; MOL – Ministry of Labour; RM – Respective Ministry; RD – Respective Department; Bk – Banks; FI – Financial Institutions
Source: Author's compilation.

8.4.5. Audit and reporting

The debt management function of the RBI is subjected to internal audit and the statutory external audit.

Accounting for the debt management operational is done by the government's Controller General of Accounts, the accounts are subject to the audit by the Comptroller and Auditor General of Accounts, a constitutional body.

The Comptroller General of Accounts does the accounting of debt management operations; the Comptroller and Auditor General of Accounts, a constitutional body, do the audit. The internal debt management functions of the RBI are reported in the statutory Annual Report of the RBI while external debt management functions are reported in the Annual Status Report on External Debt – both presented to Parliament. The data on contingent liabilities is consolidated by the RBI and placed in its annual statutory publications though not regularly.

8.4.6. Development of the markets

The financial markets have developed since the reforms of 1991, especially the money and government securities market with the introduction of new instruments, technological innovations and effective regulation. The government both central and state could successfully undertake debt restructuring in the securities market in 2002 and 2003. The turnover in the secondary market is steadily rising since 1992 when the auction system of central government dated securities was first introduced. The borrowing requirements of the government are successfully being mobilised from the market, with no devolvement on the RBI, in recent years. The primary dealer system introduced in 1995 has also developed and the primary dealers actively participate in the primary market and also provide two-way quotes in the secondary market. The borrowing calendar, announced by the central government on a six-monthly basis since March 2002, is generally adhered to. The government securities market has adopted suitable technology and the auctions are conducted electronically. The Clearing and Settlement system has been operational since 2002 and the Real Time Gross Settlement system has been introduced since March 2004. The market stabilisation scheme was introduced in 2004 and by 2005, Negotiated Dealing System – Order Matching (NDS-OM) trading module was started. An important instrument, Separate Trading of Registered Interest and Principal Securities (STRIPS) became effective from April 2010.

Table 8.6: Interest earnings from domestic securities

Year	Interest earnings on holding of domestic securities (₹ Crore)	Surplus transferred to the government (₹ Crore)	Interest payment as percentage of surplus transferred (%)
1	2	3	4
2000-01	11314	9350	121.0
2001-02	14492	10320	140.4
2002-03	1306	8834	147.9
2003-04	4872	5400	90.2
2004-05	1607	5400	29.8
2005-06	1207	8404	14.4
2006-07	5144	11411	45.1
2007-08	4958	15011	33.0
2008-09	9056	25009	36.2
2009-10	6646	18759	35.4
2010-11	15032	15009	100.2
2011-12	32339	16010	202.0
2012-13	52306	33010	158.5
2013-14	43538	52679	82.6
2014-15	43630	65896	66.2
2015-16	43079	65876	65.4

Source: RBI.

The RBI, as a debt manager of the government and regulator of the government securities market, participates in and supports the borrowing program of the government. Though in the 1990's, with the development of the markets, net RBI credit to the government, especially the central government, has declined, yet the interest receipts of RBI on account of holding central government securities ranged between 14.4 per cent and 202.0 per cent of its profits in the last decade and half (Table 8.6).

8.4.7. Coordination between RBI, government and markets

To coordinate the activities of debt management with fiscal authorities, various committees function in RBI. The Cash and Debt management committee, consisting of officials from the MOF and RBI meets regularly to discuss the operational details of market borrowings for the Central Government. The issues pertaining to the State Governments are discussed in a semi-annual meeting with the officials from MOF, DOF and RBI. The Technical Committee on Money and Government Securities, consisting of representatives from market, academia, government, banks, and RBI, meet regularly and advise the RBI on development and regulation of the government securities market.

8.4.8. Need for a separation of debt and monetary management

In India, the separation of debt would provide the RBI with necessary independence in monetary management and an environment to pursue an inflation target. The separation of debt management would also provide focus to the task of asset-liability management of government liabilities, undertake risk analysis and also help to prioritise government expenditure through higher awareness of interest costs. The need for setting up a specialised framework on public debt management which will take a comprehensive view of the liabilities of government, and establish the strategy for low-cost financing in the long run has been advocated by various expert committees since late 1990s (Table 8.7).

Table 8.7: Timeline: Separation of debt management

Year	Source	Recommendations
1	2	3
1997	Report of the Committee on Capital Account Convertibility (Chairman: S. S. Tarapore)	Setting up of an Office of the Public Debt (OPD)
1997	A working group on Separation of Debt Management from Monetary Management (Chairman: V. Subrahmanyam)	Separate Debt management office as a company under the Indian Companies Act
2000	The Advisory Group on Transparency in Monetary and Financial Policies	Independent Debt Management Office, in a phased manner.
2001	The RBI Annual Report 2000–01	Separate DMO.
2001	The Internal Expert Group on the Need for a Middle Office for Public Debt Management, (Chairman: A. Virmani)	Establishing an autonomous Public Debt Office.
2004	The Report on the Ministry of Finance for 21st Century (Chairman: Vijay Kelkar)	National Treasury Management Agency.
2004	The Fiscal Responsibility and Budget Management (FRBM) Act	Prohibits the Reserve Bank from participating in the primary market for Central Government securities with effect from April 2006.
2006	Fuller Capital Account Convertibility (Chairman: S.S. Tarapore)	Set up of Office of Public Debt outside RBI
2007	The Union Budget 2007–08	Establishment of a DMO in the government.
2008	The High Level Committee on Financial Sector Reforms (Chairman: Raghuram Rajan)	Structural change of public debt management, such that it minimises financial repression and generates a vibrant bond market. Set up independent DMO.
2008	Internal Working Group on Debt Management (Chairman: Jahangir Aziz)	Establishing a DMO.

Table continued

Table 8.7: Timeline: Separation of debt management

Year	Source	Recommendations
1	2	3
2009	Committee on Financial Sector Assessment (Chairman: Rakesh Mohan)	Setting up DMO.
2012	Report of the Working Group on Debt Management Office (Chairman: Govind Rao)	Independent DMO.
2012	The Financial Sector Legislative Reforms Commission Approach Paper	Separation of debt management with specialised investment banking capability for public debt management.
2013	The Financial Sector Legislative Reforms Commission (Chairman: B.N. Srikrishna)	Specialised framework to analyse comprehensive structure of liabilities of the Government, and strategizing minimal cost techniques for raising and servicing public debt over the long term within an acceptable level of risk.

Source: Various Reports, GoI and RBI.

Despite consistency in recommendations of separating debt management from monetary management, there has been hesitancy on part of the RBI and GOI, as documented in speeches by the top management and arguments offered in the annual reports of the RBI. The main arguments advanced are that there already is a separate department within the RBI and that during these critical economic years, need for coordination would be immense and that the government may not have the necessary experience or expertise.

In this context, important water shed in the institutional arrangements of debt management was the setting up of the middle office in the Ministry of Finance in 2008, to formulate debt management strategy for the central government. Again the Union Budget 2011–12 had stated that the government was in the process of setting up an independent Debt Management Office (DMO) in the Ministry of Finance. The DMO was entrusted with the responsibilities of piloting the evolution of legal, governance and comprehensive risk management framework suitable for independent debt office, formulation of strategies regarding long term debt management and annual debt issuance; and maintaining centralised data base on government liabilities and dissemination of debt related information to public. Similarly, the Union Budget for 2012–13 proposed to move the Public Debt Management Agency Bill in the Parliament.

However, an important re-think in the whole process was required because the RBI was not convinced that the separation would be useful for the financial markets. The proposed argument was that in the post crisis period there has been an increased need for close coordination between monetary policy, financial stability and debt management. Debt management, according to Khan (2012), was a difficult exercise in a developing country and was not simply raising resources from the market. The size and dynamics of government borrowing has a wider influence on interest rate movements, and liquidity and credit growth. Therefore, focus only on the cost factors may not be an appropriate way to manage debt. He had also argued that policy coordination may not be operationally effective especially, if the fiscal deficit was high. According to Subbarao (2011), despite a large borrowing program, the RBI was able to complete successfully market borrowings in a cost efficient manner and with average maturity of 10 years, amongst the longest maturity profiles in the world. Merely shifting the debt management to a different agency in an uncertain environment and with large size of deficit would not help as the pressure on the central bank would continue to ensure government borrowing at low cost. The remedy is fiscal consolidation and not separation of debt management, according to him. Also, significant capital flows require close coordination between debt management and monetary policy, especially when sterilisation through government bonds has to be undertaken by the central bank.

Earlier, Mohan (2003), had also opposed separation of debt management from the RBI, arguing that given the federal structure of India, debt management of the state governments is difficult. In the case of state governments, a substantial amount of deficit financing is through government borrowings. In view of the size of the borrowings by the state and central government, it is necessary to harmonize the annual borrowing program of the government. A separation from the central bank would make such harmonisation difficult.

There are also other views as to why the two functions should not be separated.[10] These can be summarised as follows:-

a. high level of fiscal deficit and over-all government debt to GDP ratio;
b. conflict of interest between debt manager and the government's role as an owner of public sector banks;
c. close interlinkages between debt and monetary management roles;

---

10 Some of these are those reasons that were offered by the Committee on Financial Sector Assessment (GOI and RBI, 2009).

d. difficulty in harmonising operations of debt issue and redemptions, SLR maintenance and Market Stabilisation Scheme;
e. existing expertise available in the RBI; and
f. inappropriateness of state debt management by a central government entity.

The above issues are debatable and need to be analysed. A separate debt management office will help to consolidate all debt-related activities of the government in one office. At present, various schemes operate, some under the government of India and few under states, many of which are independently managed by different governments. There are no economies of scale being explored and little interaction or synchronisation of activities occurs between these offices and their practices.

Further, the argument that because the central government has an ownership share in public sector banks, debt management should not be placed under the same government needs further analysis. If the central bank regulates and supervises the government securities market then in a similar vein it can be argued that there is a conflict between regulation and supervision and participation in the market, as the RBI participates in the government securities markets as a dealer/trader too. Earlier, RBI was a participant in the primary market too. Similarly, as the central bank is a regulator and supervisor of commercial banks there could emerge a conflict of interest to strengthen the balance sheet of commercial banks, therefore RBI may prescribe higher stipulations of holding government bonds. The central bank could also use its influence over the regulated entities to subscribe to flotations that it manages on behalf of the government. Goodhart (2010) goes further and questions the necessity of entrusting the role of setting interest rate on Central Bank which already handles the essential role of liquidity management and financial stability in the country.

The argument is weak on the issue of conflict emerging due to ownership pattern on select institutions in the financial sector, mainly public sector banks because of following reasons –

a. RBI had a share in State Bank of India (SBI) for many years, and that never diluted the RBI's supervision or regulation of SBI.
b. The share of ownership of the government in public sector bank, has been declining over the years and is expected to decline even further. Also, if re-privatisation of public sector banks is initiated as is being debated in the country now.

c. The government, even if is not the owner, is finally responsible for the operations of the commercial banks, as demonstrated by the recent financial crisis in many countries in the US and Europe.
d. The share of public sector banks in holding of government securities has been declining in recent years while the share of non-public sector banks has been rising.
e. There are different techniques to ensure an arms length's distance between ownership of public sector banks and administration of separate debt management office, most important being public dissemination of information and transparency in operations.

Finally, despite the ownership, performance of public sector banks, in terms of NPAs or return on assets are not significantly different when compared with other banks operating in India. Even if there is a separate department, with the requisite 'firewall' conducting debt management, within the central bank, the markets will still suspect the influence of inside information on interest rates. This 'joint family approach' does not augur well for transparency in management of debt and monetary policy formulation. And when the central bank is balancing different objectives of debt and monetary management, accountability is difficult to fix.

A separate debt management office also ensures that there are alternative views of the economic situation of the markets and the economy, and not just that special view which has been formed by the central bank through its trading desk and market intelligence. The debt manager has also to build capacity for understanding the economy to successfully operate in the financial markets. Through proper coordination between the central bank and debt manager, a better view of the financial markets and the economy can be formed. The arguments against the separation like difficulty in harmonising the operations, could basically be resolved by better coordination between various agencies, similar to the type of informal as well as institutionalised coordination between the RBI and the Ministry of Finance. A separated agency has an advantage that it will bring in transparency in the operations of debt management. It will also help in focusing on the communication policy as well as dissemination of debt related information to the market.

On the issue of lack of expertise to manage the DMO, as in other countries, the government could consider hiring experts, temporarily or permanently, that are available in the RBI or from rest of the world. Incidentally, it may be considered that in the central bank, in absence of any specialised cadre of debt management recruits, staffs is transferrable and generally moved to different desks. In contrast, in a proposed DMO, the staff will be completely dedicated to activities of debt management and gain specialisation and expertise on the job. On a long term basis, certification courses to ensure specialised training to individuals in the DMO could be considered.

Finally, the benefits of separating debt from monetary management are significantly large. First, given that fiscal deficits are large and that debts are substantial, a focussed approach will be useful. In the last decade, government borrowings (centre and states) have increased from Rs. 1,657 billion in 2007–08 to Rs. 7,537 billion in 2016–17. Such a substantial increase of annual borrowings of market loans from 3.3 per cent of GDP to 4.9 per cent, over a decade would require careful examination and analysis which a specialised institution can provide (–Figure 8.1). Second, given the focused approach, specifically tailored schemes for different segments of the population can be simulated. Illustratively, the outstanding amount of small savings schemes like Senior Citizen Scheme and Public Provident Fund have increased from Rs. 414 billion in 2007–08 to Rs. 2,416 billion in 2016–17 but the ownership pattern remains unknown because of which, it becomes difficult to tailor social security schemes for the elderly in terms of interest rates and maturity. This also applies to other social security schemes which result in increasing liabilities of the government. Third, an autonomous DMO would imply an annual statutory report and consequent public scrutiny, and dissemination of information. This would ensure that the government does not take undue advantage of being the owners of public sector banks and does not practise fiscal profligacy by access to easy borrowing at low rates of interest.

Figure 8.1: Combined market borrowings of centre and state (as a percent of GDP)

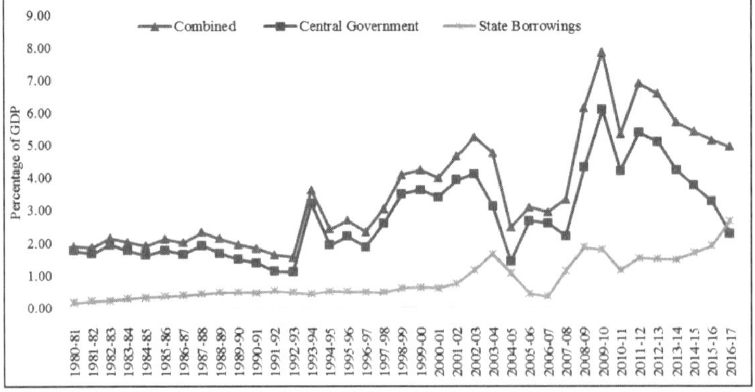

Source: RBI.

8.4.9. Advantages from the separation of debt management from the RBI

The separation of debt and monetary management in India has been considered since 1997 (RBI, 1997; Reddy, 2004). The RBI has acknowledged the need for such separation, based on the fiscal performance of the government and development of the financial markets. The assignment of the function of debt management to a separate agency, would help to establish specific accountability and responsibility on the debt manager. This would lead to professional management of government debt liabilities and a mandate to operate on commercial basis. Expectations have an important role to play in debt management (Calvo, 1988) and such a separation would reinforce the commitment of the government to fiscal discipline and consolidation. The establishment of a separate agency, away from political interference, will also be beneficial, as it will help avoid the impact of political business cycles on debt management (Rajaraman, 2004; Khemani, 2000).

The separation of debt management from monetary policy will help the central bank to focus exclusively on price stability (RBI, 1997),[11] which will provide transparency in its operations (Blinder, 2004) and thereby enhance its credibility (Wagner, 1998), rather than having to focus on multiple objectives, which makes the central bank subservient to the government (Goodhart, 1994). The development of focused and credible debt management strategy could also ensure that the funds are available to the government at competitive rates of interest. The availability of financial resources to the government at commercial rates of interest will lead to expenditure prioritisation and to fiscal discipline in budget making.[12]

The separation of the two functions can also facilitate the regulation and supervision of the secondary markets more objectively by the RBI. The markets in developed countries are generally either regulated by the central bank or a separate independent authority but not by the debt manager, who simply assumes the role of another player in the debt market. The primary

---

11 "Although price stability is an important economic policy objective by itself, there are several difficulties in adopting such a single goal of monetary policy in India. Given the need to manage the Government borrowing programme, the Reserve bank would have to balance, often times, its internal debt management function with the monetary." (Paragraph 3.8, Annual report 1999–2000, RBI).

12 Though Smith (1791) and Ricardo (1951) argue in the context of war finance, the logic can be extended to government expenditure on many projects, which do not result in adequate returns.

dealers, under the contractual arrangement with the debt manager, could continue to be market makers participating in the primary auctions and trading in the secondary market but regulated by the central bank.

There can also arise a conflict in the role of supervising the banks and being the debt manager of government securities. The banks and financial institutions, which are regulated by the RBI, and generally subscribe to market loans, could be under an unstated pressure to make the borrowing programme of the government a success. This unstated pressure could impede the discovery of a competitive price as also the genuine demand of securities in the market. The RBI as a debt manager under an agreement with each state government also endeavours to ensure the success of the floatation of each state, despite the insufficiency of demand for some of the bonds. If debt management is separated from the RBI, its supervisory role can be strengthened in terms of defining the composition and weights of government securities or guaranteed bonds in the asset portfolio of the commercial banks. The commercial banks will need to assess the risk and commercial viability of each project and of each state government before investing in guaranteed bonds. The separation of debt management can also facilitate the retailing of government securities, purely on a commercial basis, by the banking sector. The state government bonds and the guaranteed bonds would have to be traded on commercial basis in such an environment, which will provide incentive to the respective governments to achieve higher credit ratings through better fiscal discipline.

8.4.10. Middle office

In the Union Budget speech of 2007–08, the Finance Minister had proposed to set up an autonomous Debt Management Office (DMO). Many a developments have occurred since then except the formation of DMO. Earlier, since 1997, various groups of experts set up by the RBI and the GOI had consistently suggested hiving of debt management function from the RBI to an independent entity. The middle office was set up in the Ministry of Finance but the hiving-off has not been undertaken. The reasons advanced for the hesitancy were that the global circumstances were not conducive in terms of volatile capital flows and need for intervention/sterilisation; deficits and debt levels were still high; staff of the proposed DMO may not have the requisite skills; and there could be a conflict between the role of government as a debt manager and owner of public sector banks.

8.4.11. Public debt management agency

In the Union Budget Speech on 28 February 2015, Union Finance Minister announced setting up of that the Government of India would set up a Public Debt Management Agency (Box 8.1). The agency was to issue government securities,

---

Box 8.1

Public debt management agency – structure and objectives

Objectives

The Financial Sector Legislation Reforms Commission (FSLRC) recommended in its 2013 Report that the Public Debt Management Agency (PDMA) be responsible for 'minimising the cost of raising and servicing public debt over the long-term within an acceptable level of risk at all times.' In the opinion of the Commission, this would direct the PDMA to manage public debt, contingent liabilities and cash of the central government while remaining an agent of the latter and practicing independent goals with transparency and accountability. The intention was to coordinate fiscal policy, monetary policy and public debt management seamlessly.

Structure

FSLRC suggested a two-tiered setup to manage the operations and administration of a Public Debt Management Agency. A lean organisation was recommended and should ideally recruit specialised personnel with expertise in sovereign bond market. The agency should have autonomy over both selection and salary structures of employees, while maintaining a limited staff. It was also specified that expertise and functions of the agency should be focused solely on the narrow mandate of public debt management.

One of the tiers is an advisory council (AC) that comprises of experts in finance, law, and public debt management with the purpose of advising and issuing opinions (by way of a consensus decision) on any matter related to the objectives, functions, strategies and policies of the public debt management agency, financing plans submitted by the agency to the central government, as well as the agency's annual report.

The lower tier of the organisation structure would be a management committee (MC) that supervises and controls daily operations and follows standard governance practices as well. However, seniority in rank lies with the advisory council. By virtue of exercising general supervision and managing the business of the agency, the management committee should meet more frequently than the advisory council to take operational decisions.

Accountability

The FSLRC opines that the agency abide by the central government's instructions although the details of the implementation are left to the agency's discretion. In case that the objectives of the agency do not match with the government instructions, the agency can object the government's orders through a feedback process. However, in the case of any continued disagreement, the agency would have to implement the instructions after having recorded its objections.

Source: FSLRC, Vol.1, Government of India.

maintain and manage the register of holders of these securities; collect and publish information about public debt, including other borrowings by the central government; purchase, re-issue and trade in government securities; carry out other transactions required for management of public debt; manage the contingent liabilities of the central government; and undertake cash management for the central governmen[13]. However, on 30 April 2015, the Finance Minister announced that PDMA provisions would be removed from Finance Bill. While the proposal for separate management of government debt from the RBI's monetary functions was mooted by the RBI itself in its Annual Report of 2000–01, the Government decided to prepare a detailed roadmap for setting up such an agency at a later date. On 4 October 2016, the Public Debt Management Cell was established in place of the PDMA in the Ministry.[14] It was set up as an interim arrangement in place of the establishment of an independent and statutory debt management agency called Public Debt Management Agency (PDMA), which would be set up in due course. The PDMC will allow separation of debt management functions from RBI's monetary functions and transfer the authority to PDMA in a gradual and seamless manner, without causing market disruptions. It is anticipated that the PDMC will be upgraded to PDMA within two years' time. The extant Middle Office, existing in the Ministry of Finance since September 2008 would be subsumed into the PDMC.

---

13   For other functions, refer to Finance Bill 2015, 38.

14   For further details, refer to Office Memorandum No. 1/1/2010 MO, Ministry of Finance.

The PDMC will have advisory functions which include planning of borrowings of the GoI, managing central government liabilities, monitoring cash balances of the government and the foreign exchange market, and fostering an efficient and liquid market for government securities. It is also expected to develop an integrated debt database system as a central database of all government liabilities. It will also undertake research work, advice on matters of capital market operations, administrate interest rate on small savings as well as loans and advances given by the government, and external debt proposals and hedging requirements.

8.5. Conclusion

The objective of debt management, as generally defined, is raising resources from the market at the minimum cost while containing the risks. In contrast, the objective of monetary policy in India is to maintain a judicious balance between price stability, economic growth and financial stability. Thus, the objective of debt management is subsumed in the overall objectives of monetary policy in India, if the two functions are not separated.

To implement the specifically focussed debt management strategy, and choosing to separate debt from monetary management, governments seek to emphasise the role assigned to debt management, to preserve the integrity and independence of their central banks, to shield debt management from political interference, and to ensure transparency and accountability in public borrowing. Hence, the choice of separating debt from monetary management by many countries while ensuring that their activities are coordinated. The overall conclusion from recent research is that there is an extensive interaction between debt management, monetary policy and financial policy in mutually reinforcing ways. Such interactions become intense during strained macro-economic policy conditions and therefore there is a need for close coordination between the three organs of economic policy.

In India, high volume of domestic debt as a per cent of GDP is a matter of concern, despite attempted fiscal correction and success of financial sector reforms since 1991. The market related rates of interest on government securities has led to diversification of ownership pattern and increasing absorption of government securities by market. The rise in contingent liabilities, however, is an area of concern.

The interest rates in the financial markets are converging and the markets are becoming integrated as they are developing. The interest rate spread between different segments of the market is beginning to narrow down and trading volumes have increased. Thus, debt management functions and practices have developed substantially since 1991, though still being managed by a department within the RBI. In view of the developments in the markets and the commitment on the part of the central government to contain the fiscal deficit, it would be appropriate to consider the separation of monetary and debt management.

The task of debt management can now be assigned to a separate agency, preferably under the Ministry of Finance, initially. The assignment of tasks to the debt agency can be strategised, beginning with the debt management operations of the central government. This could lead to an integrated and more professional management of all government liabilities, currently dispersed in different offices, with a focussed mandate to operate on sound economic and commercial principles. The strategy could ensure that resources are available to the government at competitive market rates of interest prompting expenditure prioritisation and fiscal discipline in budget making. Eventually, in a pre-conceived time frame, management of all debt and cash obligations, of all levels of government should be assigned to this agency for operational efficiency and better coordination. In later stages, the independent debt agency can also provide expert advice to public sector undertakings to manage cash and debt obligations. The separation of debt management would provide focus to the task of asset-liability management of government liabilities, undertake risk analysis and also help to prioritise government expenditure through higher awareness of interest costs. The separation of debt and monetary management accompanied with better transparency will enhance credibility of the RBI and the government.

Appendix 8.1: Case studies

Debt management office in UK

Debt Management Office (DMO) in UK took over the responsibility for debt management on 1 April 1998. The objective of the government's debt management policy is to minimise its financing cost over long term, taking into account the risk, to manage the daily cash needs in the most cost-effective way, to provide loans to local authorities and to financially manage certain public sector entities (DMO, 2003 and 2005). Prior to this separation of

DMO, the formal objective, set in 1995 after the 'Debt Management Review', was to support and complement monetary policy, and subject to this, to avoid distorting financial markets, and to fund the government at least cost and risk (DMO, 2017).

The Treasury and the DMO, jointly determine the market-borrowing program for the next year, which earlier was outlined in the annual Debt and Reserves Management Report (DRMR) which was part of the Budget Report. It is now stated in the annual Debt Management Report (DMR) since 2016. The DMO also advises the Treasury in its selection of an appropriate debt issuance strategy. The DRMR details the breakdown of maturity and instruments, gilt auction calendar, and short-term debt sales, including Treasury bills and the debt portfolio. The market participants are consulted during the formulation of these plans. The gilt market operates through a primary dealer system (gilt-edged market makers, GEMMs). The GEMMs have certain benefits in the auction bidding and for preferred counterparty status and a number of market-making and market participation obligations. The services of gilt inter-dealer broker (GIDB) are limited to GEMMs and their main purpose is to support liquidity in the secondary market by helping GEMMs to unwind any unwanted gilt positions. However, the DMO may directly deal with the GIDB in the case of near maturity gilts (DMO, 2017). The auctions are the exclusive means by which the gilts are issued – multiple for conventional gilts and uniform for index-linked. In addition, DMO may occasionally issue stock through a conversion offer or a switch or reverse auction, with the objective to build benchmark securities. The DMO attaches a high priority to risk management and has developed a set of policies to limit its exposure to risk in the achievement of its objectives. The framework of risk management includes the Accounting Officer, Credit and Market Risk Committee, Operational Risk Committee, Controls Group, Risk Management Unit, Senior Risk Owners and the Internal Audit function.[15]

DMO assumed full responsibility for Exchequer cash management on 3 April 2000. DMO estimates significant net cash flows into and out of central government on daily basis and then monitors the actual cash flows as they occur. The Treasury also makes the cash flow forecasts. DMO aims to manage these flows primarily through bilateral dealing in a range of money market

---

15   More details in DMO's Annual Reports and Accounts 2015-16, July 2016, 41

instruments (borrow from and lend to wholesale money market participants under bilateral arrangements and also repo/reverse repo) and by the issuance of Treasury bills (weekly tenders on the last business day of each week) without influencing the interest rates, markets or trading patterns. In its bilateral dealings with the market, DMO is a price-taker. The DMO has also replaced the Bank of England for conducting Treasury bill tenders since 14 January 2000. Most of cash management of the government is completed early in the morning but sizable unanticipated cash movements that take place late in the day are smoothened by bilateral trading arrangements in the money market. The current arrangement of cash management has replaced the ways and means advances account at the Bank of England (BOE).

DMO has no contact with the Monetary Policy Committee with regard to interest rate decisions. DMO and BOE coordinate their activities to ensure that the operations of DMO do not impact the BOE's monetary policy operations. The BOE acts as DMO's agent for gilt settlement and gilts registration.

The DMO is legally and constitutionally part of HM Treasury. The structure of DMO and its relationship with the treasury is outlined in the DMO's Executive Agency Framework document setting out the DMO's objectives, targets, and structural framework for its operations (DMO, 1999 and 2005).[16] The Minister responsible for the DMO is the Chancellor of the Exchequer who is responsible to Parliament for the work of the DMO. The Chancellor determines the policy and operational framework within which DMO operates but delegate's operational decisions on cash and debt management to the Chief Executive (CE). The advisory board, which meets monthly, advises the managing committee/board which meets weekly, but its proceedings are not published. The CE, accountable to the Chancellor is appointed, through open competition, for a period of five years. DMO is subject to the jurisdiction of the Parliamentary Commissioner for Administration. The CE has to establish an Audit Committee from outside the DMO. DMO is organised into different business units – Policy and Research;

---

16 The Framework Document outlines the following – status, aim and objectives; accountability and relationships with the Treasury; accountability to Parliament; role of the permanent secretary to the Treasury and of the Chief Executive responsible for day-to-day management of DMO; internal management of DMO; responsibility for the preparation of the annual business plan, corporate plan and the annual report and accounts; financial arrangements, auditing and human resource policies of the DMO; and review arrangements.

Debt Management; Cash Management; Fund Management; Hedging and Balance Sheet Management; Lending to local Government; Settlements; Risk management; CEO's Office, Business Delivery, Finance Facilities and HR. The Business Plan, including the targets, for the year is prepared and published (subject to deletion of any sensitive information). DMO also is expected to prepare and publish every year its Annual Report and Accounts. The budget of DMO is funded through the Treasury's Parliamentary Vote. DMO is subject to an external audit by the Comptroller and Auditor General and internal audit that reviews the systems of internal control, including financial controls. DMO's working is subject to regular reviews in consultation with the Treasury and Cabinet Office.

Debt management in New Zealand

The New Zealand Debt Management Office (NZDMO), responsible for managing the government's debt, overall net cash flows, and some of its interest bearing assets, was established in July 1988. New Zealand was the first country to create a separate debt management office with private sector ethos and as a strategic component of public policy with the focus on risk quantification and management in public debt. It also happens to be the only country with a fully integrated Sovereign Asset and liability Management (SALM) framework (Koc, 2014). Since 1997, NZDMO is a part of Asset and Liability Management Branch of the Government. The objective of NZDMO is to maximise the long term economic return on the government's financial assets and debt in the context of government's fiscal strategy and to balance the likely risks incurred in minimising cost (New Zealand Treasury, 2013). In terms of managing the government's debt portfolio, NZDMO adopts a risk-averse approach.

The major responsibilities of NZDMO include financing government's gross borrowings; settling and accounting for all debt transactions; debt management (domestic and external); cash management; risk management in accordance with the fiscal strategy; facilitating and executing derivative transactions; disbursing cash to government departments and facilitating departmental cash management; undertaking lending to government organizations and state owned enterprises; providing advice to New Zealand Treasury, government departments, government organizations and capital markets; and maintaining relationships with investors, financial intermediaries, and credit-rating agencies.

NZDMO is committed to transparency, neutrality and even-handedness which it believes helps in lowering the cost of borrowing by reducing price uncertainty and encouraging competitive bidding, and that these gains outweigh short-term gains available through opportunistic borrowing in the domestic market. The types of securities issued include nominal bonds, Inflation-indexed bonds and Treasury bills which can also be issued through private placements and syndication (NZDMO, 2016). The annual auction calendar with annual requirement, dates and size of the auctions ensure transparency, while neutrality and even-handedness is promoted through the auction process – conventional bonds through multiple price auction and indexed bonds through uniform price auction.

NZDMO coordinates with other parts of Treasury and follows the principles set out in The Fiscal Responsibility Act, 1994. The Reserve Bank of New Zealand (RBNZ) and NZDMO have a close working relationship, which is formalised in agency agreements. An agency agreement clearly delineates the responsibilities of both organisations, including the action in the event of foreign exchange intervention. The RBNZ acts as NZDMO's issuing agent, registrar, and paying agent in the domestic market. RBNZ conducts auctions of Treasury bills and government bonds on NZDMO's behalf, but NZDMO retains the responsibility for pricing decisions. RBNZ also disseminates information on government securities. RBNZ also offers advice to NZDMO on the borrowing program of the government, market conditions and preferences based on its network as well as periodic surveys. An important provision in the agency agreement is that all functions carried out by RBNZ as agent for NZDMO are conducted without reference to monetary policy considerations. Exchange reserves of the RBNZ are protected by the foreign currency debt of NZDMO (Grimes, 2001).

The Secretary of the Treasury is directly responsible to the Minister of Finance for the working of NZDMO. The head of NZDMO is a Treasurer who reports to Deputy Secretary in-charge of Asset and liability Management Branch. The Advisory Board (comprising of three members) oversees the operations of NZDMO and provides the secretary with quality assurance of activities of NZDMO, risk management framework and business plan (Controller and Auditor General, 2007). The responsibilities of NZDMO are not codified in legislation but it operates independently, as a matter of custom. The NZDMO has three major groups with separate front, middle and back office – Portfolio Management, Risk Policy and Balance Sheet,

Business Information, NZ Export Credit Office, and Accounting and Transactional Services, with legal and administrative services being provided within Treasury. The information management system integrates the front, middle and back offices. NZDMO has a system of wholesale investors and retail investors that are responsible for the primary issuance and distribution of government securities, respectively.

Swedish national debt office

Sweden has a separate debt office, Swedish National Debt Office (SNDO), since 1789 but a major reform was undertaken in 1998. The core principles and rules for debt management are given in the legislation titled State Borrowing and Debt Management Act, enacted by Parliament in 1998. The Act specifies the objective to borrow and the government delegates the mandate to borrow to SNDO and the government is liable for any loans undertaken by SNDO with or without approval from the State.[17] The objective of debt management is to minimise long-term costs while taking risks into account and taking into consideration the operations of the monetary policy. The guidelines for debt management, after accommodating the comments of Riksbank, have to be prepared annually on 1 October. The government has to submit an annual report on debt management to parliament, which is also released to the public. The guidelines give three year rolling plan, consistent with the time frame used in budget making. The government during the year can change the guidelines if circumstances so desire, but this is done through amended guidelines, which then become public documents. Swedish law requires the government to evaluate the management of central government debt in a written communication to the Parliament.[18] Evaluation is both quantitative (comparing the actual cost with that provided in the guidelines) and qualitative (performance on daily basis, including market maintenance) and can cover five-year periods (Government Offices of Sweden, 2017). The gross debt position of Sweden is analysed and reported monthly by the SNDO (IMF, 2000).

In the gilt market, SNDO has taken an active role in the development of the market. The strategy is to concentrate on borrowings in a few large issues. Bond auctions are bi-weekly, and auction and volume are announced a week

---

17   Awadzi, 2015, 52.
18   IMF, 2003, 217 for more on SNDO guidelines.

in advance. SNDO has three separate dealer systems, one each for nominal bonds, treasury bills, inflation-linked and foreign currency bonds. The authorised dealers are committed to enter bids on behalf of investors. Repo and reverse repo are regular features of the operations by SNDO. SNDO also undertakes cash and guarantees management for the government.

The advisory board (Board of Directors) of SNDO, consisting of external members (half of them are members of Parliament), makes strategic decisions while the operational management is conducted by SNDO, led by director general, appointed by the government. The Director General is assisted by a Deputy Director General; a Policy Group and a Management Group discuss and take day-to-day decisions and strategic policy issues, respectively. The board monitors and evaluates the operational aspects of debt management and reports directly to the government. There is clear organisational separation between front, middle and back office. In addition, the internal audit department directly reports to the board. The SNDO also comprises of departments such as Scientific Advisory Council, Financial Stability and Consumer Protection, Guarantees and Lending, Cash Management, Debt Management, Economic Analysis and Information Technology. The government funds the SNDO. SNDO makes hiring decisions and establishes the salaries of all employees, other than the director general and the deputy director general (where the government sets the compensation).

Appendix 8.2: Salient features of a debt management office[19]

Governance

The legal authority to borrow in the name of the central government generally rests with the Parliament or congressional legislative body and in most of the cases limits on borrowings are prescribed. The public debt management functions are increasingly being centralised either in a separate department under the Ministry of Finance (MoF) or in an independent agency reporting directly to the Minister of Finance or to a Council of Ministers, for reasons of accountability to Parliament and the link with the budget-making office (Carracedo and Dattels, 1997).

---

19 I have benefited from discussions with Magnusson, T. I. (World Bank), Olden, B., Thomas, T. and Filipsson, M. (IMF), Giavazzi, F. (Universita Bocconi, Italy), and Goldfajn, I. (Central Bank, Brazil).

Scope

The scope of debt management encompasses the domestic financial obligations of the government and the trend is to include all types of government debt under a single agency – sub-national governments, external debt, cash management and contingent liabilities. The concentration of all debt management activities in a single agency helps in lowering the costs of raising resources, better coordination and risk management. It also facilitates gathering of information and analysing market intelligence for understanding the needs of different components of the market – designing of instruments, preparing a maturity profile of debt, introducing suitable regulatory provisions, and developing a compatible infrastructure for overall debt management.

Clear objectives

In the provisions of the legislation itself, generally clear and detailed objectives for debt management are delineated. Clarity and transparency in debt management objectives makes the debt manager more accountable and less susceptible to political pressure that may result in sub-optimal debt management policies. The clarity and transparency helps to reduce uncertainty among investors and intermediaries and enhances the confidence of the market in debt management initiatives. Clarity in the role and objectives of the debt management office also helps to minimise the potential conflicts between monetary, fiscal and debt management policies. The objectives vary across countries – minimise long-term borrowing cost (Australia, Belgium, Denmark); debt management subject to constraint of monetary policy (Sweden, UK); maximise long-term economic return on the government's financial assets and debt, given the fiscal strategy and risk aversion (New Zealand); and meet the fiscal requirements of the government as also to protect liquidity, contain the costs and exposure to risks, and outperform a shadow portfolio or benchmark (Ireland). Some countries prescribe strategic targets for components of debt management policy – currency composition (Australia, Belgium, Denmark, New Zealand, UK, USA); interest rate in terms of fixed and floating (France, Italy, New Zealand) and in terms of modified duration (Australia, Belgium, Denmark, Italy, Sweden); and refinancing requirements (Denmark, Sweden). The management of debt takes place within the framework imposed by monetary policy requirements.

Organization of the debt office

The organisational framework for separate debt management agency is precisely specified, has a legal authority to represent the government, and the roles and mandates of important functionaries are well articulated. The legislation generally defines the administrative process for debt management, including specification of the function, procedure for record keeping, frequency of reporting to the authorities and dissemination policy to the public.

The debt management office is generally provided with a sufficient degree of functional autonomy to fulfil its mandate without political pressure. Such autonomy is permitted along with the requirement that the debt management office be accountable, and transparent in its operations, procedures and results. The activities of the agency are supervised by a special advisory board, which provides guidance on strategic and technical issues to the chief executive of a separate agency, regularly monitors its activities and reports directly to the concerned authority. The board is generally expected to spell out the strategy for undertaking such activities as benchmarking of securities and their size, introduction of new instruments, and major policy developments. The advisory board could also earmark some risk limits relative to agreed benchmarks for the chief executive to track. The constitution and functioning of the advisory board lends credibility to the operations, which is necessary for robust market expectations (Calvo, 1988; Diamond and Dybvig, 1983). The membership of the advisory board is generally broad based with representatives from the government, market, academia, and the central bank, to function in a transparent and effective manner. The tenure of the members is generally long, and expiry of the term is on a rotational basis to provide consistency to policy and strategy of debt management.

The chief officer executes the operational aspects and the office is mainly organised as an independent entity covering operational work, policy and planning, risk assessment, regulations and audit. The front office is responsible for resource mobilisation, executing transactions in financial markets, including the management of auctions and other forms of borrowing, and all other funding operations, including guarantee operations, hedging, and derivative transactions of the government. The middle office undertakes risk analysis and assesses the performance of the debt managers against any strategic benchmarks. It also undertakes portfolio analysis, develops a risk management strategy, formulates a borrowing policy – annual and long-term, assesses and manages different types of risks, and compares the emerging debt indicators with agreed benchmarks. The debt managers undertake extensive research studies and prepare alternate debt scenarios to ensure that the rate of growth and level of debt is sustainable over time and can be serviced under a wide range of circumstances while meeting cost/risk objectives. The back office handles the settlement of transactions and the maintenance of financial records (debt registry, disbursements, and debt-service payments). Disaster recovery plans are an important component of any debt management office.

The overall debt management activity is supported by an accurate and comprehensive management information system (MIS) with proper safeguards, including accurate debt recording and reporting systems. The MIS is expected to capture all relevant cash flows, with up-to-date reporting of servicing and redemptions, ownership pattern and maturity profile of government securities, and is expected to be fully integrated into the government's accounting system.

Policy and planning

The policy and planning unit is considered the most important component of the debt management office as it has to forecast the budgetary gap, and then to plan for the currency mix, maturity profile, indexed or nominal issues, and the type of auctions. The borrowing requirement is a function of the flows of government revenue and expenditure over time. The forecasts of the budgetary gap on daily, weekly and monthly basis help to optimise cost-effective arrangements for financing temporary imbalances or long-term deficits. The maturity mix of government securities would need to be assessed, based on the fiscal situation, market conditions and the expectations of investors. Long-term bonds are preferred to stabilise the market while large issuance of short-term bonds would raise the refinance risk. Giovannini (1997) argues that longer the maturity, greater is the gain from debt deflation. The other issue is the choice between nominal and indexed bonds, and domestic and foreign bonds. Barro (1999) argues that short-term nominal bonds can lessen the impact of inflation on the budget, but then shortening the maturity enhances the sensitivity to variations in real interest rates. Bohn (1988) shows that conventional nominal bonds provide a hedging device against shocks and help to smooth tax rates while Bohn (1990) argues that changes in the price level have a greater impact on long-term nominal bonds than on short-term bonds.

Theoretically, long-term index-linked bonds minimise costs and are preferable to nominal bonds and foreign currency debt (Barro, 1999); empirically, Australia, Canada, New Zealand, Sweden, UK and USA prefer such bonds (Barro, 1995 and 1997; Shiller, 2003). The issuance of index-linked bonds indicates that the government does not intend to inflate which helps to stabilise the markets (Giovannini, 1997).[20] Barr and Campbell (1996) show that better inflation forecast could be obtained from the index-linked bonds, which is useful information for the debt manager and the central bank.[21] However, pricing of the index-linked bonds is difficult and therefore trading in the market is generally restricted.[22] The absence of index-linked loans/advances in the portfolio of the banks and financial institutions could be another reason for lack of interest in index-linked bonds in some countries. McCray (2002) reports mixed experience on the performance of indexed bonds, based on the survey of some OECD countries – satisfied (Iceland, France, UK and USA), uncertain (Australia, Canada, Sweden), and disappointed (New Zealand) – while Kleiman (1988) observes that indexation significantly reduced the economic effects of inflationary uncertainty in Israel. Miller (1997) shows that foreign currency denominated debt is useful if foreign and domestic economies are positively correlated. The requirements of market participants in different countries would differ depending on the level of development of the financial markets, regulatory and supervisory specifications for the major investors, banking facilities and the social security system, which the debt office has to factor into its policy formulation.[23] The banks and financial

---

20 In Chile and Israel, where inflation-indexed securities accounted for 89 per cent and 66 per cent, respectively, of the total outstanding securities as at end-2000, the objective was to signal the commitment of the government to its anti-inflationary strategy (Mihaljek, Scatigna and Villar, 2002).

21 ECB (2004) also gives the method of computing inflation expectations from the index-linked bonds.

22 In view of the fact that inflation-linked bonds indicate a commitment to a low inflation regime, these could be useful in inflation targeting countries. In an economy where, historically, the inflation rate is not restricted to a narrow band, and which has not adopted the inflation target approach, pricing would be difficult and trading limited.

23 In the Indian market, the banks typically require relatively short-term securities with a fixed nominal return, a liquid market with a short settlement time, and therefore a wholesale, dematerialised payments and settlements system is suitable. Non-bank financial institutions typically have a medium- to long-term time horizon. They may prefer a mix of fixed-cash-flow and zero-coupon discount bonds to meet their long-term liabilities. Insurance companies prefer long term bonds while provident and pension funds may prefer indexed securities. Resident corporates would like a short-term risk-free instrument while individuals opt for a medium-term horizon to invest

institutions that are supervised entities assign different weights to different debt instruments.

Though, theoretically, all types of auctions yield similar results, in practice, different auction systems are preferred in different countries depending on the development of the financial markets, prevalence of institutional investors and market conditions. In a well-developed market, multiple price auctions may be preferred but in a developing market, a uniform auction with no winners' curse may be attractive. Similarly, in the case of conventional instruments and in normal market situations, multiple price auctions may be preferable while a uniform auction may be used for non-conventional instruments, (e.g. indexed bonds), or when the markets are volatile.

In different market conditions, the horizon for debt issuance is generally weekly, monthly or quarterly, depending on the cash flow of the government and the needs of investors. While very short term swings in government requirements are met through the overdraft facility from commercial banks or even the central bank, medium to long-term requirements are met from the market. To avoid refinancing risk, a manageable size of each issue is floated.

The other important issue is the assessment of risk which depends on the size of government debt, maturity profile and currency composition. The most important risks, which are required to be managed, are market, liquidity and refunding risk, followed by credit, operational, legal, political and reputational risk. In some countries, limits on the deviation from the benchmark portfolio have been prescribed to contain risk while in others passive debt management policy is pursued. The debt management office develops the risk management policy and the tolerance limits are generally approved and set by the responsible minister or secretary (Financial Markets Division, 2002). A number of debt managers use derivative products (currency and interest rate swaps, forward contracts, futures and options) to contain the risks and adhere to the prescribed benchmarks (Cassard and Folkerts-Landau, 1997).

Audit

External auditors or government's audit agency regularly audit the activities of debt management annually, which are then made public according to a

---

their personal savings and may also prefer non-tradable securities (post office saving certificates). Non-residents would focus on reserve currencies while some investors may seek arbitrage opportunities. Such investors will prefer liquid markets with quick payments and settlement systems.

pre-announced schedule. In the case of New Zealand, the audit is quarterly. Internal audit of debt management activities is regularly undertaken and reports are directly submitted to the supervisory board.

Financial markets

Debt managers have an obligation to assure that the financial market is functioning smoothly and efficiently, characterised by liquid and deep markets, so as to minimise debt-service costs (Piga, 1988). The existence of an efficient financial market is important for various reasons – (i) financing needs of the government can directly be met from the market rather than from the central bank; (ii) borrowings can be raised by the government in its own currency and exchange risk can be avoided, (iii) domestic borrowers are able to access resources, even in times of global financial instability; and (iv) debt management decisions are not perceived to be influenced by inside information on interest rate decisions.

The central bank generally undertakes the government market-borrowing programme as an agent of the government. Adopting market-based methods for the primary issuance of government debt helps in the development of primary market. In the primary issuance, announcement of a reasonably stable and explicit calendar lends credibility to debt management and lowers the cost of borrowings (Piga, 1998). The calendar would depend on the forecasting capabilities and planning process. The need for computerised auctioning mechanism and accounting system involving registration and payments also play an important role in the development of primary market.

The development of secondary market is important for the debt manager, especially when government borrowing is substantial and professional and institutional investors dominate the market. A well-developed secondary market ensures liquidity of investment and setting of prices on daily basis for risk evaluation purposes (Piga, 1998). Ideally, the debt manager provides electronic clearing and settlement system to guard against counterparty risk. This function is generally coordinated by the central bank to ensure security and development of delivery-versus-payment system. The central bank is generally the depository, operating the book-entry system.

Primary dealers

In many countries, the institutional arrangement of establishing dealers in government securities has helped to develop the primary market. Primary dealers are useful as advisers to the debt manager and provide crucial feedback from the market. The primary dealer's network can also be a useful market maker providing two-way quotes on government securities in the secondary market.

Coordination committees

The function of debt management requires close coordination between monetary, debt and fiscal policies. Therefore, the sharing of information and consultations between the debt management office, government, and central bank and market participants is very important. The coordination between the central bank and debt manager has to focus on the cash management program and the schedule of Treasury bill and long dated borrowing programme being undertaken. The central bank generally continues to be the fiscal agent of the government. The central banks in many developing countries also supervise and regulate the financial markets and therefore have important information to share with the debt manager. The development of the secondary market for debt instruments is also the primary responsibility of the debt manager and the central bank. The debt manager would be operating in various segments of the secondary market but the central bank generally would operate at the short end through the overnight interest rates.

The objective of close coordination is that the activities of the central bank and debt manager should not be providing conflicting signals to the market and should be operating independently and exclusively. Therefore, the borrowing program and various scenario analyses for debt management prepared by the debt manager are generally reviewed by the central bank before finalisation. The risk structure of the government debt is also discussed with the central bank, as it is generally responsible for the supervision of the banks and other financial institutions – major investors in government securities. The central bank continues to be the regulator and supervisor of the market while the debt manager assumes the role of a primary dealer of the government.

Regular reporting to the Treasury

The debt office is required to prepare a regular (weekly/fortnightly/monthly) consolidated funding report for the Treasury, in which credit risk, market risk and funding risk on borrowings are discussed. The report includes details about the completed borrowing programme, deviations from the estimated targets, sensitivity analysis and the trajectory for the ensuing period. This information is also shared with the central bank.

Dissemination policy and activities

In many countries with developed government securities market, a borrowing calendar for both the money and gilt market, along with the total target amount to be borrowed is disseminated in the beginning of the year to provide certainty to the borrowing schedule and to help the market participants to plan their investment. This annual calendar may be indicative and a precise calendar may be issued quarterly or monthly. The mode of auction – multiple or uniform, for different instruments – is also indicated along with the calendar to minimise uncertainty for the market participants. The debt management office regularly publishes comprehensive information after every auction/borrowing event (swap, switch) to avoid any information asymmetry as also the quarterly/annual report of all activities undertaken during the period.

Staffing pattern

The staffs of the separate debt office is subject to a code-of-conduct and conflict-of-interest guidelines regarding the management of their personal financial affairs, to allay fears of the market participants and the investors that personal financial interests may undermine sound debt management practices.

9

Conclusions and Policy Implications

The process of planned development, in terms of the Five Year Plans, started in India in 1951. The main objective of the Five Year Plans was to attain a high growth with equitable income distribution. The emphasis in the plans was laid on high government investment for development purposes. In the drive for higher investment, in view of the unavailability of financial resources from tax revenues due to the low economic base, and inadequate surpluses from public sector enterprises, the government resorted to borrowed funds – domestic as well as external. The increasing reliance on external borrowing had important economic and political implications. Therefore, since the early 70s, after the war between India and Pakistan in 1971 and the oil shock in 1973, the dependence on external borrowing declined and the government increasingly resorted to domestic borrowing. In periods of financial strain, increasing reliance was placed on borrowing from RBI, resulting in monetisation of debt. The domestic debt situation became critical by the mid 80s, mainly because government was able to garner resources, at low rates of interest, from RBI and markets, and fiscal profligacy was rampant.

The objective of this study was to look at the trends and investigate the implications of domestic debt on Indian economy. The period of the empirical work has been restricted to the earlier exhaustive work done in 1997. The descriptive analysis broadly pertains to the period 1951–2017 where data was available while the empirical analysis varies from 1951–95 to 1971–95, depending on the availability of consistent time series data.

In India, the central and the state governments incur domestic debt. Therefore, the appropriate measure is the consolidated debt position of the central and the state governments to analyse the implications of domestic debt on the macro-economic aggregates in the economy. Domestic debt of the government, in addition to market loans and bonds, also includes Treasury bills, small saving schemes, provident funds, and reserve funds and deposits. The component, reserve funds and deposits, refer to domestic debt which includes depreciation, developmental, contingency or similar funds, which are not strictly liabilities but more of financial obligations in the regular course of the conduct of government business. Therefore, this component has been excluded while empirically analysing the impact of domestic debt on the macro aggregates. Further, the government borrows from the public and also RBI, the implications of which are different for the economy and, therefore, the analysis is conducted separately.

Domestic debt held by the public can influence the consumption pattern through the operation of the wealth effect. The study stresses the need for an appropriate underlying consumption function for testing the hypothesis of Ricardian equivalence. The study concludes that the permanent income hypothesis, incorporating rational expectations, is the appropriate specification to test for the Ricardian Equivalence Hypothesis. Further, on the crucial issue of par and the market value of domestic debt in empirical work, the study provides empirical estimates to demonstrate that the results are not sensitive to use of either series of debt variable. This conclusion is useful, especially for developing countries where money markets may not be developed and government securities may not be actively traded, and therefore market value of government debt is not computed.

In case of monetised debt, implications of open economy model for a small economy are derived. The Indian economy, during 1951 to 1995, can be characterised to be a closed economy with trade restrictions, strict exchange control measures, nearly fixed exchange rates and administered interest rates. The result of rising reserve money and money supply in these conditions, are predicted to lead to increase in price level. The analysis is extended to study the relationship between monetised debt, an important component of reserve money and the price level.

The overall conclusions of the study on Ricardian equivalence in India are mixed. In India, domestic debt and consumption do not support the Ricardian equivalence behaviour. The increasing monetisation of debt does not directly affect the movements in the money supply and the price level. Reserve Money directly affects changes in the price level as well as causes changes in the monetised debt and narrow money supply. The close relationship between the money supply and prices is further established by the empirical results. Cointegration and the Granger causality tests support the Ricardian Equivalence Hypothesis between domestic debt and growth.

The analysis in this study suffers from a limitation due to non-availability

Conclusions and Policy Implications

of data. The study is mainly based on domestic debt of government – both central and state. In India, in addition to government debt, local bodies like municipal corporations and public sector undertakings like electricity boards or road transport corporations are also permitted to borrow from the market. These securities are also eligible instruments for consideration of statutory liquidity ratio and therefore, are held by banks and other financial institutions. The amount annually borrowed by these undertakings is small but the details of the amount outstanding, and the ownership pattern of such borrowing is not published. Therefore, in this study, borrowings by local bodies and by public sector undertakings are not included in analysis. However, for future research, these borrowing can also be considered if data is available.

The Indian economy is presently in the process of further and second round of liberalisation, after the initial wave in 1991. The exchange rates and the interest rates are still being liberalised in a phased manner. The government securities market is developed compared to 1992. The government is also introducing a large number of new instruments – short and long term, which should further encourage growth in the market for government securities. The suggestions for further research would therefore be to focus on the crowding out of private sector investment as a result of the rising participation of the government to mobilise financial resources from the open market.

The results of further liberalisation and evolvement of the financial sector and the market determined rates of interest are expected to cause many changes in the composition of domestic debt and its ownership pattern. The private holders, with the market determined rate of interest on government securities, may begin to hold domestic debt for capital gains. The impact of domestic debt on the consumption pattern can therefore become important in future.

The financial viability of the new debt instruments and the rising coupon rate on government securities needs to be assessed with a long term objective in consideration. The increase in the interest burden with the market related yields on the government securities and Treasury bills will have an immediate impact on budget. The increasing dependence on Treasury bills for long period of time, though low in terms of the interest burden as compared to the dated securities, have a hidden cost pertaining to consistent roll-overs, creation and destruction. In view of the immediate concern to reduce the interest payment burden on national exchequer, the government has experimented regularly with floated zero coupon bonds and inflation indexed securities but not with much success. These bonds may hide the inherent interest cost in the short run, but in the long run, the interest burden would be similar to the regular borrowing of government loans on coupon rates if inflation is not stable and so, also, inflation expectations. Further, given the rational expectation hypothesis, the impact of these instruments on the economy may not be different from the traditional instruments.

The financial deregulation and the liberalisation of interest rates and exchange rates will result in greater integration of the Indian economy with the global economy. Therefore, India requires a flexible and efficient monetary policy which necessitates lowering of the statutory liquidity ratios. The process of financial liberalisation has led to market related rates of interest on government debt.

Both central and state governments, followed the fiscal responsibility legislations since 2003. In this case, the states have been more successful in fiscal responsibility but centre, mainly due to great recession, had to be accommodative. Finally, the union government, appointed a committee to review the need and performance of fiscal responsibility legislation in force since 2003.

The objective of debt management is raising resources from the market at minimum cost while containing the risks, while that of the monetary authority is to achieve price stability. In the years preceding the financial crisis of 2008, separation of debt and monetary management was a settled norm and a number of countries with liberalised financial markets and high levels of government debt sought to adopt professional debt management techniques to save cost and to provide policy signals to the market. Separation of debt management is essential to preserve the integrity and independence of the central bank, to ensure transparency and accountability, and to improve debt management by entrusting it to portfolio managers with expertise in modern risk management techniques. In India, debt is managed by the central and state governments, and the RBI. The separation of debt management would provide focus to the task of asset-liability management of government liabilities, undertake risk analysis and also help the government to prioritise public expenditure through higher awareness of interest costs. The separation would also be helpful for the borrowing programme which would have to be completed without the support of the regulatory or supervisory authority. This may lead to widening of investor base and market-friendly yield curve. But after the great financial recession of 2008, the issue has re-emerged as in many countries, especially the advanced economies, the scope of fiscal operations was expanded, and the debt to GDP ratios have increased substantially. Similarly, in view of the sensitiveness of the issue, especially amidst less developed financial

Conclusions and Policy Implications

markets, there has been some rethinking on the issue; in India, the RBI has also been rethinking the separation issue and seems reluctant given the present context of the economy.

Bibliography

Abbot, C. C. 1953. *The Federal Debt: Structure and Impact.* New York: McGraw-Hill.

Abel, A. B. and F. S. Mishkin. 1983. 'An Integrated View of Tests of Rationality, Market Efficiency and the Short-run Neutrality of Monetary Policy.' *Journal of Monetary Economics* 11: 3–24.

Agell, J. and M. Persson. 1992. 'Does Debt Management Matter?.' In *Does Debt Management Matter?*, edited by J. Agell., M. Persson and B. M. Friedman, Oxford: Clarendon Press.

Aghevli, B. B. 1977. 'Money, prices and the Balance of Payments: Indonesia 1968–73.'" *Journal of Development Studies* 13: 37–57.

Aghevli, B. B. and M. S. Khan. 1977. 'Inflationary Finance and the Dynamics of Inflation: Indonesia, 1951–72.' *American Economic Review* 67: 390–403.

_____. 1978. 'Government Deficits and the Inflationary Process in Developing Countries.'" *IMF Staff Papers* 25: 383–416.

Ahluwalia, I. J. 1979. 'An Analysis of Price and Output Behaviour in the Indian Economy: 1951–73.' *Journal of Development Economics* 6: 363–390.

Akaike, H. 1969. 'Fitting Autoregressive Models for Prediction.' *Annals of the Institute of Statistical Mathematics* 21: 243–247.

_____. 1970. 'Statistical Predictor Identification.' *Annals of the Institute of Statistical Mathematics* 22: 203–217.

_____. 1974. 'A New Look at the Statistical Predictor Identification.' *IEEE Transactions on Automatic Control* AC-19: 717–723.

Akerlof, G. A. and R. D. Milbourne. 1980. 'The Short Run Demand for Money.' *Economic Journal* 90: 885–900.

_____. 'Irving Fisher on His Head II: The Consequences of the Timing of Payments for the Demand for Money.' *Quarterly Journal of Economics* 95: 145–157.

Akhtar, M. A. and D. S. Wilford. 1979. 'The Influence of the United Kingdom's Public Sector Deficit on its Money stock, 1963–76.' *Bulletin of Economic Research* 31: 3–13.

Akhtar, M. A., H. P. Bluford. and D. S. Wilford. 1979. 'Fiscal Constraints, Domestic Credit, and International Reserve Flows in the United Kingdom, 1952–71.' *Journal of Money, Credit, and Banking* 11: 202–208.

Alesina, A., A. Prati. and G. Tabellini. 1990. 'Public Confidence and Debt Management: A Model and A Case Study of Italy.' In *Public Debt Management: Theory and History* edited by R. Dornbusch. and M. Draghi, 94–121. Cambridge: Cambridge University Press.

Alesina, A. and L. H. Summers. 1993. 'Central Bank Independence and Macroeconomic Performance: Some Comparative Evidence.' *Journal of Money, Credit and Banking* 25(2): 151–162.

Allen, S. and Smith, M. 1983. 'Government Borrowing and Monetary Accommodation.' *Journal of Monetary Economics* 12: 605–616.

Ando, A. and F. Modigliani. 1963. 'The Life Cycle Hypothesis of Saving: Aggregate Implications and Tests.' *American Economic Review* 53: 55–84.

Approach Paper. 2012. Financial Sector Legislative Reforms Commission. New Delhi: Ministry of Finance, Government of India.

Aschauer, D. A. 1985. 'Fiscal policy and Aggregate Demand.' *American Economic Review* 75: 117–127.

Attfield, C. L. F., D. Demery. and N. W. Duck. 1981. 'A Quarterly Model of Unanticipated Monetary Growth, Output and the Price Level in the U.K. 1963–78.' *Journal of Monetary Economics* 8: 331–350.

Bade, R. and M. Parkin. 1980. 'Central Bank Laws and Monetary Policy.' *University of Western Ontario*, Unpublished.

Bagchi, A. 1990. 'Debt, Deficits and Taxation in India's Government Finance: Perspective for the Eighth Plan.' *National institute of Public Finance and Policy*. New Delhi, India.

Bailey, M. J. 1971. *National Income and the Price Level*, 2nd edition. New York: McGraw Hill.

Balakrishnan, P. 1991. *Pricing and Inflation in India*. New Delhi: Oxford University Press.

Banerjee, A., S. Cole. and E. Duflo. 2003. 'Bank Financing in India.' *Mimeo*, MIT Press.

Bank of England and HM Treasury. 1995. *Report of the Debt Management Review*. United Kingdom: Debt Management Office.

Barman, K. 1978. *India's Public Debt and Policy since Independence*. Allahabad: Chugh Publications.

_____. 1986. *Public Debt Management in India*. New Delhi: Uppal Publishing House.

Barr, D. G. and J. Y. Campbell. 1996. 'Inflation, Real Interest Rates, and the Bond Market: A Study of UK Nominal and Index-Linked Government Bond Prices.' *Working Paper No 5821*. National Bureau of Economic Research

Barro, R. J. 1974. 'Are Government Bonds Net Wealth.' *Journal of Political Economy* 82: 1095–1117.

_____. 1976. 'Rational Expectations and the Role of Monetary Policy.' *Journal of Monetary Economics* 2: 1–32.

_____. 1977. 'Unanticipated Money Growth and Unemployment in the United States.' *American Economic Review* 67: 101–115.

_____. 1978a. 'Comment from an Unreconstructed Ricardian.' *Journal of Monetary Economics* 4: 569–581.

_____. 1978b. 'Unanticipated Money, Output, and the Price Level in the United States." *Journal of Political Economy* 86: 549–580.

_____. 1978c. *The Impact of Social Security on Private Saving*. Washington: American Enterprise Institute for Public Policy Research.

_____. 1979.'On the Determination of the Public Debt.' *Journal of Political Economy* 87: 940–971.

_____. 1980a. 'Federal Deficit Policy and the Effects of Public Debt Shocks.' *Journal of Money, Credit, and Banking* 12: 745–762.

_____. 1980b. 'Unanticipated Money and Economic Activity in the United States.' In *Money, Expectations, and Business Cycles*. New York: Academic Press.

_____. 1981a. 'Output Effects of Government Purchases.' *Journal of Political Economy* 89:1086–1121.

_____. 1981b. 'Public debt and Taxes.' In *Money, Expectations, and Business Cycles*. New York: Academic Press.

_____. 1983. *Macroeconomics*. New York: John Wiley and Sons.

_____. 1986. 'U.S. Deficits Since World War I.' *Scandinavian Journal of Economics* 88: 195–222.

_____. 1987. 'Government Spending, Interest Rates, Prices, and Budget Deficits in the United Kingdom, 1701–1918.' *Journal of Monetary Economics* 20: 221–247.

_____. 1989a. *Modern Business Cycle Theory*. Cambridge: Harvard University Press.

_____. 1989b. 'The Ricardian Approach to Budget Deficits.' *Journal of Economic Perspectives* 3(Spring): 37–54.

_____. 1989c. 'Interest-Rate Targeting.' *Journal of Monetary Economics* 23: 3–30.

_____. 1989d. 'The Neo-Classical Approach to Fiscal Policy.' In *Modern Business Cycle Theory*, edited by R. J. Barro. Cambridge: Harvard University Press.

_____. 1995. 'Optimal Debt Management.' *Working Paper No. 5327*. National Bureau of Economic Research,

_____. 1997. 'Optimal Management of Indexed and Nominal Debt.' *Working Paper No. 6197*. National Bureau of Economic Research.

_____. 1999. 'Notes on Optimal Debt Management.' *Mimeo*, Harvard University, May.

Barro, R. J. and D. B. Gordon. 1983a. 'A Positive Theory of Monetary Policy in a Natural Rate Model.' *Journal of Political Economy* 91(4): 589–610.

_____. 1983b. 'Rules, Discretion and Reputation in Monetary Policy.' *Journal of Monetary Economics* 12: 101–121.

Barsky, R. B., N. G. Mankiw. and S. P. Zeldes. 1986. 'Ricardian Consumers with Keynesian Propensities.' *American Economic Review* 76: 676–691.

Barth, J. R. and J. T. Bennett. 1974. 'The Role of Money in the Canadian Economy: An Empirical Test.' *Canadian Journal of Economics* 8: 306–311.

Barth, J. R., G. Iden. and F. S Russek. 1984. 'Do Federal Deficits Really Matter?' *Contemporary Policy Issues* 3: 79–95.

_____. 1986. 'Government Debt, Government Spending, and Private sector Behaviour.' *The American Economic Review* 76: 1158–1167.

Bean, C. R. 1986. 'The Estimation of "Surprise" Models and the "Surprise" Consumption Function.' *Review of Economic Studies* 53: 497–516.'

Belongia, M. T. 1996. 'Measurement Matters: Recent Results from Monetary Economics Reexamined.' *Journal of Political Economy* 104: 1065–1083.

Bernanake, B. S., and F. S. Mishkin. 1997. 'Inflation Targeting: A New Framework for Monetary Policy?' *Working Paper No. 5893*. National Bureau of Economic Research.

Bernanke, B. S. and M. Gertler. 1999. 'Monetary Policy and Asset Volatility.' *Federal Reserve Bank of Kansas City, Economic Review*, Fourth Quarter.

Bernheim, B. D. 1987. 'Ricardian Equivalence: An Evaluation of Theory and Evidence.' In *Macroeconomics Annual,* edited by S. Fischer for NBER. Cambridge: MIT Press.

Bernstein, E. M. and I. G. Patel. 1952. 'Inflation in Relation to Economic Development.' *IMF Staff Papers* 2: 363–398.

Beveridge, S. and C. R. Nelson. 1981. 'A New Approach to Decomposition of Economic Time Series into Permanent and Transitory Components with Particular Attention to Measurement of the Business Cycle.' *Journal of Monetary Economics* 7: 151–174.

Bhalla, S.S. 1980. 'The Measurement of Permanent Income and its Application to Savings Behaviour.' *Journal of Political Economy* 88: 722–744.

_____. 1981a. 'The Transmission of Inflation into Developing Economies.' In *World Inflation and the Developing Countries,* edited by W. A. Cline and Associates, 52–101. Washington: Brookings Institution.

_____. 1981b. 'India's Closed Economy and World Inflation.' In *World Inflation and the Developing Countries,* edited by W. A. Cline and Associates, 136–165. Washington: Brookings Institution.

Bhattacharya, B. B. and S. Guha. 1990. 'Internal Public Debt of Government of India: Growth and Composition.' *Economic and Political Weekly* 25: 780–788.

_____. 1992. 'The Behaviour of Public Debt in India: A Macroeconometric Analysis.' *Journal of Quantitative Economics* 8: 29–50.

Bhattacharya, B. B. and P. D. Sharma. 1985. 'Relationship between Money and Price in India: Some Evidence from Bivariate Causality Tests.' *Journal of Quantitative Economics* 1: 285–298.

Bhole, L. M. 1985. *Impacts of Monetary Policy.* Bombay: Himalaya Publishing House.

Bilson, J. F. O. 1980. 'The Rational Expectations Approach to the Consumption Function.' *European Economic Review* 13: 273–299.

Biswas, B. and P. J. Saunders. 1990. 'Money and Price Level in India: An Empirical Analysis.' *Indian Economic Journal* 38: 103–114.

Blanchard, O. J. 1985. 'Debt, Deficits, and Finite Horizons.' *Journal of Political Economy* 93: 223–47.

Blejer, M. I. 2013. 'Central Bank's Outdated Independence.' *Project Syndicate,* April 17.

Blinder, A. S. and A. Deaton. 1985. 'The Time series Consumption Function Revisited.' *Brookings Papers on Economic Activity* 2: 465–521.

Blinder, A. S. and R. W. Solow. 1973. 'Does Fiscal policy Matter?' *Journal of Public Economics* 2: 319–337.

Blinder, A. S. 1997. 'Distinguished Lecture on Economics in Government: What Central Bankers Learn from Academics – and Vice Versa.' *Journal of Economic Perspectives* 11: 3–19.

_____. 1999. *Central Banking in Theory and Practice.* Cambridge: MIT Press.

_____. 2004. *The Quiet Revolution: Central Banking Goes Modern.* New Haven: Yale University Press.

Blommestein, H. J. and E. C. Thunholm. 1997. 'Institutional and Operational Arrangements for Coordinating Monetary, Fiscal and Public Debt Management in OECD Countries.' In *Coordinating Public Debt and Monetary Management,* edited by V. Sundararajan., P. Dattels., and H. J. Blommestein, IMF.

Blommestein, H. J. and P. Turner. 2012. 'Interactions Between Sovereign Debt Management and Monetary Policy Under Fiscal Dominance and Financial Instability.' *OECD Working Papers on Sovereign Borrowing and Public Debt Management*, No. 3, OECD Publishing.

Bohn, H. 1988. 'Why Do We Have Nominal Government Debt?.' *Journal of Monetary Economics* 21(1): 127–40.

———. 1990. 'Tax Smoothing with Financial Instruments.' *American Economic Review* 80(5): 1217–30.

Boskin, M. J. 1988. 'Concepts and Measures of Federal Deficits and Debt and Their Impact on Economic Activity.' In *The Economics of Public Debt*, edited by K. J. Arrow, and M. J. Boskin, 77–115. U.K.: Macmillan Press.

Brahmananda, P. R. 1972. 'Monetary Theory in an Indian Setting.' *Prajnan*, Journal of Social and Bank Management Sciences, NIBM, Pune, Volume 1.

———. 1974. 'The Nature and Genesis of the Indian Stagflation and its Control.' In *Inflation*, edited by S. L. N. Simha. Bombay: Vora Publications.

———. 1977. *Determinants of Real National Income and Price Level in India*. Bombay: University of Bombay.

———. 1980. *Growthless Inflation by means of Stockless Money*. Bombay: Himalaya Publishing House.

Brannen, P. P. and E. F. Ulveling. 1981. 'The Implication of the Rational Expectations Hypothesis for Monetary Policy.' *Indian Economic Journal* 29: 55–64.

Brockie, M.D. 1954. 'Debt Management and Economic Stabilization.' *Quarterly Journal of Economics* 68: 613–628.

Brunner, K. and A. H. Meltzer. 1972. 'Money, Debt, and Economic Activity.' *Journal of Political Economy* 80: 951–977.

Buchanan, J. M. 1958. *Public Principles of Public Debt*. Homewood: Irwin.

———. 1967. *Public Finance in Democratic Process*. Chapel Hill: University of North Carolina Press.

———. 1976. 'Barro on Ricardian Equivalence Theorem.' *Journal of Political Economy* 84: 337–342.

Buchanan, J. M. and R. E. Wagner. 1977. *Democracy in Deficit*. New York: Academic Press.

———. 1978. 'Dialogues Concerning Fiscal Religion.' *Journal of Monetary Economics* 4: 627–636.

Buiter, W. H. and U .R. Patel. 1992. 'Debt, Deficits, and Inflation: An application to the Public Finances of India.' *Journal of Public Economics* 47: 171–205.

Buiter, W. H. and J. Tobin. 1979. 'Debt Neutrality: A brief Review of Doctrine and Evidence.' In *Social Security versus Private Saving*, edited by G. M. von Furstnberg, 39–63. Cambridge: Ballinger Publishing Company.

Burdekin, R. C. K. and L. O. Laney. 1988. 'Fiscal Policy Making and Central Bank Institutional Constraint.' *Kyklos International Review for Social Sciences* 41(4) (November): 647–662.

Bureau of Economic Analysis, U.S. Department of Commerce. 1993. *National Income and Product Accounts of the United States: Volumes 1 and 2, 1929–88*. Washington: U.S. Government Printing Office.

Cagan, P. 1956. 'The Monetary Dynamics of Inflation.' In *Studies in the Quantity Theory of Money*, edited by M. Friedman. Chicago: University of Chicago Press.

Calvo, A.G. 1988. 'Servicing the Public Debt: The Role of Expectations.' *The American Economic Review* 78(4): 647–661.

Calvo, A. G. and P. E.Guidotti. 1990. 'Indexation and Maturity of Government Bonds: An Exploratory Model.' In *Public Debt Management: Theory and History*, edited by R. Dornbusch and M. Draghi, 52–93. Cambridge: Cambridge University Press.

Campbell, J. Y. and N. G. Mankiw. 1989. 'Consumption, Income and Interest Rates: Reinterpreting the Time Series Evidence.' *Working paper No. 2924*. National Bureau of Economic Reasearch.

Carr, J. and M. R. Darby. 1981. 'The Role of Money Supply Shocks in the Short-run Demand for Money.' *Journal of Monetary Economics* 8: 183–199.

Carracedo, M. F., and P. Dattels. 1977. 'Survey of Public debt Management Frameworks in Selected Countries.' In *Coordinating Public Debt and Monetary Management*, edited by V. Sundararajan., P. Dattels. and H. J. Blommestein, 96–162. Washington, DC: IMF.

Cassard, M. and D. F. Landau. 1997. 'Risk Management of sovereign Assets and Liabilities.' *IMF Working Paper, No. 166*. Washington, DC: IMF.

Cecchetti, S. G. 1998. 'Policy Rules and Targets: Framing the Central Banker's Problem.' *FRBNY Economic Policy Review* (June): 1–14.

Central Statistical Organisation, Ministry of Planning, Government of India. 1989. *National Accounts Statistics – Sources and Methods*. Faridabad: Government of India Press.

Chan, L. K. C. 1983. 'Uncertainty and the Neutrality of Government Financing Policy.' *Journal of Monetary Economics* 11: 351–72.

Chelliah, R. J. 1991. 'Growth of Indian Public Debt – Dimensions of the Problem and Corrective Measures.' *IMF Working Paper, No. 91/72*. Washington, DC: IMF.

Chitre, V. S. 1986. 'Quarterly Prediction of Reserve Money Multiplier and Money Stock in India.' *Artha Vijnana*, Reprint Series No. 10. Pune: Gokhale Institute of Politics and Economics.

Christ, C. F. 1968. 'A Simple Macroeconomic Model with a Government Budget Restraint.' *Journal of Political Economy* 76: 53–67

Clearing Corporation of India. 2006. 'Money, G-Secs and Forex Markets: Pressure on Primary Dealers.' *Economic and Political Weekly* 41(32) (12 August): 3450–3451.

Cobham, D. 1980. 'The Influence of the United Kingdom's Public Sector Deficit on its Money Stock, 1963–76: Some Comments.' *Bulletin of Economic Research* 32: 121–129.

Committee on the Global Financial System. 2011. 'Interaction of Sovereign Debt Management with Monetary Conditions and Financial Stability, Lessons and Implications for Central Banks.' *CGFS Papers*, No. 42, May.

Cottarelli, C. 1993. 'Limiting Central Bank Credit to the Government: Theory and Practice.' *Occasional Paper, No. 110, IMF*. Washington, DC: IMF.

Cottarelli, C. and M. Mecagni. 1990. 'The Risk Premium on Italian Government Debt, 1976–88.' *IMF Staff Working Papers* 37: 865–880. Washington, DC: IMF.

Cox, W. M. 1985. 'The Behaviour of Treasury Securities: Monthly, 1942–1984.' *Journal of Monetary Economics* 16: 227–40.

Cuddington, J. T. 1982. 'Canadian Evidence on the Permanent Income – Rational Expectations Hypothesis.' *Canadian Journal of Economics* 15: 331–335.

Cukierman, A. 1986. 'Central Bank Behaviour and Credibility: Some Recent Theoretical Developments.' *Federal Reserve Bank of St. Louis* (May): 5–17.

_____. 1992. *Central Bank Strategy, Credibility, and Independence: Theory and Evidence.* Cambridge: The MIT Press.

_____. 1994. 'Central Bank Independence and Monetary Control.' *The Economic Journal* 104(427):1437–1448.

Cukierman, A., S. B.Webb. and B. Neyapti. 1992. 'Measuring the Independence of Central banks and its Effect on Policy Outcomes.' *The World Bank Economic Review* 6(3): 353–398.

Currie, E., J. J. Dethier. and E. Togo. 2003. 'Institutional Arrangements for Public Debt Management.' *Policy Research Working Paper, No. 3021.* The World Bank.

Dalaya, C. 1966. *Internal Debt of the Government of India.* Bombay: Vora and Company.

Darby, M. R. 1978. 'The Consumer Expenditure Function.' *Explorations in Economic Review* 4: 645–674.

_____. 1979. *The Effects of Social Security on Income and the Capital Stock.* Washington: American Enterprise Institute.

Darrat, A. F. 1988. 'Have Large Budget Deficits caused Rising Trade Deficits?' *Southern Economic Journal* 54: 879–887.

Deadman, D. and S. Ghatak. 1981. 'On the Stability of the Demand For Money in India.' *Indian Economic Journal* 29: 41–54.

Deaton, A. 1987. 'Life-Cycle Models of Consumption: Is the Evidence Consistent with the Theory?' In *Advances in Econometrics*, edited by T. F. Bewley, 121–148. Cambridge: Cambridge University Press.

_____. 1992. *Understanding Consumption.* Oxford: Clarendon Press.

Debelle, G., and S. Fischer. 1994. 'How Independent Should a Central Bank be?' In *Goals, Guidelines, and Constraints Facing Monetary Policymakers*, edited by J. C. Fuhrer, 195–221. Boston, Massachusetts: Federal Reserve Bank of Boston.

Demetriades, P. and K. Luintel. 1997. 'The Direct Costs of Financial Repression: Evidence from India.' *Review of Economics and Statistics* 79: 311–320.

Demopoulos, G. D., G. M. Katsimbris. and S. M. Miller. 1987. 'Monetary Policy and Central Bank Financing of Government Budget Deficits: A Cross-Country Comparison.' *European Economic Review* 31: 1023–1050.

Diamond, D. W. and P. H. Dybvig. 1983. 'Bank Runs, Deposit Insurance, and Liquidity.' *The Journal of Political Economy* 91(3): 401–419.

Diamond, P. A. 1965. 'National Debt in a Neoclassical Growth Model.' *American Economic Review* 55: 1126–1150.

Dicky, D. A., D. W. Jansen. and D. L. Thornton. 1991. 'A Primer on Cointegration with an Application to Money and Income.' *Federal Reserve Bank of St. Louis* 73: 58–78.

Dincer, N. N. and B. Eichengreen. 2013. 'Central Bank Transparency and Independence: Updates and New Measures.' *BOK Working paper, No. 2013-21*. September.

Domar, E. D. 1944. 'The "Burden of the Debt" and the National Income.' *American Economic Review* 34: 798–827.

Dreze, J. H. and F. Modigliani. 1972. 'Consumption Decisions under Uncertainty.' *Journal of Economic Theory* 5: 308–35.

Dutton, D. S. 1971. 'A Model of Self-Generating Inflation.' *Journal of Money, Credit, and Banking* 3: 245–262.

Dwyer, G. P. 1982. 'Inflation and Government Deficits.' *Economic Inquiry* 20: 315–329.

Eaton, J. and H. S. Rosen. 1980. 'Taxation, Human Capital, and Uncertainty.' *American Economic Review* 70: 705–15.

El-Erian, M. A. 2013. 'The Threat to the Central - Bank Brand.' *Project Syndicate*, June 4.

Engle, R. F. and C. W. J. Granger. 1987. 'Co-integration and Error Correction Representation, Estimation, and Testing.' *Econometrica* 55: 251–76.

EPW Research Foundation. 2006. 'Can Primary Dealers Replace RBI in Security Issues?' *Economic and Political Weekly* 41(17) (29 April): 1604–1610. .

Eschweiler, B. and M. D. Bordo. 1993. 'Rules, Discretion, and Central Bank Independence: The German Experience 1880–1989.' *Working Paper No. 4547*. National Bureau of Economic Research.

European Central Bank. 1999. 'Deriving Inflation Expectations from Inflation Index-linked Bonds.' *ECB Monthly Bulletin*, February, 16.

Evans, P. 1985. 'Do Large Deficits Produce High Interest Rates?' *American Economic Review* 75: 68–87.

_____. 1988. 'Are Consumers Ricardian? Evidence for the United States.' *Journal of Political Economy* 96: 983–1004.

Feige, E. L. and D. K. Pearce. 1976. 'Economically Rational Expectations: Are Innovations in the Rate of Inflation independent of Innovations in Measures of Monetary and Fiscal Policy?' *Journal of Political Economy* 84: 499–522.

_____. 1979. 'The Causal Relationship between Money and Income: Some Caveats for Time Series Analysis.' *Review of Economics and Statistics* 61: 521–533

Feldstein, M. 1974. 'Social Security, Induced Retirement and Aggregate Capital Accumulation.' *Journal of Political Economy* 82: 905-926.

_____. 1976. 'Perceived Wealth in Bonds and Social Security: A Comment.' *Journal of Political Economy* 84: 331–36.

_____. 1988. 'The Effects of Fiscal Policies When Incomes are Uncertain: A contradiction to Ricardian Equivalence.' *American Economic Review* 78: 14–23.

_____. 1982. 'Government Deficits and Aggregate Demand.' *Journal of Monetary Economics* 9: 1–20.

Feldstein, M. and D. W. Elmendorf. 1990. 'Government Debt, Government Spending and Private Sector Behaviour: Comment.' *American Economic Review* 80: 589–599.

Feldstein, M. and A. Pellechio. 1979. 'Social Security and Household Wealth Accumulation: New Microeconometric Evidence.' *Review of Economics and Statistics* 61: 361–368.

Ferguson, J. M. 1964. *Public Debt and Future Generations*. Chapel Hill: University of North Carolina Press.

Financial Markets Division of the Department of Finance of Canada. 2002. 'Risk Management Practices Concerning Assets and Liabilities of Debt Managers in OECD Countries.' In *Debt Management and Government Securities Markets in the 21st Century*, 135–147. Paris: OECD.

Fischer, S. (ed.). 1978. *Rational Expectations and Economic Policy*. Chicago: University of Chicago Press.

———. 1982. 'Seigniorage and the Case for a National Money.' *Journal of Political Economy* 90: 295–313.

Fisher, D. 1988. *Monetary and Fiscal Policy*. London: Macmillan.

Flavin, M. A. 1981. 'The Adjustment of Consumption to Changing Expectations about Future Income.' *Journal of Political Economy* 89: 974–1009.

———. 1985. 'Excess Sensitivity of Consumption to Current Income.' *Canadian Journal of Economics* 18: 117–136.

———. 1987. 'Ricardian Equivalence: An Evaluation of Theory and Evidence: Comment.' In *Macroeconomics Annual*, edited by S. Fischer, 304–309. National Bureau of Economic Research. Cambridge: MIT Press.

Flemming, J. M. 1962. 'Domestic Financial Policies under Fixed and under Floating Exchange Rates.' *IMF Staff Papers* 9: 369–379.

Frenkel, J. A. 1977. 'The Forward Exchange Rate, Expectations, and the Demand for Money: The German Hyperinflation.' *American Economic Review* 67: 653–70.

Geweke, J. 1982. 'Measurement of Linear Dependence and Feedback between Multiple Time series.' *Journal of the American Statistical Association* 77: 304–324.

———. 1984a. 'Inference and Causality in Economic Time Series Models.' In *Handbook of Econometrics*, edited by Z. Griliches, and M. D. Intriligator, 1145–1212. New York: North-Holland.

———. 1984b. 'Measures of Conditional Linear Dependence and Feedback Between Time Series.' *Journal of the American Statistical Association* 79: 907–915.

Geweke, J. and R. Meese. 1981. 'Estimating Regression Models of Finite But Unknown Order.' *International Economic Review* 22: 55–70.

Geweke, J., R. Meese., and W. Dent. 1983. 'Comparing Alternative Tests of Causality in Temporal Systems: Analytic Results and Experimental Evidence.' *Journal of Econometrics* 21: 161–194.

Ghatak, A. and S. Ghatak. 1993. 'Budgetary Deficits and the Ricardian Equivalence: The Case of India: 1950–1986.' Discussion Papers in Economics No. 93/5. University of Leicester.

Ghuge, V. B. 1977. *The Burdens and Benefits of India's National Debt, 1941–74*. Bombay: Himalaya Publishing House.

Ghose P. 2013. 'Inflation Indexed Bonds.' *CCIL Monthly Newsletter*, September.

Ghose, P. and S. Rajaram. 2015. 'Two Decades of Primary Dealer Operations in India.' *CCIL Monthly Newsletter*, May.

Giavazzi, F. and M. Pagano. 1990. 'Confidence Crises and Public Debt Management.' In *Public Debt Management: Theory and History*, edited by R. Dornbusch and M. Draghi. Cambridge: Cambridge University Press.

Giovannini, A. 1997. 'Government Debt Management.' *Oxford Review of Economic Policy* 13(4): 43–52.

Goldfeld, S. M. 1973. 'The Demand for Money Revisited.' *Brookings Papers on Economic Activity* 3: 577–646.

Goldsmith, R. W. 1956. *A Study of Savings in the United States*. Princeton: Princeton University Press.

Gomez, C. 2008. *Financial Markets, Institutions and Financial Services*. New Delhi: PHI Learning Private Limited.

Goodhart, C. 1989. 'The Conduct of Monetary Policy.' *Economic Journal* 99(396) (June): 293–346.

_____. 1999. *'Monetary Policy and Debt Management in the UK.'* In *Government Debt Structure and Monetary Conditions*, edited by K. A. Chrystal. Bank of England, London.

_____. 2010. 'The Changing Role of Central Banks.' *BIS Working Paper*, No. 326.

_____. 2012. 'Monetary Policy and Public Debt.' *Financial Stability Review*. No. 16.

Goodhart, C. A. E. 1994. 'What Should Central Banks Do? What Should be Their Macroeconomic Objectives and Operations.' *The Economic Journal* 104:1424–1436.

Gopala Krishnan, S. 1989. *Economic Development in India*. New Delhi: Anmol Publications.

_____. 1991. 'Effect of Domestic Government Debt on Private Consumption and Saving in India.' Working Paper No. 2. New Delhi: National Institute of Public Finance and Policy.

Gordon, D. F. 1978. 'Debts, Keynes, and our Present Discontents.' *Journal of Monetary Economics* 4: 583–589.

Government of India and Reserve Bank of India. 2009. India's Financial Sector an Assessment. Executive Summary Volume I. Committee on Financial Sector Assessment.

Government of India. 1951. *The First Five Year Plan*. New Delhi: Planning Commission.

_____. 1956. *The Second Five Year Plan*. New Delhi: Planning Commission.

_____. 1961. *The Third Five Year Plan*. New Delhi: Planning Commission.

_____. 1963. *Economic Survey – 1962–63*. New Delhi: Ministry of Finance.

_____. 1966. *Economic Survey – 1965–66*. New Delhi: Ministry of Finance.

_____. 1969. *The Fourth Five Year Plan*. New Delhi: Planning Commission.

_____. 1972. *Economic Survey – 1971–72*. New Delhi: Ministry of Finance.

_____. 1973. *Economic Survey – 1972–73*. New Delhi: Ministry of Finance.

_____. 1974a. *The Fifth Five Year Plan*. New Delhi: Planning Commission.

_____. 1974b. *Economic Survey – 1973–74*. New Delhi: Ministry of Finance.

_____. 1979. *Economic Survey – 1978–79*. New Delhi: Ministry of Finance.

_____. 1980. *The Sixth Five Year Plan*. New Delhi: Planning Commission.

_____. 1985. *The Seventh Five Year Plan*. New Delhi: Planning Commission.

_____. 1990. *Economic Survey – 1989–90*. New Delhi: Ministry of Finance.

_____. 1992a. *Economic Survey – 1991–92*. New Delhi: Ministry of Finance.

_____. 1992b. *The Eighth Five Year Plan*. New Delhi: Planning Commission.

_____. 1995. *Economic Survey – 1994–95*. New Delhi: Ministry of Finance.

_____. 1997. *The Ninth Five Year Plan*. New Delhi: Planning Commission.

_____. 2002. *The Tenth Five Year Plan*. New Delhi: Planning Commission.

_____. 2003. *Fiscal Responsibility and Budget Management* Act. New Delhi: Ministry of Finance.

_____. 2004a. *FRBM Rules*. New Delhi: Ministry of Finance.

_____. 2004b. *FRBM Rules*. New Delhi: Ministry of Finance.

_____. 2007. *The Eleventh Five Year Plan*. New Delhi: Planning Commission.

_____. 2011. *Report of the Committee on Comprehensive Review of National Small Savings Fund*. Ministry of Finance.

_____. 2012a. *The Twelfth Five Year Plan*. New Delhi: Planning Commission.

_____. 2012b. 'Public Finance'. In *Economic Survey*. New Delhi: Department of Economic Affairs, Ministry of Finance.

_____. 2013a. Middle Office (Debt Management). New Delhi: Department of Economic Affairs, Ministry of Finance.

_____. 2013b. *Union Budget Speech*. New Delhi: Ministry of Finance.

_____. 2013c. Middle Office (Debt Management). New Delhi: Department of Economic Affairs, Ministry of Finance.

_____. 2013d. *Report of Financial Sector Legislative Reforms Commission*. Volume I, Analysis and Recommendations. New Delhi: Ministry of Finance.

_____. 2013e. *Report of Financial Sector Legislative Reforms Commission*. Volume II, Draft Law. New Delhi: Ministry of Finance.

_____. 2014. *Fourteenth Finance Commission Report*. Volume I. New Delhi: Ministry of Finance.

_____. 2017. 'Cabinet approves the exclusion of States from the investments of National Small Savings Fund from 1.4.2016.' New Delhi: Cabinet, Press Information Bureau, 18 January.

Granger, C. W. J. 1969. 'Investigating Causal Relations by Econometric Models and Cross-Spectral Methods.' *Econometrica* 37: 424–438.

_____. 1980. 'Testing for Causality: A personal Viewpoint.' *Journal of Economics and Control* 2: 329–352.

_____. 1986. 'Developments in the Study of Cointegrated Economic Variables.' *Oxford Bulletin of Economics and Statistics* 48: 213–239.

_____. 1988. 'Some Recent Developments in a Concept of Causality.' *Journal of Econometrics* 39: 199–211.

Grilli, V., D. Masciandaro. and G. Tabellini. 1991a. 'Institutions and Policies.' *Economic Policies* 13.

_____. 1991b. 'Political and Monetary Institutions and Public Financial Policies in the Industrial Countries.' *Economic Policy* 6: 342–392.

Guilkey, D. K. and M. K. Salemi. 1982. 'Small Sample Properties of Three Tests for Granger-Causal Ordering in a Bivariate Stochastic System.' *Review of Economics and Statistics* 64: 668–680.

Gujarati, D. 1968. 'The Demand for Money.' *Journal of Development Studies* 5: 59–64.

Gulati, I. S. 1993a. 'Reducing the Fiscal Deficit: Soft and Hard Options.' *Economic and Political Weekly* 28: 1721–1722.

_____. 1993b. 'Tackling the Growing Burden of Public Debt.' *Economic and Political Weekly* 26; 1883–1886.

Gupta, A. P. 1993. 'Reforming Deficit Measurement: The Indian Case.' *Economic and Political Weekly* 28: 345–353.

Gupta, K. L. 1984. *Finance and Economic Growth in Developing Countries*. London: Croom Helm.

———. 1992. *Budget Deficits and Economic Activity in Asia*. London: Routledge

Gupta, S. B. 1979. *Monetary Planning for India*. Delhi: Oxford University Press.

Hafer, R. W. 1981. 'Selecting a Monetary Indicator: A Test of the New Monetary Aggregates.' *Federal Reserve Bank of St. Louis Review* 63: 12–18.

———. 1982. 'The Role of Fiscal Policy in the St. Louis Equation.' *Federal Reserve Bank of St. Louis Review* 64: 17–22.

Hamburger, M. and B. Zwick. 1981. 'Deficits, Money, and Inflation.' *Journal of Monetary Economics* 7: 141–150.

Hamiliton, J. D. and M. A. Flavin. 1986. 'On the Limitations of Government Borrowing: A Framework for Empirical Testing.' *American Economic Review* 76: 808–819.

Hannan, E. J. and B. G. Quinn. 1979. 'The Determination of the Order of an Autoregression.' *Journal of the Royal Statistical Society, Series B* 41: 190–195.

Hansen, L. P., and K. J. Singleton. 1982. 'Generalized Instrumental Variables Estimation of Nonlinear Rational Expectations Models.' *Econometrica* 50: 1269–1286.

Haug, A. A. 1990. 'Ricardian Equivalence, Rational Expectations, and The Permanent Income Hypothesis.' *Journal of Money, Credit, and Banking* 22: 305–326.

Hausman, J. A. 1978. 'Specification Tests in Econometrics.' *Econometrica* 46: 1251–1271.

Hayashi, F. 1982. 'The Permanent Income Hypothesis: Estimation and Testing by Instrumental Variables.' *Journal of Political Economy* 90: 895–916.

———. 1985a. 'The Permanent Income Hypothesis and Consumption Durability: Analysis based on Japanese Panel Data.' *Quarterly Journal of Economics* 100: 1083–1113.

———. 1985b. 'Tests for Liquidity Constraints: A Critical Review.' *Working Paper No. 1720*. National Bureau of Economic Research.

Hein, S. E. 1981. 'Deficits and Inflation.' *Federal Reserve Bank of St. Louis Review* 63: 3–10.

Hess, G. 1998. 'The Maturity Structure of Government Debt and Asset Substitutability in the UK.' *Mimeo*, Bank of England Conference on the Relationship between the Level and Composition of Government Debt and Monetary Policy.

Holmes, J. M. and P. A. Hutton. 1992. 'A New Test of Money-Income Causality.' *Journal of Money, Credit, and Banking* 24: 338–355.

Hsiao, C. 1981. 'Autoregressive Modelling and Money-Income Causality Detection.' *Journal of Monetary Economics* 7: 85–106.

International Monetary Fund and The World Bank. 2001. *Developing Government Bond Markets – A Handbook*. Washington DC: IMF and WB.

———. 2003. *Guidelines For Public Debt Management – Accompanying Document and Selected Case Studies*. Washington DC: IMF and WB.

———. 2009. *Managing Public Debt: Formulating Strategies and Strengthening Institutional Capacity*, March.

International Monetary Fund. 2010. *Stockholm Principles: Guiding Principles for Managing Sovereign Risk and High Levels of Public Debt*. IMF Forum.

Jacobs, R. L. 1977. 'Hyperinflation and the Supply of Money.' *Journal of Money, Credit, and Banking* 9: 287-303.

Jadhav, N. 1994. *Monetary Economics for India*. Delhi: Macmillan.

Jain, I. 1988. *Resource Mobilisation and Fiscal Policy in India*. New Delhi: Deep and Deep Publications.

Jena, P. R. 2004. 'Integration of Financial Markets in India: An Empirical Analysis.' *Indian Journal of Economics and Business* 3(1): 63–77.

Joyce M., M. Tong. and R. Woods. 2011. 'The UK's Quantitative Easing Policy: Design, Operation and Impact.' *Quarterly Bulletin* Bank of England, Q 3.

Kalderen, L. 1977. 'Debt Management Functions and Their Location.' In *Coordinating Public Debt and Monetary Management*, edited by V. Sundararajan., P. Dattels., and H. J. Blommestein, 79–95. Washington, DC: IMF.

Kalderen, L., and H. Blommestein. 2002. 'The Role and Structure of Debt Management Offices.' In *Debt Management and Government Securities Markets in the 21st Century*, 101–134. Paris: OECD.

Kanagasabapathy, K. and C. Singh. 2013. 'A Separate Debt Management Office: Rationale, Scope and Structure.' *IIMB Working Paper, No. 431*. Washington, DC: IMF.

Kanagasabapaythy, K., C. Singh. and S. Shimpi. 2016. 'Need to Rationalize Rising Interest Burden on Public Debt of the Central Government.' *IIMB Working Paper, No. 501*, January.

Karras, G. 1994. 'Government Spending and Private Consumption: Some International Evidence.' *Journal of Money, Credit, and Banking* 26: 9–22.

Kearney, C. and R. MacDonald. 1985. 'Public Sector Borrowing, The Money Supply and Interest Rates.' *Oxford Bulletin of Economics and Statistics* 47: 249–273.

Kendrick, J. W. 1976. *The Formation and Stocks of Total Capital*. New York: National Bureau of Economic Research.

Khan, H. 2012. 'Role of State in Developing Debt Markets.' *RBI Monthly Bulletin*. RBI.

Khan, M. S. 1974. 'The Stability of the Demand-for-Money Function in the United States 1901–1965.' *Journal of Political Economy* 82: 1205–1219.

Khemani, S. 2000. 'Political Cycles in a Developing Economy: Effect of Elections in the Indian States.' *Policy Research Group, Working Paper No. 2454*. The World Bank.

King, R. G. and C. I. Plosser. 1985. 'Money, Deficits and Inflation.' *Carnegie-Rochester Conference Series on Public Policy* 22: 147–96.

Kingston, G. 1991. 'Should Marginal Tax Rates be Equalised Through Time?' *Quarterly Journal of Economics* 106: 911–924.

Kleiman, E. 1988. 'Benefits and Burdens of Indexed Debt: Some Lessons from Israel's Experience.' In *The Economics of Public Debt*, edited by K. A. Arrow. and M. J. Boskin, 264–291. London: The Macmillan Press Ltd.

Kochin, L. A. 1974. 'Are Future Taxes Anticipated by Consumers.' *Journal of Money, Credit and Banking* 6: 85–394.

Kopits, G. and S. Symansky. 1998. 'Fiscal Policy Rules.' *Occasional papers, No. 162*. Washington, DC: IMF.

Kormendi R. C. and P. G. Meguire. 1984. 'Cross-Regime Evidence of Macroeconomic Rationality.' *Journal of Political Economy* 92: 875–908.

_____. 1985. 'Macroeconomic Determinants of Growth: Cross-Country Evidence.' *Journal of Monetary Economics* 16: 141–163.

_____. 1986. 'Government Debt, Government Spending, and Private Sector Behaviour: Reply.' *American Economic Review* 76: 1180–1187.

_____. 1990. 'Government Debt, Government Spending, and Private Sector Behaviour: Reply and Update.' *American Economic Review* 80: 604–617.

Kormendi, R. C. 1983. 'Government Debt, Government Spending, and Private Sector Behaviour.' *American Economic Review* 73: 994–1010.

_____. 1984. 'Does Deficit-Financing Affect Economic Growth? Cross-Country Evidence.' *Journal of Banking and Finance, Supplement: Studies in Banking and Finance* 2: 243–255.

Kotlikoff, L. J. 1988. 'Intergenerational Transfers and Savings.' *Journal of Economic Perspectives* 2: 41–58.

Kotlikoff, L. J. and H. L. Summers. 1981. 'The Role of Intergenerational Transfers in Aggregate Capital Accumulation.' *Journal of Political Economy* 89: 706–732.

Krishnamurthy, A. and A. V. –Jorrgensen. 2011. 'The Effect of Quantitative Easing on Interest Rates: Channels and Implications for Policy.' *National Bureau of Economic Research, Working Paper No. 17555.*

Kumar, S. and R. Kumar. 2012. 'Sovereign Debt Management and Monetary Policy in India: An Empirical Investigation of Conflict of Interest Argument.' *Department of Economic Policy Research.* RBI.

Kydland, F. E. and E. C. Prescott. 1977. 'Rules Rather than Discretion: The Inconsistency of Optimal Plans.' *The Journal of Political Economy* 85(3): 473–492.

_____. 1980. 'A Competitive Theory of Fluctuations and the Feasibility and Desirability of Stabilization Policy.' In *Rational Expectations and Economic Policy*, edited by S. Fischer, 169–198. Chicago: University of Chicago Press.

_____. 1982. 'Time to Build and Aggregate Fluctuations.' *Econometrica* 50: 1345–1370.

Lal, S. N. 1978. *Problems of Public Borrowing in Underdeveloped Countries.* Allahabad: Chugh Publications.

Laney, L. and Willet, T. 1983. 'Presidential Politics, Budget Deficits, and the Money Supply in the United States: 1960–1976.' *Public Choice* 40: 53–69.

Laumas, G. S. and P. S. Laumas. 1976. 'The Permanent Income Hypothesis in an Underdeveloped Economy.' *Journal of Development Economics* 3:289–297.

Laurence, H. 1986. *Monetary Theory.* New York: McGraw-Hill.

Layton, A. P. 1984. 'A Further Note on the Direction of Granger Instantaneous Causality.' *Journal of Time Series Analysis* 5: 15–18.

Leiderman, L. 1980. 'Macroeconometric Testing of the Rational Expectations and Structural Neutrality Hypothesis for the United States.' *Journal of Monetary Economics* 6: 69–82.

Leiderman, L. and M. I. Blejer. 1988. 'Modelling and Testing Ricardian Equivalence.' *IMF Staff Papers* 35: 1–35.

Leiderman, L. and A. Razin. 1988. 'Testing Ricardian Equivalence in an Intertemporal Stochastic Model.' *Journal of Money, Credit, and Banking* 20: 1–21.

Leimer, D. R. and S. D. Lesnoy. 1982. 'Social Security and Private Saving: New Time Series Evidence.' *Journal of Political Economy* 90: 606–629.

Leland, H. E. 1968. 'Saving and Uncertainty: The Precautionary Demand for Saving.' *Quarterly Journal of Economics* 82: 465–73.

Leone, A. 1991. 'Effectiveness and Implications of Limits on Central Bank Credit to the Government.' In *The Evolving Role of Central Banks* edited by P. Downes. and R. V. Zadeh, 363–413. Washington, DC: IMF.

Levy, M. 1981. 'Factors Affecting Monetary Policy in an Era of Inflation.' *Journal of Monetary Economics* 7: 351–373.

Lewis, K. A. 1974. 'A Note on the Interest Elasticity of the Transactions Demand for Cash.' *Journal of Finance* 29: 1149–1152.

Lohmann, S. 1992. 'The Optimal Commitment in Monetary Policy: Credibility versus Flexibility.' *American Economic Review* 82.

Lucas, R. E. 1976. 'Econometric Policy Evaluation: A Critique.' In *The Phillips Curve and Labour Markets*, edited by K. Brunner and A. H. Meltzer, 19–46. Amsterdam: North Holland.

Lucas, R. E. and N. L. Stokey. 1983. 'Optimal Fiscal and Monetary Policy in an Economy without Capital.' *Journal of Monetary Economics* 12: 55–93.

MacKinnon, J. G. and R. D. Milbourne. 1984. 'Monetary Anticipations and the Demand for Money.' *Journal of Monetary Economics* 13:. 263–274.

Magnusson, T.1999a, 'Sovereign Financial Guarantees.' *Workshop on Management of a Debt Office in Tbilisi*. UNCTAD, UNDP and UNITAR.

_____. 1999b. 'Legal Arrangements for a Debt Office.' *The Swedish National Debt Office*, June.

_____. 2001. 'The Institutional and Legal base for Effective Debt Management.' *Third Inter-regional Debt Management Conference in Geneva*. UNCTAD.

Mahajan, Y. L. 1979. 'Stability of the Demand For Money in India.' *Indian Economic Journal* 27: 95–109.

Mankiw, N. G. 1982. 'Hall's Consumption Hypothesis and Durable Goods.' *Journal of Monetary Economics* 10: 417–425.

_____. 1985. 'Consumer Durables and the Real Interest Rates.' *The Review of Economics and Statistics* 67: 353–62.

Mankiw, N. G. and M. D. Shapiro. 1985. 'Trends, Random Walks, and Tests of the Permanent Income Hypothesis.' *Journal of Monetary Economics* 16: 165–174.

McCallum, B. T. 1984. 'Are Bond-Financed Deficits Inflationary? A Ricardian Analysis.' *Journal of Political Economy* 92: 123–135.

McCray, P. 2002. 'Experience with Index-linked Bonds in OECD Countries.' In *Debt Management and Government Securities Markets in the 21st Century*. Paris: OECD.

McMillin, W. D. and F. Koray. 1989. 'An Empirical Analysis of the Macroeconomic Effects of Government Debt: Evidence from Canada.' *Applied Economics* 21: 113–124.

McMillin, W. D., and R. E. Parker. 1990. 'Federal Debt, Tax-Adjusted q, and Macroeconomic Activity.' *Journal of Money, Credit, and Banking* 22: 100–109.

Mehra, Y. P. 1977. 'Money wages, Prices, and Causality.' *Journal of Political Economy* 85: 1227–1244.

Meltzer, L. A. 1951. 'Wealth, Saving, and the Rate of Interest.' *Journal of Political Economy* 59: 93–116.

Middleton, P. E. 1981. 'The Relationships between Monetary and Fiscal Policy.' In *Essays in Fiscal and Monetary Policy*, edited by M. J. Artis and M. H. Miller. London: Oxford University Press.

Mihaljek, D., M. Scatigna. and A. Villar. 2002. 'Recent Trends in Bond Markets.' In *The Development of Bond markets in Emerging Economies*, Monetary and Economic Department, BIS Papers No. 11. BIS.

Milbourne, R. D., P. Buckholtz. and M. T. Wasan. 1983. 'A Theoretical Derivation of the Functional Form of Short Run Money Holdings.' *Review of Economic Studies* 50: 531–541.

Miller, M. H. and C. W. Upton. 1974. *Macroeconomics: A Neoclassical Introduction*. Homewood: Irwin.

Miller, V. 1997. 'Why a Government Might Want to Consider Foreign Currency Denominated Debt.' *Economic Letters* 55: 240–250.

Minhas, B. S. 1987. 'The Planning Process and the Annual Budgets: Some reflections on Recent Indian Experience.' *Indian Economic Review* 22: 115–149.

Mishan, E. J. 1963. 'How to Make a Burden of the Public Debt.' *Journal of Political Economy* 71: 529–544.

Mishra, D. K. 1985. *Public Debt and Economic Development in India*. Lucknow: Print House.

Modigiliani, F. 1961. 'Long run Implications of Alternative Fiscal Policies and the Burden of the National Debt.' *Economic Journal* 71: 730–755.

Modigliani, F. and T. Jappelli. 1987. 'Fiscal Policy and Saving in Italy since 1860.' In *Private Saving and Public Debt*, edited by M. J. Boskin, J. S. Fleming and S. Gorini, 126–170. Oxford: Basil Blackwell.

Modigliani, F. and A. Sterling. 1986. 'Government Debt, Government Spending and Private Sector Behaviour: Comment.' *American Economic Review* 76: 1168–79.

_____. 1990. 'Government Debt, Government Spending and Private Sector Behaviour: A Further Comment.' *American Economic Review* 80,

Mohan, R. 2003. 'Fiscal Issues and Central Banks in Emerging Markets: an Indian Perspective.' *BIS Papers, No. 20*. BIS.

Mohanty, M. S. 1995. 'Budget Deficits and Private Saving in India: Evidence on Ricardian Equivalence.' *Reserve Bank of India Occasional Papers* 16: 1–27.

Muellbauer, J. 1983. 'Surprises in the Consumption Function.' *Economic Journal, Supplement*, 34–50.

Muellbauer, J. 1985. 'Habits, Rationality and the Life-cycle Consumption Function.' *Working Paper*. Oxford: Nuffield College,.

Mundell, R. A. 1968. *International Economics*. New York: Macmillan.

Nachane, D. M. and R. M. Nadkarni. 1985. 'Empirical Testing of Certain Monetarist Propositions via Causality Theory: The Indian Case.' *Indian Economic Journal* 33: 13–41.

National Council of Applied Economic Research. 1965. *Management of Public Debt in India*. New Delhi: NCAER.

National Stock Exchange. 2009. *Debt Market Workbook*. Mumbai.

Nelson, C. R. and C. I. Plosser. 1982. 'Trends and Random Walks in Macroeconomic Time Series.' *Journal of Monetary Economics* 10: 139–162.

Nelson, C. R. and G. W. Schwert. 1982. 'Tests for Predictive Relationships between Time-series Variables: A Monte Carlo Investigation.' *Journal of the American Statistical Association* 77: 11–18.

Niskanen, W. 1978. 'Deficits, Government Spending, and Inflation.' *Journal of Monetary Economics* 4: 591–602.

O'Driscoll, G. P. 1977. 'The Ricardian Nonequivalence Theorem.' *Journal of Political Economy* 85: 207–210.

OECD. 2002. *Debt Management and Government Securities Markets in the 21st Century*. Paris: OECD.

Olivera, J. H. G. 1967. 'Money, Prices and Fiscal Lags: A Note on the Dynamics of Inflation.' *Banca Naz. Lavoro Quarterly Review* 82:. 258–67.

Owoye, O., A. A. Nyatepe-Coo. and O. A. Onafowora. 1995. 'Another look at the Evidence on the Efficacy of Monetary and Fiscal Policies in Developing Countries: An Application of the St. Louis Equation.' *Indian Economic Journal* 43: 127–139.

Pagan, A. 1984. 'Econometric Issues in the Analysis of Regressions with Generated Regressors.' *International Economic Review* 25: 221–247.

Pagano, M. and M. J. Hartley. 1981. 'On Fitting Distributed lag Models Subject to Polynomial Restrictions.' *Journal of Econometrics* 16: 171–198.

Pandit, V. 1978. 'An Analysis of Inflation in India, 1950–75.' *Indian Economic Review* 13: 89–115.

Pathak, D. S. 1978. 'Central Monetary Authority and Money Supply - A Post-Keynesian Analysis.' *Indian Economic Journal* 25: 129–138.

Patinkin, D. 1989. *Money, Interest, and Prices*. Cambridge: MIT Press.

Paul, M. T. 1981. 'The Demand for Money and the Variability of the Rate of Inflation.' *Indian Economic Journal* 29: 65–74.

Persson, T. and L. E. O. Svensson. 1984. 'Time-Consistent Fiscal Policy and Government Cash-Flow.' *Journal of Monetary Economics* 13:. 365–374.

Pesaran, M. H. 1982. 'A Critique of the Proposed Tests of the Natural Rate-Rational expectations Hypothesis.' *Economic Journal* 92: 529–554.

_____. 1987. *The Limits to Rational Expectations*. New York: Basil Blackwell.

Pierce, D. A. and L. D. Haugh. 1977. 'Causality in Temporal Systems: Characterizations and a Survey.' *Journal of Econometrics* 5: 265–293.

Piga, G. 1998. 'In search of an Independent Province for the Treasuries: How should Public Debt be Managed?.' *Journal of Economics and Business* 50(3): 257–275.

Pigou, A. C. 1928. *A Study in Public Finance*. London: Macmillan.

Plosser, C. I. 1982. 'Government Financing Decisions and Asset Returns.' *Journal of Monetary Economics* 9: 325–352.

Poterba, J. M. 1988. 'Are Consumers Forward Looking? Evidence from Fiscal Experiments.' *American Economic Review* 78: 413–418.

Protopapadakis, A. A. and J. J. Siegel. 1987. 'Are Money Growth and Inflation Related to Government Deficits? Evidence from Ten Industrialised Economies.' *Journal of International Money and Finance* 6: 31–48.

Raghavachari, M. V. 1979. 'Growth of Budgetary Subsidies of Central Government.' *Economic and Political Weekly* 14: 522–528.

Rajaraman, I. 2004. 'Fiscal developments and Outlook in India.' *Working Paper No. 15*.. New Delhi: National institute of Public Finance and Policy.

Ramachandra, V. S. 1983. 'Direction of Causality between Monetary and Real Variables in India - An Empirical Result.' *Indian Economic Journal* 31: 65–76.

Rangarajan, C. 1995. 'Monetary Management: The Changing Framework.' *Indian Economic Journal* 43: 1–10.

Rangarajan, C. and A. Singh. 1984. 'Reserve Money: Concepts and Policy Implications for India.' *Reserve Bank of India Occasional papers*, Vol. 4, 1–26.

Rangarajan, C. and V. Sundararajan. 1982. 'Government Expenditure and Money Supply Multipliers under Alternative Conditions.' *Indian Economic Journal* 30: 1–14.

Rangarajan, C., A. Basu. and N. D. Jadhav. 1989. 'Dynamics of Interaction between Government Deficit and Domestic Debt in India.' *Reserve Bank of India Occasional Papers*, Vol. 10, 163–220.

Rao, D. C. 1980. 'The Statutory Liquidity Ratio – Its Role and Some Policy Issues.' *Reserve Bank of India Bulletin*, Vol. 34, 860–870.

Rao, D. C., T. R. Venkatachalam. and A. Vasudevan. 1981. 'A Short-term Model to Forecast Monetary Aggregates – Interim Results.' *Reserve Bank of India Occasional Papers* 2: 113–140.

Rao, V. K. R. V. 1953. 'Deficit Financing, Capital Formation and Price Behaviour in an Under-developed Economy.' *Eastern Economist Pamphlets,* No. 20.

Rasche, R. H. 1993. 'Monetary Aggregates, Monetary Policy and Economic Activity.' *Federal Reserve Bank of St. Louis* 75: 1-41.

Ray, D. and K. S. Namboodri. 1988. 'Granger's Causality – An Indian Experience.' *Journal of Quantitative Economics* 4: 279–291.

Reddy, Y. V. 2002. 'Developing Bond Markets in Emerging Economies – Issues and Indian Experience.' *Asian Conference*, Bangkok, March, 11.

Reddy, Y. V. 2004. 'Monetary and Financial Sector Reforms in India.' In *India's Emerging Economy*, edited by K. Basu, 61–81. Cambridge: MIT Press.

Reserve Bank of Australia. 1993. 'The Separation of Debt Management and Monetary Policy.' *Reserve Bank of Australia Bulletin* (November): 1–5.

Reserve Bank of India. 1960. 'Absorption and Pattern of Ownership of Government Debt in India.' *Reserve Bank of India Bulletin* 14: 1–25.

_____. 1961a. 'Pattern of Ownership of Government Debt as at the end of March 1959 and 1960.' *Reserve Bank of India Bulletin* 15: 328–355.

_____. 1961b. *Report of the Working Group on Money Supply*. Bombay: Reserve Bank of India.

_____. 1962. 'Pattern of Ownership of Government Debt as at the end of March 1961.' *Reserve Bank of India Bulletin* 16: 506–520.

_____. 1963. 'Ownership and Distribution of Funded Government Debt in India, 1930–56.' *Reserve Bank of India Bulletin* 17: 312–313.

_____. 1964. 'Pattern of Ownership of Government Debt. March 1963.' *Reserve Bank of India Bulletin* 18: 1–13.

_____. 1965. 'Pattern of Ownership of Government Debt. March 1964.' *Reserve Bank of India Bulletin* 19: 43–55.

_____. 1966. 'Pattern of Ownership of Government Debt. March 1966.' *Reserve Bank of India Bulletin* 20: 1466–1473.

_____. 1968. 'Pattern of Ownership of Government Debt. March 1967.' *Reserve Bank of India Bulletin* 22: 283–294.

_____. 1969. 'Pattern of Ownership of Government Debt. March 31, 1968.' *Reserve Bank of India Bulletin* 23: 996–1015.

_____.1970. *Functions and Working*. Bombay: Reserve Bank of India.

_____. 1971. 'Pattern of Ownership of Government Debt, March 31, 1969.' *Reserve Bank of India Bulletin* 25: 1036-1040.

_____. 1975. 'Ownership of Central and State Government Securities as on March 31, 1973.' *Reserve Bank of India Bulletin* 29: 1036–1040.

_____. 1977. *Money supply In India: Concepts, Compilation and Analysis – Report of the Second Working Group*. Bombay: Reserve Bank of India.

_____. 1981. *Report on Currency and Finance – 1980–81, Vol. I*. Bombay: Reserve Bank of India.

_____. 1982. 'Ownership of Government Debt: March 31, 1978 and Preliminary Trends in 1979 and 1980.' *Reserve Bank of India Bulletin* 36: 248–300.

_____. 1985. *Report of the Committee to Review the Working of the Monetary System*. Bombay: Reserve Bank of India.

_____. 1991. *Report on Currency and Finance – 1990–91, Vol. II*. Bombay: Reserve Bank of India.

_____. 1994a. *Annual Report – 1993–94*. Bombay: Reserve Bank of India.

_____. 1994b. 'Finances of State Governments: 1993–94.' *Reserve Bank of India Bulletin* 48: 125–353.

_____. 1994c. 'Ownership of Government Rupee Securities: Outstanding as on March 31, 1990 and Preliminary Trends in 1991 and 1992.' *Reserve Bank of India Bulletin* 48: 1517–1579.

_____. 1994d. *Report on Currency and Finance – 1993–94, Vol. 1*. Bombay: Reserve Bank of India.

_____. 1995. *Report on Currency and Finance – 1994–95, Vol. 1*. Bombay: Reserve Bank of India.

_____. 1997. *Report of the Committee on Capital Account Convertibility.* Mumbai: Reserve Bank of India.

_____. 1998. *Report of the Advisory Committee on Ways and Means Advances to State Governments*, Mumbai: Reserve Bank of India.

_____. 2001, *Report of the Expert Committee to Review the System of Administered Interest Rates and Other Related Rates.* Mumbai: Reserve Bank of India.

_____. 2003a. *Report of the Advisory Committee on Ways and Means Advances to State Governments*, Mumbai: Reserve Bank of India.

_____. 2003b. *Report of the Working Group on Instruments of Sterilisation.* Mumbai: Reserve Bank of India, December.

_____. 2003c. *Report of the Working Group on Liquidity Adjustment Facility.* Mumbai: Reserve Bank of India.

_____. 2004a. *Discussion Paper on Capital Indexed Bonds.* Mumbai: Reserve Bank of India, May.

_____. 2004b. Launching of Market Stabilisation Scheme. *Press Release*, February 23.

_____. 2005a. *Report of the Internal Technical Group on Central Government Securities Market.* Mumbai: Reserve Bank of India. July.

_____. 2005b. *Report of the Advisory Committee on Ways and Means Advances to State Governments*, Mumbai: Reserve Bank of India.

_____. 2006. *Report on Currency and Finance.* Mumbai: Reserve Bank of India.

_____. 2008. *Reserve Bank of India Bulletin.* Mumbai: Reserve Bank of India.

_____. 2012a. *Annual Report.* Mumbai: Reserve Bank of India.

_____. 2012b. *Handbook of Statistics on Indian Economy.* Mumbai: Reserve Bank of India.

_____. 2012c. *Report on Trend and Progress of Banking in India* 2011-12. Mumbai: Reserve Bank of India.

_____. 2012d. *State Finance Reports: A Study of Budgets*, Mumbai: Reserve Bank of India.

_____. 2013a. *Annual Report.* Mumbai: Reserve Bank of India.

_____. 2013b. *Handbook of Statistics on the Indian Economy.* Mumbai: Reserve Bank of India.

_____. 2013c. *The Reserve Bank of India - 1981-1997.* Volume 4, New Delhi: Academic Foundation, August, 17.

_____. 2013d. *Reserve Bank of India Bulletin.* Mumbai: Reserve Bank of India.

_____. 2014a. *Annual Report.* Mumbai: Reserve Bank of India.

_____. 2014b. *Macroeconomic and Monetary Developments, Third Quarter Review 2013-14.* Mumbai: Reserve Bank of India, January.

_____. 2015a. *Government Securities Market, A Primer.* Mumbai: Reserve Bank of India, June.

_____. 2015b. *Report of the Advisory Committee on Ways and Means Advances to State Governments*, Mumbai: Reserve Bank of India, November.

_____. 2016a. *Market Stabilisation Scheme – Revision of ceiling for 2016-17.* December 2.

---. 2016b. *Master Direction – Operational Guidelines for Primary Dealers.* Mumbai: Reserve Bank of India, July 1.

---. 2016c. *MSS Ceiling for 2016-17 fixed at ₹ 30,000 crore.* June 22.

---. 2017. *Macroeconomic Impact of Demonetisation – A Preliminary Assessment,* Mumbai: Reserve Bank of India, March 10.

Ricardo, D. 1951. 'Principles of Political Economy and Taxation.' In *The Works and Correspondence of David Ricardo,* edited by P. Sraffa. Cambridge: Cambridge University Press.

Roberts, D. L. and S. Nord. 1985. 'Causality Tests and Functional Form Sensitivity.' *Applied Economics* 17: 135–141.

Roberts, P. C. 1978. 'Idealism in Public Choice Theory.' *Journal of Monetary Economics* 4: 603–615.

Robinson, D. J. and P. Stella. 1988. 'Amalgamating Central Bank and Fiscal Deficits.' In *Measurements of Fiscal Impact: Methodological Issues,* edited by I. B. Mario. and K-Y. Chu, Occasional Paper, No. 59. Washington, DC: IMF.

Rotemberg, J. J., J. C. Driscoll and J. M. Poterba. 1995. 'Money, Output, and Prices: Evidence from a New Monetary Aggregate.' *Journal of Business and Economic Statistics* 13: 67–83.

Roubini, N. and X. S-I. Martin. 1991. 'Financial Repression and Economic Growth.' *Working paper No. 3876.* National Bureau of Economic Research.

Samuelson, P. A. 1958. 'An Exact Consumption-Loan Model of Interest with or without the Social Contrivance of Money.' *Journal of Political Economy* 66: 467–82.

Sandmo, A. 1970. 'The Effect of Uncertainty on Savings Decisions.' *Review of Economic Studies* 37:. 353–360.

Sargan, J. D. and A. Bhargava. 1983. 'Testing Residuals from Least Squares Regression for Being Generated by the Gaussian Random Walk.' *Econometrica* 51: 153–174.

Sargent, T. J. and N. Wallace. 1973. 'Rational Expectations and the Dynamics of Hyperinflation.' *International Economic Review* 2: 328–350.

Schwarz, G. 1978. 'Estimating the dimension of a Model.' *Annals of Statistics* 6: 461–464.

Seater, J. J. 1981. 'The Market Value of Outstanding Government Debt, 1919–75.' *Journal of Money, Credit and Banking* 8: 85–101.

---. 1982. 'Are Future Taxes Discounted.' *Journal of Money, Credit and Banking,* 14: 376–389.

---. 1985. 'Does Government Debt Matter: A Review.' *Journal of Monetary Economics* 16: 121–131.

---. 1993. 'Ricardian Equivalence.' *Journal of Economic Literature* 31: 142–190.

Seater, J. J. and R. S. Mariano. 1985. 'New Tests of the Life Cycle and Tax Discounting Hypothesis.' *Journal of Monetary Economics* 17: 195–215.

Seshadri, R. K. 1976. 'Gilt-Edged Investments.' *Reserve Bank of India Bulletin* 30: 627–633.

Seshan, A. 1987. 'The Burden of Domestic Public Debt in India.' *Reserve Bank of India Occasional Papers* 8: 1–18.

Sharma, R. L. 1978. 'The Demand for Money in India: An Empirical Analysis.' *Indian Economic Review* 13: 33–43.

_____. 'Causality between Money and Price Level in India: An Empirical Analysis.' *Indian Economic Review* 19: 213–221.

Shiller, R. J. 2003. 'The Invention of Inflation-Indexed Bonds in Early America.' *Working Paper No. 10183*. National Bureau of Economic Research.

Shrivastava, N. N. 1972). *Evolution of the Techniques of Monetary Management in India*. New Delhi: Somaiya Publications.

Sidrauski, M. 1967. 'Rational Choice and Patterns of Growth in a Monetary Economy.' *American Economic Review* 57: 534–544.

Sims, C. A. 1972. 'Money, Income, and Causality.' *American Economic Review* 62: 540–552.

Singh, A., S. L. Shetty. and T. R. Venkatachalam. 1982. 'Monetary Policy in India: Issues and Evidence.' *Supplement to Reserve Bank of India Occasional Papers*, Vol. 3.

Singh, B. 1989. 'Money Supply-Prices: Causality Revisited.' *Economic and Political Weekly* 24; 2613–2615.

Singh, C. 1999a. 'Monetized Debt, Monetary Aggregates and Price Level in India.' *Prajnan*, Journal of Social and Bank Management Sciences, NIBM, Pune, 27(4).

_____. 1999b. 'Domestic Debt and Economic Growth in India.' *Economic and Political Weekly* 34: 1445–1453.

_____. 2005. 'Financial Sector Reforms and State of Indian Economy.' *Working Paper*. SCID.

Singh, C., P. R. D. Prasad and K. K. Sharma. 2017. 'Should Revenue and Capital Account be Shown Separately in the Union Budget?.' *IIMB Working Paper*, No. 536, January.

Singh, C., P. R. D. Prasad, K. K. Sharma and K. S. Reddy. 2017. 'A Review of the FRBM Act.' *IIMB Working Paper*, No. 550, June.

Singh, G. N. 1976. *Public Debt and Indian Economic Development*. Calcutta: Blackie (India) Employees' Cooperative Industrial Society Limited.

Singh, T. 1990. 'Modelling the Demand for Money in India.' *International Journal of Development Banking* 8: 33–41.

Singh, T. and B. Singh. 1994–95. 'Money, Income and Causality: An Indian Experience.' *Prajnan* 23: 431–457.

Smith, A. 1791. *An Inquiry into the Nature and Causes of the Wealth of Nations*. London: A. Strahan and T. Cadell.

Sreekantaradhya, B. S. 1972. *Public Debt and Economic Development in India*. New Delhi: Sterling Publishers.

Stock, J. H. and M. W. Watson. 1988. 'Variable Trends in Economic Time Series.' *Journal of Economic Perspectives* 2: 147–174.

_____. 1989. 'Interpreting The Evidence on Money – Income Causality.' *Journal of Econometrics* 40: 161–181.

Subbarao, D. 2011. 'Implications of the Expansion of Central Bank Balance Sheets.' Speech, Special Governors meeting, Kyoto, Japan, January 31.

Sundararajan, V., and P. Dattels. 1997. 'Coordinating Public Debt and Monetary Management in Transition Economies: Issues and Lessons from Experience.' In

Coordinating Public Debt and Monetary Management, edited by V. Sundararajan., P. Dattels. and H. J. Blommestein, 3–56. Washington, DC: IMF.

Sundararajan, V., P. Dattels. and H. J. Blommestein. 1997. *Coordinating Public Debt and Monetary Management*. Washington, DC: IMF.

Swinburne, M. and M. C. Branco. 1991. 'Central Bank Independence and Central Bank Functions.' In *The Evolving Role of Central Banks*, edited by P. Downes. and R. V. Zadeh. Washington, DC: IMF.

Tanner, J. E. 1970. 'Empirical Evidence on the Short-Run Real Balance Effect in Canada.' *Journal of Money, Credit, and Banking* 2: 473–485.

_____. 1979a. 'An Empirical investigation of Tax Discounting.' *Journal of Money, Credit, and Banking* 11: 214–218.

_____. 1979b. 'Fiscal Policy and Consumer Behaviour.' *Review of Economics and Statistics* 61: 317–321.

Tanzi, V. and M. I. Blejer. 1988. 'Public Debt and Fiscal Policy in Developing Countries.' In *The Economics of Public Debt*, edited by K. J. Arrow and M. J. Boskin, 230–263. London: Macmillan.

Tanzi, V., M. I. Blejer. and M. O. Teijeiro. 1987. 'Inflation and the Measurement of Fiscal Deficits.' *IMF Staff Papers* 34: 711–738.

Taylor, J. B. 1998. 'Monetary Policy and the Long Boom.' *Federal Reserve Bank of St. Louis* (November–December): 3–11.

Thimmaiah, G. 1985. 'Fiscal Management.' In *India's Economic Development Strategies*, edited by J. N. Mongia, 153–198. Holland: D. Reidel.

Thompson, E. A. 1967. 'Debt Instruments in Both Macroeconomic Theory and Capital Theory.' *American Economic Review* 57: 1196–1210.

Thornton, D. L. and D. S. Batten. 1985. 'Lag-Length Selection and Tests of Granger Causality between Money and Income.' *Journal of Money, Credit, and Banking* 17: 164–178.

Tobin, J. 1963. 'An Essay on Principles of Debt Management.' In *Fiscal and Debt Management Policies*. A Series of Research Studies prepared for the Commission on Money and Credit. Englewood Cliffs: Prentice Hall.

_____. 1978. 'Comment From an Academic Scribbler.' *Journal of Monetary Economics* 4: 617–625.

_____. 1980. *Asset Accumulation and Economic Activity*. Chicago: University of Chicago Press.

Tobin, J., and W. Buiter. 1980a. 'Long Run Effects of Fiscal and Monetary Policy on Aggregate Demand.' In *The Government and Capital Formation*, edited by G. M. von Furstenberg. Cambridge: Ballinger.

_____. 1980b. 'Fiscal and Monetary Policies, Capital Formation, and Economic Activity.' In *The Government and Capital Formation*, edited by G. M. von Furstenberg. Cambridge: Ballinger.

U.K. Debt Management Office. 1999. *Debt Management Report – 1999–2000*. March.

U.K. Debt Management Office. 2003. *Debt Management Account Report and Accounts – 2002–2003*. July.

Vasudevan, A. 1979. 'Demand for Money in India, 1961–62 to 1976–77.' *Economic and Political Weekly* 14: 1170–1172.

――――――. 1991. 'Analytics of Monetary Management.' *RBI Occasional Papers* 12: 183–208.

Velayudham, T. K. 1978. 'Funding of Treasury Bills in India.' *Economic and Political Weekly* 13: 771–775.

Velayudham, T. K. 1986. *Treasury Bills in India – A Critical Analysis*. New Delhi: Corporate Investment Research and Consultancy Bureau.

Vickers, J. 1999. 'Monetary Policy and Asset Prices.' *Bank of England Quarterly Bulletin*, November.

Wagner, H. 1998. 'Central Banking in Transition Countries.' *IMF Working Paper, No. 98/126*. Washington, DC: IMF.

Walsh, C. E. 1995a. 'Is New Zealand's Reserve Bank Act of 1989 an Optimal Central Bank Contract?' *Journal of Money, Credit and Banking* 27(4): 1179–1191.

――――――. 1995b. 'Optimal Contracts for Central Bankers.' *American Economic Review* 85(1): 150–167.

Wilcox, D. W. 1989a. 'Social security Benefits, Consumption Expenditure, and the Life Cycle Hypothesis.' *Journal of Political Economy* 97: 288–304.

――――――. 1989b. 'The Sustainability of Government Deficits: Implications of the Present-value Borrowing Constraint.' *Journal of Money, Credit, and Banking* 21: 291–306.

Yawitz, J. B. and L. H. Meyer. 1976. 'An Empirical Investigation of the Extent of Tax Discounting.' *Journal of Money, Credit, and Banking*, Vol. 8, pp. 247–54.

Yotsuzuka, T. 1987. 'Ricardian Equivalence in the Presence of Capital Market Imperfections.' *Journal of Monetary Economics* 20: 411–436.

Zeldes, S. P. 1989. 'Consumption and Liquidity Constraints: An Empirical Investigation.' *Journal of Political Economy* 97: 305–346.

Index

ad hoc Treasury bills, 38–40
annual domestic borrowing from the public (ADBP), 193–194
Articles of Constitution
 Art. 246(1), 1
 Art. 246(3), 1
 Art. 292, 1–2
 Art. 293, 1
Aschauer's study of Ricardian equivalence, 110–111
Asian Crisis of 1997, 212
auction method of government securities, 32–35
 price-based auctions, 33
 yield-based auctions, 33
auction system of borrowing, 23
Auditor General of Accounts, 230
Augmented Dickey-Fuller test, 120–121, 124, 202

Barro's intergenerational model, 65–66
basic model with government debt, 68–70
budget constraint equations, 69
budget equation for members of generation, 66–67
Buiter and Tobin's study of Ricardian equivalence, 103–104

Canara Bank, 31
Capital Indexed Bonds, 23–24
capital mobility in India, 146–147
captive market, 28, 28n21

Cash and Debt Management Committee, 22
cash reserve ratio, 28, 155
central bank, independence of, 221–224
central governments WMA, 42
Clearing and Settlement system, 231
Cointegrating Regression Durbin Watson (CRDW), 202–203
cointegration, 189
Cointegration test, 6
Committee on Administered Rates on Small Savings, 48
commodity market clearing condition, 68
composition of domestic debt, 18
 annual average growth (1952-2016), 19
 internal debt, 19
 as per cent to total internal liabilities (1952-2016), 18
 trend, 18
Comptroller General of Accounts, 230
Consolidated Fund of India, 1–2
consumption function, 76–79, 260
 under permanent income hypothesis, 79–80
 under Ricardian Equivalence Hypothesis, 76–79. *see also* empirical studies on Ricardian equivalence in India
contingent liabilities of government, 56–57
coupon rates
 on government securities, 30
 on market bonds, 23

currency to money supply in India, 187n8

dated loans, 20
182-day/364-day Treasury bills, 40
91-day Treasury bills, 36–38
   low discount rate on, 38
   ownership pattern, 38
debt crises of 1982, 212
debt management, 213, 262
Debt Management Office (DMO)
   audit and reporting, 230, 255
   back office, 227
   coordination between RBI, government and markets, 232
   coordination committees, 257
   development of markets, 230–232
   dissemination policy and activities, 258
   features of a, 225–227
   financial market functioning, 256
   front office, 227
   functional autonomy of, 226
   governance, 250
   institutional arrangement of establishing dealers, 256–257
   management of pension and provident funds, 226
   middle office, 227, 240
   in New Zealand, 247–249
   objectives, 251
   organisational framework, 252–253
   placing of contingent liabilities, 226
   policy and planning, 253–255
   report preparation, 257
   role of RBI, 225, 227–230
   scope, 251
   staffing pattern, 258
   in Sweden, 249–250
   in UK, 244–247
deficit financing, 186–188, 187n5–6
demand for money function in India, 147

Department of Government and Bank Accounts (DGBA), 229
Department of Internal Debt Management (DIDM), 228–229
development planning, 188
devolvement on PDs, 34–35
Dickey-Fuller test, 198
Discount and Finance House of India Ltd. (DFHI), 31
domestic debt of the government, 259
   annual growth, 1952-2016, 10
   composition of. *see* composition of domestic debt
   data analysis, 1951 to 2017, 4
   data base and methodological issues, 198–201
   decadal rate of growth, 1952-2016, 10
   economic growth and, 184–186, 190–197
   effect of deficit financing undertaken, 186
   empirical literature, 189–192
   financing of rising government expenditure, 193
   financing pattern in Five Year Plans, 12
   formulation of testable hypothesis, 188–189
   GDP *vs*, 10
   growth of, 193–195
   held by public, 194–196, 199–202, 205, 260
   Keynesian view, 185n1
   macroeconomic implications of, 3–4
   major cause of rising, 11
   method of decomposing growth of money supply, 191
   raised in open markets, 4
   rate of annual increase, 8–9
   ratio of annual accruals of, 193
   ratio of annual domestic borrowing from the public (ADBP), 193

Index

relationship between growth and, 5–6
Ricardian view, 185–186
test of cointegration, 197–198
traditional view, 185
trends, 8–17
unanticipated component of domestic debt and growth, 190–191, 205–209

economic impact of public debt, 1, 3, 259
  role for borrowing, 11
effective revenue deficit, 58
empirical studies on Ricardian equivalence in India
  coefficient of lagged consumption, 141
  estimation of debt and wealth functions, 136–137
  estimation of wealth and domestic debt functions, 137–139
  issues in data specifications and period of estimation, 134–136, 143–145
  literature review of, 130–131
  test for stationarity of domestic debt and wealth, 139–140
  testing for Ricardian equivalence under permanent income, 131–134
  testing of robustness of results, 1971-95, 141–142
Engle-Granger Cointegration Test, 197–198, 202–203
Euler equation method, 89, 100
exchange rate in India, 146, 149–150
external borrowing, 259

Feldstein's study of Ricardian equivalence, 105–108
financial liberalisation, 23, 25, 28, 35, 48, 146–147, 261–262
fiscal deficit and revenue deficit of centre and states (1982-2016), 14
fiscal policy, 6

Fiscal Responsibility and Budget Management Act, 2003, 29, 31, 57–60, 211
  implementation of, 58
  Medium Term Expenditure Framework Statement in, 58
  objectives of, 57–58
  Preamble to, 58
Fiscal Responsibility and Budget Management (FRBM) Act, 2003, 2
fiscal responsibility legislation in India, 59–60
floating multiple loans, 21–22
Fourteenth Finance Commission (FFC), 50

GDP, percentage of
  defence expenditure, 11
  direct taxes of centre and states, 1950-2016, 13
  domestic liabilities, total expenditure, and tax revenue, 13
  expenditure on administrative services, 11
  food subsidy, 11
  indirect taxes of centre and states, 1950–2016, 13
  public and the private sector, 1962–95, 197
  public sector in national accounts aggregates, 197
  tax ratio, 11
  vs domestic debt, 10
Gold Bonds, 21
government securities, 4, 57, 153, 212, 217, 227, 229–231, 261
  auctions of, 21, 32–35
  as collateral, 221
  coupon rates on, 30
  demand for, 28
  interest rates on, 149

292   Index

market determined yields on, 48
market stabilisation scheme and, 35
maturity pattern of, 26–27
primary and secondary market for, 31–32, 213
RBI holding, 27n20, 29
redemption yield on, 135–136, 138n16
by a separate debt office, 225
as special securities, 50
Granger causality in economics, 6, 197–198, 203–205
  broad money (M3) and prices (P), 180–181
  causality between monetary aggregates and prices, 160–162
  causality test, 203–205, 208–209
  cross-correlation tests, 158
  cross-spectral tests, 158
  data base and methodological issues, 163–169
  definition of causality, 158
  direct tests, 158
  lag length, determining, 162
  literature review, 160–162
  methods of lag selection for causality tests, 160
  monetised debt (MD) and broad money (M3), relationship between, 173
  monetised debt (MD) and narrow money (M1), relationship between, 172
  monetised debt (MD) and prices (P), relationship between, 175
  monetised debt (MD) and reserve money (RM), relationship between, 170–171
  narrow money (M1) and prices (P), relationship between, 179–180
  procedure of test, 159
  relationship between monetised debt and prices, 160
  relationship between reserve money and prices, 162
  reserve money (RM) and prices (P), relationship between, 176–178
  result on direction of causality, 169–183
  selection of lag lengths, 165–169
  selection of the appropriate lag length, 159–160
  stationarity of time series data, 164–165
  tests, 158–160
G-secs, 24

Hyderabad State Loans, 21

ICICI Securities and Finance Company Ltd. (I-SEC), 31
Indian economy, 145–146, 261–262
  capital mobility, 146–147
  demand for money function, 147
  domestic interest rates, 148
  exchange rate, 146, 149–150
  interest rate structure, 147
  rate of inflation, 149
  relationship between monetised debt and price level, 148–150
  relationship between money supply and prices, 150
  trade restrictions, 146–147
inflation, 6, 23–24, 39, 108n31, 148–149, 187, 190n11, 219, 221–222, 224, 232, 253–254, 254n20, 254n22
inflation-adjusted growth rates of revenue and capital accounts, 17
Inflation Indexed Bonds, 23–24
Inflation Indexed National Saving Securities-Cumulative (IINSS-C), 24
Inflation Indexed National Security Certificates, 24
interest payments and interest receipts, 14–15
  as percentage, 16

Index

interest rate structure in India, 147
internal debt
  components, 20
  market loans and bonds, 20–36
Iyengar, H.V.R., 39

Jarque-Bera asymptotic LM normality test, 122–123

Keynesian consumption function, 77, 91, 97
Keynesian model of pump-priming, 188
Kisan Vikas Patras, 49
Kochin's study of Ricardian equivalence, 101–102
Kormendi's study of Ricardian equivalence, 108–110, 108n31
Krishnamachari, T. T., 39

life cycle hypothesis, 78
Liquidity Adjustment Facility (LAF), 32
loans from banks and other institutions, 47, 47n49

marketable debt, 20
market borrowings. *see also* market loans (rupee loans); Treasury bills
  formulating, 21–22
  loans from banks and other institutions, 47
  provident Funds and other accounts, 50–55
  reserve funds and deposits, 55–56
  small savings, 47–53
  special floating and other loans, 41
  special securities, 40–41
  through loans and bonds as per cent of GDP (1952-2016), 26
  ways and means advances (WMA), 41–47

market loans (rupee loans), 20–36
  auction method of government securities, 32–35
  maturity pattern, 26–27
  ownership pattern of, 27–31
  primary and satellite dealers, 31–32
  structure of interest rates - long term (1960-2016), 30
  trends, 25–26
market stabilisation scheme, 35–36
members of generation
  budget constraints, 69
  budget equation for, 66–67
  choice problem for, 69–70
  consumption and asset holding of, 68
  current asset market clearing condition, 70
  endowment for, 69
minimum Final Prediction Error, 189
Modigliani and Sterling's study of Ricardian equivalence, 111–113
monetary policy, 6
monetary ratios, 156
monetisation of debt in India
  analytical framework, 145–150
  as an important component of reserve money, 150–153
  money supply and prices, 153–158
  spurts in price level, 157–158
  use of, 150
money supply and prices, 153–158, 179–181
Mundell-Fleming model, 148

National Defence Bonds, 21
National Savings Certificates, 49
National Small Savings Fund (NSSF), 18, 49–50
NBFCs, 24

Negotiated Dealing System-Order Matching (NDS-OM), 24, 32
Negotiated Dealing System - Order Matching (NDS-OM), 231
net RBI credit to government (NRBIG), 151
non-developmental expenditure (NDE), 193–194
non-interest bearing reserve funds, 65n63

oil price, 157
operative intergenerational transfers, 186

permanent income, defined, 78
permanent income hypothesis, 76–78
  function of unanticipated changes in assets and disposable income, 80–83
  incorporation of rational expectations and, 79–82
  Lucas critique, 81n2
  rational consumption behaviour at time 't,' 81
Planning Commission, 11
primary and satellite dealers, 31–32
Primary Dealers Association of India (PDAI), 31
provident funds, 28, 50–55
public borrowing, 1
  external borrowings *vs* domestic borrowing, 3
public debt
  1952–2016, 9
  management, 229–230
Public Debt Management Agency (PDMA), 241–243
  accountability, 242
  objectives, 241
  structure, 241–242
Public Debt Management Cell (PDMC), 252–253

public provident fund, 54–55, 248
Punjab National Bank, 31

Rangarajan, C., 39
RBI Act 1934, 2
Real Time Gross Settlement system, 231
replication studies on Ricardian equivalence
  Aschauer's study, 110–111
  Buiter and Tobin's study, 103–104
  Feldstein's study, 105–108
  Kochin's study, 101–102
  Kormendi's study, 108–110, 108n31
  Modigliani and Sterling's study, 111–113
Reserve Bank of India (RBI), 2, 22
  credit to banks, commercial sector, and governments, 151, 151n10
  as a debt manager, 225, 227–230, 240
  efforts to manage the forex movement and liquidity, 35
  efforts to rein in inflation, 39
  gross foreign exchange assets of, 151n13
  holdings of government debt, 151
  investments, 151n12
  owned funds of, 151n15
  phasing out of *ad hoc* Treasury bills, 38–39
  profits transferred to central government, 228
  role in borrowing program, 22
  role in debt management, 2
reserve funds and deposits, 55–56, 55n62
reserve money, 150–154, 176–178
  growth in (1952-95), 152–153
reserve money multiplier in India, 147n7
revenue expenditure and capital expenditure of centre and states (1982-2016), 14
revenue to capital expenditure, ratio of, 16–17

Index

Ricardian Equivalence Hypothesis, 4–6
  appropriate measure of government debt, 85
  assumptions in equating tax finance and bond finance, 64–65
  basic model with government debt, 68–70
  basic model without government debt, 66–68
  case of bond finance, 64
  choice of an appropriate equation, 89–90
  coefficient of government spending, 97
  coefficient of transfer payments, 97
  concept of, 62–63
  consumption function and, 76–79
  decomposition of variables, 88–89
  discount rates, 71
  econometric methodology, 85–90
  Feldstein's study, 98, 98n12
  finite lives and Barro's intergenerational model, 65–66
  fundamental logic, 62–64
  general issues, 84
  Hall's study, 100
  imperfect private capital markets and, 70–72
  incorporation of rational expectations and, 82–83
  issue of par and market value, 114–117
  issue of treatment of trend, 88
  issue of using data on debt series in terms of par values or market values, 85
  issues concerning simultaneity, 88
  issues of data specifications, 86–88
  Kochin's study, 99
  Kormendi's study, 99–100
  literature review, 84–90
  lump-sum transfer to individuals, 71–72
  mathematically, 63
  measurement issues, 84–85
  misperception of future taxes, 74
  problems of identification, 86
  reduction in tax revenue, 63
  replication of some studies, 100–117
  Seater and Mariano's study, 98, 98n12
  specific consumption studies, 90–100
  testing for, 117–127
  timing of taxation, 74–75
  traditional aggregate consumption function approach, 91
  uncertainty about individuals' future and, 73–74
  volume of government expenditure, 74

satellite dealer system, 32
Securities Trading Corporation of India Ltd. (STCI), 31
Senior Citizen Scheme, 248
Separate Trading of Registered Interest and Principal Securities (STRIPS), 231
separation of debt from monetary management
  advantages, 211–212, 239–240
  central bank, independence of, 221–224
  functions, 239–240
  level of coordination, 224–225
  liquidity management and, 225
  from monetary policy, 239
  need for, 232–238
  post-crisis debate, 217–221
  timeline, 233–234
  traditional view, 213–217
Sims' test, 159
small saving scheme, 47–53
special securities, 4, 40–41
State Bank of India, 31
state borrowings, 1
state governments WMA, 43
state provident funds, 50, 54
Statutory Liquidity Ratio (SLR), 28

Subsidiary General Ledger (SGL), 32

testing for Ricardian Equivalence Hypothesis, model, 117–127
   Augmented Dickey-Fuller test, 120–121, 124
   consumption function, 124–127
   data series in the regression, 120
   data sources, 120
   specification of model, 117–119
   wealth and government debt functions, 121–124

total tax revenue of the government (TTR), 193–194

trade restrictions in India, 146–147

Treasury bills, 4, 25, 36, 153, 196, 261
   ad hoc, 38–40
   91-day, 36–38
   182-day/364-day, 40
   ownership pattern, 38
   share of, 36
   structure of interest rates, 37

unanticipated component of domestic debt, 80–83, 190–191, 205–209

ways and means advances (WMA), 41–47, 41n47, 211, 226
   central government, 42
   minimum balance and limit of, 46
   rate of interest on, 42
   recommendations by various committees, 44–45
   state governments, 43

'When Issued' market, 24

Wholesale Price Index, 24

wholesale price index (WPI), 195

'winners' curse,' 32

yield on government securities, 33